20th Century Pattern Design

TEXTILE & WALLPAPER PIONEERS

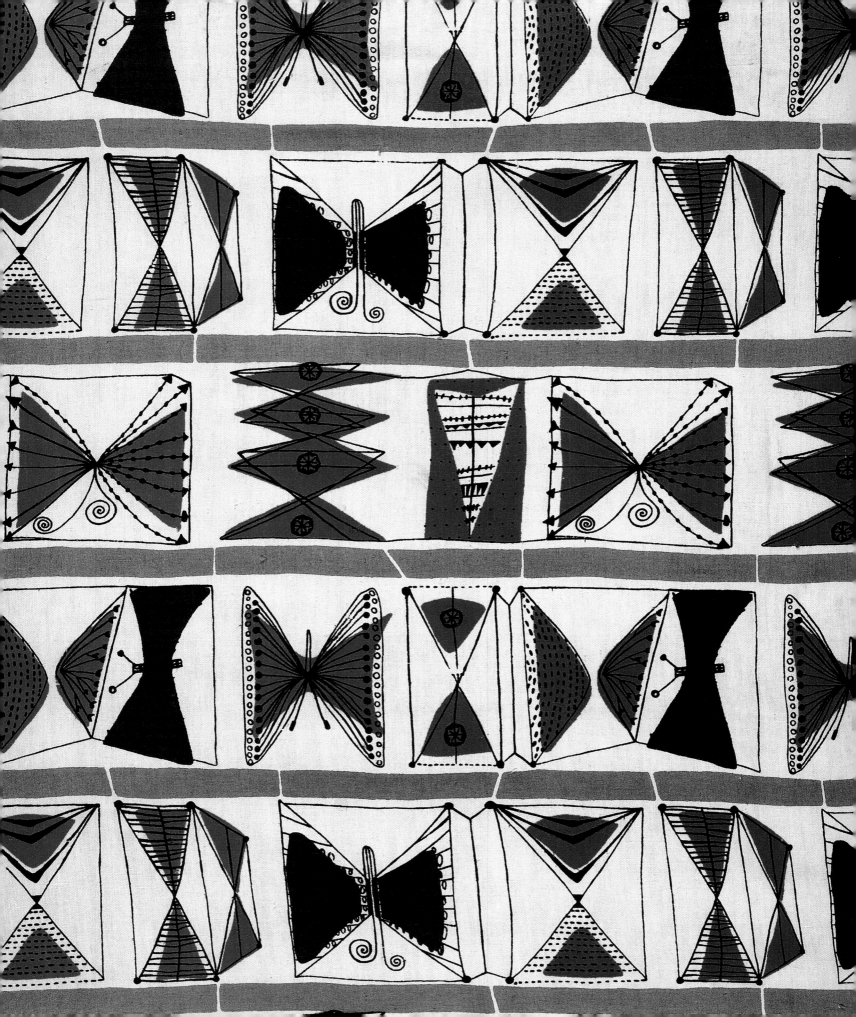

LESLEY JACKSON

20th Century Pattern Design

TEXTILE & WALLPAPER PIONEERS

MITCHELL BEAZLEY

For Ian

20th Century Pattern Design
Textile & Wallpaper Pioneers
By Lesley Jackson

First published in Great Britain in 2002 by Mitchell Beazley,
an imprint of Octopus Publishing Group Ltd,
2–4 Heron Quays, London E14 4JP

Commissioning Editor Mark Fletcher
Managing Editor Hannah Barnes-Murphy
Art Editor Christie Cooper
Designer Fiona Knowles
Editor Richard Dawes
Picture Research Christine Crawshaw
Production Angela Couchman

ISBN 1840003715

A CIP record for this book is available from the British Library

Set in Veljovic
Colour reproduction by Fine Arts Repro House Co. Ltd
Produced by Toppan Printing Co. (HK) Ltd
Printed and bound in China

Endpapers
Lustgården screen-printed linen furnishing fabric, designed by Stig Lindberg, produced by Nordiska Kompaniet, 1947.

p.1
Jerusalem by Night printed fabric wall hanging, designed and produced by Piero Fornasetti, c.1950.

p.2
Fritillary screen-printed linen furnishing fabric, designed by Lucienne Day, produced by Liberty, 1954.

Opposite
Heinä screen-printed cotton furnishing fabric, designed by Maija Isola, originally produced by Marimekko, 1957, reprinted by Marimekko, 2001.

Contents

Preface

Given the obvious visual appeal of textiles and wallpapers, it has always surprised me that surface pattern has so often been marginalized within mainstream histories of 20th-century design. While the achievements of William Morris during the 19th century are widely recognized, very few pattern designers since then have been awarded the same degree of attention. As a result, the true significance of this rich seam of creativity has been unjustly downplayed. In my previous books I have attempted to redress the balance by featuring textiles and wallpapers alongside other areas of the applied arts. However, the wealth and diversity of this subject in its own right has finally prompted me to write a book devoted to 20th-century pattern design.

Twentieth-century pattern is a gargantuan topic, and although I have ranged widely within this field, for practical reasons I have limited myself to working within certain parameters. Firstly, as the subtitle of the book indicates, I have decided to focus on textiles and wallpapers, particularly the designers and producers I regard as the most innovative from a creative point of view, the design pioneers. Secondly, within the vast arena of textiles, I have concentrated mainly on printed rather than woven fabrics, as it is here that pattern has been most forcefully expressed over the past hundred years. Thirdly, I have chosen to focus mainly (although not exclusively) on furnishing fabrics, because, in my opinion, this has been the most consistently ground-breaking area of printed textile design over the last century. However, where significant initiatives have originated in dress fabrics, or where there has been active cross-fertilization between dress and furnishing fabrics, I have touched upon this. For the sake of clarity, picture captions indicate the intended application of the fabric.

The rapid season-by-season turnover in the fashion industry makes it much more difficult to document fabric production in this area, and while this in no way invalidates the end products, it is undoubtedly much easier – although still by no means straightforward – to trace the threads of stylistic development in the field of patterned furnishing fabrics. This is what I have endeavoured to do. There is also an intrinsic logic to studying furnishing fabrics and wallpapers as an entity, as they are closely related aspects of interior design, and often designers practise in both fields. Had space permitted – sadly, it did not – it would have been fascinating to branch out into carpets, laminates, and ceramics as well.

Industrial production rather than craft is the main focus of the book, although even in factories hand printing has frequently been employed alongside machine production. The work of selected small-scale designer-producers operating independently is occasionally discussed, where it is deemed to be stylistically significant or influential. Technical developments in textile and wallpaper manufacturing are not the main subject of this study, and nor have I attempted to document company histories or to

Top Fig. 0.1
Anemone flexo-printed wallpaper, designed and produced by Neisha Crosland, 1999. Since crossing over from her original field of fashion textiles, the British designer Neisha Crosland has revitalized contemporary wallpaper with her subtle, seductive, rhythmic patterns.

Above Fig. 0.2
Metro screen-printed cotton furnishing fabric, designed by Tom Hedqvist, printed by Borås Wäfveri for the Tio-Gruppen, 1993. Sweden's Tio-Gruppen have been designing high-voltage patterns since the 1970s. This design, inspired by the Bauhaus artist Josef Albers, formed part of their Homage collection.

chart the economic fortunes of the industry as a whole, although all these topics are touched upon at intervals, and there is no doubting their importance in their own right. Some of the patterns I have chosen to illustrate were best sellers, but many were produced in fairly small quantities and reached only a limited audience. Commercial success has not been used as a criterion for my selection, however, as this book is not intended as an analysis of popular taste or patterns of consumption, but as a record of the unfolding of a series of innovative styles.

The heroes and heroines of this book are the pattern designers, and from among the many thousands of practitioners active in this field over the course of the past century, I have singled out several hundred as being particularly outstanding. Some of these designers are famous already, some are moderately well known, and some are still waiting in the wings. All are worthy of wider recognition, and I hope that interest and appreciation will be stimulated as a result of discussing and illustrating their work. Many pieces have been newly photographed, and I am grateful to all the museums that have cooperated in this venture, particularly the Whitworth Art Gallery in Manchester.

The book is structured chronologically in seven chapters, and focuses mainly on Europe and the United States. The countries highlighted vary from chapter to chapter, reflecting the emergence of new pattern design superpowers at different moments in time. Thus Britain dominates the 1900s, and France, Austria, and Germany are the prime movers during the 1920s. The United States and Sweden do not enter the story until slightly later, and only emerge fully-fledged after the Second World War. Finland, a late developer, blazes a trail during the 1960s and 1970s, while the most recent creative flourish has originated in Japan. The two countries which, in my opinion, have made the most sustained creative impact on pattern design during the past century have been Britain and Sweden, which is why so much of the text, and so many illustrations, are devoted to them.

In the hope of opening up this subject to a new audience, I have endeavoured to make the text accessible to non-specialists. Designers' birth and death dates, where known, are cited in the index rather than in the main text. A short glossary is included at the end of the book. This focuses mainly on printing terms and is intended to clarify the differences between hand and machine production, so crucial to an understanding of textile and wallpaper manufacture. For reasons of space, notes are limited mainly to quotations, cross-referenced to a more extensive bibliography listing wider sources. I am deeply indebted to all the textile and wallpaper scholars around the world who have assisted me, and on whose research I have drawn. Specific acknowledgments appear at the end. Here I would particularly like to thank Lesley Hoskins for generously agreeing to read through my text.

Lesley Jackson

Above Fig. 0.3
Queen of Spain *screen-printed cotton furnishing fabric, designed by Michael Taylor, produced by Hull Traders, 1963.* Shown here in two colourways, this textile won a Cotton Board Award in 1964. Hull Traders fearlessly pushed forward the boundaries of British pattern design during its heyday in the 1960s.

Arts and Crafts, Art Nouveau, and Jugendstil

The late 19th century in Britain witnessed a remarkable flowering of pattern design – quite literally so, as most of the designs were floral, reinterpreted in arresting and imaginative new styles. The renaissance was dominated by William Morris, a one-man pattern-making phenomenon, and the founding father of the Arts and Crafts Movement. Morris released a flood of creativity, not only in his immediate circle but also among Arts and Crafts designers and manufacturers throughout the country. Building on the foundations laid by Morris, second-generation Arts and Crafts designers, such as C.F.A. Voysey and Lindsay Butterfield (fig. 1.1), extended the boundaries of pattern design in exciting new ways.

Revered in Europe as *le style anglais*, British textiles and wallpapers dominated *fin de siècle* exhibitions, magazines, and interiors, causing widespread reverberations. Adopting aspects of the Arts and Crafts style, but pushing them to new extremes, Art Nouveau and Jugendstil designers from France, Belgium, and Germany such as Hector Guimard, Henry van de Velde, and Otto Eckmann created wildly exaggerated, frenetic, whiplash patterns that provoked excitement and revulsion in equal measure.

Meanwhile, in Austria, a new school of pattern design was emerging, closely allied with the severe, geometric style of modern architecture pioneered by Charles Rennie Mackintosh in Glasgow and Josef Hoffmann in Vienna. The Austrian Secession bore fruit in the hugely creative Wiener Werkstätte (Vienna Workshops), a powerhouse of alternative pattern design that continued to grow and develop over the next two decades. Although, by 1910, the Arts and Crafts Movement was on the wane and Art Nouveau and Jugendstil were passé, the Wiener Werkstätte opened up many exciting avenues for pattern designers to explore over the coming years.

Britain: A.W.N. Pugin, Owen Jones, and Christopher Dresser

At the time of the Great Exhibition held in London in 1851 furnishings were dominated by elaborate floral chintzes and

Opposite Fig. 1.1
Block-printed linen furnishing fabric, designed by Lindsay Butterfield for G.P. & J. Baker, 1903. Lindsay Butterfield was one of the most important second-generation Arts and Crafts designers. Here he co-opts the William Morris device of superimposing primary motifs on a recessive background pattern. The flattened leaf and flower forms show the influence of his contemporary C.F.A. Voysey.

luxurious woven silks. Manufacturers tended to confuse quality with complexity, and many patterns were minutely detailed. Before this, in the 1840s, the architect A.W.N. Pugin had introduced crisp, richly coloured Gothic Revival motifs into interior decoration, applying his distinctive decorative formula to various media, including textiles, wallpapers, and tiles. Around the same time the writer John Ruskin embarked on a long and sustained campaign for aesthetic reform, influencing generations of designers, notably William Morris. He believed that Gothic art and architecture marked a high point in the history of civilization, and in *The Stones of Venice* (1851–3) he argued for a return to the spirit of creative commitment that fired the medieval age.

For pattern designers, a key publication of the mid-19th century was *Grammar of Ornament* (1856), by the architect and designer Owen Jones. This book, which illustrated decorative motifs from innumerable global sources, opened people's eyes to the wider potential of pattern design. For designers it was enormously educative, serving for many years as a primary source of reference. Later, through his woven silks for firms such as Warner, Sillett & Ramm and his wallpapers for Jeffrey & Co., Jones pioneered the introduction of disciplined patterns in which historical motifs served as a vehicle for contemporary expression.

During the 1870s many designers drew heavily on the inspiration of Japan, their interest aroused initially by the display of Japanese applied arts at the International Exhibition of 1862 in London. Chief among these were E.W. Godwin, Bruce Talbert, and Christopher Dresser, who all created textile and wallpaper designs with a new rigour in their imagery and compositions. The multi-faceted Christopher Dresser was an almost exact contemporary of William Morris, and in many ways his alter ego. Working within the industrial system rather than against it, he supplied designs to a host of manufacturers in both Britain and France in almost every field of the applied arts, including textiles and wallpapers. The activities of Owen Jones and Christopher Dresser paved the way for the professionalization of modern design. Originally trained as a botanist, Dresser was fascinated by the geometrical qualities of plants and plant growth, and approached pattern design in a quasi-scientific way. In 1859 he published a book called *Unity in Variety, as Deduced from the Vegetable Kingdom*. His appreciation, from a biological point of view, of the "oneness" of plant forms enabled him to create highly original, complex organic patterns that contrast with, but complement, those of William Morris.

Britain: William Morris

During the second half of the 19th century Britain witnessed nothing less than a revolution in the field of pattern design as a result of the work of William Morris. By going back to the basics of design and production, Morris cut a swathe through the prevailing confusion, evolving completely fresh forms of pattern. Diverting emphasis away from luxurious, jacquard-woven silk furnishing

fabrics and wall coverings at one end of the market, and cheap, roller-printed textiles and wallpapers at the other – both of which he felt had become debased in terms of design – he refocused attention on the merits of traditional craft-based hand block-printing and hand weaving. By evolving patterns that exploited the potential of these media, Morris revolutionized people's perception of home furnishings, particularly printed fabrics and wallpaper, and unlocked the floodgates of creativity in pattern design.

Prodigiously talented and tirelessly energetic, Morris exerted a huge and lasting influence on almost every area of the applied arts. As a partner in Morris, Marshall, Faulkner & Co. from 1861, and later as head of Morris & Co. from 1874 to 1896, his activities encompassed furniture, tiles, stained glass, tapestries, wallpapers, and furnishing fabrics. But his greatest achievements as a designer were undoubtedly in pattern design. He brought patterns to life through his dazzlingly inventive treatment of plant forms and the rhythmic exuberance of his compositions. His wallpapers – produced from 1864 – and his printed textiles – produced from 1873 – thoroughly revitalized these fields. Morris regarded purity and freshness of colour as essential ingredients of his printed textiles, and for this reason rejected the harsh tones of commercial aniline dyes in favour of the mellow hues of vegetable dyes. Initially he collaborated with Thomas Wardle of Leek, Staffordshire (fig. 1.2), but in 1881, after acquiring a disused silk dyeworks at Merton Abbey, just south of London, he began to block-print his own textiles. It was here that he mastered the technique of indigo discharge-printing, in which the cloth was dyed a rich dark blue, then block-printed with bleach to remove the pigment before being overprinted with other colours. Morris's early attempts to print his own wallpapers had proved unsuccessful, however, and he subcontracted this area of production to Jeffrey & Co., a manufacturer whose skills in block-printing were unparalleled and whose artistic sympathies were in line with his own (fig. 1.3).

Although Morris drew on a wide range of European, Middle Eastern, and Asian sources, he avoided the pitfalls of revivalism. A dedicated student of the decorative arts on a global level – he admired in particular French medieval tapestries, Elizabethan embroideries, Italian woven silks, Indian block-printed cottons, and Persian ceramics – he scrutinized historical pattern in minute detail, achieving a high degree of technical mastery over his compositions and repeats. Elements of these multifarious design idioms appear in his textile and wallpaper patterns, but reinterpreted in an original guise. Morris created a revolutionary hybrid form of pattern-making, quintessentially English, yet somehow exotic at the same time.

Native English plants, depicted in a refreshingly honest way, were an essential part of his design vocabulary. This in itself was completely revolutionary at a time when imitation and illusionism reigned. Stressing the importance of a deeply felt response to

Left Fig. 1.2
Tulip *block-printed cotton furnishing*
fabric, designed by William Morris,
printed by Thomas Wardle & Co. for
Morris & Co., 1875. Two distinct layers
of pattern – primary and secondary –
are clearly evident in this design,
originally conceived as a wallpaper.

Left Fig. 1.3
Jasmine *block-printed wallpaper,*
designed by William Morris, printed by
Jeffrey & Co. for Morris, Marshall,
Faulkner & Co., 1872. Fluidity and
rhythm were key elements in William
Morris's patterns. This design is
brought to life by the dynamic, furling
stems of the jasmine.

Above Fig. 1.4
Purple Bird *woven silk and wool double cloth, designed by C.F.A. Voysey, produced by Alexander Morton & Co., 1899.* Voysey deliberately reduced this pattern to its simplest elements. Motifs have clear outlines with flat infill colouring and there are no distracting details.

Right Fig. 1.5
Isis *block-printed wallpaper, designed by C.F.A. Voysey, produced by Jeffrey & Co., c.1893.* Before developing the serene minimalist style seen in *Purple Bird* (above), Voysey designed a series of wallpapers with seductive scrolling, organic forms. These patterns were highly influential on the Continent.

nature, Morris argued: "some beautiful piece of nature must have pressed itself on our notice so forcibly that we are quite full of it, and can, by submitting ourselves to the rules of art, express our pleasure to others, and give them some of the keen delight that we ourselves have felt."[1] Composed of a mass of intertwining foliage and flowers, arranged in rhythmic, S-shaped curves and twisting diagonals, his patterns were constructed as a measured interplay between assertive foreground and recessive background elements. "One should aim at combining the solidity of form and clarity of composition with the mystery emanating from the richness of details," he advised.[2] Some patterns were harmonious in colour, but exploited differences in scale. Others were complex and multi-layered, juxtaposing forceful primary motifs and intense colours against smaller, secondary decorative elements in quieter tones. Vital but never chaotic, natural but not naturalistic, stylized but not artificial, Morris's patterns were full of invigorating rhythms, stimulating colours, and seductive organic shapes. "No amount of delicacy is too great in drawing the curves of a pattern, no amount of care in getting the lines right from the first can be thrown away, for beauty of detail cannot afterwards cure any shortcoming in this," he wrote.[3]

The founding of the Art Workers Guild in 1884 and the Arts and Crafts Exhibition Society in 1888 consolidated the aesthetic reforms that Morris had initiated. By this time the Arts and Crafts Movement represented a broad spectrum of artists, architects, and designers, encompassing an extensive range of studio, workshop, and factory production. While Morris himself was at his most productive as a pattern designer during the 1870s and the early 1880s, the liberating effect of his work was at its most potent during the 1890s, reaching a peak during the decade following his death in 1896. Although Arts and Crafts patterns became more stylized and mannered towards the end of the century, the homely, down-to-earth qualities that Morris had pioneered were never lost. While delighting in nature as a source of inspiration, Arts and Crafts patterns were governed by discipline and restraint. It was this that set them apart from the more exaggerated styles that developed on the Continent, which treated plant forms in a more licentious way.

Britain: C.F.A. Voysey

The single most influential figure at the turn of the 19th century was the architect Charles Francis Annesley Voysey. Trained as an architect, Voysey set up in practice around 1882, and began designing wallpapers the following year at the instigation of his friend Arthur Heygate Mackmurdo. It soon became evident that he had outstanding natural abilities as a pattern designer, and over the next fifty years he created a large body of work. Mackmurdo's own patterns, and those of his fellow Century Guild member Herbert Horne, were distinguished by their restless, sinuous, febrile plant forms. Slightly manic in quality, they prefigured some of the more extreme manifestations of Continental Art Nouveau.

Their influence was evident in some of Voysey's early patterns, but within a short time the distinctive planar qualities of his style began to emerge, and it was in this calmer and more restful expression that he found his own voice.

What distinguishes Voysey from Morris is that his patterns are much easier to digest visually. "Simplicity in decoration is one of the essential qualities without which no true richness is possible,"[4] was one of his aphorisms. "To be simple is the end, not the beginning, of design."[5] As a draughtsman Voysey was fastidious and economical, paring down his designs to their most concentrated form. Drawing on a limited pool of recurrent motifs, he reduced individual elements to their essence, flattening the surface to produce stencil-like effects, emphasizing outline, eliminating shading, and minimizing detail (fig. 1.4).

Voysey's fame as a pattern designer was confirmed by *The Studio* magazine, which in 1896 noted: "Now a 'Voysey wall-paper' sounds almost as familiar as a 'Morris Chintz' or a 'Liberty Silk'."[6] His first wallpaper client had been Jeffrey & Co. (fig. 1.5), and ten years later, in 1893, he signed a contract with Essex & Co., for whom he created several hundred designs. Voysey's last recorded wallpaper commission was in 1930, and in the intervening years he supplied designs to many other firms, including the Anaglypta Company, Heffer, Scott & Co., Lightbown Aspinall, Lincrusta Walton, Charles Knowles, John Line, Arthur Sanderson, and William Woollams. His style was particularly well suited to block-printing, which allowed great clarity and subtlety in the rendition of mass and line. Depending on the way the blocks were inked, different textures resulted, ranging from flat, opaque colours to lightly mottled effects. Patterns varied from the extreme simplicity of *The Glade* (1897), with its isolated clumps of flowers, to lush, all-over foliage patterns such as *The Morgiana* (1901). Making a conscious decision to distance himself from the "greenery-yallery" palette associated with Arts and Crafts interiors, Voysey said: "Let us do our utmost to raise the colour sense from morbid sickly despondency to bright and hopeful cheeriness, crudity if you will rather than mud and mourning."[7] Most of his wallpapers were printed in as few as two or three colours, normally in tones of the same intensity. This, combined with Voysey's highly personal vocabulary and his distinctive graphic style, was what gave his designs their satisfying coherence.

A noteworthy feature of Voysey's work was the free crossover between different disciplines: often similar patterns were produced as both textiles and wallpapers, and sometimes adapted as carpets as well. His first textile client was Turnbull & Stockdale, for whom he created print designs in 1890. He also excelled in woven fabrics, and subsequently designed textiles for many other companies, including G.P. & J. Baker, Donald Brothers, William Foxton, A.H. Lee, Liberty, Stead McAlpin, Alexander Morton, Müntzer & Co., Newman, Smith & Newman, Morton Sundour, St Edmundsbury

Above Fig. 1.6
*Seagulls silk and wool double cloth,
designed by C.F.A. Voysey, produced
by Alexander Morton & Co., c.1895–8.*
Although Voysey exhibited this design
at the Arts and Crafts Exhibition in
1893, it was not produced as a woven
fabric until a few years later. Voysey's
patterns were often adapted for reuse
in different media.

Weavers, J.W. & C. Ward, Thomas Wardle, and Wylie & Lochhead.
His most memorable textiles are the silk, wool, and cotton double
cloths he designed for Alexander Morton from around 1895 (fig. 1.6).
Double cloth is a reversible fabric composed of two layers of cloth
woven simultaneously on the same loom. This medium, like block-
printed wallpapers, was particularly well suited to the idiom evolved
by Voysey, whose correspondence with the manufacturer suggests
that he paid careful attention to the selection of colours and yarns.

Voysey attracted many admirers in mainland Europe, including
the designer Henry van de Velde and the architect Victor Horta,
both Belgians; and in 1900 the *Journal of Decorative Art* hailed him
as the "fountain head" and "prophet" of Art Nouveau.[8] Ironically,
Voysey himself was fundamentally opposed to international cross-
fertilization. "Each country has been given its own characteristics
by its Creator and should work out its own salvation," he asserted in
the lecture "Patriotism in Architecture," given at the Architectural
Association in London in 1911. He was decidedly uncomfortable
with the idea of being associated with Art Nouveau, which he
viewed as a dangerously self-indulgent and morally dubious
trend. In 1904 he said: "I think the condition which has made
l'Art Nouveau possible is a distinctly healthy development, but
at the same time the manifestation of it is distinctly unhealthy
and revolting."[9] By this time, however, the Continental design
revolution that he had inadvertently triggered was unstoppable,
and the ripples produced by *le style anglais* were spreading all
over the Western world.

Britain: J.H. Dearle and Morris & Co.

Before the Arts and Crafts Movement, pattern design in Britain
was at a low ebb. Originality was neither valued nor nurtured, and
manufacturers trained their in-house staff to copy designs from
historical sources or from other companies, or bought patterns from
commercial studios in France. By daring to be different and single-
mindedly pursuing his vision of reform, William Morris brought
innovation into the limelight and inspired a host of other designers
and manufacturers. His aesthetic was vigorously perpetuated long
after his death through the agency of Morris & Co., which remained
in operation until 1940. Continuity was provided by his gifted
assistant, John Henry Dearle, who joined the firm in 1878 and
from the late 1880s designed most of its patterns, taking over as
manager in 1896. Although Dearle's designs were less subtle than
those of Morris in their layering and repeats, he successfully
assumed his master's stylistic mantle, generating new patterns in a
recognizable Morris idiom. Wallpapers such as *Seaweed* (c.1896–1901)
(fig. 1.7) and printed textiles such as *Briar* (1906) were remarkably
vivid and fresh. Kathleen Kersey also designed some patterns for
the company during the first decade of the century.

Britain: Walter Crane and Lewis F. Day

Although he was approaching the end of his career, Walter Crane
characterized the astonishing versatility of designers who held

sway around the turn of the century. After achieving early renown as an illustrator of children's books, Crane developed into an accomplished all-round designer. From the mid-1870s he designed a series of stunning complementary wallpapers and friezes for Jeffrey & Co., richly coloured and minutely detailed designs featuring rabbits, peacocks, swans, and cherubs. He also designed printed and woven textiles for firms such as Birch, Gibson & Co., Liberty, Thomas Wardle, and Warner. Best known for his figurative patterns combining classical imagery with an aesthetic sensibility, Crane developed a more rarefied vocabulary and style than most of his fellow Arts and Crafts practitioners. Although his most original work predates the 1900s, Crane exerted a powerful influence on the next generation through his writing, lecturing, and teaching. A tireless campaigner for design reform as well as a prolific designer, he left a legacy that remained strong until the First World War.

Lewis Foreman Day was an almost exact contemporary of Walter Crane, and applied his talents to a similarly diverse range of applied arts. Originally working in stained glass, he began to design textiles and wallpapers after setting up in private practice in 1870. In 1881 he was appointed artistic director for Turnbull & Stockdale, where he designed numerous printed textiles and oversaw the company's wide-ranging output for almost three decades (fig. 1.8). Indigo discharge-printing, the technique revived by William Morris, was one of his specialities at Turnbull & Stockdale; he used this to create patterns of great lightness and delicacy, composed from tiny dots and fine lines. In addition Day designed wallpapers for Jeffrey & Co., and printed and woven textiles for Thomas Wardle, Alexander Morton, and A.H. Lee.

As a designer Day was something of a chameleon and his artistic signature was not always easy to recognize. While displaying a quieter, more undemonstrative style than Morris and Crane, he was nevertheless a highly skilful designer with a finely tuned commercial eye. Always palatable and frequently inspirational, his designs reflected a sophisticated awareness of historical and ethnic patterns and techniques (fig. 1.27). Day was actively involved in the formation of the Art Workers Guild and the Arts and Crafts Exhibition Society, dedicating his life to the dissemination of their aesthetic aims. He wrote extensively for leading art magazines, and his influential series of design handbooks, including *Ornament and its Application* (1904), became standard teaching tools.

Britain: Lindsay Butterfield

Some twenty-five years younger than Day and Crane, Lindsay Butterfield embarked on his career at a propitious moment in the early 1890s. Influenced by Voysey, he moved freely between textiles and wallpapers, working for many leading firms, including the wallpaper producers Essex & Co. and Jeffrey & Co., and the textile manufacturers G.P. & J. Baker , Newman, Smith & Newman, Turnbull & Stockdale (fig. 1.9), Thomas Wardle, and Warner. His

Top Fig. 1.7
Seaweed block-printed wallpaper, designed by John Henry Dearle, printed by Jeffrey & Co. for Morris & Co., c.1896–1901. In this pattern, with its writhing stems and scrolling foliage, Dearle successfully emulated the style of his late master, William Morris.

Above Fig. 1.8
Tulip Tree roller-printed cotton furnishing fabric, designed by Lewis F. Day, produced by Turnbull & Stockdale, 1903. Subtle shading adds tonal interest to the flattened stylized leaves and flowers in this vibrant pattern. The white background enhances the fresh colours.

woven double cloths for Alexander Morton were particularly successful, prompting him to enter into a contract with the company in 1902. A devoted gardener and the co-author, with W.G. Paulson Townsend, of *Floral Forms in Historic Design* (1922), Butterfield created patterns that were informed by his botanical knowledge. Like Morris, he favoured plants commonly found in English gardens, such as daffodils, sweet peas, poppies, irises, and lilies. Normally focusing on just one type of flower, he was skilled at transposing them into stylized images and arranging them in dynamic and stimulating ways (fig.1.1). He often gave greater prominence to stems and leaves than petals or flower heads, and to pattern constructions based on flowing lines rather than mass (fig. 1.18). There was a refreshing naturalness and lack of pretension to Butterfield's designs, and the effects were never forced.

Britain: George C. Haité, Sidney Mawson, and Allan Vigers

Several pattern designers at the turn of the century were artists, notably George C. Haité, a versatile all-rounder who pursued a dual career as a painter and designer, working with firms such as Liberty and Warner. Trained by his father George Haité, a designer of Paisley fabrics, he put his skills as a watercolourist to good effect in his printed florals for G.P. & J. Baker, which are characterized by luminous colours and vigorous rhythmic compositions (fig. 1.10). In his woven textiles for A.H. Lee the surface of the cloth was block-printed after weaving to capture his subtle shading effects.

Such freedom was actively encouraged within Arts and Crafts circles, and another leading pattern designer, Sidney Mawson, worked also as a landscape painter. Mawson began his career designing printed textiles for Thomas Wardle in 1882, initially strongly influenced by the virtuoso stylized naturalism of William Morris. Active until the 1920s, he also designed wallpapers for Jeffrey & Co. and textiles for G.P. & J. Baker, Liberty, Morton Sundour, Turnbull & Stockdale, and Warner. His printed textiles for Liberty were particularly vibrant, encapsulating the essence of the Arts and Crafts style in a popular accessible form (fig. 1.11). For Mawson, plants were a design device rather than a personal passion, so that he had no qualms about creating generalized images or conjuring up fantasy flowers (fig. 1.28). Individual motifs were often magnified or condensed to suit his purpose, and he often juxtaposed unlikely elements, as in the medley of intertwined fruit in *The Chatsworth* (1909). Mawson remained eclectic to the end, his later designs including a series of roller-prints for Morton Sundour that featured minutely detailed Persian scenes.

The architect Allan Francis Vigers took a highly individualistic approach to pattern design, informed by his skills as an illuminator. Best known for his wallpapers for Jeffrey & Co., he specialized in intricate florals, composed of a mass of small flower heads, mounted like jewels on white or dark-blue backgrounds (fig. 1.12). At once naturalistic and highly artificial, his patterns featured typical English garden flowers, such as pansy, mallow, briar rose, and dianthus, simply and accurately depicted, but arranged in consciously artful, synchronized formations. In addition to wallpapers Vigers designed printed and woven textiles for G.P. & J. Baker, Liberty, and Alexander Morton.

Britain: Glasgow School

One surprising aspect of British turn-of-the-century pattern design was the limited direct impact of the Glasgow School. The architect Charles Rennie Mackintosh, chief protagonist of the movement, did not actually design printed textiles until around 1917, although decorative motifs from his furniture and interiors indirectly influenced prevailing styles. Even the Scottish architect and designer George Walton, who relocated from Glasgow to London in 1897, exerted only a limited effect on mainstream pattern design. In many ways Walton was not a natural pattern designer, and his wallpaper designs for Jeffrey & Co., created during the 1900s, seem strangely contrived. Concentrating mainly on stencilled patterns for specific interiors, he did not design production textiles until some years later. A third designer associated with the Glasgow School, the illustrator Jessie King, designed several printed textiles with delicate watery images for Liberty during the 1900s and 1910s, but otherwise made little impact on pattern design.

Britain: Silver Studio

One channel through which the Glasgow style was more widely disseminated was the Silver Studio, a leading London-based commercial pattern studio. Around the turn of the century it adopted some of the mannered styling associated with Mackintosh, such as stylized roses and milky secondary colours, although this was but one of many idioms in its wide-ranging and flexible repertoire. Until the 1870s most commercial pattern studios servicing the British textile industry were in France. Following the lead of Christopher Dresser, who had set up his studio in the 1860s, Arthur Silver's founding of the Silver Studio in 1880 indicated a new spirit of self-reliance in British design. Embarking on his career at the height of the Aesthetic Movement, Silver promoted Japanese-inspired imagery and established a lasting relationship with Liberty, for whom the Silver Studio created many designs.

Wallpapers and furnishing fabrics were the mainstay of the Silver Studio's output, but dress fabrics, graphics, metalwork, and floor coverings were all tackled at various times (figs. 1.14 and 1.15). Arthur Silver died in 1896, but the business was continued by his son, Rex Silver, until 1963. The creative heyday of the Silver Studio, however, was the 1890s and 1900s, when it was a powerhouse of pattern design in both the Arts and Crafts and Art Nouveau styles. During the 1890s the Studio's employees included two outstanding designers, both talented watercolourists: John Illingworth Kay and Harry Napper. The Manx designer Archibald Knox was also associated with the Silver Studio between 1897 and 1900, creating models for Liberty's Celtic Revival Cymric metalwork, as well as textile designs.

Top Fig. 1.9

Roller-printed cotton furnishing fabric, designed by Lindsay Butterfield, produced by Turnbull & Stockdale, 1901. Foliage plays an important role in many of Butterfield's designs. Here the dynamic interaction between the leaves and flowers accounts for the potency of the pattern.

Above Fig. 1.10

Block-printed linen furnishing fabric, designed by George C. Haité, produced by G.P. & J. Baker, c.1900. Stencilled wallpapers were very popular at this time, and the graduated colouring on this fabric simulates these effects. Note the seductive wavy, upward movement of the plants.

Top Fig. 1.11

***The Melbury** roller-printed cotton furnishing fabric, designed by Sidney Mawson, roller-printed by Turnbull & Stockdale for Liberty, c.1906. Magnification of different elements of the pattern to the same scale was a characteristic Mawson device. Here the trees are the same size as the flowers.*

Above Fig. 1.12

***Columbine** block-printed wallpaper, designed by Allan Vigers, produced by Jeffrey & Co., 1901. Delicate florals on dark backgrounds were a speciality of Allan Vigers. The consciously artificial arrangement of the flowers in this pattern is the wallpaper equivalent of synchronized swimming.*

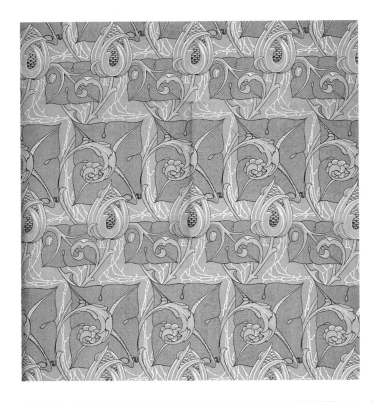

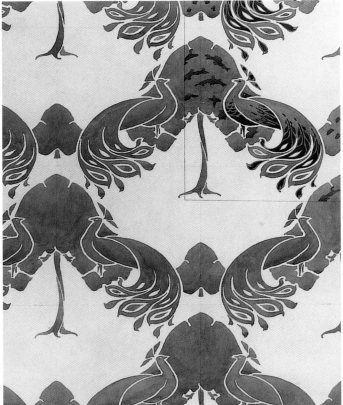

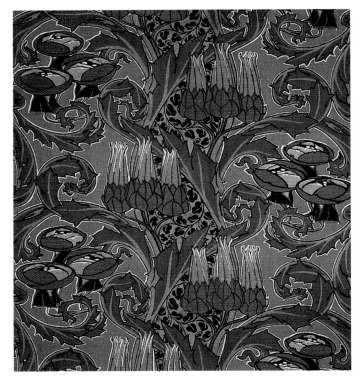

John Illingworth Kay worked at the Silver Studio from 1892 to 1900. His patterns, with their quasi-Symbolist imagery and restless compositions, had a fantastical, dreamlike quality (fig. 1.15). Harry Napper, who joined around 1893 and was head of the Studio between 1896 and 1898, specialized in patterns with a decidedly Continental flavour, characterized by sinuous, twisting stems and exaggerated fringed leaves and petals. Tailoring his imagery to suit the mood of Art Nouveau, he later expanded his vocabulary to include weeds and poisonous plants (fig. 1.16). After turning freelance in 1898, Napper continued to sell some of his patterns through the Silver Studio, and maintained his contacts with a number of French manufacturers. During the 1900s and 1910s his British textile clients included G.P. & J. Baker, Liberty, Alexander Morton, Simpson & Godlee, Turnbull & Stockdale, and J.W. & C. Ward, and he also designed stencilled wallpapers for Alexander Rottmann. From 1900 to 1916 the Studio's chief designer was Harry Silver, Rex Silver's brother, who produced many accomplished patterns in a measured English version of Continental Art Nouveau. Although the Studio was operating in a commercial environment, the thousands of textile and wallpaper designs it created remained remarkably vivid and imaginativeup until about 1908. Its legendary professionalism helped it to attract many loyal clients, among them G.P. & J. Baker, A.H. Lee, Alexander Morton, Newman, Smith & Newman, Simpson & Godlee, Stead McAlpin, F. Steiner, Turnbull & Stockdale, J.W. & C. Ward, Thomas Wardle, and Warner. The Silver Studio was equally active in the field of wallpapers, where its clients included Essex & Co., Jeffrey & Co., Lightbown Aspinall, John Line, C. & G. Potter, Alexander Rottmann, and Sanderson.

In 1897 *The Studio* reported that *le style anglais* was invading France, and that "the majority of designers and manufacturers are content to copy and disfigure English patterns."[10] One way for European manufacturers to tap directly into the English style was to purchase designs from the Silver Studio, and by 1906 the proportion of the firm's designs being sold to European manufacturers had risen to 40 percent. During the 1900s its European customers included Bergerot Dupont & Cie, Ferdinand Leborgne, Koechlin Baumgartner & Cie, Vanoutryve & Cie, and Nouveaux Tissages Belges, while American clients included Cheney Brothers and Marshall, Field & Co. The Silver Studio played a key role in popularizing the Arts and Crafts style internationally and infusing the market with an anglicized interpretation of Art Nouveau (fig. 1.13).

Britain: Jeffrey & Co. and Essex & Co.

At the turn of the century the relationship between design and industry in Britain was extremely fertile. A wealth of talented designers allowed manufacturers to choose with whom they collaborated, while the designers themselves enjoyed unparalleled opportunities to work with a wide variety of receptive firms.

Just as significant as the designers who forged the Arts and Crafts style were the enlightened manufacturers who put their work into production. In 1896 *The Studio* noted that the factory-made goods shown in the Arts and Crafts Society Exhibition that year were "admirable and satisfactory in all respects."[11] Jeffrey & Co., the most pre-eminent Arts and Crafts wallpaper manufacturer, was founded in 1836. It flourished under the direction of Metford Warner, who joined the firm in 1866, purchased it in 1871, and remained in charge for over fifty years. Having already been entrusted by William Morris and Owen Jones with the production of their wallpapers, Jeffrey & Co. began to collaborate with other leading architects and designers. During the late 19th and early 20th centuries contributors included William Burges, W.J. Neatby (fig. 1.17), and George Heywood Sumner, as well as Crane, Day, Godwin, Mawson, Talbert, Vigers, Voysey, and Walton. From the early 1900s Metford Warner's sons, Albert and Horace Warner, also began to design for the company (fig. 1.19). Albert later became a partner, while Horace succeeded his father as head of the firm. Jeffrey & Co. was renowned for its superb quality printing and great care was taken to ensure that patterns were accurately and sensitively reproduced. The company set the trend for crediting designers personally – one reason why it attracted such an impressive array of talent.

Equally highly respected was Essex & Co., founded by R. Walter Essex in 1887. In addition to its enviable alliance with Voysey, the company commissioned wallpapers from other designers, such as Butterfield (fig. 1.18) and Haité. Printed and stencilled friezes became one of its specialities, produced in a department run from 1900 to 1922 by John Illingworth Kay. In 1899 Essex & Co. joined the Wall Paper Manufacturers Ltd (WPM), an industrial joint-stock company created from the amalgamation of thirty-one factories. In 1923 it was subsumed within the Sanderson branch of the WPM, along with Jeffrey & Co., marking the end of a glorious era of British wallpapers. The WPM became a virtual monopoly, stifling creativity and annihilating competition.

Opposite top left Fig. 1.13
Roller-printed cotton furnishing fabric, possibly designed by the Silver Studio, produced by Liberty, c.1900–5. With its flat, squared leaves and rectilinear composition, this pattern has a decidedly Continental flavour. Liberty had opened a shop in Paris in 1890 and its fabrics were sold throughout Europe.

Opposite bottom left Fig. 1.14
Design for a printed textile, Silver Studio, 1903. Peacocks and peacock feathers had been fashionable "Aesthetic" motifs since the 1870s, and were still in vogue thirty years later. This diagonal trellis pattern, possibly by Harry Silver, has a strong Arts and Crafts flavour in its colouring, content, and composition.

Opposite top right Fig. 1.15
Design for a wallpaper, attributed to John Illingworth Kay at the Silver Studio, 1893. Clusters of trees with broad canopies were a recurrent feature of John Illingworth Kay's designs, which accounts for this attribution. Note the restless fluidity of the sinuous pattern and the way the design is sucked upwards.

Opposite bottom right Fig. 1.16
Convolvulus and Seed Pod *block-printed cotton furnishing fabric, designed by Harry Napper at the Silver Studio, produced by G.P. & J. Baker, 1898.* The overtly sombre colouring of this intense and mannered Art Nouveau pattern adds to the claustrophobia generated by the composition.

Top Fig. 1.17
Lancaster Frieze block-printed
wallpaper frieze, designed by W.J. Neatby,
produced by Jeffrey & Co., 1904. The
attenuated thorny stem and stylized
rose heads in this Art Nouveau design
reflect the influence of the Glasgow
School, although the orange colouring
is noticeably brighter.

Above Fig. 1.18
Design for Hawkweed wallpaper,
Lindsay Butterfield, produced by Essex &
Co., 1902. In this sprightly, linear Art
Nouveau pattern the spindly stems and
narrow, scrolling leaves are the most
prominent and dynamic features of the
composition, rather than the flower
heads, which are more static.

Top Fig. 1.19
The Mill Stream block-printed wallpaper
frieze, designed by Horace Warner,
produced by Jeffrey & Co., 1904. Created
at the height of the fashion for pictorial
wallpaper friezes, this atmospheric
silhouetted design creates its effect by
juxtaposing strong horizontal and
vertical elements.

Above Fig. 1.20
Eltham block-printed and stencilled
wallpaper, probably designed by William
Shand Kydd, produced by Shand Kydd,
c.1905. Similar in some respects to the
Lancaster Frieze (top left), this pattern
suggests the influence of the Glasgow
School in its stylized rose motifs and
muted colouring.

Britain: Shand Kydd, Liberty, and WPM

The leading firms in the WPM during the early 20th century were Lightbown Aspinall, C. & G. Potter, and Arthur Sanderson & Sons, the latter originally founded as an importer of luxury French wallpapers in 1860, becoming a producer during the 1870s. One company that managed to remain independent for longer, however, was Shand Kydd, established by William Shand Kydd in 1891 and largely responsible for the fashion for wallpaper friezes that began in the mid-1890s. Drawing on a combination of hand block-printing for outlines and stencilling for infill, Shand Kydd produced wallpapers (fig. 1.20) and friezes that were characterized by vivid colours and subtle graduated effects, achieved by brushing, sponging, or dabbing with chamois leather. Early frieze designs featured classic Aesthetic Movement motifs such as peacocks, or *fin de siècle* lilies, poppies, or roses. Full-blown Art Nouveau patterns composed of loops of scrolling acanthus were a Shand Kydd speciality, often in russet and gold. The depth of the friezes varied, as did the structure and width of the repeat. Shand Kydd's influence extended to the lower end of the market, and its products were widely emulated by other firms. Rivals used cheaper processes, such as machine surface-printing and, later, aerograph spraying, to simulate the company's hand block-printed and stencilled effects.

During the 1900s the craze for pictorial friezes infiltrated the mass market. Themed decoration was actively promoted, and included woodland scenes for dining rooms and seascapes for bathrooms. Stylized landscapes, juxtaposing vertical trees with horizontal rivers, were particularly fashionable (fig. 1.19). Nursery friezes – popular until the 1930s – were commissioned from illustrators of children's books, such as Walter Crane. In 1898 Liberty, which had established a Paper-Hanging Department in 1887, commissioned a series of mural panels from the artist Cecil Aldin and the celebrated poster designer and book illustrator John Hassall. "The object is to place before children such pictures as are well drawn and well coloured, and thus train the eye in infancy to discriminate and enjoy artistic work. The present series consists of bold and simple Outline Pictures illustrating Nursery Rhymes, Domestic and Farmyard Animals etc.," explained *The Liberty Bazaar*.[12] During the 1910s this formula was widely employed by other firms using mass-production techniques. C. & G. Potter reproduced drawings by the children's writer Mabel Lucie Attwell, for example, while Lightbown Aspinall teamed up with Will Owen, famous for his *Punch* illustrations and Bisto gravy advertisements (fig. 1.21).

Britain: A.H. Lee and Warner

At the start of the 20th century Britain had the largest textile industry in the world, serving huge global export markets. Manufacturers excelled at both printed and woven textiles, with spinning, weaving, and printing of cottons centred in Lancashire, while Yorkshire specialized in woollen cloths, although there were also many mills in other parts of the country. In the field of woven textiles, one of the most innovative companies was A.H. Lee &

Top Fig. 1.21
Bo Peep *(above) and **Simple Simon** (below) roller-printed nursery wallpaper friezes, designed by Will Owen, produced by Lightbown Aspinall, 1910.* Will Owen's skills as both poster designer and illustrator are reflected in the graphic clarity and directness of these designs, machine-printed for mass consumption.

Above Fig. 1.22
Woven silk and wool furnishing fabric, designed by Harry Napper, produced by J.W. & C. Ward, c.1900. The influence of Voysey is clearly discernible in this design, particularly in the flattened, angular leaves. Rectilinear compositions became increasingly popular during the early 1900s.

Above Fig. 1.23
*Woven silk and wool double cloth,
designed by Gavin Morton, produced by
Alexander Morton & Co., c.1895–1900.*
The exaggerated wiriness of the stems,
the sweeping motion of the tulip
petals, and the pallid mauve and
yellow colouring of this masterly
woven design are all characteristic
features of Art Nouveau.

Sons, established by Arthur Henry Lee at Warrington in 1888 and subsequently relocated to Birkenhead. Lee specialized in sophisticated jacquard-woven wool, silk, and cotton furnishing fabrics, and developed an interesting hybrid technique that involved block-printing on woven fabrics to produce tonal effects. Closely associated with leading protagonists from the Arts and Crafts Movement, the company numbered among its designers Arthur Lee's brother-in-law, George Faulkner Armitage, in addition to Crane, Day, Haité, Mackmurdo, and Voysey.

J.W. & C. Ward of Halifax, who produced woven fabrics by Dresser, Napper (fig. 1.22), Talbert, Voysey, and the Silver Studio, was also remarkably progressive at this time. Less adventurous, but still significant, was Warner & Sons, established in 1891 as the successor to a long line of silk-weaving companies run by Benjamin Warner since the 1860s. Originally based at Spitalfields in east London, the company relocated to Braintree, Essex, in 1895 after taking over a large silk-weaving mill previously operated by one of its chief rivals, Daniel Walters & Sons. Woven silk damasks and brocades were Warner's main speciality, although some cheaper furnishing fabrics woven from cotton and wool were also produced. Priding itself on the accuracy of its historical reproductions, the company specialized primarily in traditional designs. Occasionally, however, it ventured into the field of modern design, collaborating with Owen Jones, E.W. Godwin, and Bruce Talbert during the 1870s and 1880s, and later producing designs by Butterfield, Crane, Haité, Mackmurdo, Mawson, and the Silver Studio.

Britain: Alexander Morton and Morton Sundour

One of the chief protagonists in the design renaissance at the turn of the century was the Scottish weaving company Alexander Morton & Co. Founded in Ayrshire in 1870, it manufactured a wide variety of woven textiles and carpets. Although the firm initially pursued largely traditional formulae, designs were commissioned from Day, Dresser, and Talbert, and during the 1880s it produced coloured madras muslins and wool tapestries for Morris & Co.

In 1895 Alexander Morton's son, James Morton, became a partner in the company, and it was at his initiative that closer links were established with the artistic avant-garde in Britain. During the late 1890s and early 1900s he enlisted an impressive roll-call of designers, including his cousin Gavin Morton (fig. 1.23), William Shand Kydd, Sidney Mawson, Harry Napper, John Scarratt Rigby, M.H. Baillie Scott, George Heywood Sumner, Charles Harrison Townsend, Frederick Vigers, and the Silver Studio. The two most high-profile designers, however, were C.F.A. Voysey and Lindsay Butterfield, both of whom entered into contracts with the company: Voysey from around 1896 and Butterfield from 1902. Their designs, produced in the form of wool, silk, and cotton double cloths, as well as heavier wool tapestries, proved extremely popular, and were sold through outlets such as Liberty, Morris & Co., and Wylie & Lochhead.

In 1900 Alexander Morton began to shift its operations to Carlisle, Cumbria, and from this date James Morton turned his attention to improvements in synthetic dyestuffs. This led to the launch of Sundour Fabrics in 1906, a range of printed and woven textiles dyed with a specially formulated and rigorously tested range of "guaranteed unfadable" colours. The initiative was so successful that in 1914 a new company called Morton Sundour Fabrics was created, by which time the Sundour trade name was famous all over the world. Initially printing had been subcontracted, but in 1912 block-printing facilities were established at the company's headquarters in Carlisle, with roller-printing added in 1921. Many patterns were designed by Ronald D. Simpson, who joined the company in 1908, while its Arts and Crafts associations were perpetuated during the 1920s through long-standing alliances with Mawson, Voysey, and Sidney Haward of the Haward Studio.

Britain: Thomas Wardle and Liberty

During the early 20th century fashions in interior design were changing rapidly. Jocelyn Morton, in his chronicle of the Morton textile dynasty, has noted that there was "a move away from the heavier 'tapestries' for curtains and toward bright printed goods."[13] By devoting an increasing part of its production to printed textiles, Morton Sundour was following the lead not only of Morris & Co., but also of an emergent group of companies who, from the 1870s, had used this medium as a vehicle for creativity in textile design. The dyer and printer Thomas Wardle, who collaborated enthusiastically with William Morris during the 1870s in Morris's experiments with vegetable dyes, played a key role in raising the profile of printed textiles. Fascinated by the techniques and imagery of Indian block-printed textiles, Wardle created hybrid products using imported Indian tussore and Mysore silks, which were then dyed in a range of exquisite colours and hand block-printed with "Oriental" patterns at his factory in Leek, Staffordshire. Hugely influential in shaping artistic taste, these fabrics were sold through Wardle's London shop, as well as prestigious outlets in the capital such as Heal's and Liberty. Wardle later produced contemporary Arts and Crafts designs, including some by his son, Thomas Wardle Jnr, and others by Butterfield, Crane, Day, Mawson, Voysey, Cecil Millar, and Léon Solon.

Liberty & Co., the fashionable London store founded by Arthur Lasenby Liberty in 1875, played a decisive role in disseminating and generating Arts and Crafts textiles. The store, originally established in response to the Aesthetic Movement's mania for all things Japanese, promoted textiles, particularly Chinese, Japanese, and Indian coloured silks, as a key area of its merchandise from the outset. Within a couple of years the term "Liberty Art Fabrics" was appearing in advertisements, denoting products superior to run-of-the-mill commercial manufacture. From the late 1870s Liberty began to establish relationships with leading British textile companies, including Thomas Wardle and, later, Alexander Morton, both of which supplied exclusive designs.

The success of Liberty Art Fabrics led, around 1880, to the direct commissioning of patterns (figs. 1.24 and 1.26). Some of the earliest were by Christopher Dresser and the Silver Studio, and with the latter this special relationship continued for many years. In addition Liberty selected innovative patterns from the *crème de la crème* of freelance designers, including Butterfield, Crane, Day, Haité, Mawson, Napper, Vigers, and Voysey, as well as Jessie King, John Scarratt Rigby, and Arthur Willcock. John Llewellyn, who joined the Silks Department in 1889 and later became a director of the company, was responsible for commissioning many of these designs. Others were initiated by textile manufacturers and then supplied to Liberty on an exclusive basis. John W. Howe, another Liberty director, commented in 1898: "It is no matter to us where a design comes from, so long as it possesses merits worthy to be put before the public by the House of Liberty. We collect designs from all quarters, and our manufacturing friends are only too pleased for us to suggest the designs which should be taken up."[14] Companies with whom Liberty collaborated included G.P. & J. Baker, David Barbour, Turnbull & Stockdale, and Warner. Tight quality control standards were enforced, and all textiles were sold anonymously under the Liberty Art Fabrics name. From 1904 Liberty began to print much of its own cloth, after taking over the printworks of Edmund Littler at Merton Abbey, who had been one of its chief commission printers since the 1890s.

Liberty's printed linen and cotton furnishing textiles, sometimes produced as reversible duplex fabrics, were renowned for the originality of their patterns and for the clarity and freshness of their colours. Greens were a speciality during the 1890s, followed by cool blues during the 1900s, both printed on a crisp white ground. During the early 20th century Liberty's patterns became simpler and more relaxed, often generously spaced and printed in monochrome. Lush stylized florals in the late Arts and Crafts style were produced until the First World War and beyond. Progressive without being exaggerated or alienating, Liberty prints were steeped in a reassuring Englishness, yet had a daring Continental edge (fig. 1.13). Speaking of the range in 1898, John Llewellyn observed: "These and other similar characteristic patterns are now all the rage, not only in England, but on the continent, and, indeed, throughout the World. Just in the same way as there was a Louis XVI period, so we flatter ourselves that we have created a new 'English' period."[15] By this time Liberty had opened its own shop in Paris and was also supplying Siegfried Bing's L'Art Nouveau gallery in the French capital. Liberty Art Fabrics were also sold through outlets in other European cities, prompting the use of the Italian term "*Stile Liberty*" to describe Art Nouveau.

Britain: G.P. & J. Baker and Turnbull & Stockdale

One of Liberty's commission printers was G.P. & J. Baker, which evolved from an Anglo-Turkish trading company established by George Baker in the mid-19th century. The name G.P. & J. Baker was adopted in 1884 after his sons, George Percival Baker and

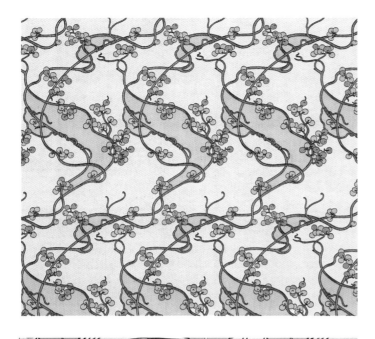

Top Fig. 1.24
Roller-printed cotton furnishing fabric, produced by Liberty, 1894. This pattern, with its writhing, sinuous composition, embodies the restless energy of Art Nouveau, and hints at the lingering influence of japonaiserie. Liberty prints such as this were celebrated for the freshness of their colours.

Above Fig. 1.25
*Design for **Waterlilies** block-printed furnishing fabric, Harry Napper, produced by G P & J. Baker, 1905.* The stylization of the water in this pattern suggests an awareness of Japanese prints. The enduring influence of Voysey is also apparent in the flatness of the lily pads.

Above Fig. 1.26
Roller-printed furnishing fabric, designed by the Silver Studio, produced by Liberty, c.1899. The Silver Studio supplied numerous designs for Liberty Art Fabrics. This pattern, with its insistent upward movement, exemplifies the tempered Art Nouveau style for which Liberty was admired.

Above Fig. 1.27
Block-printed linen furnishing fabric, designed by Lewis F. Day, produced by Turnbull & Stockdale, 1903. Strongly curvilinear compositions define the structure of this design and the two Liberty prints on the opposite page. This Persian-inspired pattern juxtaposes motifs on two different scales.

Above right Fig. 1.28
Block-printed cotton furnishing fabric, designed by Sidney Mawson, produced by Turnbull & Stockdale, 1906–7. This richly coloured Indian-inspired design provides an excellent vehicle for Turnbull & Stockdale's superb printing, as well as highlighting Sidney Mawson's skill as a pattern designer.

Above Fig. 1.29
Block-printed wallpaper frieze, designed by Maurice Dufrène, produced by Joseph Petitjean, 1900. This French pictorial wallpaper frieze shares similar characteristics with the British example in Fig. 1.19. Maurice Dufrène explored a variety of fashionable styles during his long career.

Above Fig. 1.30
Woven silk wall covering and gilded beechwood furniture with embroidered upholstery, designed by Georges de Feure, 1900. In this ensemble, created for Siegfried Bing's Pavillon de l'Art Nouveau at the Exposition Universelle in Paris, the legacy of the French Rococo style is clearly apparent.

Above right Fig. 1.31
Woven silk furnishing fabric, probably designed by Édouard Colonna for Cornille Frères, c.1900. This textile illustrates the type of formal compositions favoured by French designers. Although there are echoes of plant motifs, the pattern is not intended to be naturalistic.

Right Fig. 1.32
Printed cotton velveteen furnishing fabric, designed by Eugène Gaillard, 1900. This fabric was displayed at the Exposition Universelle in Paris. The pallid colours and the undisguised artificiality and exaggeration of the motifs in this pattern are distinctively French features of the composition.

James Baker, entered into partnership and began to produce textiles in Britain. In 1893 they leased the Swaisland Print Works at Crayford, Kent, where block-printed and roller-printed fabrics were produced, decorated with stunning patterns by leading designers such as Butterfield (fig. 1.1), Haité, Mawson, Napper (fig. 1.25), Vigers, Voysey, and the Silver Studio. George Percival Baker was a keen gardener, and many of the textiles he commissioned celebrated English fruit and flowers.

Another leading manufacturer of block-printed and roller-printed textiles was Turnbull & Stockdale, established by William Turnbull and William Stockdale at Ramsbottom, Lancashire, in 1881. The creative direction of the company was undertaken by Lewis F. Day, who was chief designer and artistic director from 1881 to 1910. Day himself designed many patterns during this period, including indigo discharge-prints and reversible duplex-printed cottons (figs. 1.8 and 1.27). He also commissioned patterns from other designers, including Butterfield, Mawson (fig. 1.28), Napper, Voysey, O.B. Bryan, Alfred Carpenter, and Samuel Rowe. The firm enjoyed an enviable reputation for quality, and, in addition to producing its own ranges, undertook commission printing for a number of retailers, including Liberty, Goodyer, and Maple's.

Britain: CPA and F. Steiner

As in the case of the wallpaper industry, the character of the textile industry changed significantly in 1899 after the creation of a large printed textile combine, the Calico Printers Association (CPA). Initially composed of forty-six printworks and thirteen merchants, the CPA concentrated on the production of cheap apparel fabrics for export, particularly to Africa. But although it initially controlled 85 percent of the textile printing trade, the organization did not thrive, and by 1910 its share had fallen to 60 percent. Along with Turnbull & Stockdale, one of the few Lancashire printing firms to remain independent of the CPA was F. Steiner & Co. Originally founded during the 1840s as a dyer and printer by the chemist Frederick Steiner, the company responded enthusiastically to the vogue for Art Nouveau, producing fabrics with extravagant compositions in astringent colours. The unusual character of some patterns suggests that they may have been purchased from France or Belgium. Others were supplied by British studios familiar with the Continental market, among them the Christopher Dresser Studio and the Silver Studio.

France and Belgium: Art Nouveau

The unbridled creativity of British Arts and Crafts pattern design at the turn of the century acted as an inspiration and catalyst for European Art Nouveau. But while some British designers, such as Harry Napper, entered into the spirit of creative exchange, others, such as Voysey, were alarmed at how their ideas were co-opted and distorted by rivals in mainland Europe. In 1909 Frank Warner, director of Warner & Sons, described Art Nouveau as "a Continental nightmare of design and colour... a vulgar parody on English art."[16]

Art Nouveau first manifested itself at the Paris Exposition Universelle of 1889, and was initially a sculptural phenomenon, embodied in exaggeratedly organic glass, metalwork, and furniture. By the turn of the century, however, the style was fully fledged, and had spread to other media, including surface patterns. Championed by architects such as Hector Guimard in Paris and Victor Horta in Brussels, it also exerted a strong effect on the development of German Jugendstil. Its chief promoter in France, and the instigator of much international exchange and cross-fertilization between disciplines, was Siegfried Bing. His remarkable gallery, L'Art Nouveau, brought together creations by leading British, European, and American protagonists in a wide range of media.

France: Édouard Colonna, Georges de Feure, and Eugène Gaillard

Bing's greatest triumph was his Pavillon de l'Art Nouveau at the Paris Exposition Universelle in 1900, which featured six interiors with furniture and furnishings by the architects Édouard Colonna, Georges de Feure, and Eugène Gaillard. The textiles in these room settings, produced in the form of woven silks and printed cotton velveteens, represented the summation of French Art Nouveau pattern design (fig. 1.30). French *fin de siècle* fabrics differed markedly from British Arts and Crafts textiles, their most striking feature being a reverence for tradition, particularly formal mirror repeats. Édouard Colonna's patterns were the most overtly modern and the most abstract, with their dancing, linear, rhythmic structures (fig. 1.31). Large in scale and exuberant in mood, Georges de Feure's florals were ostentatious and exotic (fig. 1.30), while Eugène Gaillard's sickly, etiolated plant forms had a restless, feverish quality (fig. 1.32). Distinguished from their British counterparts by the extreme artificiality of their imagery, they were also set apart by their exaggerated paleness and limited tonal variety. Colonna, de Feure, and Gaillard were not primarily pattern designers, and this was reflected in their approach to textiles. Produced as set pieces as part of a luxurious ensemble, their creations were never intended for the mass market, although they did exert some influence on the output of receptive manufacturers, such as the Lyons silk weavers Cornille Frères.

France: Hector Guimard

In Britain many leading Arts and Crafts architects were also accomplished textile and wallpaper designers, and pattern design had a major impact on interiors. By contrast, in France, three-dimensional design provided a much more fruitful avenue for Art Nouveau and patterns tended to be more incidental. The difference between the French and British approach is demonstrated by Hector Guimard – creator of the flamboyant ironwork entrances to the Paris Métro stations – who dabbled with pattern in some of his buildings. He created several wallpapers for the Castel Béranger in Paris (1894–8), some in the form of printed designs, others simulating low-relief plasterwork using the Lincrusta technique. The wild, squiggly motifs with which they were decorated were a

literal translation of the rampant organic vocabulary that he had originated in his architecture and metalwork. Guimard, like many French architects, was not really interested in designing patterns for general consumption. His aim was to create a *Gesamtkunstwerk*, a one-off work of art in which he controlled every element of the design, including the patterns on the ceilings and walls.

France: Alphonse Mucha, Émile-Allain Seguy, and Félix Aubert

The Czech-born graphic artist Alphonse Mucha, who lived in Paris, is frequently cited as a leading Art Nouveau pattern designer. His most tangible contribution was a group of printed textile panels featuring *fin de siècle femmes fatales*, which closely resembled his posters. He also published an album called *Documents Décoratifs* (1902), featuring fantastical designs for furniture, metalwork, ceramics, carpets, and wallpapers. However, although highly original, these patterns were never actually produced. Self-promotional publications of this kind, often bearing little relation to what was manufactured, were a common feature of the European design scene at this date, another example being Émile-Allain Seguy's *Les fleurs et leurs applications décoratives* (1901).

One of the few independent French pattern designers comparable to successful English practitioners was Félix Aubert. Using the standard vocabulary of Art Nouveau, Aubert created patterns composed of sinuous, long-stemmed flowers and ribbon-like motifs. He worked in a crisp but sometimes rather wooden style, designing printed fabrics for companies such as Pilon et Cie, and wallpapers for firms such as Gillou & Fils (fig. 1.33). Maurice Dufrêne, chief designer at La Maison Moderne, also designed fabrics and wallpapers for various firms (fig. 1.29).

Belgium and Germany: Henry van de Velde

The European obsession with dynamic whiplash motifs owed much to the theories of the Belgian Henry van de Velde. A symbolist painter turned architect-designer, he designed many textiles and wallpapers for companies in the Netherlands, Belgium, Germany, and France. Keen to establish closer links between artists and industry, van de Velde worked in Germany from 1899 to 1917, where he created designs for several manufacturers of jacquard-woven dress and furnishing fabrics, including Wilhelm Vogel of Chemnitz and Deuss & Oetker of Krefeld (fig. 1.34).

In 1894 van de Velde published his romantic personal manifesto *Le Déblaiement de l'Art* (Clearing the Way for Art), in which he coined the term *"dynamographique."* Putting this theory into practice, he promoted an overtly rhythmic, linear approach to design, applied across a wide range of media, including furniture, ceramics, and textiles. For van de Velde, vigorous, thrusting movement was a direct expression of spontaneity and life. Assertively rhythmic, sometimes perversely so, his patterns darted and danced in unexpected directions, denying visual repose. Although he confined

Top Fig. 1.33
Block-printed wallpaper frieze, designed by Félix Aubert, probably produced by Gillou & Fils, 1898. The extreme simplicity and flatness of this design suggest the influence of Japanese wood-block prints. The distinctive palette reflected the French preference for chalky tones.

Above Fig. 1.34
Woven artificial silk damask dress fabric, designed by Henry van de Velde, produced by Deuss & Oetker, 1901. This dynamic, linear pattern, with its twisting and darting motifs, illustrates van de Velde's belief that design should embody the energetic forces of the natural world.

himself largely to abstract motifs, his designs evoked unfurling leaves and stems, suggesting the irresistible forces of rising sap in the spring.

Germany: Hermann Obrist and Otto Eckmann

Munich was a hotbed of artistic activity during the 1890s and 1900s, and it was in this city that the radical breakaway art movement known as the Secession took place in 1893, four years before that in Vienna. It was out of the Secession that Jugendstil emerged, the German variant of Art Nouveau, taking its name from the title of the magazine *Die Jugend* (Youth), launched in Munich in 1896. One of the most influential figures in the city at this time was the embroidery designer Hermann Obrist, who had studied medicine, botany, ceramics, and painting before establishing his embroidery studio in 1892. Flying in the face of convention, Obrist injected nature with a heightened electrical charge, the exaggerated organic imagery of his embroideries signalling a radical departure for textile design. *Peitschenhieb* (c.1895), depicting an uprooted plant, pulsating with ferocious rhythmic undulations, became an icon of Jugendstil, influencing other pattern designers (fig.1.35).

Another leading proponent of Jugendstil, and a fellow member of the Munich Secession, was Otto Eckmann. After abandoning his career as a painter in 1894, Eckmann turned to woodcuts and tapestry, exploiting these forms as vehicles for fantastical symbolist imagery inspired by Japanese prints. Later he applied his talents to patterns, designing woven fabrics with restless organic imagery for Deuss & Oetker, and machine-printed wallpapers with flamboyant, rhythmic, curvilinear motifs for H. Engelhard of Mannheim (fig. 1.36). Long-stemmed flowers, drooping foliage, and emblematic

Above left Fig. 1.35
Surface-printed ceiling wallpaper, produced by G. Hochstädter, c.1905. The looping, tentacle-like stems in this design are characteristic of Jugendstil, the uninhibited German variant of Art Nouveau. Jugendstil flowered at Darmstadt, where the manufacturer of this wallpaper was based.

Above Fig. 1.36
Hellebaus surface-printed wallpaper, designed by Otto Eckmann, produced by H. Engelhard, 1900. Strongly influenced by Japanese prints, Otto Eckmann arrived at textile and wallpaper design via painting, woodcuts, and tapestry. His approach to colour and composition was highly idiosyncratic.

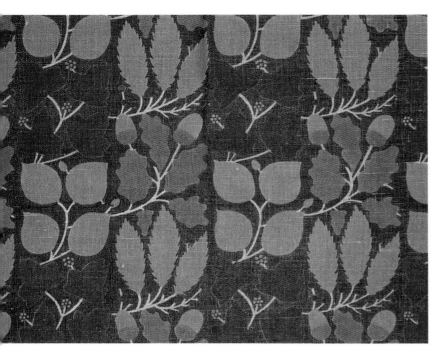

Top Fig. 1.37
Block-printed linen furnishing fabric, designed by M.H. Baillie Scott, produced by the Deutsche Werkstätten, c.1910. The British architect Baillie Scott, who had great success in Europe, originally developed this square pattern-making formula for stencilled wall coverings in the houses he designed.

Above Fig. 1.38
Block-printed cotton furnishing fabric, designed by Richard Riemerschmid, produced by the Deutsche Werkstätten, 1907. Rejecting the decadence of Jugendstil, Richard Riemerschmid created easily digestible, practical, and down-to-earth modular patterns based on small, repeated, stylized units.

birds, particularly swans, were key elements in his vocabulary. Other noteworthy Jugendstil artist-wallpaper designers included Walter Leistikow and Hans Christiansen.

Germany: Deutsche Werkstätten

The two most significant German pattern designers of the early 20th century were Adelbert Niemeyer and Richard Riemerschmid. Both were based in Munich and closely involved with the Deutsche Werkstätten (German Workshops), which had its roots in the Dresdner Werkstätten für Handwerkskunst (Dresden Workshops for Art Handicraft), founded by Karl Schmidt in Dresden in 1898. In 1907 the Dresdner Werkstätten merged with the Werkstätten für Wohnungseinrichtung, which was based in Munich and had been co-founded in 1902 by Karl Bertsch, Adelbert Niemeyer, and Willy von Beckerath. The new organization was called the Deutsche Werkstätten für Handwerkskunst GmbH, Dresden und München, but the name was shortened to Deutsche Werkstätten AG in 1913.

Although inspired by the aesthetic and social ideals of the British Arts and Crafts Movement, the Deutsche Werkstätten embraced machine production alongside handicrafts. Its showcase project was the garden city of Hellerau, designed from 1906, and in 1910 the workshops were transferred to a new factory in the city, designed by Riemerschmid. Block-printed and woven textiles formed a significant part of the Deutsche Werkstätten's activities from the outset, and from 1910 there was greater emphasis on printed textiles, including simple flat leaf patterns by the British Arts and Crafts architect Mackay Hugh Baillie Scott (fig. 1.37). Beckerath, Bertsch, Niemeyer, and Riemerschmid all contributed designs, and other textile designers during the early years included Lilly Erk, Margarethe Junge, and Carl Strathmann.

Richard Riemerschmid originally practised as a Symbolist painter, but turned to architecture and design during the late 1890s. Furniture became his main discipline, although he also designed glass, ceramics, carpets, lighting, and graphics. Tackling both printed and woven furnishing fabrics, Riemerschmid produced patterns that were generally small in scale, with compact structures and intense repeats (fig. 1.38). Many designs were composed of small circular, triangular, or diamond-shaped motifs in dense, interlocking arrangements. Leaves, berries, and flower heads, all pared down to their most reduced forms, were key components of Riemerschmid's design vocabulary – an extreme reaction against the excesses of Jugendstil.

The Deutsche Werkstätten had close links with the Deutscher Werkbund (German Work Association), an alliance of artists, craftsmen, and industrialists founded in Munich in 1907. This organization encouraged manufacturers to produce everyday goods that were well-made and functional, and which embraced the aesthetics of modern design. Machine production was actively endorsed as a way of rationalizing manufacture and bringing costs

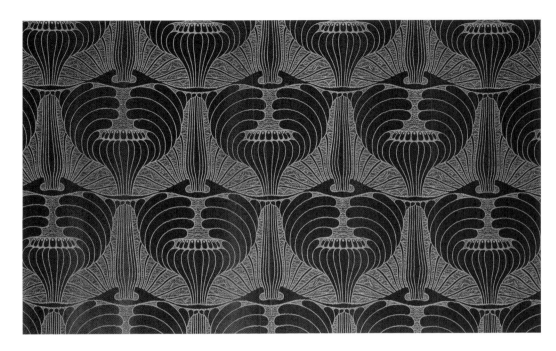

Left Fig. 1.39
Mohnköpfe woven silk, cotton, and viscose rayon furnishing fabric, designed by Koloman Moser, produced by Johann Backhausen & Söhne, 1900. Although based on poppy heads, the organic motifs in this pattern are so stylized as to be almost unrecognizable. What is important in this composition is the dynamic thrust and rhythm.

down. The Werkbund's aspirations, summed up by the word *Sachlichkeit* (meaning "objectivity" and "matter of factness"), were perfectly embodied in the unassuming but stimulating patterns of Riemerschmid. In addition to textiles, he designed surface-printed wallpapers for Erismann & Cie of Breisach, an active Werkbund member. Like his textiles, these were characterized by small, tightly organized, stylized plant motifs, and their overtly repetitive patterns were intended as an honest reflection of the fact that they were machine-produced.

Like Riemerschmid, Adelbert Niemeyer had trained as a painter, but excelled as a designer of furniture, interiors, ceramics, glass, posters, textiles, and wallpapers. Niemeyer designed woven fabrics for Wilhelm Vogel of Chemnitz and printed fabrics for Hahn & Bach of Munich (both Werkbund members), before channelling his activities into the Deutsche Werkstätten from 1907. His early textile patterns were mainly abstract, featuring linked rings and criss-crossing bands. Niemeyer's talented pupil, Emmy Seyfried, also designed imaginative woven textiles for these two firms.

Germany: Peter Behrens

The architect Peter Behrens, another Munich Secession artist, was also briefly active in textiles at this time. In 1898 he became a founding member of the Vereinigte Werkstätten für Kunst im Handwerk (United Workshops for Art in Handicraft) in Munich, another organization that brought together artists, designers, and architects committed to raising standards of design. This prompted him to start designing ceramics, glass, metalwork, and furniture, and in 1901 he built a house for which he designed every detail of the furnishings at the artists' colony in Darmstadt. At this time

Behrens was still working in the flamboyant Jugendstil style, but after moving to Düsseldorf in 1903 to become director at the Kunstgewerbeschule (School of Arts and Crafts), he developed a simpler, plainer idiom. His printed textiles, designed around that time for Gebrüder Elbers of Hagen, were created at this transitional stage in his career. Printed in muted colours, they featured geometric columns suggestive of totems, and flat, stiff, quasi-symbolic birds.

Austria: Koloman Moser and Josef Hoffmann

Artistic life in Vienna was electrified in 1897 with the founding of the Vienna Secession, which was created in direct opposition to the Vienna Academy. The Secession provided a forum for radical artists, architects, and designers who wanted to break with tradition, their aim being to develop new forms of contemporary expression and to foster creative cross-fertilization between different branches of the visual arts. In painting the prime mover was Gustav Klimt, and in design the pivotal figures were the architect Josef Hoffmann and the painter and graphic artist Koloman Moser. Hoffmann and Moser's ground-breaking textiles for Johann Backhausen & Söhne marked the birth of a distinctive new Viennese school of pattern design.

Backhausen produced a wide range of textiles, including carpets and woven and printed fabrics. Moser's patterns for the company, created between 1898 and 1904, deliberately eschewed both the seductive floral imagery of the English Arts and Crafts style and the decadent, sinuous flourishes of Franco-Belgian Art Nouveau. Instead, his key source of inspiration was *katagami* (the mulberry-bark stencils used by Japanese dyers to transfer patterns on to

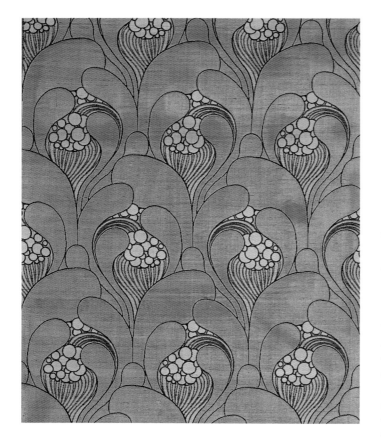

cloth), an interest nurtured through his study of the collections in the Österreichische Museum für Kunst und Industrie. Moser's patterns, which were intense, inward-looking, and fantastical, were characterized by flattened, abstracted, organic imagery and fluid, interlocking forms, evoking tentacles, stamens, and waves. Designed to cover every inch of the cloth, these curiously exotic patterns, with their repetitive and tightly structured compositions, can be directly attributed to the influence of *katagami*. Plants were the main subject, but condensed into fluid, rhythmic, biological, abstract forms, as with the poppy heads in *Mohnköpfe* (1900) (fig. 1.39). Symbolist painting, which was at the peak of its popularity in Europe during this period, was another pervasive influence, and is clearly discernible in *Blumenerwachen* (1899), with its quasi-mystical interpretation of natural phenomena (fig. 1.40). Mysticism was also evident in the work of another Backhausen designer, the painter and architect Robert Oerley, who created a pattern called *Kosmischer Nebel* (1899) evoking swirling balls of mist (fig. 1.41).

In 1901 Moser published a portfolio of textile and wallpaper patterns called *Flächenschmuck* (Surface Decoration), featuring highly stylized and condensed compositions of leaves, flowers, animals, and birds. Ingeniously conceived and intricately drawn, these patterns were more abstract than organic, more graphic than decorative, and once again the Japanese influence was particularly strong. Many were composed as mirror images, sometimes in the form of positive-negatives, while others were multiplied as if seen through a kaleidoscope. Obsessively repetitive in a mathematical way, they were an exercise in pure theoretical pattern design, presaging the graphic experiments made by M.C. Escher several decades later.

Josef Hoffmann's approach was completely different to that of Moser. Originally trained as an architect at the Vienna Academy under Otto Wagner, with whom he later worked, Hoffmann was appointed Professor of Architecture at the Kunstgewerbeschule in Vienna in 1899. He went on to become the most influential designer in Austria, applying his talents to many diverse fields and collaborating with a host of manufacturers in Austria, Germany, and Bohemia (later part of Czechoslovakia). In 1903, after securing financial backing from the banker and industrialist Fritz Waerndorfer, Hoffmann and Moser co-founded the Wiener Werkstätte (Vienna Workshops). Created as a multi-disciplinary alliance between like-minded designers and craftsmen in a wide range of media – including ceramics, glass, furniture, metalwork, jewellery, textiles, and bookbinding – the Werkstätte stated that its aim was to "intervene whenever the struggle is engaged against outdated or ossified art forms and to replace them by forms adapted to their uses; logical, economic forms, corresponding to aesthetic needs."[17] Moser withdrew from the Wiener Werkstätte in 1907, but Hoffmann played a key role as the artistic director of the enterprise from 1903 to 1931, pushing its creative work forward on all fronts, including pattern design.

Two major architectural projects, the Purkersdorf Sanatorium near Vienna (1903–5) and the Palais Stoclet in Brussels (1905–11), dominated the Wiener Werkstätte's early activities. Each was conceived as a *Gesamtkunstwerk*, an attempt to create the ultimate coordinated building, perfectly harmonized in all aspects of its furniture and furnishings. Hoffmann's early textiles took the form of woven upholstery fabrics and carpets for these interiors, although he also supplied designs independently to Backhausen, both before and after the founding of the Wiener Werkstätte. His first patterns, dating from 1901, marked a decisive shift away from the prevailing curvilinear Art Nouveau and Jugendstil idioms. Composed of rectangles, squares, ovals, and triangles, suspended within a rhythmic arrangement of parallel or intersecting lines, they had a stark geometry that reflected the cross-fertilization between Vienna and Glasgow at this time (fig. 1.42). Charles Rennie Mackintosh had participated in the Vienna Secession in 1900, and the grid patterns that characterized his furniture were translated by Hoffmann into a comprehensive vocabulary of two- and three-dimensional design. There are also similarities between Hoffmann's patterns and the stained-glass windows of the American architect Frank Lloyd Wright. Neither Mackintosh nor Wright, however, was creating patterns during this period, whereas pattern-making was a key element in the wider design vocabulary of Hoffmann and the Wiener Werkstätte.

Ultimately it was the stark, geometric patterns developed by Hoffmann, rather than the stylized organic designs of Moser, that became the prevailing Viennese idiom. The new style was also embodied in patterns created by several other Backhausen designers during the 1900s, notably Otto Prutscher, a former pupil of Hoffmann. Subsequently Hoffmann himself expanded his vocabulary to include geometricized organic motifs. By the end of the decade he had developed his familiar leaf and lattice patterns, a recurrent feature in his later printed textiles for the Wiener Werkstätte, with their insistent all-over designs. Stylized plant motifs were also a leitmotif of Hoffmann's wallpapers, manufactured from around 1908 by Erismann & Cie. His wallpapers were much lighter and airier than his textiles, however, and were typically composed of small sprigs framed within a large, rectangular grid. Like his textiles, these were often printed in black and white, although the wallpaper patterns were more recessive. Because they were produced by machine surface-printing rather than by hand block-printing, they could be sold for reasonable prices, thereby helping to disseminate Hoffmann's distinctive design ideas to a broader market.

The Wiener Werkstätte's involvement in pattern design took on added momentum in 1910 with the establishment of its in-house textile and fashion departments. From this time printed textiles became its main focus, and over the next two decades, with input from a growing number of contributors, its patterns became increasingly ambitious and diverse.

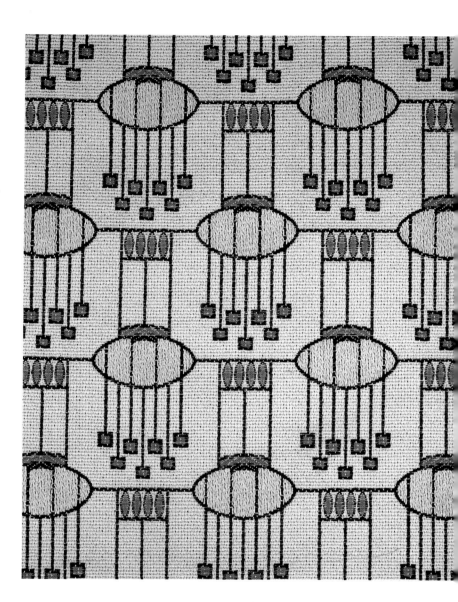

Opposite top Fig. 1.40
Blumenerwachen woven cotton, silk, and wool furnishing fabric, designed by Koloman Moser, produced by Johann Backhausen & Söhne, 1899. A symbolic interpretation is invited by the title's reference to "awakening flowers." Japanese *katagami* stencil prints were the main stylistic influence.

Opposite bottom Fig. 1.41
Kosmischer Nebel woven silk and cotton furnishing fabric, designed by Robert Oerley, produced by Johann Backhausen & Söhne, 1899. The "cosmic fog" of the pattern's title reflects the intensity of this depiction of balls of mist.

Above Fig. 1.42
Lampen woven cotton and viscose rayon furnishing fabric, designed by Josef Hoffmann, produced by Johann Backhausen & Söhne, 1906. In stark contrast to Koloman Moser's seductive organic designs, Josef Hoffmann favoured crisp, geometric motifs and taut, punchy, repetitive patterns.

Proto-Modernism, Modernism, and Moderne

Opposite Fig. 2.1

Surface-printed wallpaper, designed by Henri Stéphany, produced by the Société Charles Follot, c. 1929. This wallpaper demonstrates the dramatic impact of Cubism on pattern design during the 1920s. Plant forms are deconstructed and then reassembled in an energetic striped, rhythmic composition. The intensity of the colours, particularly the use of several variations of the same tone, characterizes the decorative exuberance of the Jazz Age.

In 1908 the Austrian architect Adolf Loos published a polemical pamphlet called "Ornament and Crime" in which he announced that decoration was superfluous to the needs of the rational modern age. However, while Loos's extreme ideas clearly influenced the architects of the Modern Movement and the founders of the Bauhaus, many other designers instinctively rejected his bleak message – notably the *artistes décorateurs* in Paris (fig. 2.1) and the proto-Modernist pattern designers of the Wiener Werkstätte in Vienna – and it was their work that was celebrated in the *Exposition Internationale des Arts Décoratifs et Industriels Modernes*, held in Paris in 1925.

After the exhibition the Americans enthusiastically embraced the French "Moderne" style, or Art Deco as it has since become known. Meanwhile, in Britain, another type of proto-Modernism surfaced in the Omega Workshops, triggered by the catalyst of Post-Impressionist painting. Rampant decoration flourished alongside emergent Modernism during the 1910s and 1920s, a period of great diversity and innovation for pattern design. In fact, many leading practitioners, such as Josef Hoffmann, expressed themselves in both idioms, without any sense of awkwardness or compromise. In many ways the two prevailing trends – Modernism and Moderne – were complementary. It was not until the 1930s that Modernist dogma came into the ascendant, sending pattern design into partial retreat.

Austria: Wiener Werkstätte

Originally established by Josef Hoffmann and Koloman Moser in 1903 to produce artist-designed furniture and furnishings, the Wiener Werkstätte exerted a huge influence on the decorative arts over the next three decades. Gradually the emphasis shifted from

Top Fig. 2.2
Amsel block-printed linen dress fabric, designed by Koloman Moser, produced by the Wiener Werkstätte, 1910–11. The Wiener Werkstätte played a pivotal role in pattern design's evolution during the 1910s and 1920s, developing electrifying new forms of abstraction. This pattern predates Op Art by fifty years.

Above Fig. 2.3
Stichblatt block-printed dress and furnishing fabric, designed by Ugo Zovetti, produced by the Wiener Werkstätte, 1910–11. Often limited to one or two colours, with sharp contrasts between light and dark, many early Wiener Werkstätte patterns were characterized by punchy rhythms and insistent repetition.

exclusive furnishings for specific interiors to a broader range of products. With the establishment of its textile and fashion departments around 1910, and the shift from woven to printed textiles, the Wiener Werkstätte's involvement in pattern design greatly increased. Over the next twenty years 1,800 textiles were created by around a hundred designers.

By 1910 the original high-minded ideals of the Wiener Werkstätte had been somewhat diluted, and there was greater pragmatism in the running of the organization. Creative standards remained high, however, and Hoffmann continued to play a key role as artistic director, although Moser, who opposed the growing diversification and commercialization of the Werkstätte, had left in 1907. By increasing its range and scale of production, the Werkstätte disseminated its aesthetic ideas more widely. Despite its proximity to Germany, its activities appear to have been surprisingly little affected by the First World War, and the 1910s and 1920s were an astonishingly buoyant and creative period.

During the early years the Wiener Werkstätte had relied heavily on Backhausen & Söhne to produce its fabrics – at that time mainly woven upholstery textiles – while some Werkstätte designs were manufactured on a larger scale by Backhausen under its own name. From 1910, however, the Werkstätte took direct control over the marketing of its own textiles, registering its official trademark in 1913. Production now encompassed both dress and furnishing fabrics – often treated as interchangeable – printed on silk, cotton, and linen, and some patterns were also used to decorate accessories such as lampshades and umbrellas. The textile and fashion departments, although administratively separate, were closely related creatively and commercially. Many designers had input into both departments, among them Eduard Josef Wimmer-Wisgrill, who joined the Werkstätte in 1906 and was head of fashion from around 1910 to 1922. From the outset the fashion department drew extensively on the printed fabrics produced by the textile department, such as Koloman Moser's *Amsel* (1910–11), with its quasi-optical diamond effects (fig. 2.2).

Woven textiles, because of the mechanical processes they involve, tend to foster designs of a formal nature, whereas block-printed fabrics offer more creative scope. The simple fact of moving from one medium to another, therefore, had a radical effect on the output of the Wiener Werkstätte, encouraging much greater freedom and experimentation in design. Some Werkstätte patterns were printed using as many as twenty-four blocks, an indication of the high level of sophistication possible using this medium, although it was equally well suited to simpler and more modest effects. In general the shift from woven to printed textiles encouraged a more consciously graphic approach to pattern-making. Carl Otto Czeschka created patterns that were easily digestible but memorable, using colour to emphasize the rhythms of simple shapes, as in *Wasserorgel* (1910–12) (fig. 2.4). Ugo

Zovetti's intense abstracts and teaming organic patterns, such as *Stichblatt* (1910–11) (fig. 2.3) and *Konstantinopel* (1910–12), were highly compressed.

The establishment of the textile department acted as a catalyst for the emergence of new idioms, both abstract and representational, and this coincided with a move towards greater ornamentation in design. Josef Hoffmann led the way, employing a more relaxed and overtly decorative vocabulary in place of his earlier rigid geometric designs. In general patterns became more colourful, playful, and energetic, as in the jazzy abstracts of Mitzi Friedmann, with their chevrons, zigzags, and serrated motifs. Even tiny dress prints, such as *Blitz* (1910–11) by Carl Krenek, were full of explosive energy, contrasting rounded shapes with jagged motifs (fig. 2.6). Progressive abstraction flourished alongside nostalgic lyricism, the latter stimulated by the growing interest in Austro-Hungarian folk art. Traditional florals were reinterpreted in lively and imaginative ways by designers such as Lotte Frömel-Fochler (fig. 2.8) and Wilhelm Jonasch (fig. 2.7), who developed a new vocabulary of flattened, geometricized motifs and heightened colours. Primitivism and exoticism were central to the patterns of Ludwig Heinrich Jungnickel, such as *Urwald* (c.1910–11) (fig. 2.9). Other liberating influences included Fauvism, Cubism, and Expressionism, as well as the Ballets Russes, which visited Vienna in 1912–13.

The Wiener Werkstätte acted as an umbrella for many individual talents, and there was no approved house style. New blood was regularly injected, and it was the constant stream of new ideas which resulted that made the group into such a powerful force for so long. Many designers had been taught by Hoffmann at Vienna's Kunstgewerbeschule, and were based in the Kunstlerwerkstätte (Artists' Workshops), established in 1913 to provide subsidized workspace for artists who had recently left the school. Here, supervision was provided by the Wiener Werkstätte's master craftsmen and chief designers, and in return the Werkstätte had first refusal on all designs. Draughtsmen were employed to prepare the artists' designs for the block-cutters. The fabrics were printed by commission printers in Austria, Switzerland, Germany, and France.

Josef Hoffmann, who devised around seventy-five patterns over three decades, provided the creative backbone for the Wiener Werkstätte (fig. 2.12). Generating and absorbing ideas in equal measure, he played a decisive role in shaping the Werkstätte's overall approach to pattern and in recruiting new designers. In his own designs, organic motifs such as leaves and flowers were often reduced to their simplest elements, then juxtaposed with abstract motifs in the form of squares, diamonds, and triangles, and slotted into a geometric framework like building bricks. The interplay between the organic and geometric was arresting, exaggerated by the startling contrast between light and dark. Hoffmann's approach to pattern was consciously architectural and overtly graphic at the same time.

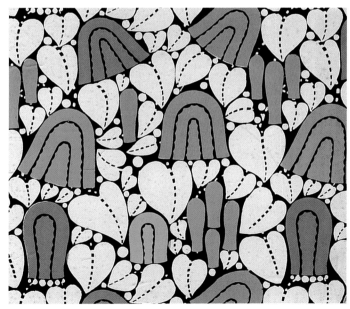

Top Fig. 2.4
Wasserorgel *block-printed dress fabric, designed by Carl Otto Czeschka, produced by the Wiener Werkstätte, 1910–12.* Carl Otto Czeschka was an accomplished and influential graphic designer. This pattern, alluding to hydraulic organs, has great visual immediacy and was used for both fashion and bookbinding.

Above Fig. 2.5
Jagdfalke *wallpaper, designed by Josef Hoffmann, block-printed by Max Schmidt for the Wiener Werkstätte, 1913.* Originally designed as a printed furnishing fabric in 1910–11, this pattern was part of the Wiener Werkstätte's first wallpaper collection in 1913. It features Hoffmann's hallmark heart-shaped leaves.

Top Fig. 2.6
Blitz block-printed dress fabric, designed by Carl Krenek, produced by the Wiener Werkstätte, 1910–11. The lightning to which the title refers is evoked through the jagged zigzag motifs. Carl Krenek's background as a graphic artist perhaps accounts for the dynamic and vigorous intensity of this design.

Above left Fig. 2.7
Krieau block-printed furnishing fabric, designed by Wilhelm Jonasch, produced by the Wiener Werkstätte, 1910–11. This colourful, folksy floral, which was much larger in scale than *Blitz* (top left), was used to upholster the benches in Josef Hoffmann's Grabencafé in Vienna in 1912.

Above Fig. 2.8
Grünfink block-printed furnishing fabric, designed by Lotte Frömel-Fochler, produced by the Wiener Werkstätte, 1910–11. The Wiener Werkstätte evolved a distinctive and influential new genre of floral pattern design, characterized by flat, geometricized motifs and densely packed, colourful compositions.

Above Fig. 2.9
Urwald block-printed linen furnishing fabric, designed by Ludwig Heinrich Jungnickel, produced by the Wiener Werkstätte, c.1910–11. The chevron-patterned tree trunks, with their spiky foliage, inject visual dynamism into this exotic, folk art-inspired pattern, while the monkeys add a note of fun.

Top Fig. 2.10
Irrgarten block-printed furnishing fabric, designed by Dagobert Peche, produced by the Wiener Werkstätte, 1913. The title of this airy, balletic pattern, which means "maze," suggests the ingenuity of the composition. The blade-like motifs make the design both spiky and feathery at the same time.

Above Fig. 2.11
Flut block-printed fabric, designed by Dagobert Peche, produced by the Wiener Werkstätte, 1911–16. The title of this pattern, "Incoming Tide," suggests that it depicts lapping water. Fine black outlines edged with colour – here blue to evoke the sea – were a characteristic device of Dagobert Peche.

Dagobert Peche, who dominated the Werkstätte from 1913 until his untimely death in 1923, exerted a particularly significant impact on pattern design. During this period he created over a hundred textile and wallpaper patterns, as well as designing ceramics, glass, ivory, leather, jewellery, metalwork, and fashion. He introduced a completely new style of pattern-making, stimulating and provocative, yet free-flowing and relaxed (figs. 2.10 and 2.11). Consciously artificial in character, but full of grace and fluidity, Peche's images dance, float, and waft effortlessly with airy, Neo-Rococo charm. Although chiefly associated with stylized vegetation patterns, he also created some highly original abstracts, composed of sinuous, painterly scrolls or angular, snaking lines. Blade-like leaves preponderated – sometimes feathery, as in *Wicken* (1919), sometimes spiky, as in *Irrgarten* (1913) (fig. 2.10) – all drawn in a light, delicate, linear style. Some patterns, such as *Daphne* (1918), were created as positive-negatives, printed either in light colours on a dark background or dark colours on a light background.

During the 1920s approximately half of the Wiener Werkstätte's patterns were abstract and half were stylized, decorative designs. Designers such as Maria Likarz, who created more than 200 designs, and Max Snischek, who took over the fashion department in 1922, moved freely between these two idioms, and there was growing cross-fertilization between their work and that of the European artistic avant-garde. Likarz's early patterns included a bold abstract geometric called *Irland* (1910–13) (fig. 2.13), presaging the textiles of Sonia Delaunay, and there were further similarities in her later dynamic folksy abstracts composed of coloured bands, chevrons, and stripes. Working in a confident modern idiom, Snischek created strikingly adventurous abstracts that prefigured the "Contemporary" style of the 1950s. Often these were characterized by overlapping strips of colour or maze-like patterns of fine lines (fig. 2.15).

Two other prolific designers of the 1920s were Mathilde Flögl and Felice Rix, who combined a delicate, spindly graphic style with whimsical and fanciful organic and figurative motifs (fig. 2.14). Abstract patterns also formed part of the repertoire of both designers. Rix specialized in bold, criss-crossing diagonals, while Flögl's forte was richly coloured patchworks. Clara Posnanski, who ran a textile finishing business in Vienna, added another interesting dimension to the late Werkstätte oeuvre. Specializing in *Spritzdrucke* (sprayed prints), a stencil process in which dyes were applied using fine aerograph sprays, she created geometric patterns with distinctive granular shaded effects (fig. 2.16).

Heightened activity in one area of pattern design naturally prompted cross-fertilization with others, paving the way for the Wiener Werkstätte's expansion into wallpapers in 1913. The first collection, printed by Max Schmidt in Vienna, featured existing textile designs adapted as wall coverings, including Eduard Wimmer-Wisgrill's Neo-Biedermeier striped floral sprig pattern

Ameise and Josef Hoffmann's stylized tulip design *Jagdfalke* (fig. 2.5) (both 1910–11). Subsequently the Wiener Werkstätte collaborated with other European wallpaper manufacturers, who surface-printed their designs by machine on a larger scale. The German firm Flammersheim & Steinmann produced special collections by Dagobert Peche in 1922 and Maria Likarz in 1925, while the Swiss-German firm Salubra produced a collection by Mathilde Flögl in 1929. A distinctive feature of Peche's wallpapers was the contrast between the spikiness of the leaves and flowers and their graduated striped backgrounds that dissolved from one colour into another.

Electrifyingly modern in its outlook, the Wiener Werkstätte demonstrated what could be achieved when designers set up as manufacturers and seized the artistic reins. Challenging the conventions of accepted design idioms, Werkstätte patterns were important in two key respects. First, they explored the exciting new vocabularies of abstraction. Secondly, they injected new life into traditional floral motifs, giving them punch and zest. Characterized by diversity rather than homogeneity, the Werkstätte's output cannot be neatly characterized. As Waltraud Neuwirth has pointed out, their designs encompassed a series of apparently irreconcilable opposites: "tectonics and movement, classicism and baroque/rococo, absence of ornamentation and decorative excess, austerity and ecstasy, monochrome and excessive colour, and, if we wish to use the classical antithesis, Apollonian and Dionysian."[1]

Austria: Josef Frank

Although the Wiener Werkstätte was the dominant force in Austria during the first three decades of the 20th century, acting as a magnet for the most talented pattern designers, another important company operating in Vienna during the late 1920s was Haus & Garten. Co-founded in 1925 by Oskar Wlach and the architects Josef Frank and Walter Sobotka, this was an upmarket home furnishings company producing furniture, lighting, and printed textiles. Josef Frank, Haus & Garten's chief designer, trained as an architect at the Technische Hochschule in Vienna during the first decade of the century and, after the First World War, was appointed Professor of Building Construction at the Kunstgewerbeschule. The joyful, vividly coloured, block-printed linen furnishing fabrics he designed for Haus & Garten during the late 1920s were extremely popular, and he consciously swam against the tide of the increasingly doctrinaire Modernist age.

A master of floral pattern design, Frank combined the ingenuity of William Morris, whose work he greatly admired, with the energy of the Wiener Werkstätte, to which he had supplied several patterns during the 1910s. As with Morris, it was Frank's keen interest in botany that accounted for the freshness of his imagery. But whereas Werkstätte designers depicted imaginary flowers as a vehicle for decorative abstract infill patterns, Frank adopted a more authentically scientific approach. Several patterns, including

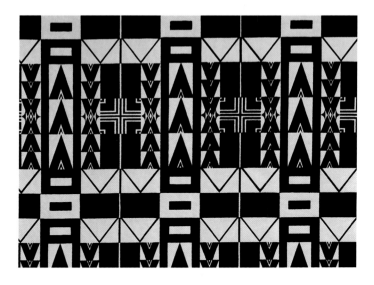

Top left Fig. 2.12
Santa Sofia block-printed silk and cotton furnishing fabric, designed by Josef Hoffmann, produced by the Wiener Werkstätte, 1910–12. This design shows Hoffmann's customary use of geometric motifs in a grid-like framework.

Centre left Fig. 2.13
Irland block-printed furnishing fabric, designed by Maria Likarz, produced by the Wiener Werkstätte, 1910–13. The geometric abstraction of the 1920s is heralded by this pre-war pattern.

Left Fig. 2.14
Gespann block-printed cotton furnishing fabric, designed by Felice Rix, produced by the Wiener Werkstätte, 1925. The doodle-like quality of Rix's linear pattern gives it a feeling of informality.

Top right Fig. 2.15
Berggeist block-printed silk furnishing fabric, designed by Max Snischek, produced by the Wiener Werkstätte, 1924. With its spindly lines and strips of colour, this pattern foretells an aesthetic more often associated with the 1950s.

Above right Fig. 2.16
Paul aerograph-sprayed stencilled furnishing fabric, designed and printed by Clara Posnanski for the Wiener Werkstätte, 1927. Here graduated colouring was achieved by spraying dyes on to stencils.

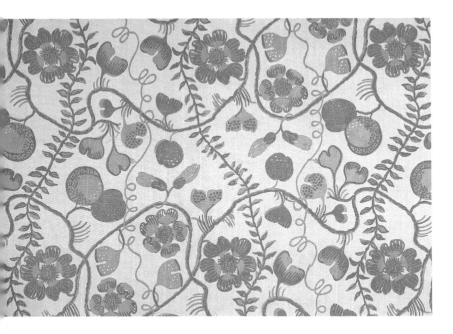

Mirakel and *Orangenzweige* (both 1925–30), were dominated by long, snaking stems weaving through the design and binding it together, a device characteristic of Morris's work (fig. 2.17). Sometimes these stems were vertical or horizontal, but at other times were twisted on the diagonal, with rotational pattern repeats.

Mille fleurs patterns, inspired by French medieval tapestries, were another recurrent feature, characterized by lush carpets of minutely detailed flowers, as in *Kitzbühel* (1925–30), depicting an Austrian alpine meadow. Sometimes the flowers were vertically aligned as if springing up from flowerbeds, as in *Primavera* (1920–25); at other times they were strewn in different directions, as in *Tulipan* (1925–30), as if in aerial view (fig. 2.18). The overriding effect was one of informality, and repeats were cleverly disguised. *Tang* (1925–30) was rather different in character, contrasting geometric starfish motifs with the fluid, undulating outlines of seaweed. Haus & Garten continued in operation until 1935, but Frank, who was Jewish, emigrated to Sweden in 1933, the year in which Hitler came to power.

Germany: Deutsche Werkstätten

Outside Austria the most receptive market for Wiener Werkstätte textiles was Germany, and it was in Munich – birthplace of the Deutsche Werkstätten and the Vereinigte Werkstätten – that artistic trends most closely paralleled those in the cultural hothouse of Vienna. Textiles had been a significant element of the Deutsche Werkstätten's activities since its creation in 1907, with Richard Riemerschmid and Adelbert Niemeyer playing a key role in formulating its early style. Block-printed textiles became increasingly important after 1910. From 1923 textile production was expanded with the founding of the Deutsche Werkstätten-Textilgesellschaft mbH (DEWE-TEX), established in cooperation with the Gottlob Wunderlich factory at Waldkirchen-Zschopautal.

By this time Richard Riemerschmid was less actively involved, having taken up the post of director at the Kunstgewerbeschule in Munich in 1913, but Adelbert Niemeyer continued to produce designs. Dense, all-over, stencil-like patterns of massed flowers and foliage, printed in bright colours with strongly defined outlines, were characteristic of his work during the 1910s (fig. 2.19). Some patterns had a Neo-Biedermeier flavour, with cut-out motifs arranged in formal garlands or vertical bands. Others were composed of tiny repeated images of feathers or leaves.

A towering figure at the Deutsche Werkstätten from 1922 was Professor Josef Hillerbrand, who taught at the Staatsschule für Angewandte Kunst (State School for Applied Art) in Munich. Originally trained as an architect and mural painter, Hillerbrand subsequently developed into a talented all-round designer of textiles, carpets, ceramics, glass, metalwork, furniture, lighting, and interiors. Pattern design was his most outstanding area, and in addition to his numerous printed textiles, he designed wallpapers

Top Fig. 2.17
Orangenzweige *block-printed linen furnishing fabric, designed by Josef Frank, produced by Haus & Garten, 1925–30.* Although based in Vienna, Josef Frank developed a style of pattern-making more closely allied with William Morris than the Wiener Werkstätte, as reflected in these undulating stems.

Above Fig. 2.18
Tulipan *block-printed linen furnishing fabric, designed by Josef Frank, originally produced by Haus & Garten, 1925–30, reprinted by G.P & J. Baker for Svenskt Tenn, mid-1930s.* Many of Josef Frank's earlier designs were reissued after he emigrated to Sweden in 1933. This one was printed in Britain.

Above left Fig. 2.19
Block-printed linen furnishing fabric, designed by Adelbert Niemeyer, produced by the Deutsche Werkstätten, c.1910. Flat, stencil-like patterns featuring dense clusters of foliage with strongly defined outlines were common just before and after the First World War.

Left Fig. 2.20
Block-printed cotton furnishing fabric, designed by Josef Hillerbrand, produced by the Deutsche Werkstätten, c.1922–30.

Josef Hillerbrand had a natural flair for pattern-making. This design, with its disembodied plant motifs and striking colouring, has a rather surreal quality.

Above Fig. 2.21
Block-printed furnishing fabric, designed by Josef Hillerbrand, produced by the Deutsche Werkstätten, 1926. With its heightened colouring and the decorative intensity of its geometricized, organic patterns, this striking design shows Hillerbrand at the height of his powers.

for Erismann & Cie. Although clearly indebted to Dagobert Peche for aspects of his imagery and style, Hillerbrand was a highly accomplished and original pattern designer (figs. 2.20 and 2.21). His early patterns were characterized by graceful, balletic, linear motifs, often sparsely arranged on a white or black ground. During the mid-1920s stylized leaves and flowers became a recurrent theme, used as a vehicle for geometricized infill patterns, with a lively interplay between flat colour and fine line. Ostensibly naturalistic, although frequently fantastical, his patterns were subtly avant-garde in their exploration of abstraction and adventurous in their use of colour. Strongly coloured grounds were a feature of many designs, and colours were sometimes limited to variants of one intense shade (fig. 2.21). Hillerbrand also designed printed and woven textiles in subtle colours with simple checks and stripes.

Working alongside Hillerbrand at DEWE-TEX was a group of talented artists, architects, and designers, including Ernst Böhm, Fritz August Breuhaus de Groot, Ruth Hildegard Geyer-Raack, Lisl Bertsch-Kampferseck, Richard Lisker, Tommi Parzinger, Elisabeth Raab, Robert Raab, Heinrich Sattler, Berta Senestréy, Wolfgang von Wersin, Else Wenz-Viëtor, and Franz Wiedel. In printed textiles, designers tended to fall into one of two camps, reflecting the dichotomy in Hillerbrand's output. One group specialized in colourful jaunty stylized plant patterns; the other produced subtle striped or plaid designs. Some crossed over between the two.

Germany: Vereinigte Werkstätten für Kunst im Handwerk and Deutscher Farbmöbel

Another collective that sprang up in Munich at the same time as the Deutsche Werkstätten was the Vereinigte Werkstätten für Kunst im Handwerk (United Workshops for Art in Handicraft). Founded in 1898 by a group of artists and architects, the Vereinigte Werkstätten produced modern furniture and furnishings, including restrained, graceful printed and woven textiles by the architect and furniture designer Bruno Paul. After Paul shook off the influence of Jugendstil, his textiles took on strong Neo-Classical overtones, and he often arranged his motifs in neat vertical bands or trellis-like frames (fig. 2.22).

After the First World War the mood changed and more vigorous, colourful, and dynamic styles developed in both printed and woven textiles, created by the studio of Fritz August Breuhaus de Groot and by other designers, including E. Engelbrecht, Paul László, Anneliese May, Maria May, and Tommi Parzinger. Several designers also contributed to the Deutsche Werkstätten, and Josef Hillerbrand's influence was strongly felt. The architect and furniture designer Paul László created patterns with bold, graphic, stylized plant motifs, but switched at will from highly patterned to minimalist effects. Like Hillerbrand, many designers were also active in the field of wallpapers. László and Parzinger both collaborated with Flammersheim & Steinmann, for example, while Maria May designed a special collection for Rasch in 1932.

Top Fig. 2.22
Block-printed linen furnishing fabric, designed by Bruno Paul, produced by the Vereinigte Werkstätten, c.1910. The restrained classicism of this Neo-Biedermeier design was common before the First World War. German designers later began to explore the language of geometric abstraction.

Above Fig. 2.23
Starnberg 2 *block-printed cotton furnishing fabric, designed by Elisabeth Raab, produced by Deutsche Farbmöbel, 1925.* Pattern-making in Germany assumed a contradictory character during the 1920s, when minimalist geometrics appeared alongside playful, decorative, stylized floral designs.

Hillerbrand's influence was also evident at the Deutsche Farbmöbel, a printed textile firm established in Munich in 1925 by Wilhelm Marsmann and Viktor von Rauch. Both of these designers created colourful patterns composed of stylized leaves and flowers, although Marsmann's vocabulary also extended to collage-like designs incorporating fish and birds. Counterbalancing these decorative patterns were the severe abstracts of Elisabeth Raab (fig. 2.23).

Germany: Bauhaus

In 1983 the Italian designer Andrea Branzi observed: "Industrial design and the Modern Movement have always been nagged by the 'question of decoration,' a complex question that has never really been cleared up, and over which a battle has been fought in the name of that cleanness of form that is indispensable to the civilized development of industrial society."[2] Battle lines were drawn up by Adolf Loos with the publication of his polemical pamphlet *Ornament and Crime* (1908), and battle commenced with the creation of the Bauhaus in 1919. The stated aim of the Bauhaus was to foster cross-fertilization between artists, craftsmen, and architects, but its hidden agenda was the elimination of superfluous decoration. Pattern design was strategically omitted from the school's syllabus, and surface decoration – other than carefully chosen colours – was virtually outlawed.

Given the Bauhaus's reluctance to acknowledge the validity of pattern, it is somewhat ironic that wallpapers became the most successful mass-produced item to emerge from the school. This apparent anomaly is explained by the fact that wallpaper design grew out of the activities of the mural painting workshop, which formed part of the interior design department. The workshop was headed by the artist and colour designer Hinnerk Scheper. Scheper was a friend of Maria Rasch, a former Bauhaus student and the sister of Dr Emil Rasch, director of the wallpaper firm Gebr. Rasch of Bramsche. Having produced a lively group of patterns by the Cologne-based JEKU Artists' Studio called Neuartige Eigenheim Tapeten (New Home Wallpapers) in 1925, Rasch had already demonstrated its receptiveness to modern design. Following negotiations, a contract was drawn up between the company and the Bauhaus in 1929, and production of the first *Bauhaus-tapeten* (Bauhaus wallpapers) began the following year (fig. 2.24).

Intended as low-cost, machine-produced, "standard" products, suitable for use in the new large-scale social housing developments being built at this time, Bauhaus wallpapers were deliberately understated and recessive. They were created as flexible colour and texture tools that could harmonize with a range of interiors and furniture, rather than as vehicles for personal expression, and the first collection consisted of designs developed by students in the interior design department. What was radical about the *Bauhaus-tapeten* was that they were not decorated with patterns in the conventional sense, but with mottled, flecked, or combed markings and painterly textural effects, printed in three different

Top Fig. 2.24
Four surface-printed wallpapers, designed by students at the Bauhaus, produced by Rasch, 1930. Decorated with subtly coloured, understated, textural effects, Rasch's *Bauhaus-tapeten* marked a concerted attempt by early Modernists to challenge the dominance of conventional patterned furnishings.

Above Fig. 2.25
Silk and cotton damask hanging, designed and hand-woven by Gunta Stölzl at the Bauhaus, 1926–7. Composed using an "approved" vocabulary of elementary forms, this hanging was created before the self-imposed clampdown on personal expression at the Bauhaus. Later, pattern was virtually outlawed.

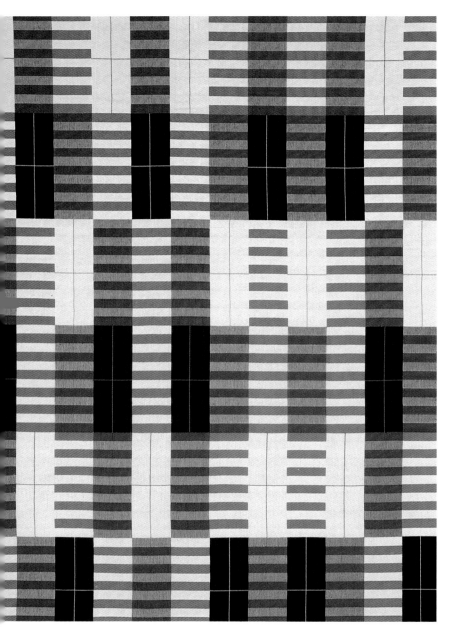

Above Fig. 2.26
*Triple-weave hanging, designed and
hand-woven by Anni Albers at the
Bauhaus, 1926.* Albers limited herself to
four colours in this characteristically
austere and disciplined, yet visually
stimulating design. Where the cloth
lies double, it is raised in relief, adding
a sculptural dimension.

tones of the same colour. The wallpapers were initially produced
in various shades of red, orange, yellow, blue, grey, pink, and
brown, but the range of colours was later expanded. The collection
grew to be lastingly successful and, after being relaunched in 1948,
is still in production in a modified form today. During the 1930s
the *Bauhaus-tapeten* activated a shift away from patterned
wallpapers to monochrome and embossed wall coverings. They
also fuelled the fashion for *Effekttapeten*, wallpapers characterized
by subdued mottled designs with a subliminal pattern element.
These paralleled the "porridge" effects popular in other countries.

From the outset the Bauhaus treated textiles as a purely structural
medium, although it took some time before pattern was
successfully eliminated. During the early 1920s, drawing on the
theories of Johannes Itten, the weaving department created
carpets and tapestries decorated with an "approved" vocabulary
of elementary forms (circles, squares, and triangles) in primary
colours. Paul Klee also exerted a powerful influence through his
teaching on design theory, prompting further experimentation in
woven textiles with layering and stripes. Gunta Stölzl used colour,
rhythm, and geometric form in an overtly expressive and dynamic
way in her tapestries from this period (fig. 2.25). Anni Albers,
who studied at the Bauhaus from 1922 to 1930, exemplified a
more restrained approach, limiting herself to a more sober palette
and grid-like compositions of bands and stripes (fig. 2.26).

After the Bauhaus moved to Dessau in 1925, emphasis shifted from
craft production to industrial design, and the school now began
to consider tapestry as self-indulgent. Renouncing the decorative
nature of her earlier work, Stölzl, who was appointed head of the
weaving department in 1927, now focused on designing woven
furnishing fabrics for industrial production, eliminating pattern
in favour of colour and texture. In 1930 a contract was signed with
the Berlin-based firm Polytex, which produced Bauhaus textiles
under licence. "The good designer is the anonymous designer,
the one who does not stand in the way of the material; who sends
his products on their way to a useful life without an ambitious
appearance," wrote Anni Albers a few years later.[3]

Stölzl's successor in 1931 was the interior designer Lilly Reich.
Ironically, shortly before the Bauhaus closed, Reich introduced
a new course, "Combination exercises in material and colour,"
which opened the door for experimentation with printed textiles.
The emphasis was on simple, low-cost patterns for machine
production, and designs by current and former students, including
Hajo Rose, were sold to companies such as M. van Delden of
Gronau. Some *Bauhaus-tapeten* designs were also manufactured as
printed textiles, but the initiative proved short-lived as the Bauhaus
was shut down by the Nazis in 1933.

Not surprisingly, the school disapproved of the *Exposition des Arts
Décoratifs et Industriels Modernes* held in Paris in 1925. Its staff and

students alike rejected the basic premise of the exhibition – that design could be purely decorative – and made clear their fundamental opposition to prevailing trends. However, although the anti-pattern sentiments of the Bauhaus found little favour among mainstream textile and wallpaper manufacturers, the school's "less is more" aesthetic and "truth to materials" ethic had a lasting impact on hand weavers internationally, including Ethel Mairet in Britain and Hélène Henry in France.

France: Paul Poiret and Atelier Martine

Significantly, the first steps towards the evolution of Art Deco patterns in France were taken not by an architect, artist, or designer, but by a couturier, Paul Poiret, who established his fashion house in 1903. Rejecting formality, Poiret revolutionized women's fashion with his loose Empire-line dresses, Egyptian tunics, and Persian *jupes culottes*, or divided skirts. Vibrant colours and rich patterns were key features of his garments, which were often trimmed or lined with patterned fabrics or embroidery. Embracing eclecticism, Poiret was inspired by "the Orient," a loose term encompassing Asia, eastern Europe, and the Middle East. The orientalist craze was further fuelled by Sergei Diaghilev's Ballets Russes, which took Paris by storm during 1909–10, with their exotic costumes and set designs by Léon Bakst.

Already hailed as the most brilliant couturier in Europe, Poiret had ambitions to revitalize interior decoration, inspired by seeing the Wiener Werkstätte's printed textiles while on a trip to Vienna in 1910. His enthusiasm prompted two separate but related initiatives in Paris, a decorating workshop called the Atelier Martine, which operated from 1911 to 1929, and the "Petite Usine," a short-lived textile workshop led by Raoul Dufy. The Atelier Martine consisted of a group of teenage girls who produced lively, colourful "primitive" drawings of flowers and vegetation, used as the basis for printed textiles and wallpapers (figs. 2.27, 2.28, and 2.30). Plucked from humble backgrounds and lacking any artistic education, the girls were never formally trained, Poiret's aim being to nurture their instinctive creativity and foster an authentic modern school of "folk art." For inspiration they were sent out to sketch in the countryside, and they also visited fruit and vegetable markets, botanical gardens, and the Paris aquarium. Many of the girls came and went over the years, two of the most outstanding being Alice Rutty and Agnès Jallot, whose drawings Poiret held in particularly high regard.

The Atelier Martine's vivid, uninhibited, and invigorating style of pattern-making caused a sensation at the Salon des Artistes Décorateurs in 1912 and was widely influential over the next two decades (fig. 2.29). Exuding a raw naïvety, its printed textiles – used for both curtains and upholstery – were decorated with bold, simplified floral patterns or stylized vegetation. Martine wallpapers, manufactured by Paul Dumas, although not as brightly coloured as the fabrics, were still extremely potent, and were often characterized

Top Fig. 2.27
Two block-printed silk dress fabrics, designed by the Atelier Martine, 1919. These vibrant printed fabrics, designed by untrained young girls at Paul Poiret's Atelier Martine, show the unpretentious style of floral pattern-making nurtured by the couturier. The draughtsmanship is authentically childlike.

Above Fig. 2.28
***Les Pavots** wooden roller-printed wallpaper, designed by the Atelier Martine, printed by Paul Dumas, c.1912.* Rejecting the polish and sophistication of patterns created by commercial studios, Paul Poiret sought to capture the naïve spontaneity of childhood in his Atelier Martine textiles and wallpapers.

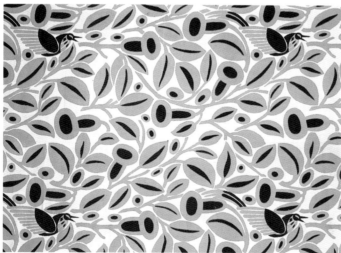

Top Fig. 2.29
Surface-printed wallpaper from the Nouveautés pattern book, produced by A. Glatigny & Cie, 1927-8. These flower heads are similar in outline to those in Fig. 2.27, confirming the powerful impact of the Atelier Martine style on mainstream producers during the 1920s. The colours are likewise bold.

Above Fig. 2.30
Block-printed silk fabric, designed by the Atelier Martine, 1924. Produced towards the end of Paul Poiret's involvement with the Atelier Martine, this design is more sophisticated than the studio's early patterns and appears to reflect stylistic cross-fertilization from the Wiener Werkstätte.

by dark grounds and dynamic foliage, producing riotous jungle effects. Branching out into furniture, carpets, and other applied arts, the workshop evolved into a successful decorating firm, undertaking commissions for complete interiors. A radical new departure was to combine curtains, upholstery fabrics, and wallpaper, all in the same bold pattern, thereby intensifying the impact of the already powerful designs.

The first Atelier Martine shop opened in Paris in 1912, and other outlets followed in Berlin, London, Philadelphia, and Biarritz. The First World War had a catastrophic effect on Poiret's career, however, and although the popularity of the Atelier Martine continued unabated during the early 1920s, Poiret himself was never able to re-establish his glittering pre-war reputation. At the Paris Exposition of 1925, in a final bid to renew his fortunes, three luxurious barges were decked out with Martine fabrics and furniture. Beset by financial problems, Poiret was obliged to sell the Atelier Martine in 1926, and soon after the Wall Street crash of 1929 it closed down permanently.

France: Raoul Dufy

Poiret's second contribution to the history of pattern design was his role in prompting the artist Raoul Dufy to embark on a career in textile design. Dufy and Poiret, who met in 1909, shared an enthusiasm for contemporary Austrian pattern design. Realizing that Dufy's Fauvist paintings and wood engravings were readily translatable into textile patterns, Poiret encouraged him to start designing fabrics. In 1911, shortly after establishing the Atelier Martine, Poiret set up a small textile printing works, known as the "Petite Usine," to produce Dufy's designs. The artist's dramatic early patterns, such as the giant flower-and-leaf pattern *La Perse* (1911), were used for cushions and curtains, as well as being incorporated into Poiret's coats and dresses.

So compelling were Dufy's patterns that, within a year, he was tracked down by Charles Bianchini of the Lyons silk firm Bianchini-Férier and offered a contract. Although this forced the closure of the Petite Usine, some of Dufy's original designs, such as *La Chasse* and *La Danse* (both 1911), were later produced by Bianchini-Férier, and Poiret continued to use Dufy's fabrics for his garments. Dufy's partnership with Bianchini-Férier proved very successful, both commercially and creatively, and between 1912 and 1928 he designed over 2,000 patterns. Originally established in 1888 as Atuyer, Bianchini et Férier, the company specialized in jacquard-woven dress and furnishing silks. As well as designing for these ranges, Dufy created patterns for the block-printed linen and cotton furnishing textiles produced at Bianchini-Férier's branch factory at Tournon, near Lyons.

Although stylized foliage formed the basis for many patterns, Dufy's vocabulary was wide-ranging, encompassing narrative, figurative, and abstract designs (figs. 2.31 and 2.32).

Quintessentially modern, yet historically aware, Dufy was equally at home in a variety of genres, although his primary source of inspiration was *toiles de Jouy*, textiles printed from engraved copper plates, associated with the Oberkampf factory at Jouy-en-Josas during the late 18th century. Drawing on his experience of wood engraving, Dufy reinterpreted this genre in a bolder, heavier contemporary idiom, giving rise to the term *toiles de Tournon*. Two of his earliest examples were *Fruits d'Europe* and *Fruits d'Afrique* (both 1912) (fig. 2.32). Printed in monochrome, these designs were notable for the exoticism of their imagery, and the crispness of their graphic style, particularly the heightened contrasts between white line patterns and flat coloured planes. Several designs produced around 1920 – *L'Amour*, *La Moisson*, and *La Pêche* – were based on much earlier wood engravings, and Dufy's familiarity with this medium informed his pattern-making style.

Fundamental to the appeal of Dufy's textiles were their dynamic compositions, with motifs often arranged in opposing diagonals. In *La Moisson* (1920) a harvester was camouflaged by giant sheaves of wheat, their vigorous criss-crossing forms creating a quasi-Futurist effect. Blade-shaped leaves were a recurrent motif, their rhythmic curves serving to bind elements of the pattern together. Another Dufy characteristic was the device of highlighting minor elements of the pattern by magnifying and condensing them in size. In *Fruits d'Europe* sheaves of corn, pumpkins, flowers, foliage, and birds were all equalized in size, while in *Paris* (1923) flowers were blown up to the same scale as figures and buildings, creating surreal juxtapositions. In *Longchamps* (1923) all the different elements of the composition – jockeys, horses, pavilions, giant rose blooms, and parading society ladies – were crammed together, jostling for attention. By camouflaging key elements of the design, Dufy aroused the curiosity of the viewer. Wit and ingenuity were important features of his patterns, which were intended to stimulate the mind as well as the eye.

In 1920 Dufy observed: "The decorative tendencies in contemporary painting, aided by new methods of manufacture, have brought the art of fabric printing to an unparalleled degree of perfection... Synthetic colours, contrary to widely held opinion, if treated correctly, can be compared with the vegetable dyes employed in other times. These brilliant works will tell posterity of today's magnificent renaissance in the art of printed fabrics."[4] Dufy's textiles dominated Bianchini-Férier's collections from 1913, influencing a whole school of French pattern design. He continued to design for the company until around 1928 and then designed for the House of Onondaga in New York between 1930 and 1933, after which he devoted himself again to painting.

France: Bianchini-Férier and Soieries Ducharne

Bianchini-Férier also collaborated with several other designers, including Paul Iribe (fig. 2.33), A.F. Lorenzi, Charles Martin, and the illustrator Robert Bonfils. Working in the Dufy idiom, the firm

Top Fig. 2.31
Block-printed linen furnishing fabric, designed by Raoul Dufy, produced by Bianchini-Férier, c.1925. Drawing on his experience of wood engraving, Raoul Dufy often used overtly graphic devices in his textiles, as in this lively pattern, designed on the diagonal, with its white lines cut into solid shapes.

Above Fig. 2.32
Fruits d'Europe *block-printed linen furnishing fabric, designed by Raoul Dufy, produced by Bianchini-Férier, 1912.* This design, complementing another called *Fruits d'Afrique*, demonstrates Dufy's characteristic ploy of magnifying and condensing different elements of a pattern to the same scale.

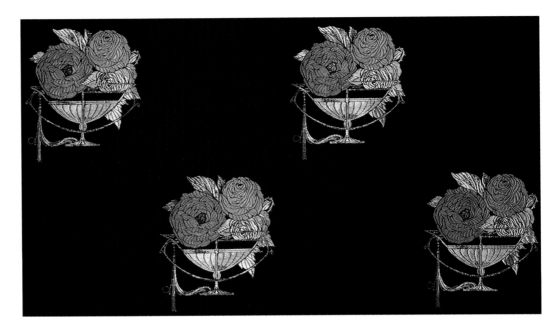

Coupes de Roses woven silk brocade with gold thread, designed by Paul Iribe, produced by Bianchini-Férier, 1914. Paul Iribe, celebrated for his stylish fashion illustrations for Paul Poiret, created several iconic textile designs before the First World War that paved the way for Art Deco. In this luxurious fabric the contrasts between the pink and orange flowers, the gold cups, and the black background are extremely dramatic.

created contemporary pictorials, such as Lorenzi's *La Promenade* (1926) and lively fruit and foliage designs, such as *Oasis* (1925–9) by Bonfils. Later, after Cubism succeeded Fauvism as the dominant artistic style, Bonfils adopted the abstract geometric Moderne idiom in mechanistic patterns such as *Variations* (c.1931), composed of fragmented concentric circles, chevrons, and broken stripes.

The productive alliance between Raoul Dufy and Bianchini-Férier inspired other companies, notably Soieries Ducharne, which employed the talented Michel Dubost as its chief designer from 1922 to 1933. Established in 1920 by François Ducharne, the firm specialized in jacquard-woven dress silks. Dubost, who was in charge of its Paris studio, created dynamic florals, Franco-Moorish abstracts, and dazzling patterns that combined representational motifs with advanced abstraction, including *La Forêt est pleine d'Oiseaux*.

France: Artistes Décorateurs

At this time most French textile and wallpaper manufacturers were serviced by commercial design studios, such as Kittler, Libert, Pollet, and Wolfsperger, who produced vast quantities of technically perfect designs. Often family-run operations, the studios tended to perpetuate a traditional aesthetic, although, as a service industry, they were obliged to turn their hand to both traditional and Moderne. But although the 1920s marked the heyday of the studios, it was not they, nor the manufacturers they serviced, who were responsible for Art Deco. The originators were the independent *artistes décorateurs* (multi-disciplinary, artist-led decorating companies). Furnishings were but one of a number of subsidiary activities for *artistes décorateurs*, their primary activity being furniture. Bypassing manufacturers, they established direct

contact with clients through regular exhibitions organized by the Société des Artistes Décorateurs, which was founded in 1901.

With the evolution of *artistes décorateurs* into *ensembliers* shortly before the First World War, the French began to diverge from the German concept of *Gesamtkunstwerk*. Instead of designing every element of a building in a consistent and unified style, *ensembliers* assembled interiors from a range of disparate but complementary elements. In a climate of historical revivalism, references to Rococo and Neo-Classicism abounded, and the Empire period in particular was celebrated as a golden era in French design. The textiles and wallpapers produced by *artistes décorateurs* were as stylistically inconsistent as their furniture. They were sometimes designed by the *artistes décorateurs*, and sometimes commissioned from fashionable artists, illustrators, and pattern designers, the diversity of contributors adding to the eclecticism of the designs. Although many patterns were unashamedly traditional, others assimilated Ballets Russes colouring, Atelier Martine imagery, or Cubist abstraction, a vocabulary known collectively as Moderne.

France: Süe et Mare and André Groult

Süe et Mare, the most famous of the *artistes décorateurs*, were renowned for their collaborations with artists. Originally founded by Louis Süe in 1912 as L'Atelier Français, the company was renamed La Compagnie des Arts Français in 1919 after Süe joined forces with André Mare. Although best known for their furniture, both men had originally trained as painters and included textile design among their extensive repertoire of accomplishments (fig. 2.40). They also commissioned textiles from other artists and designers, including Marianne Clouzot, Jacques Drésa (the professional name of André Saglio), Marguérite Dubuisson,

Gustave-Louis Jaulmes, Charles Martin, Maurice Taquoy, and Paul Véra. More progressive than Süe et Mare was the *ensemblier* René Herbst, who founded the Union des Artistes Modernes (UAM) in 1929. Before embracing Modernism at UAM, he displayed great flair in his use of bold, stylized floral textiles and wallpapers, applying them liberally to walls, ceilings, floors, windows, and furniture.

Even more significant in terms of pattern design was the company run by André Groult, which, although multi-disciplinary, was particularly noted for its textiles and wallpapers. Groult had previously worked for the Paris shop La Maison Moderne, where he had led the shift from Art Nouveau towards more restrained Classical styles. Pattern design was his speciality, and in 1910, when he was setting up his own decorating company, the facilities included a block-printing workshop, enabling him to produce coordinated textile and wallpaper designs. In addition to creating his own patterns he commissioned designs from the illustrator Paul Iribe (fig. 2.34) and the portrait painter Marie Laurencin. Other designers included Albert André, Arlègle, Jacques Drésa, Erté, Georges d'Espagnet, Jean-Émile Laboureur, Constance Lloyd, and Louis Süe. Modern in spirit, although moderate in tone, Groult's patterns ranged from stencil-like, flat, stylized flower and fruit patterns to Dufyesque narrative *toiles*.

France: Primavera, La Maîtrise, and Pomone

Several Parisian department stores also established their own decorating studios, producing modish textiles and wallpapers in eclectic and hybrid styles. In 1913 Les Magasins du Printemps created Primavera, whose wallpapers ranged in style from pseudo-primitive to Cubist Moderne. Les Galeries Lafayette set up La Maîtrise in 1921, with Maurice Dufrêne, formerly of La Maison Moderne, as artistic director. A founder member of the Société des Artistes Décorateurs, Dufrêne created designs in many different styles. In addition to creating his own patterns, he commissioned upholstery tapestries from Jean Beaumont and wallpapers from Palyart. Finally, in 1923, Au Bon Marché secured the services of another veteran designer, Paul Follot, to run its decorating studio, Pomone. One of the most fashionable and prolific *artistes décorateurs* of the 1900s and 1910s, Follot was the son of the wallpaper manufacturer Félix Follot (of the Société Charles Follot), so pattern design naturally formed part of his repertoire (fig. 2.38). Follot designed both textiles and wallpapers, shifting effortlessly between traditional and Moderne styles.

France: Émile-Allain Seguy, René Gabriel, and Henri Stéphany

The heightened interest in textiles and wallpapers at this time led to the emergence of specialist pattern designers. Chief among these were Émile-Allain Seguy, René Gabriel, and Henri Stéphany, whose work was much sought after by both manufacturers and *artistes décorateurs*. Seguy had been producing very original patterns since the turn of the century, published in the form of stencil-printed

Top Fig. 2.34
Block-printed linen furnishing fabric, designed by Paul Iribe, produced by André Groult, 1910. The stylized roses in this printed fabric, exhibited at the Salon d'Automne in 1910, are similar to those in Iribe's *Coupes de Roses* (opposite). Rose accessories also often adorned the dresses of Paul Poiret.

Above Fig. 2.35
Design for a wallpaper, Émile-Allain Seguy, produced by the Société Isidore Leroy, 1925–6. One of the most original designers of the period, Émile-Allain Seguy used bright colours and exotic imagery to striking effect, creating dazzling and memorable patterns with a heightened decorative intensity.

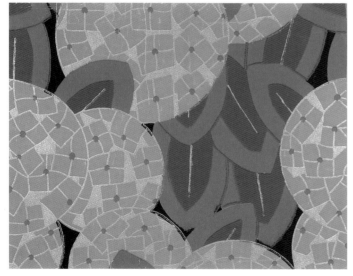

pochoir albums. During the mid-1920s his dazzling, stylized insect and bird patterns were translated into wallpapers by the Société Isidore Leroy (fig. 2.35), while the American firm Schumacher produced woven silk textiles. Seguy's wallpapers were arresting in their imagery and colouring, featuring surreal juxtapositions of birds, butterflies, or insects against a curtain of leaves or flowers.

René Gabriel block-printed his own wallpapers in his workshop Au Sansonnet during the 1920s, and subsequently supplied patterns to Nobilis and Papiers Peints de France. Stylistically his designs ranged freely from full-blown, jazzy abstraction (fig. 2.36) to graceful, calligraphic landscapes and florals. Henri Stéphany excelled in the vibrant Moderne idiom, designing woven silks for Cornille Frères and Schumacher, and wallpapers for Desfossé et Karth, the Société Française des Papiers Peints, and the Société Charles Follot. His wallpapers for the Société Française des Papiers Peints included dynamic fractured patterns of abstracted blossoms printed in metallic pigments (fig. 2.37). For Follot, Stéphany designed striped foliage patterns (fig. 2.1) and a pattern called *Constructions Arabes* (1925–9), a Cubist-inspired Moorish roofscape.

France: Paul Dumas, Société Charles Follot, Société Francaise des Papiers Peints, and Nobilis

Wallpapers emerged as a particularly buoyant art form in France during the 1920s, reflecting the heightened decorative intensity of French pattern design. Paul Dumas ran a large textile and wallpaper factory at Montreuil sous Bois where, in addition to printing wallpapers for Atelier Martine, he produced designs by, among others, Paul Follot (fig. 2.38), Lina de Andrada (fig. 2.39), and Lucie Renaudot. The Société Charles Follot, established in 1859, also produced artist-designed, surface-printed wallpapers, ranging in style from Rayonist to Delauneyesque to sub-Wiener Werkstätte. Apart from Stéphany (fig. 2.1), other notable designers during the late 1920s and early 1930s were Édouard Bénédictus, Paul Follot, and the decorative painter Adrien-Jacques Garcelon.

The Société Française des Papiers Peints, established by Jules Roger in 1881, produced classic Art Deco wallpapers by some of the most fashionable *artistes décorateurs* and designers of the period, such as Émile-Jacques Ruhlmann, Henri Stéphany (fig. 2.37), and Süe et Mare. Ruhlmann's patterns, such as *Les Roses* (1923–4) (fig. 2.41), which featured a profusion of stylized flowers, were striking in their vivacity. The designs of Süe et Mare were more conventional, with their elegant arrangements of ribbons, roses, and swooping birds (fig. 2.40). The Parisian wallpaper *éditeur*, or publisher, Nobilis was originally founded by Adolphe Halard in 1928 as a shop selling imported wallpapers. It established its artistic credentials in the 1930s with designs by Suzanne Fourcade, René Gabriel, Pierre Lardin, Jacques Le Chevalier, Paule Marot, and Charles Portel. In 1930, after joining forces with the textile designer Suzanne Fontan, the company expanded into furnishing fabrics, and after the Second World War it was renamed Nobilis-Fontan.

Top Fig. 2.36
Tombouctou *block-printed wallpaper, designed by René Gabriel, produced by Papiers Peints de France, 1925.* During the 1920s chevron patterns were a feature of Moderne designs, symbolizing the rhythms of the Jazz Age. René Gabriel, a leading wallpaper designer, explored diverse modish styles.

Above Fig. 2.37
Surface-printed wallpaper, designed by Henri Stéphany, produced by the Société Française des Papiers Peints, c.1925. Cubism was enthusiastically embraced by French pattern designers as a purely decorative device. The fractured blossoms in this wallpaper look more like glittering baubles than flowers.

Far left top Fig. 2.38
Surface-printed wallpaper, designed by Paul Follot, produced by Paul Dumas, 1930. Many strands of contemporary art influenced French pattern design during the 1920s. Raoul Dufy and Fauvism were clearly important inspirations for Paul Follot in this expressive painterly wallpaper, also produced as a printed textile.

Far left bottom Fig. 2.39
Les Joueurs de Tennis *surface-printed wallpaper, designed by Lina de Andrada, produced by Paul Dumas, 1925.* This design, depicting glimpses of two tennis courts in aerial view, was machine-printed at the large textile and wallpaper factory run by Paul Dumas. Raoul Dufy's influence is apparent in the unusual composition.

Left top Fig. 2.40
Surface-printed wallpaper, designed by Louis Süe and André Mare, produced by the Société Française des Papiers Peints, 1922–3. Süe et Mare were leading *artistes décorateurs*, who designed textiles and wallpapers as well as furniture. This pattern, although apparently traditional, is depicted in an informal modern style.

Left bottom Fig. 2.41
Les Roses *surface-printed wallpaper, designed by Émile-Jacques Ruhlmann, produced by the Société Française des Papiers Peints, 1923–4.* Ruhlmann, like many *artistes décorateurs*, moved freely between historical and contemporary idioms. The massed roses in this pattern have an almost abstract quality.

France: Édouard Bénédictus and Paul Rodier

Although pattern designers frequently moved between textiles and wallpapers, they tended to develop allegiances in one particular area. Édouard Bénédictus, for example, designed wallpapers for the Société Charles Follot, but was primarily associated with textiles. Originally trained as a painter, he designed rugs and woven textiles during the 1920s in an upbeat, fantasy style. A keen advocate of artificial fibres, Bénédictus collaborated in 1925 with Brunet-Meunié et Cie, a Paris-based firm of *éditeurs,* founded in 1815, that specialized in this field. Best known for his ebullient fountain design *Les Jets d'Eau* (fig. 2.42), an iconic image from the Paris Exposition of 1925, he injected the liveliness and dynamism of printed fabrics into the static medium of woven textiles. Bénédictus also designed cotton and viscose damasks for Tassinari & Chatel, and around 1926–7 he published an album of exuberant Moderne patterns called *Nouvelles Variations.*

Another high-profile and influential design-led textile manufacturer was Paul Rodier, best known for his woven fabrics made from unusual combinations of yarns. Already celebrated for his hand-woven dress fabrics, Rodier expanded into furnishing fabrics during the 1920s, and in 1927 he supplied some of the textiles for the luxury liner *Île de France.* One of the few manufacturers to make "authentic" Cubist fabrics, Rodier produced some woven abstracts designed by Picasso for the interior designer Jean-Michel Frank.

France: Exposition Internationale des Arts Décoratifs et Industriels Modernes

All the different creative threads in French pattern design came to a head in the *Exposition Internationale des Arts Décoratifs et Industriels Modernes* of 1925. This was largely conceived as a propaganda exercise to re-establish international confidence in French design, and two-thirds of the site in Paris was devoted to French production, with displays by all the leading *artistes décorateurs*, department stores, and textile manufacturers. Austria also played a prominent role, showing installations by the Wiener Werkstätte and Haus & Garten. Although Germany and the United States were absent, Britain, Denmark, Greece, Italy, Japan, Poland, Spain, Sweden, Switzerland, Turkey, and the Soviet Union all mounted displays or erected pavilions. The exhibition also provided a platform for radical architects such as Le Corbusier, Robert Mallet-Stevens, and Konstantin Melnikov, and avant-garde artists such as the Italian Futurists and Sonia Delaunay. Although the *arts décoratifs* far outweighed the *arts industriels*, the exhibition marked the culmination of a host of trends that had been bubbling up in France and Austria since 1910.

France: Sonia Delaunay

One of the biggest sensations of the Paris Exposition was the Boutique Simultanée, a remarkable collaboration between the artist Sonia Delaunay and the couturier Jacques Heim. Born in the Ukraine, Delaunay had come to Paris in 1905 to study painting.

She and her husband, Robert Delaunay, were important early pioneers of abstraction, which they felt opened up new realms of perception. Through her "colour rhythm" paintings, first produced in 1912, Sonia Delaunay sought to provoke a simultaneous response to colour, form, and movement.

Her artistic ideas were closely linked with fashion from the outset, after she began to make Cubist-inspired, multicoloured patchwork garments. Later an invitation to design costumes for the Ballets Russes prompted her to experiment with integrated shapes and geometric patterns, and this led to her theory that "Construction, the cut of a dress, is to be conceived at the same time as its decoration."[5] Pattern was the key to this fusion of art and fashion, leading to the development of her *"tissus simultanés."* Although conceived as early as 1911, her textile designs dated from around 1923–7, after she was commissioned to create a group of fifty patterns for a Lyons silk manufacturer. Loosely painted, they consisted of small-scale, abstract patterns, usually squares, triangles, stripes, spots, or wavy lines, printed in a dynamic palette of contrasting colours that she described as "colour scales" (fig. 2.43). "The rhythm is based on numbers, for colour can be measured by the number of vibrations," she explained.[6]

Delaunay's importance to the history of pattern design lay in her promotion of pure geometric abstraction, and her application of the theory of "simultaneity" to printed textiles. Her *"tissus simultanés"* electrified the garments into which they were incorporated, highlighting the importance of pattern in everyday life. In a lecture given at the Sorbonne in 1927 on "The Influence of Painting on the Art of Clothes," Delaunay stated: "A movement is now influencing fashion, just as it influences interior decoration, the cinema, and all the visual arts, and it overtakes everything that is not subject to this new principle which painters have spent a century seeking; we are only at the beginning of the study of these new colour relationships, still full of mystery to unravel, which are at the base of a modern vision... There is no going back to the past."[7]

Soviet Union: Liubov Popova, Varvara Stepanova, and Thematic Textiles

Interesting parallels to the theories of Sonia Delaunay surfaced in the Soviet Union during the early 1920s, where the painter Liubov Popova and the graphic artist Varvara Stepanova tackled the issue of textile and fashion reform. After the Revolution the two women embraced the concept of Productivism, believing that it was more productive for artists to design functional objects than to pursue individual artistic expression. Popova, who had studied painting abroad, was strongly influenced by Cubism and Futurism. Stepanova, who had trained at the Kazan Art School, had gained professional experience as a dress designer. Together they developed a new democratic "uniform" for the populace, which amalgamated bold, geometric textile patterns with angular, sculptural forms.

In 1923 they designed a group of printed textiles for the First State Textile Factory in Moscow, which, like Sonia Delaunay's *"tissus simultanés,"* were conceived as an integral component of the garments themselves. These patterns were extremely radical, consisting of brightly coloured, interlocking and overlapping, flat, abstract geometric motifs. Forcefully graphic in character, they were composed from dynamic, rhythmic arrangements of circles, squares, stripes, chevrons, and grids (figs. 2.44 and 2.46). The idea was to develop a completely new vocabulary devoid of historical and cultural associations, symbolizing the positive aspirations of the emancipated Soviet Union.

Perhaps somewhat predictably, the masses did not respond with any great enthusiasm to these rarefied concepts, and the Soviet authorities became increasingly suspicious of abstraction after the Paris Exposition, which highlighted the alarming similarities between Soviet Constructivism and what was perceived as Cubism's degenerate capitalist aesthetics. By now Popova had died, and Stepanova increasingly turned her attention to typography and book design. Subsequently Constructivism fell out of official favour, and a more accessible narrative vocabulary, known as "thematic" design, was evolved. These symbolic and propaganda patterns, widely applied to printed dress fabrics at the end of the 1920s and in the early 1930s, featured Communist motifs such as hammers and sickles, and images of factories and tractors, promoting the objectives of the first Five Year Plan of 1929–34.

Printed on cheap cotton cloth at mills in and around Moscow and Ivanovo, "thematic" designs reached the peak of their popularity between 1927 and 1931. The patterns were created by established factory-trained designers such as Sergei Burylin (fig. 2.47), as well as by teachers and graduates of Vchutein, the textile faculty of the Institute of Arts and Industrial Design in Moscow, including Oskar Griun and D. Preobrazhenskaya (fig. 2.45). Although small in scale, and often limited to a single colour, many patterns were highly ingenious. Industrial motifs predominated, often depicted in a consciously mechanistic, jagged style, ranging from steam trains and ships to cogwheels and light bulbs (the latter celebrating the national programme of electrification). The imagery was usually so abstracted that its literal meaning was eclipsed by its graphic impact. Parades and sporting activities were also on the approved list of subjects, and designers excelled at creating energetic, repetitive patterns from images of rowers, swimmers, skaters, and marching figures. Arranged in tight-knit, rhythmic sequences, sometimes in opposing diagonals, "thematic" designs were visually punchy and dynamically charged.

Britain: Omega Workshops

In 1912 the artist and critic Roger Fry announced his plans for establishing a decorative workshop specializing in artist-designed furniture and furnishings: "Already in France Poiret's École Martine shows what delightful new possibilities are revealed in this

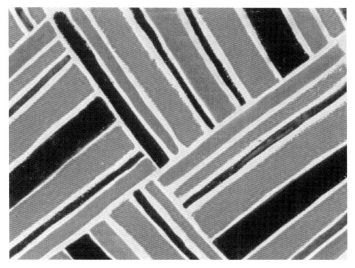

Top Fig. 2.42
Les Jets d'Eau woven silk and rayon furnishing fabric, designed by Édouard Bénédictus, produced by Brunet, Meunié et Cie, 1925. Glittering fountains and cascades of flowers are melded in this iconic textile, which was displayed in the French Embassy pavilion at the Paris Exposition in 1925.

Above Fig. 2.43
Design for a printed silk dress fabric, Sonia Delaunay, 1927. Sonia Delaunay believed that dresses and dress fabrics should be conceived at the same time, and used the term *"tissus simultanés."* Rhythm, expressed through dynamic abstract compositions and "colour scales," was central to her aesthetic.

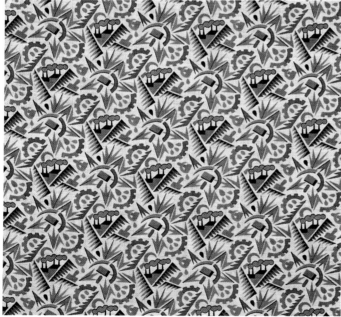

Top Fig. 2.44

Design for a printed dress fabric, Varvara Stepanova, c.1923. After the October Revolution, idealistic young Soviet designers evolved a new decorative vocabulary that broke decisively with the past. This radical and dynamic abstract pattern was conceived as a dress fabric for the liberated proletariat.

Above Fig. 2.45

Industry *roller-printed cotton dress fabric, designed by D. Preobrazhenskaya, produced by Ivanovo-Voznesensk Mills, 1930.* Cogs, saw blades, hammers, sickles, and factories are all jumbled together in this lively "thematic" mass-produced dress fabric intended to promote the first Five Year Plan.

Top Fig. 2.46

Design for a printed dress fabric, Liubov Popova, 1923–4. Conceived as a new visual language for fashion, both this pattern and that by Stepanova (top left), employ arresting graphic devices. The chopping up and reassembling of geometric motifs presages the visual tricks of Op Art forty years later.

Above Fig. 2.47

Tractor *roller-printed cotton dress fabric, designed by Sergei Burylin, produced by Ivanovo-Voznesensk Mills, 1930.* The short-lived marriage between Soviet propaganda and avant-garde graphic design prompted some of the most exciting textile patterns of the period. Here the tractor celebrates the worker.

direction, what added gaiety and charm their products give to an interior."[8] In 1913 the Omega Workshops was founded, and although this operated on different lines to the Atelier Martine in employing artists rather than untrained girls, there were close philosophical and aesthetic correspondences between the two organizations. Both were set up as a challenge to the perceived dullness and formality of interior decoration, and both sought to energize the decorative arts by promoting a more spontaneous and painterly approach. A passionate advocate of Post-Impressionist painting, Fry aimed to promote the work of British artists working in Fauvist and Cubist styles.

Operating from its headquarters in Bloomsbury, central London, the Omega Workshops employed up to twenty "artist decorators" on a part-time basis for a fixed daily or weekly rate. Their main areas of activity were furniture, ceramics, and textiles, but they also undertook murals and decorated complete interiors. Craft skills were not an issue and, unlike the Arts and Crafts Movement, the Omega Workshops were not underpinned by socialist ideals or by any desire to engage in wider reform of industrial design. In the preface to a catalogue for the Workshops, Fry stated that the aim was to "try to keep the spontaneous freshness of primitive or peasant work while satisfying the needs and expressing the feelings of modern cultivated man."[9]

Many artists and designers were temporarily or peripherally involved, although Roger Fry, Duncan Grant, and Vanessa Bell formed the core nucleus of the group. Textiles played a key role from the start, and the launch collection included printed and woven furnishing fabrics and hand-painted silk scarves. Six printed linens – *Amenophis*, *Margery*, *Maud*, *Mechtilde*, *Pamela*, and *White* – were printed at the Maromme Printworks near Rouen, in France, while a jacquard-woven woollen fabric, *Cracow*, was produced by A.H. Lee. Specific designers were not recorded, although individual patterns have been ascribed to Roger Fry (fig. 2.49) and Frederick Etchells (fig. 2.48), and others are attributed to Grant and Bell. Omega textiles were distinguished by the freedom, vigour, and painterliness of the designs. Some featured linear or geometric patterns, while others were overtly Fauvist, composed of arcs and blades. The outbreak of the First World War seriously affected the viability of the Omega Workshops, which, after failing to recover, closed in 1919.

Britain: Foxton

In 1937 the textile designer Antony Hunt reflected on changing fashions in pattern design. His comments, written at a time when Art Nouveau was deeply unfashionable, help to explain the strength of the reaction that took place subsequently: "Barely fifty years ago we were in the throes of l'Art Nouveau, in which form William Morris and his associates made their sincere attempt to evolve a style of design compatible with the economic and cultural needs of the period. Their departure from the accepted standards of their

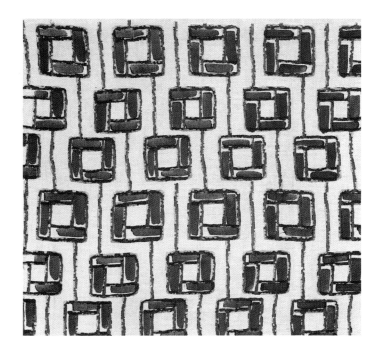

Top Fig. 2.48
Mechtilde block-printed linen furnishing fabric, possibly designed by Frederick Etchells, printed at the Maromme Printworks for the Omega Workshops, 1913. The Omega Workshops provided a vehicle for impoverished artists to supplement their income by creating decorative painterly designs.

Above Fig. 2.49
Amenophis block-printed linen furnishing fabric, probably designed by Roger Fry, printed at the Maromme Printworks for the Omega Workshops, 1913. This pattern relates to a painting by Fry, which explains the attribution. The printing subtly replicates the spontaneity of the artist's brushstrokes.

time, though now often ignorantly belittled, in reality provided almost as great a shock to the complacency of their contemporaries as did the advent of cubism, functionalism, and the architectural theories and practices of Le Corbusier, or the early fabrics of Rodier. By 1920 all active interest in Art Nouveau was dead, and buyers were off 'birds and honeysuckle'. The Queen Anne mongers returned to 'period' and a state of Sheraton stupor."[10]

During the 1910s and 1920s, in the face of mounting foreign competition, Britain lost its position as the dominant textile producer on the international stage. As the industry shrank in size, loss of commercial confidence had a direct effect on design. What had been the great strength of British design during the Arts and Crafts period – floral imagery – became its downfall. As Antony Hunt reflected: "with the advent and onrush of the chintz, cretonne, and flowers-at-all-costs craze, repetition started on a grand scale with a consequent decline in the whole level of floral design."[11]

The only British firm to rival the creativity of the Austrians and the French was W. Foxton Ltd., established by William Foxton in 1903. Excelling in high-quality printed silks, cottons, and linens, it used commission printers such as Stead McAlpin to print its cloth. Early designs were block-printed, and even after production was transferred to roller-printing during the 1920s, the distinctive block-printed aesthetic was retained. William Foxton was an early member of the Design and Industries Association (DIA), an organization modelled on the Deutscher Werkbund, which brought together architects, craftsmen, designers, educators, manufacturers, and retailers to discuss measures for raising standards of design. It was shortly after the founding of the DIA in 1915 that Foxton began to commission patterns from innovative freelance designers.

The company's most important early contributor was Claud Lovat Fraser, a painter, illustrator, graphic artist, and highly acclaimed theatre designer, whose wide-ranging activities fed into his zestful approach to pattern design (fig. 2.50). It was Fraser who initiated the inspirational series of pattern papers produced by the Curwen Press during the 1920s. At Foxton his electrifying abstract patterns had a liberating effect, and he also designed textiles for Liberty. It may have been Fraser who introduced Foxton to Charles Rennie Mackintosh, whose potential as a pattern designer was hitherto untapped. Mackintosh's textile designs, created between around 1917 and 1920, amply demonstrate his confident and original handling of abstraction, highlighting the designer's strong graphic instinct and fearless use of colour (fig. 2.51).

Over the next decade Foxton consolidated its reputation by putting into production a host of inspirational patterns by designers such as Gladys Barraclough, Percy Bilbie, Albert Griffiths, Eric Haward, Take Sato, Charles Shannon, and C.F.A Voysey. Constance Irving supplied numerous designs throughout the 1920s, including both Wiener Werkstätte-inspired florals and strong, colourful, abstract

patterns that helped to define the distinctive Foxton style (fig. 2.52). In his search for fresh talent, Foxton was drawn to the Central School of Arts and Crafts in London, where many of the best designers were being trained. The multi-talented Dorothy Hutton, an accomplished illuminator, letterer, and lithographer, designed engaging animal nursery prints and painterly floral cretonnes from around 1918. Minnie McLeish, a freelance textile designer, pioneered a free-thinking, painterly approach to pattern, characterized by thick, brown outlines and enamel-like infill colours (fig. 2.53).

F. Gregory Brown, another major contributor during the 1920s, was both a commercial artist and a textile designer. One of the first to introduce Vorticist and Cubist-inspired abstraction into mainstream pattern design, he won a gold medal for his textiles at the Paris Exposition of 1925 (fig. 2.54). Particularly impressive were his forceful, angular designs depicting woodcutters and horse riders, produced in the early 1930s (fig. 2.55). Writing in 1939, H.G. Hayes Marshall singled out William Foxton as a pivotal and inspirational figure, who "ploughed a lonely furrow" in the British textile industry during the 1920s, fostering an appreciation of colour and design: "No man ever had a greater desire to improve the standards of design in Furnishing Textiles in England. No man ever worked so hard for this end – no man had so little help and encouragement. His only mistake was being 20 years too soon."[12]

Britain: CPA, Grafton, Sefton, and Tootal

Dress fabric manufacturers tended to purchase designs from commercial studios in Paris, the aim being to keep abreast of the latest fashions. Consequently, as the Art Deco style took hold in France, it filtered through in a diluted form in Britain, prompting patterns featuring dense clusters of generalized floral motifs, and exotic imagery such as Japanese lanterns and sea urchins. Another feature of the imported cocktail was an electric palette, dominated by orange, often combined with vivid purplish-blue and pink on a dark background. "Immediate post-war reaction was colour at all costs – jazz and forgetfulness," noted Antony Hunt.[13] However, another factor influencing the use of strong colours was the new synthetic dyes that came on to the market at this time.

In 1910 the large combine that dominated dress fabric production, the Calico Printers Association (CPA), controlled about two-thirds of the printed textiles industry. The number of firms in the CPA dwindled, however, and by 1935 there were only twelve. One of the most forward-looking was F.W. Grafton, founded in 1855, of the Broad Oak Printworks at Accrington, Lancashire, which specialized in roller-printed cottons. The influence of French Art Deco was particularly apparent in the firm's patterns from around 1920, with their strong outlines, rich colours, and intense decorative effects. Grafton also produced furnishing fabrics designed by Percy Bilbie.

Two of the most imaginative independent companies were Sefton and Tootal. Belfast-based Sefton produced designs by Charles

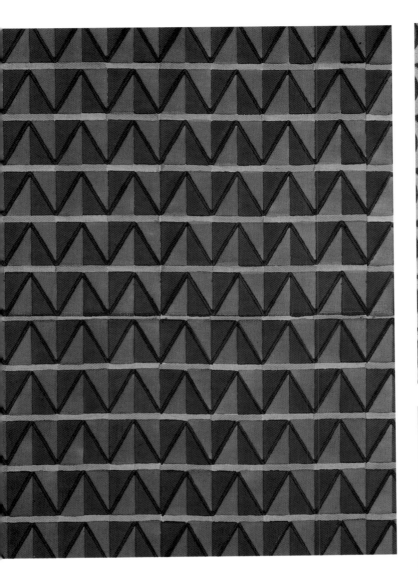

Above Fig. 2.50

Roller-printed cotton furnishing fabric, designed by Claud Lovat Fraser, produced by William Foxton, 1920. Deceptively simple yet visually intense, this style of all-over abstract geometric pattern-making would have seemed radically new and original at the time, and it still looks modern now.

Above right Fig. 2.51

Block-printed silk, designed by Charles Rennie Mackintosh, produced by William Foxton, 1918. Daring combinations of orange, purple, and black are exploited in both this and Claud Lovat Fraser's pattern (above). The cascading segment motifs generate lively rhythms.

Right Fig. 2.52

Roller-printed cotton furnishing fabric, designed by Constance Irving, produced by William Foxton, 1921. Ribbons of pattern, alternating with black stripes, account for the forceful impact of this design. Although regular, the pattern is not mechanical. Overtly hand-painted markings are a feature of the print.

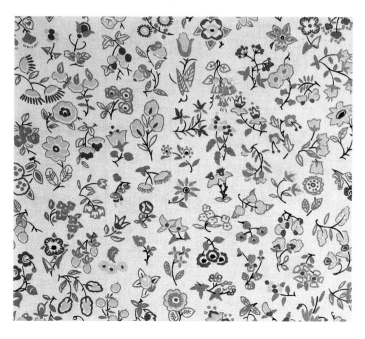

Top Fig. 2.53

Roller-printed cotton furnishing fabric, designed by Minnie McLeish, produced by William Foxton, 1920. Seeking to revitalize British printed furnishing fabrics, William Foxton, a leading figure in the Design and Industries Association, sought out some of the most talented freelance designers of the day.

Above right Fig. 2.55

Roller-printed linen furnishing fabric, designed by F. Gregory Brown, produced by William Foxton, c.1931. Evoking the aesthetic of block-printing, but through lower cost roller-printing, this vigorous pattern reflects the influence of contemporary artistic genres such as Cubism and Vorticism.

Above Fig. 2.54

Block-printed linen furnishing fabric, designed by F. Gregory Brown, produced by William Foxton, 1922. This fearlessly modern pattern was one of the textiles shown by Foxton at the Paris Exposition in 1925. Not surprisingly, F. Gregory Brown was awarded a gold medal.

Right Fig. 2.56

Heartsease *roller-printed cotton furnishing fabric, designed by John Tunnard, produced by Tootal Broadhurst Lee, 1921–6.* John Tunnard, the designer of this rustic floral cretonne, worked in the textile industry during the 1920s before becoming an artist.

Rennie Mackintosh, and captivating, watercolour-like florals by the decorative painter and theatre designer George Sheringham. Sheringham also designed for Tootal Broadhurst Lee, based in Manchester, whose output, although not modern in the conventional sense, was nonetheless highly original. The artist John Tunnard worked for Tootal from 1921 to 1926, producing attractive stylized floral cretonnes (heavy cottons resembling linen) (fig. 2.56). T.C. Dugdale was head of the design studio, and other designers included Jacqueline Cundall, George Day, Helen McKenzie, Elsie McNaught, John and Lucy Revel, A.M. Talmage, and A.R. Thomas. During the 1920s Tootal produced a distinctive collection of contemporary narrative prints in the *toiles de Jouy* manner, composed of individual vignettes linked by a theme. A typical example was *The Open Road* (1925) by George Day, which contained images of gypsy caravans, open-topped buses, cyclists, fishermen, and picnickers, dotted among a landscape of trees and fields. While these whimsical, nostalgic designs could hardly be called progressive, they parallel compositional features in the textiles of Raoul Dufy.

Britain and the United States: Wall Paper Manufacturers Ltd and M.H. Birge

After the First World War deep wallpaper friezes went out of fashion in Britain and the United States, to be replaced by narrower decorative borders, usually applied below the picture rail but sometimes framing the whole wall. Art Nouveau styling was now rejected in favour of Art Deco, and two different types of borders dominated production: one featuring stylized floral garlands, the other with jazzy, abstract patterns in the so-called "Modernistic" style. The strident oranges and blues that characterized modern dress fabrics also appeared in wallpapers, where Moderne allegiances were denoted by the use of metallic colours (fig. 2.57).

A feature of British and American domestic interiors throughout the interwar years was "cut-outs," borders with one straight edge and the other side cut along the outline of the actual pattern. Festoons of leaves and flowers were popular, but some cut-outs were even more elaborate, composed of landscapes with buildings and trees. Such designs particularly appealed to the American market, leading to the fashion for full-blown landscape wallpapers, or "scenics." In the desire to satisfy this new market, one leading American manufacturer, M.H. Birge, founded in 1878 by Martin H. Birge, enlisted the services of Charles Burchfield. This artist, who later pursued a successful career as a watercolourist, worked for Birge from 1921 to 1929, creating panoramic landscapes and lyrical nature studies, including woodland scenes.

Although the rise of the feature border was accompanied by the gradual decline of patterned filling papers, densely ornamented polychrome florals, known as "tapestry" wallpapers, remained extremely popular in both Britain and the United States during the 1910s and 1920s. A.J. Baker, of C. & G. Potter, and Edgar Pattison,

Above Fig. 2.57
Four block-printed and stencilled wallpaper borders, produced by Hayward & Son, late 1920s or early 1930s. Jazzy, abstract wallpaper borders such as this design, printed in silver and gold with stencilled infill colouring, illustrate the delayed impact of French Moderne patterns on the British market in the years after the Paris Exposition of 1925.

The Cheviot

of Jeffrey & Co., both specialized in dazzlingly naturalistic patterns of this kind. The Silver Studio also adopted this more florid, ostentatious style, its main clients being members of the Wall Paper Manufacturers Ltd (WPM), such as Potter and Lightbown Aspinall. Sidney Haward, who had originally trained at the Silver Studio and later ran the Haward Studio, also produced busy, naturalistic florals in a debased version of the Arts and Crafts style.

After the Paris Exposition, however, the innate conservatism of the British wallpaper industry was challenged by Moderne trends from France. Rex Silver went on a fact-finding mission to the exhibition, returning with new source material for his team at the Silver Studio. Freelance designers such as William Nairn Walker, who supplied patterns to the WPM also absorbed decorative ideas from France. By the late 1920s many companies, including Sanderson, were producing what were described as "semi-plains": textured papers printed in faint colours with a hotchpotch of jumbled squares and patches of broken cross-hatching, interspersed with the odd spiky leaf or flower. The 1930s also witnessed the rise of "porridge": embossed wallpapers printed with muted, mottled textural effects. In Britain cut-outs remained in vogue until the end of the 1930s, often in the form of Cubist-floral hybrids. Consumers were encouraged by both manufacturers and decorators to create their own coordinated interior schemes (fig. 2.58).

United States: Cheney Brothers and Schumacher

During the first two decades of the 20th century American textiles were overshadowed by imported stylistic influences. From around 1915, however, a concerted attempt was made to stimulate a specifically American school of pattern design. Spurred on by the enthusiastic Morris de Camp Crawford, design editor of *Women's Wear*, designers were encouraged to use museum artefacts as a source of inspiration for textile patterns. Native American, South American, and African objects, including pottery, textiles, and baskets, were particularly recommended, and between 1916 and 1922 *Women's Wear* organized a series of five design competitions. These attracted entries from the batik artists Marion Dorn and Ruth Reeves, both of whom later turned to industrial design, and a number of patterns were manufactured by firms such as Belding Brothers, Cheney Brothers, and H.R. Mallinson.

Cheney Brothers, of South Manchester, Connecticut, was founded in 1838 and specialized in woven and printed silk dress and upholstery fabrics. Until the First World War most patterns were bought from French studios, and the company favoured mainly traditional styles. In 1918, however, it established its own Paris-based art studio, run by Henri Créange, prompting a flurry of colourful patterns inspired by Poiret and Dufy that revolutionized the company's image. In 1925 Cheney produced a collection called Prints Ferronière, inspired by Edgar Brandt's ironwork decoration at its magnificent new showroom on Madison Avenue, New York. The following year it launched a range of Cubist-inspired dress fabrics called Vitraux Prints, inspired by the stained-glass windows of Maumejean Frères. Other designs were based on illustrations by Kees van Dongen and watercolours by Marie Laurencin. Although France remained the fountainhead for all this creativity, the channelling of pure unadulterated Art Deco into the United States had a stimulating effect on American design.

Another firm that jumped on the Art Deco bandwagon was F. Schumacher & Co., which had long-standing connections in France. Founded in New York in 1889 by a French émigré, Frederic Schumacher, the company initially imported European printed and woven fabrics. From 1895, after it acquired the Waverly Mill in Paterson, New Jersey, imports were supplemented by its own printed and woven designs. In 1900 Schumacher imported Art Nouveau fabrics from the Paris Universal Exhibition. Later, at the time of the Paris Exposition of 1925, the company commissioned a collection of designs from Paul Follot, Émile-Allain Seguy, and Henri Stéphany. Produced in the form of rayon damasks, brocades, and lampas, patterns included *Leaves* by Follot, *Butterflies* by Seguy, and *The Doves* by Stéphany. Pierre Pozier, Frederic Schumacher's French artist nephew, who commissioned these designs, also created Moderne woven patterns such as *Les Gazelles au Bois* (1927). Schumacher later collaborated with Édouard Bénédictus and Paul Poiret, the latter producing a group of printed fruit and flower patterns in the Atelier Martine style around 1930. The first American designer to be associated with Schumacher was Cy Clark, whose low-cost chintzes, known as Waverly fabrics, were produced from 1923. Waverly Fabrics became a separate division of the company in 1935.

United States: Stehli Silks

The design sensation of the decade was the Americana Prints collection produced by the Stehli Silks Corporation between 1925 and 1927, featuring some of the most avant-garde and outlandish patterns of the day. A consciously nationalistic exercise, the collection consisted of a large and stylistically varied group of patterns on American themes, commissioned from artists, designers, cartoonists, and celebrities. The project was initiated and overseen by Kneeland "Ruzzie" Green, who joined Stehli Silks as a stylist in January 1925 and later became a director. Although the United States declined to participate in the Paris Exposition of that year, Green formed part of the US Commission that visited the event, which clearly stimulated the collection. The patterns were startling for their daring exploitation of contemporary imagery and their radical experimental artistic styles. Green's patterns included *Cheerio* and *It* (the latter a euphemism for sex appeal). Both exploited jumbled typography as the basis for their designs, a sly reference to the early Cubist paintings of Picasso and Braque.

The most revolutionary patterns were those by the photographer Edward Steichen, who, with the help of carefully staged lighting, transposed still-life photographs of banal, everyday objects into

Top Fig. 2.59
Moth Balls and Sugar roller-printed silk dress fabric, designed by Edward Steichen, produced by Stehli Silks, 1926. This abstract pattern has its origins in a still-life photograph by Edward Steichen. Steichen was one of a number of celebrities who contributed to Stehli Silks' Americana Prints series.

Above Fig.2.60
Aspirin roller-printed silk dress fabric, designed by Kneeland "Ruzzie" Green, produced by Stehli Silks, 1927. "Ruzzie" Green joined Stehli Silks as a stylist in 1925, and oversaw the innovative Americana Prints series. This design, featuring a mass of pills, is in a similar idiom to the Steichen pattern (top).

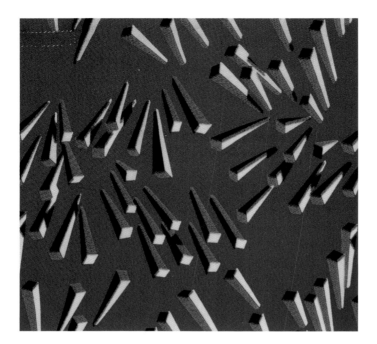

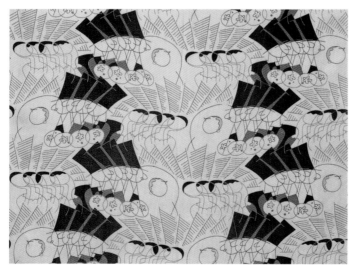

surreal but mesmerizingly beautiful abstract textile designs, including *Buttons and Thread*, *Carpet Tacks*, and *Moth Balls and Sugar* (fig. 2.59). According to *Vogue*: "The designs are not only effective in themselves, but they have the requirements of good patterns... they are undoubtedly the forerunner to a new school of industrial art."[14] Reinforcing this assertion, another design in a similar idiom was *Aspirin* by "Ruzzie" Green (fig. 2.60). Also related was *Pegs* by the printmaker, illustrator, and theatre designer Charles Buckle Falls (fig. 2.61), which simulated the effect of still-life photography through artful perspective drawing.

The influence of Italian Futurism was evident in two architectural designs featuring buildings that fly off at diagonals, suggesting the dynamism of modern life. One was *Manhattan* by the artist Clayton Knight, and the other was *Flying Buttresses* by the industrial designer Walter Dorwin Teague. Also giving a light-hearted nod to Futurism – in this case Giacomo Balla's *Dynamism of a Dog on a Leash* – was *Gentlemen Prefer Blondes* by the cartoonist Ralph Barton (fig. 2.62). The title referred to the novel by Anita Loos that Barton had recently illustrated, and his design showed a group of men transfixed by a blonde girl. Another cartoonist, John Held, whose work appeared regularly in *Vanity Fair* and *The New Yorker*, created *Rhapsody*, depicting a jazz band. This design, the title of which refers to Gershwin's *Rhapsody in Blue*, is a compelling evocation of the Jazz Age.

Celebrity contributors to the Americana Prints included Helen Wills, the legendary Wimbledon tennis champion, who created two entertaining patterns on the theme of tennis, one featuring sketches of tennis players, the other a playful decorative composition of rackets and courts. The fashion illustrator Helen Dryden designed a pattern in a similar vein called *Accessories*, which depicted everyday objects such as drums, cars, teapots, and umbrellas. Other contributors to the collection included F.V. Carpender, Rene Clarke, Neysa McNein, Katherine Sturges, Dwight Taylor, and Edward A. Wilson. Fascinating not only for their ground-breaking approach to pattern design, but also as a record of ephemeral fashions, the Americana Prints were witty and original, reflecting the confidence and ebullience of American society before the Wall Street crash of 1929.

Italy: Fortuny

Design history is not a linear process, and quite often there are contradictory things happening at the same time. The force of progress is matched by the pull of tradition, and many designers seek inspiration from the past. The Spanish-born theatre designer, painter, and couturier Mariano Fortuny, who spent most of his life in Italy, falls into this category. His work, although steeped in historical associations, was celebrated alongside that of the European avant-garde at the Paris Exposition of 1925, where it achieved equal acclaim. Best known for his loose, sheath-like dresses and sculptural, pleated silk fabrics, Fortuny also designed

Top Fig. 2.61
Pegs roller-printed silk dress fabric, designed by Charles Buckle Falls, produced by Stehli Silks, 1927. Charles Buckle Falls was a leading printmaker, illustrator, mural painter, and stage designer, which perhaps accounts for the illusionistic qualities of this *trompe l'oeil* pattern. The design was part of the Americana Prints, which were intended to encourage manufacturers to use American designers instead of buying in patterns from France.

Above Fig. 2.62
Gentlemen Prefer Blondes roller-printed silk dress fabric, designed by Ralph Barton, produced by Stehli Silks, 1926. This pattern takes its title from the novel by Anita Loos, which Ralph Barton had recently illustrated. It shows a group of men transfixed by a passing blonde, depicted in a cartoon version of the Futurist style. Humour played a key role in many of the Americana Prints.

Left Fig. 2.63
Silk velvet hand-printed with silver and gold pigments, designed and produced by Mariano Fortuny, 1927. Bucking the trend towards Modernism and the Moderne, Fortuny produced richly decorated printed fabrics, steeped in historical allusions. The motifs in this design were derived from 16th-century Italian woven textiles.

an extensive range of printed textiles that are reminiscent of 15th-century Italian velvets and brocades (fig. 2.63).

Fortuny's family had collected antique textiles, and his patterns were derived from many sources, encompassing European and Oriental imagery and ranging from Gothic to Baroque. Motifs varied from twining foliage to formal strapwork and stiff rosettes. Operating from a large workshop in Venice, Fortuny combined embossing, hand painting, block-printing, and an early form of screen-printing to create relief-patterned decoration on silk, cotton, and velvet. By mixing rich vegetable dyes with lustrous gold pigments, he achieved ravishing, sumptuous, theatrical effects. His fabrics, popular among a wealthy elite, stood wholly apart from contemporary developments, and made no attempt to comply with prevailing decorative or Moderne trends.

Functionalism
and Industrial Art

In 1939 the British textile designer H.G. Hayes Marshall observed that "modern influence has begun to conquer the traditional in Textile Design and the feeling for abstract form, first expressed in our time in the work of Picasso, has finally made itself felt in decoration and specially with regard to textile design."[1] The 1930s was a period of consolidation in pattern design, when many of the ideas that had surfaced in France, Austria, and Germany during the 1920s were disseminated further afield. Britain, Scandinavia, and the United States were the main recipients, responding positively to both Functionalist Modern and decorative Moderne. In fact, at the time the two styles were often confused – combined under the all-embracing title "Cubism," even though they were ideologically poles apart.

The fashion for Cubist patterns, reflected internationally in both textiles and wallpapers, was closely linked to emergent trends in architecture, such as more boxlike rooms and horizontal glazing. "A new style of house demands a new style of furniture and fabrics," confirmed Antony Hunt in 1937. In his book *Textile Design* Hunt succinctly summarized international furnishing trends since the First World War. "The anti-Morris, anti-classic post-war style came in as 'Cubism.' It concentrated upon abstract form, and studiously avoided any floral motifs... From France came light, loose cloths mostly of rayon – all spikes, triangles, and crescents, and from Germany heavier, rather simpler designs with squared formations. America with its characteristic enthusiasm for any live new movement quickly plunged into the vortex of Continental Cubism. England sceptically deferred until much later."[2]

Although Modernism in its purest form was vehemently anti-pattern, Functionalism – the more widely adopted practical manifestation of the Modern Movement – was more receptive to pattern, albeit in a restrained form. It was this tempered variant of Modernism, known in Britain as Industrial Art, that took hold during the 1930s, ensuring that pattern was by no means eclipsed (fig. 3.1). In Britain plain, functional furniture was promoted alongside

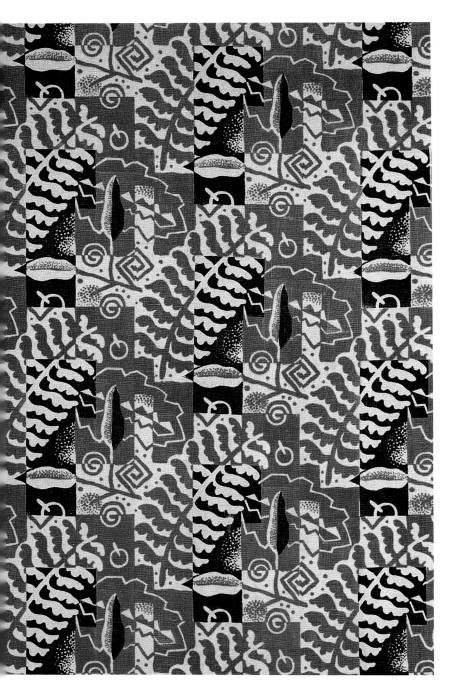

Above Fig. 3.2
*Block-printed linen furnishing fabric,
designed by Bernard Adeney, produced
by Allan Walton Textiles, c.1931–2.*
During his time as head of textiles at
the Central School of Arts and Crafts
in London, from 1930 to 1947, the
painter Bernard Adeney nurtured the
talents of many young designers.

measured stylized or abstract decoration, stimulating a new wave
of creativity in British textiles, despite the Depression (fig. 3.2). The
artist-led block-printing revival that had been gaining momentum
during the 1920s also bore fruit during the 1930s (fig. 3.3), while in
Sweden designers embraced Functionalism and devoted themselves
to producing "more beautiful everyday things." In Paris the *Exposition
Internationale des Arts et Techniques dans la Vie Moderne* of 1937
recognized the dual importance of Functionalism and decoration.
According to the exhibition's manifesto, it aimed to demonstrate
that "no incompatibility exists between Usefulness and Beauty,
and that Art and Technology should be indissolubly linked."

Many French manufacturers, particularly those catering to the
luxury market in the United States, were hit extremely hard by
the Wall Street Crash of 1929. The decline of France as a design
superpower was indicated by the much lower profile of the 1937
exhibition compared with the extravaganza of the *Exposition
Internationale des Arts Décoratifs et Industriels Modernes* of 1925.
Meanwhile the formerly buoyant applied-art industries in Austria
and Germany were increasingly disrupted. The early 1930s saw the
closure of both the Wiener Werkstätte and the Bauhaus, the first for
commercial reasons, the second as a result of political repression.
From this time modern design was increasingly stigmatized in
both countries and many talented designers fled abroad, along
with skilled craftsmen and industrialists. The dispersal of émigrés
led to the dissemination of progressive design ideas in formerly
conservative countries such as Britain and the United States,
although in the latter, hindered by the Depression, it took another
decade for them to take root. Speaking at the launch of a range
of artist-designed Constructivist fabrics produced by Edinburgh
Weavers in October 1937, Alastair Morton reflected: "In recent years
events on the continent have largely stifled advance in architecture
and decoration. Indeed some countries which formerly led the
modern movement have gone back, and even in France they
have been so concerned with other things that there has been
next to no development. It seemed therefore that the leadership
in contemporary decoration had passed over to this country."[3]

Britain: Textile Design

After the First World War British textiles had been sapped of
creative energy, but the 1930s witnessed a major creative revival.
This renaissance took two distinct forms, one artist-led and
expressed through craft production, and the other reflected in the
positive new alliance between freelance designers and the textile
industry. "To the older established designing Studios came the
newer generation of artist designers who knew that there was
nothing incompatible about designing and art," explained Hayes
Marshall.[4] Although prejudices about the superiority of French
design persisted in Britain, in reality the balance of creative
power was shifting. Commercially, too, the situation improved
significantly at the beginning of the decade, after the British
government introduced tariffs to protect the textile trade. As a

result, confidence returned, and with it a flood of new design ideas: "The enthusiasm came from the architects, decorators and fashion experts, and the manufacturers rose to the occasion and made full use of the benefits accruing to them by the import duties. Nowadays textile buyers from Overseas look at English production first," noted Hayes Marshall in 1939.[5]

The impact of the Industrial Art Movement was felt in two important ways. First, patterns became simpler and more architectural. Secondly, a quieter palette was adopted in place of the exotic colours of the Jazz Age. "Since 1928 the general tendency has been for paler and more uncommon colours," noted Antony Hunt in 1937, linking the fashion for "beigery" to the development of subtler tones of guaranteed fadeless dyes. "The beige craze passed into one of still greater pallor, and white and off-white even for coverings became the public's taste... Fashion became still more anaemic, and flats like whited sepulchres vaunted chalk-like chairs and pallid curtaining. Then, blood returning to the cheeks and money to the pockets, colour re-entered."[6]

Urging designers to build on the progress made in recent years towards the adoption of a more rigorous aesthetic, Hunt wrote: "Let us hope that all design is not again to be submerged in a pall of fulsome fruitage, or that sentiment once more will triumph over intellect, and a new craze for coziness exterminate the new hard-won foundations of more rational design."[7] Although, if this rhetoric is to be believed, Modernism was clearly in the ascendant by the mid-1930s, not all areas of pattern design were affected to the same degree. While furnishing fabrics were clearly influenced by trends in contemporary architecture, dress fabrics developed independently. The divergence between the two is indicated by the popularity of Liberty's Tana Lawn range of miniaturized florals, whose runaway success during the 1930s prompted the creation of a subsidiary, Liberty of London Prints, in 1939.

Britain: Barron and Larcher and Enid Marx

During the 1910s artist printmaking in Britain had been revitalized by an upsurge of activity in wood engraving. This, in turn, fostered a revival in block-printed textiles, as some artists were inspired to move from printmaking on paper to printing on cloth. In block-printing, patterns are cut in relief on wooden blocks (sometimes lino-faced), with multicoloured designs broken into individual elements, each requiring a separate block. Hand block-printing had long been superseded by mechanical copper roller-printing in commercial textiles and by machine surface-printing in wallpapers – both of which were much faster and more economical for long production runs – although it was still used by a few specialist printers. However, the crucial difference between factory-made and craft-produced block-printed textiles was the artist's direct involvement in the cutting of the blocks. Although labour-intensive, block-printing appealed to artists because of the control it gave them over the form, texture, and colour of the print. It also allowed flexibility,

Above Fig. 3.3
Pointed Pip *block-printed linen furnishing fabric, designed and printed by Phyllis Barron and Dorothy Larcher, c.1930–8.* Working outside the industrial system, Barron and Larcher cut their own blocks and hand-printed their own fabrics using natural dyes in their own workshop.

as the same blocks could be rotated to create diverse patterns, and different blocks could be alternated to create varied effects.

Two of the most committed adherents of block-printing during the interwar years were Phyllis Barron and Dorothy Larcher. Both had originally trained as artists in London, Barron at the Slade, Larcher at Hornsey School of Art. In 1921 Barron abandoned painting in favour of a career as an independent craft textile printer, and two years later she teamed up with Larcher. Drawing on their knowledge of traditional French and Indian block-printed textiles, the two women developed a relaxed, personal style featuring a variety of abstract, organic, and pictorial motifs. Although they fashioned their own individual design vocabularies, they worked closely together and evolved a coherent workshop style. Having distanced themselves from both commercial industry and the contemporary art world, they repositioned themselves within a global textile tradition, freely embracing elements of European, Asian, and African vernacular design.

Many of their patterns were geometric, although blocks, stripes, or diamonds were frequently softened with crimped or serrated borders. A strong vertical or diagonal axis was a common feature, as in *Small Feather* (c.1930–4), which was composed of fringed, flowing, slanting lines. Irregular graining and small spots or rings were often used as infill, adding texture and rhythm to designs such as *Pointed Pip* (c.1930–8) (fig. 3.3). Cloths varied in weight and thickness, depending on their intended application, and ranged from coarse linen and cotton furnishing fabrics to fine silk and velvet dress fabrics. Patterns were normally printed in a single colour, but occasionally two, using a limited palette of mineral and vegetable dyes. Discharge-printing was also adopted, using nitric acid on pre-dyed fabric to bleach the cloth from dark to light. Initially Barron and Larcher favoured dark, earthy tones such as indigo and iron mould, but later they supplemented these with brighter colours, including quercitron yellow and alizarin red. After relocating from London to Gloucestershire in 1930, they continued to work together until 1939, but wound down their operations after the outbreak of the Second World War.

Among their assistants in 1925 was a young artist called Enid Marx, who had developed an interest in block-printing while studying painting and wood engraving at the Royal College of Art in London. Marx was one of several artists to design pattern papers for the Curwen Press, but transferred her skills to textiles after seeing Barron and Larcher's work. In 1927 she established her own workshop in Hampstead where she printed her own textiles, mainly linens, muslins, and organdies (fine muslins), until the war. Although Marx shared her mentors' commitment to natural dyes, her patterns displayed stronger graphic qualities and a more rigorous sense of design. In addition her vocabulary was more varied, encompassing minutely detailed vignettes, such as cornucopias and baskets of flowers, as well as dynamic abstract

motifs, including crescents, ellipses, and feathered stars (figs. 3.4 and 3.5). The subtlety of Marx's patterns arose from her skill in block-cutting, expressed through delicate linear markings. But her patterns were also vigorous and rhythmic, and she was adept at creating pattern variations by rotating, alternating, or overprinting blocks. She later undertook two commissions for industrial textiles, one in 1937 for upholstery moquettes for a major London Underground design initiative, and the other for jacquard-woven cotton fabrics under the government's wartime Utility scheme.

Britain: Poulk Press and the Nicholsons
Two other prominent artists to produce hand-printed fabrics during the interwar period were Ben Nicholson and Barbara Hepworth, who both began seriously experimenting with lino-block printing in 1932–3. Some of Nicholson's blocks were later printed by Poulk Press, a textile- and paper-printing workshop established by his sister, Nancy Nicholson, in 1930. Ben Nicholson's designs – intended as an alternative to the technical sophistication of industrial production – featured crude, childlike imagery in a rough-and-ready style. Some were representational, such as *Princess* (1932–3), which featured the head of Barbara Hepworth in profile. Other patterns were composed of abstract motifs, such as *Number* (1932–3), with its loose bands of irregular typography.

Nancy Nicholson also created her own designs, produced using a combination of block-printing and stencilling and often featuring a single large image, such as a duck or a unicorn, against a wallpaper-like patterned background. In addition, between around 1936 and 1950, she printed fabrics for her sister-in-law, E.Q. Nicholson, an accomplished batik artist and former assistant to Marion Dorn. The most striking pattern, featuring flying geese (1938), was printed in many different colourways and pattern formations. Other designs were more delicate, such as *Daisy* and *Seaweed* (1949) (fig. 3.6). Some were later screen-printed by Edinburgh Weavers.

Many artists shared the Nicholsons' interest in hand-printed textiles during the interwar period, including the sculptor Frank Dobson, who designed furnishing fabrics lino-block printed by his wife, Mary, during the late 1930s. The graphic designer and calligrapher Margaret Calkin James, a contributor to the Curwen Press's pattern papers, also turned her hand to block-printed textiles between 1936 and 1950, mainly for family use. Delicate floral sprigs and calligraphic cartouches were her forte, printed in fresh, bright colours, but she also created thematic designs, including a nursery fabric decorated with children's toys and Christmas trees.

Britain: Footprints
One of the most successful block-printing enterprises of the interwar years was Footprints, a London workshop established in 1925 by two designers, Elspeth Little and Gwen Pike, with funding from Celandine Kennington. Footprints used aniline dyes rather

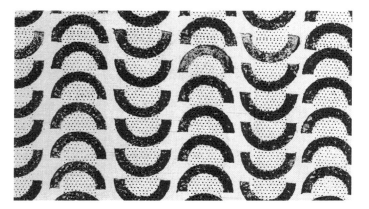

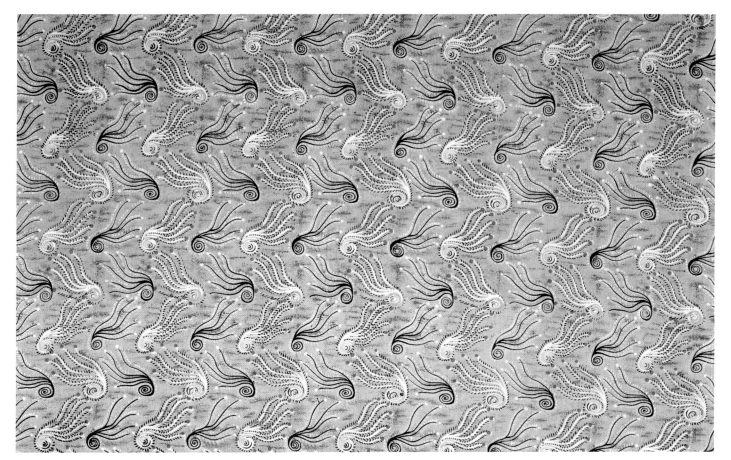

Top left Fig. 3.4
Half Moons block-printed linen, designed and printed by Enid Marx, 1930s. Enid Marx was one of many artists who experimented with hand block-printed textiles during the interwar period. This robust design was printed using just two blocks: one for the crescents and one for the dots.

Top right Fig. 3.5
Richardson (variant) block-printed linen, designed and printed by Enid Marx, 1930s. Most of Enid Marx's patterns were composed of simple repeated motifs, with the same blocks often reused in different combinations. The delicate feathered star in this design shows her skill as a block-cutter..

Above Fig. 3.6
Seaweed block-printed and stencilled cotton, designed by E.Q. Nicholson, produced by Poulk Press, 1949. The painter E.Q. Nicholson was one of several members of the Nicholson family to design textiles. Some of her patterns were later screen-printed by Edinburgh Weavers.

than vegetable dyes, and although the work was technically inferior to that of Enid Marx and Barron and Larcher, it displayed a lively, spirited approach to pattern. In addition to Pike and Little, early contributors included the artists Eric Kennington and Norman Wilkinson, and the designers Doris Scull (also known by her married name, Gregg) and Margaret Stansfield, both graduates of the newly created textile department at the Royal College of Art. Early designs were somewhat raw, typified by Margaret Stansfield's *Stream* (c.1926) and Doris Scull's *Sheep* (c.1926–9). Both designs depicted rural scenes in a primitive, graphic style, and both were arranged on the diagonal with the most basic repeats. More sophisticated was Scull's *Welwyn Garden City* (1926), depicting an abstracted townscape in a vigorous, quasi-Vorticist style.

From 1927 Joyce Clissold emerged as chief designer at Footprints, having become involved with the company while still a student at the Central School. In 1929 she took over as owner-manager, and from this time she created all the designs. Clissold's early patterns included rhythmic abstracts, such as *Cascade* (1933), but she later adopted a pictorial idiom, specializing in light-hearted narrative prints. Under her leadership Footprints grew into a substantial enterprise during the 1930s, continuing in operation until 1982, although latterly on a much-reduced scale. Lino blocks were favoured over wood because they were easier to cut and lighter to use. The firm produced finished goods such as scarves and ties, as well as dress and furnishing fabrics. Large orders were sometimes subcontracted to the commercial screen-printer Amersham Prints.

Another artist briefly associated with Footprints was Paul Nash. Inspired by the example of his friend Claud Lovat Fraser, he exhibited three designs for textiles in 1921. Among these was *Wild Cherry* (also known as *Cherry Orchard*), one of four Nash patterns subsequently printed by Footprints between 1925 and 1929 (fig. 3.7). The others were *Big Abstract*, consisting of rhythmic, interlocking, Cubist motifs, *Little Abstract* (later renamed *Terminus*) and *Pitcher*, showing a deconstructed vase of flowers. Unhappy with the quality of printing at Footprints, however, Nash later transferred three patterns to Cresta Silks, where they were reissued in 1932, along with four new designs, *Coloniale*, *Phalanx*, *Polka*, and *Ribbon*.

Britain: Cresta Silks and Cryséde

Cresta Silks, a commercial company specializing in artist-designed, block-printed dress fabrics, was an offshoot of the firm Cryséde. Established in 1920 by Alec Walker, who had previously run a Yorkshire mill producing Vigil Silks, Cryséde was initially based at Newlyn, Cornwall, but moved to St Ives in 1926. The company used bought-in silk or linen, block-printed in-house with chemical dyes and then made up into garments. The earliest patterns consisted of simple spots and stripes, but from 1923, at the suggestion of Raoul Dufy in Paris, Walker began to produce designs based on his own paintings. Although he did not cut the blocks

Above Fig. 3.7
Cherry Orchard block-printed silk crêpe de chine dress fabric, designed by Paul Nash, 1921, produced by Footprints, 1925–9. The cherry trees in this vigorous abstract pattern are evoked by arcs, dots, and forks. The same design was printed by G.P. & J. Baker for Cresta Silks from around 1932.

Opposite top Fig. 3.8
Block-printed silk dress fabric, probably designed by Alec Walker, c.1925–9, produced by Cryséde, 1930. Although at first glance this design appears to be a purely abstract pattern, it is actually a loose, painterly landscape sketch. The intense, luminous colours are typical of the work of Cryséde.

Opposite bottom Fig. 3.9
Web screen-printed rayon crêpe dress fabric, designed by Graham Sutherland, produced by Cresta Silks, 1947. The drive to involve artists in textile design that began during the 1930s was further consolidated after the Second World War. Graham Sutherland actively collaborated with several companies.

himself, he aimed "to revolutionise the art of designing and to introduce some artistic sense without which it became vulgarised and commercialised."[8]

Walker's earliest designs from the mid-1920s, such as *Russian Ballet* and *Dancer*, reflected the potent influence of the Ballets Russes. Rich, saturated colours were crucial from the outset, and fabrics were often discharge-printed with vibrant red or blue grounds (fig. 3.8). Working in a loose, spontaneous, primitive style, Walker frequently used sketches of Cornwall's towns and countryside as the basis for his designs, often drawn in aerial view. "You can take the most simple things in everyday life, and turn it into one of the most beautiful things, merely through a sense of design," he believed.[9] Crysédé was extremely successful, selling its fabrics and garments by mail order and through twenty-eight Crysédé shops around Britain. Although Walker himself withdrew from Crysédé in 1929, his work remained in production until the business ceased trading ten years later.

One of the reasons for the company's commercial success was the dynamic Tom Heron, its manager from 1924 to 1929. In 1929 he founded his own firm, Cresta Silks, at Welwyn Garden City. The main difference between the two companies was that, whereas Crysédé's cloth was printed in-house, Cresta Silks used commission printers, and screen-printing was adopted after the war. Projecting a confident, modern image, Cresta Silks adopted stylish graphics by Edward McKnight Kauffer, and ran a chain of shops designed by Wells Coates. In addition to Paul Nash, artists who produced designs for the firm during the 1930s included Elspeth Little, Cedric Morris, and Bruce Turner. Tom Heron's son, the painter Patrick Heron, began to design for Cresta Silks in 1934 and subsequently became its chief designer. His early designs were floral or figurative, but after the war he adopted a freer and more scribbly, abstract style. Designs by Mary Duncan, Lana Mackinnon, and Graham Sutherland (fig. 3.9) were also produced soon after the war, along with some reissues of Alec Walker's earlier patterns for Crysédé, to which Cresta Silks had since acquired the rights.

Britain: Curwen Press and Bardfield Papers

Mainstream British wallpaper design regressed dramatically between the wars, bogged down in a sea of "porridge," but the artist Edward Bawden made a valiant attempt to redeem the medium. Bawden, who had studied calligraphy and illustration at the Royal College of Art, was another of the contributors to the inspirational pattern papers produced by the Curwen Press during the 1920s and 1930s, and his approach to wallpaper was very much that of a graphic artist. Initially he used lino-printing to produce his own designs, but from 1926 the Curwen Press reproduced his patterns in the form of colour lithographs, printed on sheets rather than on rolls.

Flying in the face of Modernist abstraction, Bawden produced pictorial designs with accessible, entertaining subjects, treating the

Above Fig. 3.10
Woodpigeon *lithographically printed wallpaper, designed by Edward Bawden, produced by the Curwen Press, 1927.* This witty *trompe l'oeil* design, originally produced as a lino print, plays with visual conventions by cutting "portholes" in the leafy background wallpaper.

Above right Fig. 3.11
Moss *block-printed wallpaper, designed by John Aldridge, 1939, produced by Cole & Sons, 1946.* Created just before the war as part of a collection co-designed with Edward Bawden called the Bardfield Papers, this wallpaper marries contemporary surrealism with Regency pattern design.

Right Fig. 3.12
Torro *screen-printed cotton furnishing fabric, designed by Michael O'Connell, produced by Edinburgh Weavers, c.1939.* During the 1930s hand screen-printing was enthusiastically adopted by progressive British companies as a more flexible alternative to block-printing and roller-printing.

wall as a decorative mural rather than a neutral background. His patterns often had a surreal quality, as in *Desert and Camels*, showing a vista of undulating sand dunes with occasional isolated camel trains, and *Conservatory*, which juxtaposed vases of flowers with doll-like Victorian figures. Bawden's best-known design, *Woodpigeon* (1927), featured vignettes of birds and church spires emerging through windows in a "wallpaper" of leafy trees (fig. 3.10). Similarly, in *Knole Park* (1929) primitive rural vignettes were "hung" like pictures on a diagonal, oak-patterned ground. In 1933 the Curwen Press produced another collection, the Plaistow Wallpapers. These four designs, printed in muted colours, were more textural and abstract, as in *Ashlar*, simulating the appearance of dressed stone. The theatrical side of Bawden's personality resurfaced in *Facade*, depicting alternating columns and drapes.

Bawden resumed his love affair with wallpapers in 1939 when he teamed up with John Aldridge to produce the Bardfield Papers. These were initially lino-printed by the two artists, but the blocks were acquired by Cole & Sons in 1946, which successfully relaunched the collection after the war. The Bardfield Papers exploited architectural motifs such as Gothic quatrefoil windows, tracery, and stonework in a series of bold, illusionistic designs that were characterized by clever interplay between different planes. Aldridge also drew on sources such as Regency dress fabrics, reinterpreting early 19th-century motifs, such as ribbons and cornucopias, in contemporary ways. In *Moss*, with its exaggeratedly organic pattern, he subtly subverted the familiar trellis formula by adding surreal sprouting roots (fig. 3.11). Although the outbreak of the war brought this initiative to a halt, the Bardfield Papers were later relaunched, subtly influencing the direction of post-war design.

Britain: Screen-printed textiles

Just as the block-printed textile revival was reaching its peak in Britain during the early 1930s, a new technique – screen-printing – was being introduced, which would eventually eclipse both block-printing and roller-printing. In this technique, which developed out of stencilling, coloured paste is forced through a fine-mesh screen on which the pattern has been masked out with a resist medium. Much cheaper than block-printing, it was particularly useful for short runs because minimal investment was required to produce the screens. The low cost also encouraged manufacturers to take greater risks. From an artistic point of view the technique had many advantages, as it allowed much greater flexibility in terms of colour, scale, and the rendition of painterly effects (fig. 3.12). "Brushwork, stipples, dapples and etched effects can be faithfully reproduced by screen-printing and help to convey different surfaces and provide contrast and interest," advised Antony Hunt in 1937.[10] Although screen-printing was initially unsuited to bulk production, being slower and more expensive than roller-printing, as it had to be carried out by hand, eventually this problem was overcome after screen-printing was gradually mechanized following the Second World War. Mechanical flatbed screen-printing began to

Above Fig. 3.13
Crazy Lines roller-printed cotton furnishing fabric, designed by Ernst Aufseeser, produced by Turnbull & Stockdale, 1933. The metal roller used to print this Modernist pattern was hand-engraved to reproduce the textural subtleties of Ernst Aufseeser's charcoal drawing.

be adopted in the 1950s, but the big change came with rotary screen-printing, which has dominated the industry since the mid-1960s.

One of the first British companies to use screen-printing was the Barrack Fabric Printing Company, established in 1924. It was also adopted during the early 1930s by G.P. & J. Baker, which had hitherto relied on block-printing. By the mid-1930s an increasing number of artistically motivated commercial companies were exploiting screen-printing, including Donald Brothers and the Old Bleach Linen Company. The most enthusiastic advocates, however, were the new design-led companies, such as Allan Walton Textiles and Edinburgh Weavers, whose primary objective was the production of artists' designs.

Britain: Industrial Art Movement
In 1937 Antony Hunt wrote: "Textile design and production are making history. The past few years have brought changes more revolutionary and complete than in any former period… New schools of thought emerge, and strive to find their appropriate expressions in art and industry – Futurism, Cubism, Surrealism, Functionalism, all react upon and to varying degrees affect the current tendencies in architecture and furnishings, and therefore modify the forms, textures and colourings of textiles that accompany them (fig. 3.13)."[11]

One of the catalysts of this "revolution" was the Industrial Art Movement, which translated Modernist idealism into practical, tangible design reform. The campaign got under way in 1915 with the formation of the Design and Industries Association (DIA), which brought together progressive industrialists, designers, architects, craftsmen, educators, and retailers "to promote the development of British industry by encouraging good workmanship based on excellence of design and soundness of material and to educate public taste to look for such design in what they buy."[12] The movement gained further momentum in 1920 with the founding of the British Institute of Industrial Art. Apart from proselytization through the media, one of the main vehicles for raising public and commercial awareness about the value of industrial art was exhibitions. The DIA led the way with an exhibition called *British Industrial Art in Relation to the Home* at Dorland Hall in London in 1933. This was followed by *British Art in Industry*, organized by the Royal Society of Arts at the Royal Academy of Arts in 1935, and the *Exhibition of Everyday Things*, mounted by the Royal Institute of British Architects in 1936. Textiles played a key role in all three exhibitions, which brought together a wide variety of applied arts by artists and designers.

Over the course of the decade changing attitudes towards modern design were reflected by the adoption of a wider visual vocabulary. In 1937 Antony Hunt observed: "One of the soundest and most welcome features of the various contemporary styles … is the fact that they impose no limit to the subjects from which designs may

be created. No rigid tradition compels adherence to banal flora, or enslavement to the chronic charms of the acanthus. It is the sense of liberty and variety in contemporary designs which provides their interest and has to a great extent assisted them to supplant so-called 'period' designs."[13] Hunt recommended to designers three main sources of inspiration for pattern design: historical artefacts, natural history, and "theoretical designs." By the last he meant abstract-geometric patterns, and he noted that "Such designs require to be 'built' rather than drawn, architecturally or mathematically conceived rather than emotionally."[14]

Britain: Sanderson and Simpson & Godlee
One of the reasons for the strength of textile pattern design in Britain during the 1930s was the increase in the number of firms producing printed furnishing fabrics. Among the new producers was Arthur Sanderson & Sons, already established as a leading wallpaper manufacturer. Although the company had been selling bought-in textiles for some years, it was not until 1921 that it became a producer in this field, after opening a printworks at Uxbridge, west London, to which weaving facilities were added in 1934. Originally known as Eton Rural Cretonnes and then, from 1922, as Eton Rural Fabrics, the firm adopted the name Sanderson Fabrics in 1936. During the early years the French influence was particularly strong, and Sanderson's launch collection was described by the *Journal of Decorative Art* as "magnificent jazz designs, stripes and broken arrangements of orange and black, glimmering blue and gold, and jade, and rich crimson."[15] Also included were pseudo-Jacobean patterns and "exquisite arrangements of irises and crocuses." These naturalistic painterly designs, which featured massed ranks of garish cottage-garden flowers, remained popular into the following decade.

Towards the end of the 1920s Sanderson began producing a new genre of abstract designs, including radial patterns of segmented circles, arcs, and jagged fans, and vertical and horizontal designs composed of chevrons and stripes. The Austrian-born designer Mea Angerer, who had trained under Josef Hoffmann in Vienna and supplied designs to the Wiener Werkstätte, worked for Eton Rural Fabrics for eighteen months after moving to Britain in 1928, and her arrival coincided with a highly creative period. Other designers included Percy Bilbie and Cecil H. Judge, the latter described by Hayes Marshall as "a talented young designer with creative and modernistic ideas," who worked in the Sanderson studio before turning freelance.[16]

Sanderson was one of many companies that revived production of "shadow tissues" or "shadow cretonnes" during the early 1930s (fig. 3.14). These hybrid textiles, loosely resembling ikats, were created by printing a pattern on the warp threads before weaving with a one-colour weft, producing soft, fuzzy effects. The Manchester company Simpson & Godlee produced some outstanding shadow tissues early in the decade, including Cubist-inspired patchworks of

Far left Fig. 3.14
Warp-printed cotton furnishing fabric, produced by Arthur Sanderson & Sons, 1930. Popular during the early 1930s, this type of fabric, known as "shadow tissue" because of its slightly fuzzy registration, was printed on the warp threads before it was woven, rather than on the finished cloth.

Left Fig. 3.15
Roller-printed cotton furnishing fabric, produced by Turnbull & Stockdale, 1936. Working as commission printers, in addition to producing its own ranges, Turnbull & Stockdale set high standards of design for mass-produced textiles, using a variety of printing techniques.

coloured blocks. The colouring of these was particularly effective, combining neutral browns with brighter blues, greens, oranges, yellows, and reds. Reflecting the positive attitude towards modern design at this time, the firm's output also embraced painterly abstracts and gaily coloured, duplex-printed floral cretonnes.

Britain: Turnbull & Stockdale

Turnbull & Stockdale resurfaced as one of the most artistically adventurous manufacturers of the 1930s. Its shadow tissues, such as the jagged abstract *Chevron* (1933), were particularly striking. The company was admired for the quality of its printing and its willingness to experiment, and during the 1930s it used standard engraved roller-printing, surface-printing with wooden rollers, duplex-printing, discharge-printing, block-printing, and screen-printing. This had a direct impact on its patterns, which were of a diversity unparalleled by any other British manufacturer at the time (figs. 3.13, 3.15, and 3.16). Varied cloths – plain and textured, natural and artificial – were carefully chosen to complement the nature of each design. Eric Gray's evocative abstract *Skyscraper* (1933), for example, was printed on a textured rayon and cotton damask. Modernism was also embraced in Turnbull & Stockdale's woven textiles, which included, in 1933, a jacquard-woven cotton by J.C. Howarth with a distorted chequerboard pattern.

Although many of the company's fabrics were marketed anonymously, their quality and originality suggested the existence of a gifted in-house design team. Some designers were identified, however, including Frank Ormrod, whose bold, geometricized floral marked a turning point in 1929. The distinguished German designer Ernst Aufseeser, a professor of applied art in Düsseldorf from 1919 to 1933, injected a powerful shot of unadulterated Continental Modernism into British textiles with his puzzle-like linear designs, created during a brief stay in Britain. *Crazy Lines* (1933), printed in monochrome, resembled a circuit board (fig. 3.13), while *Stippule* (1933), with its stencil-like shaded effects, had a more Constructivist feel. His son Hans Aufseeser, who settled in Britain in 1930 and changed his name to Tisdall in the 1940s, adopted a more light-hearted and openly decorative approach (fig 3.16). He combined prolific activity in textile design with success as a mural painter and designer of mosaics, tapestries, and book jackets. Among other Turnbull & Stockdale designers were Josephine Cheesman, Eva Crofts, Nancy Ellis, and Christopher Heal.

Britain: Campbell Fabrics and Ramsden Wood Print Works

As Turnbull & Stockdale demonstrated, the revival of block-printed textiles was by no means confined to craft-based workshops, but also permeated industrial production. Its beneficial effects were particularly evident at Campbell Fabrics, run by the designer Nora Jean Campbell, whose patterns ranged from giant, stylized flowers and leaves (fig. 3.17) to organic and calligraphic abstract designs. Other contributors to this impressive company, whose fabrics were marketed under the name Nairn Cloth, included the rug designer Ronald Grierson, the graphic designer Ashley Havinden, and the textile designers André Bicât, Margaret Simeon, Meriel Tower, and Riette Sturge Moore. Moore, whose father was the wood engraver T. Sturge Moore, created simple and overtly graphic patterns such as *Flames* (1939), featuring isolated flame motifs.

André Bicât, whose background was in theatre design and mural painting, and who specialized in cursive linear patterns of flowers and birds, also supplied designs to the Ramsden Wood Print Works of Walsden, Lancashire. During the 1920s this company had produced patterns by W.G. Paulson Townsend, and the following decade it collaborated with a number of fashionable freelance designers, including Vere Astley, Elaine May, Erna Pinner, Philip C. Stockford, and Ursula Wakeham. Modish designs predominated, featuring motifs such as feathers, bamboo, and leaping deer, displaying the lingering influence of Art Deco.

Britain: Donald Brothers and Old Bleach Linen Company

Two well-established linen manufacturers who expanded into the field of screen-printed textiles during the 1930s were Donald Brothers and the Old Bleach Linen Company. Founded in Dundee, Scotland, in the late 19th century, Donald Brothers grew out of the local coarse jute and linen industry, and initially specialized in rugged, textured canvases and linens for use as wall coverings and furnishings. With the launch of its Old Glamis Fabrics in 1926 the firm began to produce patterned jacquard-woven fabrics and printed textiles, using subtly textured fabrics ranging from coarse linen to silky mercerized cotton to lustrous linen-rayon. Adopting the tempered elegance of the Industrial Art Movement, it produced patterns by an impressive array of designers, including Bernard Adeney, Louise Aldred, Mea Angerer, Hans Aufseeser, André Bicât (fig. 3.18), E. Victor Borton, Josephine Cheesman, Barry Costin-Nian, Eva Crofts, E. Dean, Marion Dorn, John Goodrich, Norah Hurford, Paul Nash, Mary Oliver, Grace Peat, Marianne Mahler, Barbara Pile, Astrid Sampe, P. A. Staynes, and A. Woolfe. The robustness of the firm's cloth was reflected in its choice of designers. Eva Crofts, for example, while never formally trained, displayed a natural talent for bold, primitive patterns featuring motifs such as leafy branches, flowers, and fruit (fig. 3.20). Revered by architects, Donald Brothers commissioned eight printed and woven patterns from Marion Dorn, whose stylish, large-scale patterns, such as *Stanford* (1937) and *Langton* (1938), featuring formal sprays and columns of leaves, made a dramatic impact on modern interiors.

The Old Bleach Linen Company, established by C.J. Webb at Randalstown, Northern Ireland, in 1864, was a large and successful firm which, by the 1930s, employed over 1,200 people. Household linens, dress fabrics, and machine-embroidered goods were the mainstay of production, but during the early 1930s the company expanded into furnishing fabrics, winning major commissions for work for ships and hotels. Its core furnishings range, created by talented but anonymous in-house designers, consisted of jacquard-woven linens decorated with vigorous organic and abstract-geometric patterns in the form of waves, loops, knots, scrolls, grids, and chevrons. Particularly striking was the jagged wave pattern *Sperrin* (1936), used on the liner the *Queen Mary*.

Top Fig. 3.16
Screen-printed linen furnishing fabric, designed by Hans Aufseeser, produced by Turnbull & Stockdale, c.1936. The German émigré designer Hans Aufseeser was praised by his fellow designer and stylist H.G. Hayes Marshall for possessing "a style which is distinctly decorative and entirely his own."

Above Fig. 3.17
Kew *block-printed linen furnishing fabric, designed by Nora Jean Campbell, produced by Campbell Fabrics, 1937.* Campbell Fabrics was one of the few commercial companies to retain its allegiance to block-printing throughout the 1930s. Boldness, simplicity, and clarity characterized its designs.

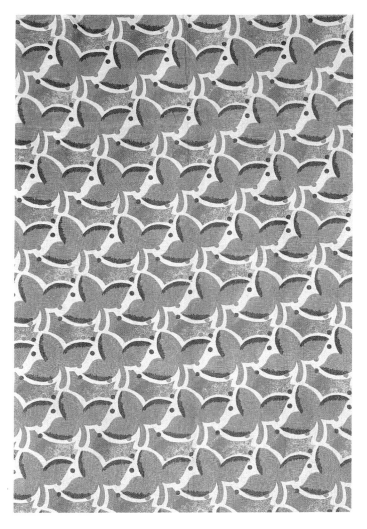

Above left Fig. 3.18
Rustic screen-printed linen furnishing fabric, designed by André Bicât, produced by Donald Brothers, 1938. Collaborating with an array of talented designers, Donald Brothers developed an enviable reputation during the 1930s for its adventurous Old Glamis range of hand screen-printed linens.

Left Fig. 3.19
Jack Tar woven linen furnishing fabric, designed by Felix Gotto, produced by the Old Bleach Linen Company, 1936. Although woven in subtle colours, this lively figurative design is full of energy and fun. It was featured in the *Exhibition of Everyday Things*, held at the RIBA in 1936.

Above Fig. 3.20
Chale screen-printed linen furnishing fabric, designed by Eva Crofts, produced by Donald Brothers, 1936. This type of coarse linen, known as crash, was a speciality of Donald Brothers. The rough texture of the cloth perfectly complements the earthy, primitive character of the pattern.

Above Fig. 3.21

*Screen-printed cotton velvet furnishing
fabric, designed by Duncan Grant,
produced by Allan Walton Textiles, 1936.*
Because screen-printing could
reproduce the subtle nuances of a
painter's brushstrokes, many artists
responded enthusiastically to the
opportunity to design for this medium.

During the 1930s the firm also began to produce screen-printed
textured linens and linen-rayons featuring abstract, figurative, and
stylized plant designs. Its design profile was greatly enhanced after it
began commissioning patterns from artists and freelance designers,
including Barry Costin-Nian, Eva Crofts, Marion Dorn, Felix Gotto,
Ronald Grierson, Ashley Havinden, H.G. Hayes Marshall, Paul
Nash, and Nancy Standley. Particularly distinctive were Felix
Gotto's designs, including *Rialto* (c.1936), a Modernist printed
pattern with graduated stripes, and *Jack Tar* (1936), woven with
angular dancing sailors (fig. 3.19). Paul Nash's *Fugue* (1936) recalled
the aesthetic of block-printing in the flatness and stiffness of its
composition. By contrast, Marion Dorn exploited the full potential
of screen-printing in a series of fluid, multi-layered designs,
sometimes printed on figured woven fabrics, as in the ribbon-like,
rhythmic *Chorale* (1936). *Aircraft* (1938), with its dynamic pairs of
darting pigeons, was used extensively on the SS *Orcades* (fig. 3.33).
Dorn's most powerful design, *Zodiac* (1939), featured outline
drawings of astrological symbols floating above flat images reserved
in the coloured ground (fig. 3.1). At the end of the decade she
produced the Ulster Group, three screen-prints called *Ulster*,
Antrim, and *Enniskillen* (c.1939), depicting scenes of Irish life.

Britain: Allan Walton Textiles

Two new companies that embodied the ethos of the Industrial Art
Movement to the full were Allan Walton Textiles and Edinburgh
Weavers. Allan Walton had originally trained as a painter and an
architect, and also practised as an interior decorator and designer.
In 1931 he became artistic director of Allan Walton Textiles, and his
brother, Roger Walton, who had worked in the family textile firm,
provided technical expertise and oversaw production at the Little
Green Dyeworks in Manchester. The company specialized in
expensive printed textiles by artists and freelance designers,
promoted through exhibitions at prestigious venues such as the
Mayor Galleries in London. Initially production was based on
block-printing, but screen-printing was adopted in 1933. As a
textile designer himself, and a contributor to his company's
collections, Allan Walton knew that the choice of cloth had a
considerable impact on the appearance of the print and the way
the fabric draped. He was particularly interested in reflective
effects, and the range of cloths used by the firm encompassed
shiny cotton-and-rayon mixes as well as linen, cotton, and velvet.

Walton's taste was eclectic, and the patterns he selected were in a
diverse range of styles. Some were designed by established artists,
including Vanessa Bell and Duncan Grant, while others were by
young textile graduates from the Central School such as Barbara
Pile and Winning Read. Bell and Grant, veterans of the Omega
Workshops, produced painterly florals and whimsical pastiche
Baroque patterns in a loose, fluid, decorative style. Bell's patterns,
printed in pastel shades, were soft and nebulous, while Grant's
designs, such as *The Winds* (1932), with its beefy cherubs and
scribbly clouds, were more robust. Particularly impressive was a

vibrant, daubed leafy pattern by Grant, printed on velvet, originally intended for the *Queen Mary* in 1936 but never used (fig. 3.21).

Some designers, such as Bernard Adeney, a teacher from the Central School, displayed their continuing allegiance to block-printing in the graphic precision of their compositions (fig. 3.2). Others, such as the flower and landscape painter Keith Baynes and the sculptor Frank Dobson, embraced the potential of screen-printing for capturing fluid brushstrokes and washes of colour. Other contributors included H.J. Bull, T. Bradley, Josephine Cheesman, Anne Cobham, J. Cockerill, Douglas Davidson, Blair Hughes-Stanton, Noel Guildford, Mary Irene Loder, Diana Low, Thomas Lowinsky, Marianne Mahler, Kenneth Martin, Margaret Moore, Cedric Morris, Barbara Pile, Helen Sampson, Margaret Simeon, Meriel Tower, Sheila Walsh, T. Picton Warlow, and Barbara Wright. Some of the most memorable designs were those by Bull and Bradley, who favoured stark, uncompromising, abstract-geometric patterns (fig. 3.22). Bull created bold, rhythmic compositions in limited colours, juxtaposing the severe angularity of triangles and stripes against the organic curves of arcs and waves. Unfortunately, the war brought this heroic enterprise to an untimely end. Allan Walton was the director of Glasgow School of Art from 1943 to 1945, but died in 1948 before the company could be revived.

Britain: Edinburgh Weavers

Edinburgh Weavers, the trail-blazing experimental subsidiary of Morton Sundour, became similarly bound up with the vision of one individual, Alastair Morton. Originally established in Edinburgh in 1928 at the initiative of his father, James Morton, Edinburgh Weavers was conceived as a research unit for exploring the links between textiles and modern architecture. According to James Morton, "just as those buildings demand a certain restraint ... so our fabrics must have in them a new simplicity and directness that calls for a restrained and cultivated handling of the new facilities of colour and mechanical manipulation that the sciences have put so easy to our hand."[17] Alec Hunter, who had hitherto worked at St Edmundsbury Weavers in Letchworth, Hertfordshire, with his father, Edmund Hunter, was enlisted to take charge of the new enterprise. He began to develop a range of modern hand-woven fabrics, initially produced at Letchworth, although the financial slump of 1930 cut short this promising initiative, and he was laid off. Edinburgh Weavers was subsequently relocated to Carlisle, and operated independently alongside Morton Sundour, drawing on the latter's production facilities and continuing to manufacture some of Hunter's designs.

After joining Morton Sundour in 1931, Alastair Morton took charge of Edinburgh Weavers and began to steer the company in new directions. He later emerged as an accomplished designer of woven textiles, but also took a keen interest in screen-printing, and under his leadership Edinburgh Weavers evolved into what Nikolaus Pevsner described as "a laboratory for the best modern textile art."

Top Fig. 3.22
Screen-printed cotton and rayon satin furnishing fabric, designed by H.J. Bull, produced by Allan Walton Textiles, 1932. This deconstructed geometric pattern reveals the influence of Cubism and Constructivism. Hard-edged abstraction remained a minority taste in Britain during the 1930s, however.

Above Fig. 3.23
Avis *woven rayon and cotton furnishing fabric, designed by Marion Dorn, produced by Edinburgh Weavers, 1938–9.* This infectiously rhythmic design, with its dynamic interplay of criss-crossing diagonals, is composed of several distinct floating layers, which give depth to the pattern.

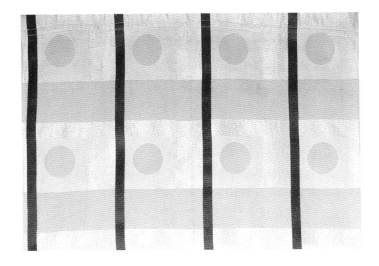

After taking up painting in 1936, Morton became friendly with the group of British artists associated with Constructivism. His interest in the movement led to the Constructivist range of fabrics, launched in October 1937, which included designs by the painters Ben Nicholson (fig. 3.24), Winifred Nicholson, Eileen Holding, and Arthur Jackson, the sculptor Barbara Hepworth (fig. 3.25), and the graphic designer Ashley Havinden. "In using pure, unassociated forms and colours the constructive artists have turned towards life and away from the symbolism of nature," wrote Eileen Holding. "They have realised that the beauty of a curve or of a straight line is not confined within the limits of a contour of a hillside or the edge of a table. Such forms are in themselves absolute, they are the basis of a perpetual evolution."[18] The Constructivist fabrics were original not only for their imagery, consisting of pure geometric patterns, but also for the sensitivity and technical ingenuity with which the subtle colours and low-relief effects were translated into woven cloth. Yarns and weaves were carefully devised to evoke subtle variations in tones, texture, and surface level. Ben Nicholson's designs included *Vertical*, *Horizontal*, and *Counterpoint*, all woven, and *Three Circles*, which was screen-printed. "In much of his work there is a peculiar stillness, not dull or static, which appeals to the intellect as well as the emotions," wrote Antony Hunt.[19]

Ashley Havinden, who was the art director of a firm of commercial artists called W.S. Crawford Ltd., as well as a celebrated rug designer, also created several other patterns for Edinburgh Weavers in addition to his Constructivist design *Segments* (1937). Among these were *Silvan* (1936), *Ashley's Abstract* (1937), and *Uccello* (1937–8), all featuring both abstract organic shapes and stylized plant and animal motifs. Conscious of the need to cater to two quite different sectors of the market, Alastair Morton commissioned both representational and non-representational designs. "Contemporary design should develop two styles," he wrote, "firstly a style built up of sensitive formalised objects having pleasing associations, such as flowers and leaves, etc … and secondly, an abstract style similar to the present constructivist paintings, depending alone on the abstract qualities of colour and form."[20] The woven designs of Marion Dorn, Riette Sturge Moore, and Margaret Simeon fell into the first of these two categories, featuring imaginative interpretations of natural motifs. *Avis* (1939), a jacquard-woven rayon by Marion Dorn, composed of angular, interlocking birds, satisfied both criteria (fig. 3.23).

Edinburgh Weavers also produced an eclectic range of screen-printed fabrics, some by John Chirnside, who had trained at Morton Sundour, but most commissioned from freelance designers such as Hans Aufseeser, Margaret Calkin James, Marianne Mahler, Michael O'Connell, John Tandy, and Miriam Wornum. Designs by Hans Aufseeser from the 1930s included a tropical foliage pattern called *Mephisto* and several jolly cartoons, such as *Charioteer* and *Sailor's Return*. John Tandy was an architect turned wood engraver, whose interest in both interiors and printmaking was evident in

Top Fig. 3.24
Vertical *woven cotton and rayon damask furnishing fabric, designed by Ben Nicholson, produced by Edinburgh Weavers, 1937.* In Edinburgh Weavers' artist-designed Constructivist collection, subtle low-relief effects were created through careful choice of yarns and by variations in the weave.

Above Fig. 3.25
Pillar *woven cotton and rayon furnishing fabric, designed by Barbara Hepworth, produced by Edinburgh Weavers, 1937.* This woven Constructivist design has, like Nicholson's pattern (top), a quiet understatement and a calm control that contrast with the restless energy of contemporary Cubist-inspired patterns.

his textile designs. Michael O'Connell, who also produced his own range of block-printed textiles under the name Mael Fabrics, specialized in theatre curtains. His designs included the loose, sunlit Mediterranean townscape *Torro* (c.1939) (fig. 3.12) and the more structured, wood-block-style *Bacchante* (c.1939–40), depicting alternating vase, plant, and Bacchus motifs. Austrian-born Marianne Mahler had trained in Vienna under Josef Hoffmann. During the 1930s she sold designs to manufacturers in France, Germany, and the United States, and her work was exhibited at the Paris Exposition in 1937. After moving to Britain that year she began working with some of the most progressive textile companies, including Donald Brothers, Edinburgh Weavers, Helios, and Allan Walton Textiles. *Treetops* (c.1939), the collage-like pattern she created for Edinburgh Weavers, featured cut-out floating trees and birds (fig. 3.26). A variant was later produced by David Whitehead Fabrics, the forward-looking company with which she collaborated after the war, working under the name Marian.

Britain: Warner

In 1925 four of Warner's staff designers – Charles Ebel, Albert Swindells, Herbert Woodman, and Bertrand Whittaker – were sent to France to see the Paris Exposition. Although the company's own contribution to the exhibition was limited to traditional damasks, brocades, and three-pile velvets, contemporary French influences later appeared in some of its designs, such as the jazzy, abstract *Excelsior* (1928), a cotton-and-rayon tissue by Albert Swindells. By this time Warner had begun to incorporate cheaper rayon yarns into some of its cloth, and was producing power-woven cotton damasks alongside hand-woven silk tissues and damasks. After taking over the Dartford Printworks in Kent in 1927, the company began to expand its range of printed textiles, including floral chintzes, cretonnes, and "Jacobean" patterns, as well as brightly coloured Moderne designs. Initially these were block-printed, but screen-printing was added in 1930.

In 1932 Alec Hunter (previously of St Edmundsbury Weavers and Edinburgh Weavers) was appointed as Warner's production manager, becoming a director in 1943. Under his direction, the firm, while continuing to cater to traditional tastes, emerged as a significant force in progressive textile design. Experimenting with unusual combinations of natural and synthetic fibres, Hunter devised methods of converting innovative hand-woven fabrics to power-loom production. He also enlisted the hand weaver Theo Moorman to establish a craft weaver's studio at the factory, which she ran from 1935 to 1939. Hunter himself was an accomplished designer of Modernist fabrics, whose woven patterns included the Cubist-inspired cotton, cotton-gimp, and jute damask *Braintree* (1932) (fig. 3.27), the circle-patterned, silk-and-rayon brocade *Discs* (1934), and *Welwyn* (1935), a silk-and-rayon brocade decorated with stylized leaves. The in-house designer Bertrand Whittaker also supplied some attractive woven designs, as did freelance designers such as Ursula Wakeham and Marion Dorn.

Above Fig. 3.26
Treetops *screen-printed cotton and rayon furnishing fabric, designed by Marianne Mahler, produced by Edinburgh Weavers, c.1939.* European émigré designers such as Marianne Mahler provide a direct link between the Wiener Werkstätte and the early post-war British "Contemporary" style.

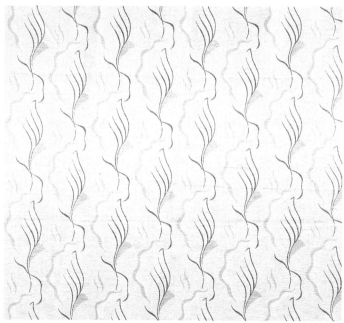

Top Fig. 3.27
Braintree no. 5 *woven cotton, cotton gimp, and jute damask, designed by Alec Hunter, produced by Warner & Sons, 1932.* Cubist-inspired upholstery fabrics such as this were influenced by French Moderne textiles of the late 1920s, interpreted in a more mellow and restrained guise.

Above Fig. 3.28
Cirrus *screen-printed silk and cotton furnishing fabric, designed by Louise Aldred, produced by Warner & Sons, 1936.* Designers in Britain during the 1930s excelled in stylized organic patterns. The calligraphic rippling lines and lapping rhythms of this design are particularly seductive.

Above Fig. 3.29
Etruscan Head *screen-printed net silk and silk noil furnishing fabric, designed by Marion Dorn, printed by Warner & Sons for Marion Dorn Limited, 1936.* In addition to selling patterns on a freelance basis, Marion Dorn established her own company to produce and market her designs.

Dorn enjoyed an unusual relationship with Warner, supplying some designs on a freelance basis, as well as commissioning the company to produce fabrics for her own enterprise, Marion Dorn Limited. In her woven textiles she reduced pattern and colour to a minimum, as in the diagonal-striped *Marywell* (1934–5), and she placed emphasis on the expression of texture through weave and yarn, including tufted and fringed effects. In her printed designs Dorn frequently played with the displacement of outline and infill, as in *Hand and Poppy* and *Acorn and Oak* (both 1935), the latter produced for the *Queen Mary*. Other patterns, such as *Etruscan Heads* (1936), explored classical imagery and displayed a more theatrical quality (fig. 3.29).

As well as producing printed patterns by Robert Artis and Herbert Woodman from its in-house studio, Warner manufactured designs by Louise Aldred, Mea Angerer, Vere Astley, Eva Aufseeser (daughter of Ernst and sister of Hans), Hans Aufseeser, Eva Crofts, Alice Sanders-Erskine, John Little, and Margaret Simeon. The work of Louise Aldred, who was also a mural painter, was particularly memorable, especially her calligraphic patterns with fluttering, ribbon-like motifs, *Cirrus* (1936) (fig. 3.28), *The Dancers* (1937), and *Hermes* (1938). At the other end of the spectrum were the traditional chintz designs by Lewis Jones from the Silver Studio. Furthermore, in addition to acting as commission printers for the designer Eileen Hunter, who ran Eileen Hunter Fabrics, Warner produced exclusive ranges for the London department store Fortnum & Mason.

Britain: Helios

After the Second World War one of the chief designers of woven textiles at Warner was Swiss-born Marianne Straub. She arrived in Britain in 1932 to study mechanized weaving at Bradford Technical College, and subsequently she worked for the hand weaver Ethel Mairet at her weaving workshop, Gospels, in Ditchling, Sussex. In 1937, after three years as consultant designer for the Rural Industries Bureau, Straub joined the progressive Bolton-based company Helios. Established in 1936 at the initiative of Sir Thomas Barlow, this was an independent subsidiary of the large Manchester firm Barlow & Jones, and was managed by Felix Loewenstein, who had previously worked at Pausa in Germany. Straub was employed as chief designer at Helios between 1937 and 1947, and then, following Loewenstein's death, as managing director until 1950, when the firm was taken over by Warner.

At Helios, Straub carried out pioneering research in the field of power-loom woven textiles for the retail market. Exploiting both dobby weaving and jacquard weaving, and using both natural and artificial fibres, she developed an innovative range of fabrics with strong visual and tactile appeal. Unusually for a weaver, Straub had a well-developed feeling for pattern, and often incorporated imagery into her designs, such as the flanged-leaf silhouettes of *Crofton* (1938) (fig. 3.30). Her later designs were more abstract, although still decidedly organic, such as the undulating, speckled

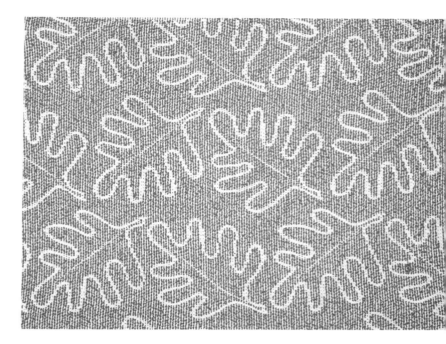

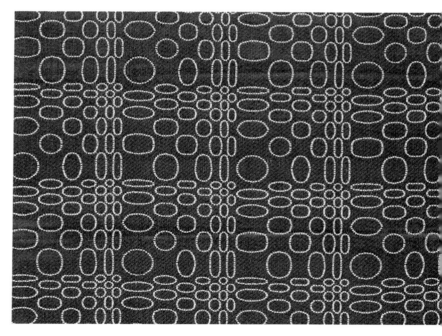

Top Fig. 3.30
Crofton rough-weave cotton furnishing fabric, designed by Marianne Straub, produced by Helios, 1938. This, like the design below it, highlights Marianne Straub's skill in creating innovative textural woven fabrics with appealing organic and abstract patterns. They were intended for the mass market.

Above Fig. 3.31
Matlock woven rayon and cotton furnishing fabric, designed by Marianne Straub, produced by Helios, 1945. Circles gradually transpose into flattened ovals in this intriguing fabric, which was used by the shipping company Cunard to furnish the cabins of its liners shortly after the war.

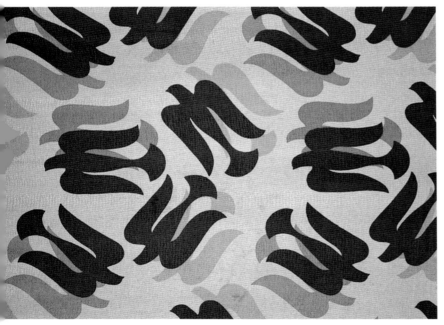

Monyash (1945). *Matlock* (1945), which featured circles mutating into ovals, was both mathematical and biological (fig. 3.31).

Under Straub's direction Helios also produced an attractive range of screen-printed textiles, drawing on the cream of British and European design talent. Dora Batty, a graphic designer with a flair for textiles who taught at the Central School from 1932, created both printed and woven fabrics for Helios. Jane Edgar, whose robust compositions reflected her interest in block-printing, was complimented by H.G. Hayes Marshall for her "strong sense of pattern, and individual feeling for rich colour." He also noted her skill in combining "a fine appreciation of period design with a sound grasp of modern decorative tendencies."[21] The Swiss designer Noldi Soland made a memorable contribution to Helios with *Wychwood* (1939), which combined fluid, linear plant motifs with flat, floating flowers (fig. 3.32). Other noteworthy contributors of printed designs during the late 1930s and 1940s were Hans Aufseeser (by this time known as Tisdall), John Farleigh, Ronald Grierson, Jacqueline Groag, Oliver Messell, Marianne Mahler, Sylvia Priestley, Margaret Simeon, and Rex Whistler. In 1940 Helios bought a rose pattern by Graham Sutherland from an exhibition of designs by artists held at the Cotton Board's newly established Colour Design and Style Centre in Manchester. This was one of several printed patterns that remained in production after Helios was taken over by Warner.

Britain: Marion Dorn

Although many talented designers were practising in Britain during the 1930s, Marion Dorn was clearly the most gifted and influential. After studying graphic arts at Stanford University, she was initially a painter, although after moving to the artists' colony of New City in New York State in 1919, she took up batik. After a trip to Paris in 1923, she settled in England with her partner, the graphic designer Edward McKnight Kauffer. Here she resumed production of her batik hangings and furnishing fabrics, which were sold through galleries such as Modern Textiles in London. From 1926 she diversified into rugs, collaborating extensively with the Wilton Royal Carpet Factory. Dorn's reputation in this field led to commissions for complete furnishing schemes, prompting her to start designing woven and printed textiles, which were produced for her by companies such as Edinburgh Weavers and Warner. In turn, they commissioned designs for their own ranges, and Dorn's growing success attracted other clients, including Donald Brothers and the Old Bleach Linen Company. Pursuing a dual career as a designer of bespoke rugs and furnishings and a freelance designer of mass-produced industrial textiles, she established her own company, Marion Dorn Limited, in 1934. The perfect exemplar of the ideals of the Industrial Art Movement, Dorn's work was featured in all the major British design exhibitions of the period.

Although never formally trained as a textile designer, Dorn displayed great skill in both printed and woven fabrics, designing

Top Fig. 3.32
Wychwood screen-printed cotton satin furnishing fabric, designed by Noldi Soland, produced by Helios, 1939. By the end of the 1930s designers were exploiting the full potential of screen-printing to create much looser and more free-flowing patterns. This is a particularly fine example.

Above Fig. 3.33
Aircraft screen-printed rayon and linen furnishing fabric, designed by Marion Dorn, produced by the Old Bleach Linen Company, 1938. Although composed of a single repeated motif, this pattern has great dynamism because of the varied orientation of the darting birds and their multicoloured silhouettes.

THE HENLEY COLLEGE LIBRARY

some extremely innovative fringed and bouclé fabrics, as well as jacquard-woven patterns combining natural and synthetic yarns. Whether printed or woven, her fabrics were conceived as architectural elements within an interior, and this affected not only her choice of imagery but also the colour, composition, and scale of her designs. Ribbon patterns, such as *Chorale* (1936) for Old Bleach, reflected a direct crossover from rug design, although Dorn created surprisingly few completely abstract textile patterns. Natural motifs – generally shells, leaves, and birds rather than flowers – were her main subject, but delineated in a consciously artificial way and often arranged in multiple layers of pattern on different planes. The interplay of colour, line, and rhythm, rather than realism, was Dorn's main design concern, and she interpreted her motifs, whether organic, figurative, or architectural, in an overtly abstract manner. As the decade progressed, her patterns became larger and more architectural. Instead of using individual scattered motifs, her compositions assumed strong vertical or diagonal emphases, as in *Langton* (1937) for Donald Brothers, with its leafy columns, and *Aircraft* (1938) for Old Bleach, with its criss-crossing diving birds (fig. 3.33). Classical imagery became more pronounced towards the end of the 1930s, although in a modernized idiom, and was again used simply as a design device rather than to evoke literal associations. Summing up Dorn's achievements in 1939, Hayes Marshall praised her "extraordinary appreciation of colour and design" and described her work as "both original and practical, reflecting the conditions and spirit of our age."[22] The outbreak of war forced Dorn to return to the United States, bringing her remarkable British career to a close.

United States: Ruth Reeves

Although the Americans chose not to participate in the Paris Exposition of 1925, selected exhibits were later shipped from Europe to the United States, where they exerted a potent effect on design. In 1932, for example, the jazzy furnishings of Radio City Music Hall in New York, which included printed aluminium wallpapers by Donald Deskey, provided a classic example of American Moderne. Another contributor to this iconic building was Ruth Reeves, who designed the foyer carpet and a large wall tapestry depicting the history of the circus and the music hall. Trained as an artist during the 1910s at the California School of Design, the Pratt Institute, and the Art Students League, the latter two in New York, Reeves subsequently worked as a batik artist and as a researcher and illustrator for *Women's Wear* magazine, before moving to Paris in 1921. Here she lived for the next seven years, studying painting with Fernand Léger and absorbing influences from textile designers such as Raoul Dufy. On returning to the United States in 1928, she embarked on a career as a textile designer, using her paintings as the basis for her patterns.

In 1930 Reeves collaborated with the textile manufacturer W. & J. Sloane on an ambitious collection of printed fabrics and wall hangings for the *International Exhibition of Decorative Metalwork and*

Top Fig. 3.34
Green Pastures *screen-printed cotton furnishing fabric, designed by Ruth Reeves, produced by W. & J. Sloane, 1930.* Originally trained as an artist, Ruth Reeves used her paintings as the basis for some of her early textile designs. These two patterns highlight the breadth of her stylistic range.

Above Fig. 3.35
Manhattan *block-printed cotton, designed by Ruth Reeves, produced by W. & J. Sloane, 1930.* A number of Ruth Reeves's designs explore issues of national identity. In this pattern the diagonal composition of individual vignettes suggests the influence of Raoul Dufy.

Cotton Textiles, held later that year at the Metropolitan Museum of Art in New York. Conceived for a series of rooms in an imaginary country house, each pattern was printed on a different type of cloth. Design in the United States was an open book at this time, and this is reflected in the remarkable diversity of styles explored in this collection, which spanned both contemporary and historical idioms. *Botanical* featured drawings of American wild flowers inspired by engravings from the 1870s, while *Pomona* suggested 18th-century Rococo prints. *Essex Hunt* depicted English fox-hunting scenes, while *Katinka*, with its brightly coloured, child-like drawings of dolls, trees, houses, and flowers, alluded to Russian toys and folk art. *Electric*, with its dynamic zigzag elements, evoked modernity, while the diamond-patterned *Polychrome*, apparently contemporary, was inspired by the tiled floors in Renaissance paintings. *Green Pastures* was a simplified landscape depicted in a flat, painterly style (fig. 3.34), while the large wall hanging *Figures with Still Life* featured monumental, Picassoesque female figures in a deconstructed Cubist interior.

Reeves followed Dufy in depicting scenes from contemporary life, several of her compositions adopting his *toile de Tournon* format, notably *Manhattan*, a bold black-and-white jigsaw of skyscrapers, factories, and city landmarks (fig. 3.35). Her most impressive design was *American Scene*, a panorama of intimate domestic episodes in the life of a typical family, woven seamlessly together. The informality of her subject matter was revolutionary in textiles at the time, the closest parallels being with the documentary murals commissioned by the Works Progress Administration (WPA) during the Depression. "It is my personal opinion that fabric design rightfully belongs in the category of the Fine Arts," Reeves stated. "As an art, it is just as important as good architecture, and certainly is more closely associated with our everyday living than are paintings. In older civilizations and among primitive people, fabric designs often had profound significance because much of the daily life of these peoples was based on religious rituals and taboos. The fabrics for our own era should, by the same token, express our contemporary life both in actual motif, where fine contemporary form seem feasible, and in feeling."[23]

Most of Reeves's subsequent designs were block-printed or screen-printed independently. Very few were manufactured commercially, apart from a group of five Guatemalan-inspired patterns produced by R.H. Macy & Company in 1935. By exploring the decorative vocabulary of South and Central American textiles, Reeves sought to cultivate an indigenous, consciously non-European style. In 1946 she commented in *Craft Horizons*: "When we ceased to be afraid of colour – for which we may thank our Mexican and South American neighbours, and made the discovery that rich, clear, singing hues do something to those who live with them, we took a long step toward health and sanity." Active until 1956, Reeves later taught at the Cooper Union Art School in New York. Several of her post-war patterns were produced by Cheney Greeff & Co., Cyrus

Clark Co., Konwiser, and Morley Fletcher. Had she received more support from manufacturers during the 1930s, however, her influence would have been much greater and she might have flourished in a similar way to Marion Dorn. "Today doors are open, ears and eyes are alert that formerly were deaf and blind to what the designer had to offer," she observed in the same article in 1946.[24]

United States: Educational Alliance

Although the Depression hampered the development of modern textiles in the United States during the 1930s, some positive initiatives arose out of the activities of the WPA. The most interesting project in the field of pattern design was a group of screen-printed textiles created by children at the Educational Alliance Art School in New York. Founded during the 1920s as a free cultural centre for Jewish immigrants, the school aimed to stimulate interest in the fine and applied arts. Courses included applied design and batik, with special emphasis on fostering creativity in children through self-expression. According to a prospectus: "The child's natural creative ability here finds an outlet. The child approaches life and expresses its impressions in art with serene naivete, amazing boldness and a freshness that is well-worth preserving." The fabrics produced at the Educational Alliance Art School, while unsophisticated, perfectly captured the innocence of the children and the idealism of the scheme (fig. 3.36).

United States: Katzenbach & Warren

In 1928 Lois and William Katzenbach were inspired to establish their own wallpaper company, Katzenbach & Warren, after a revelatory trip to Europe. "In Vienna and Munich we saw modern wallpapers for the first time … completely unlike any wallpapers we had ever seen. Wallpaper was not particularly popular in the United States at that time. The average domestic paper was still strongly influenced by the over-embellished Victorian patterns that had been so popular a generation or two before."[25] The Katzenbachs also travelled to Paris, where they saw wallpapers by André Groult and the Atelier Martine. Bowled over by the vibrancy of these patterns, they began to import wallpapers created by the Wiener Werkstätte and the Deutsche Werkstätten, and commissioned a design from Paul Poiret that was printed in the United States.

Subsequently Katzenbach & Warren began to develop its own lines, commissioning patterns from mural painters such as Franklin Hughes and James Reynolds. The early ranges also included radically simple understated designs such as *Snowflake* (1929–32) by Stewart Wheeler (fig. 3.37), commission-printed by firms such as Birge. While continuing to use block-printing and machine surface-printing, the company began to experiment with screen-printing during the mid-1930s. Always on the lookout for new talent, William Katzenbach spotted as early as 1937 the potential of the textile designer William Justema. "Anyone can design yardage; you're a wallpaper designer," Justema was told. The Justema Collection inaugurated the company's New York showroom in

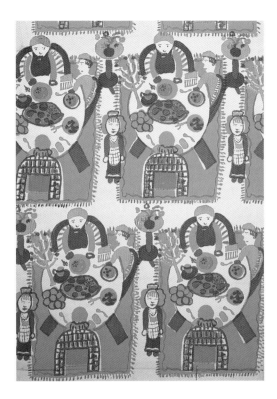

Far left Fig. 3.36
The Seder screen-printed cotton furnishing fabric, designed by A. Nedby, printed at the Educational Alliance, 1930s. Nedby was a ten-year-old child studying at the Educational Alliance, a community art school in New York which encouraged children to express their natural creativity.

Left Fig. 3.37
Snowflake surface-printed wallpaper, designed by Stewart Wheeler, produced by Katzenbach & Warren, 1929–32. Radical in its simplicity, this was one of the first modern wallpapers to be produced by Katzenbach & Warren, a company established in 1928, inspired by decorative trends in Europe.

1938.[26] In an attempt to capture a European flavour, the company included among its early designers several émigrés, such as Ilonka Karasz from Hungary and Tommi Parzinger from Germany. The Russian-born theatre designer Nicolas de Molas, who lived in Britain, also contributed patterns, and when Marion Dorn returned to her native country in 1940, not surprisingly it was with the enlightened Katzenbach & Warren that she chose to collaborate. The company also established an in-house design studio, which later produced as much as half of its designs.

Sweden: Märtha Gahn and Elsa Gullberg

In 1919 Gregor Paulsson, director of Svenska Slöjdföreningen (Swedish Society for Industrial Design) published an article encouraging Swedish designers to create "more beautiful everyday things." Sweden had excelled in woven textiles and tapestry since the late 19th century, but printed textiles lagged behind until the emergence of two pioneering female designers, Märtha Gahn and Elsa Gullberg, during the 1920s. Gahn, although principally known as a weaver, designed printed textiles for Borås Wäfveri from 1928, some of which were shown at the Stockholm Exhibition of 1930. Radical in their stark simplicity, they were composed of rows of small, stylized wild flowers depicted in an unpretentious vernacular style (fig. 3.38).

Elsa Gullberg was not only a designer but also a producer, with many years of experience in the promotion of Swedish design. In 1927 she established her own company, initially specializing in woven textiles in traditional Swedish styles. In 1935, with the help of the Austrian textile engineer Richard Künzl, she set up a small printworks – the first in Sweden to produce screen-printed textiles. Meadow-like florals, printed in fresh colours on an airy white ground, were her speciality (fig. 3.39), but she also commissioned patterns in different idioms from two leading ceramics and glass designers, Vicke Lindstrand and Arthur Percy. Between 1936 and 1948 Vicke Lindstrand, who had originally trained in graphic design, created a lively series of patterns featuring Cubist guitars and Fauvist zebras, depicted in a Scandinavian version of the Moderne style (fig. 3.40). Arthur Percy's designs included botanical plant studies resembling wood engravings, and informal painterly scenes from everyday life. After the war Gullberg adopted a low-key abstract style, creating all-over patterns with nugget-like motifs in warm colours until she retired in 1955.

Sweden: Nordiska Kompaniet and Jobs Handtryck

The 1930s witnessed the emergence of the formidable Astrid Sampe, a designer who would dominate Swedish textiles for the next four decades. Trained at the Konstfackskolan in Stockholm and the Royal College of Art in London, she began to design textiles in 1935 for the Stockholm department store Nordiska Kompaniet, founded in 1902. This prompted the creation of the Nordiska Kompaniet Textilkammare (NK Textile Design Studio), which she ran from 1937 until 1971. Her earliest printed NK patterns, with simple honeycomb and fish-scale patterns, were lino block-printed in a workshop in Stockholm in 1936, and some were

shown at the Paris Exhibition in 1937. Sampe's style, initially rather crude, quickly became more refined, and in 1937 she created the stylish *Axen*, shown at the New York World's Fair in 1939 (fig. 3.41).

From around 1937 screen-printing was introduced, initially undertaken by Borås Wäfveri and, from the mid-1940s, by Ljungbergs Textiltryck at Floda, which demonstrated great skill in translating designs into screens. Although the war hampered progress, one positive outcome was the temporary displacement to Sweden of the Danish architect Arne Jacobsen. Bucking the trend towards abstraction, minimalism, and rationalism, he created an inspirational collection of floral patterns for NK in 1944 (fig. 3.43). At once painterly and minutely detailed, Jacobsen's panoramic depictions of vegetation in forest glades and meadows were deeply romantic. Imbued with a visionary intensity, his patterns symbolized the poignancy of a world in which beauty was under threat.

Building on the success of this initiative, Sampe commissioned a group of patterns from the talented ceramics designer Stig Lindberg in 1947. Lindberg, an instinctive and spontaneous pattern designer, developed a vocabulary that was quintessentially Swedish, and he worked in an idiosyncratic, playful, decorative style. Many of his designs had a strongly organic quality, including *Abstraktion*, which was composed of rows of pods with linear motifs suggestive of leaf veins. Good-natured and witty, Lindberg delighted in storytelling, and several of his designs, such as *Lustgården*, *Melodi*, and *Poème d'Amour*, suggested folk stories or fairy tales (fig. 3.42). Other designs explore variations on a theme, as in *Pottery*, featuring his own ceramics, and *Jardinjär*, depicting casseroles containing a medley of plants, vegetables, and birds.

Among other NK designers during this formative early post-war period were Lena Fjällbäck, Börge Glahn, Tyra Lundgren, Sven Markelius, Ulla Schumacher-Percy, Sven Erik Skawonius, and the Danish designer Helga Foght. As with Lindberg and Jacobsen, many of the designers chosen by Astrid Sampe were associated with other media. For example, Sven Markelius was an architect and Ulla Schumacher-Percy was a rug designer, while Sven Erik Skawonius and Tyra Lundgren specialized in ceramics and glass.

Two other designers commissioned by Sampe during the 1940s were Lisbet Jobs-Söderlund, a potter specializing in bowls painted with informal groups of wild flowers, and her sister, Gocken Jobs. Their patterns, composed of naturalistic clumps of plants, were shown at NK in 1945 in the exhibition *When Beauty Comes to Town*. In 1946 the sisters established their own firm, Jobs Handtryck, at Leksand in Dalarna, where they perfected their distinctive approach to floral textiles, often printed in a bright polychrome palette on a black ground (fig. 3.44). Erik Zahle later referred rather dismissively to the "flower orgies" of the 1940s, but, for many textile designers, it was through immersing themselves in their native flora that they discovered the essence of Swedish design.[27]

Opposite top Fig. 3.38
Blåklocka *printed cotton furnishing fabric, designed by Märtha Gahn, produced by Borås Wäfveri, 1929.* Refreshing in their purity and simplicity, Märtha Gahn's naïve florals paved the way for a new school of Swedish pattern design.

Opposite centre Fig. 3.39
Öland *screen-printed cotton furnishing fabric, designed by Elsa Gullberg, produced by Elsa Gullberg AB, 1944.* Meadow-like, floral sprig patterns of this kind were popular in Sweden during the war. Elsa Gullberg, who ran her own company, sought to nurture a distinctively Swedish aesthetic.

Opposite bottom Fig. 3.40
Afrika *screen-printed linen furnishing fabric, designed by Vicke Lindstrand, produced by Elsa Gullberg AB, 1936.* Although best known as a glass designer, Vicke Lindstrand originally trained in graphics, and practised as an illustrator and cartoonist in the 1920s.

Above left Fig. 3.41
Axen *screen-printed rayon Vistra furnishing fabric, designed by Astrid Sampe, printed by Borås Wäfveri for Nordiska Kompaniet, 1937.* This pattern, based on an ear of wheat, was shown at the New York World's Fair in 1939.

Left Fig. 3.42
Lustgården *screen-printed linen furnishing fabric, designed by Stig Lindberg, printed by Ljungbergs Textiltryck for Nordiska Kompaniet, 1947.* Seeking escape in whimsy and nostalgia, Gustavsberg ceramics designer Stig Lindberg created an inspired group of witty modern folk art patterns.

Above Fig. 3.43
Kejsarkrona *screen-printed cotton furnishing fabric, designed by Arne Jacobsen, originally printed by Ljungbergs Textiltryck for Nordiska Kompaniet, 1944, reprinted 1995.* Exiled in Sweden during the war, the Danish architect Arne Jacobsen designed many intense, visionary floral patterns.

Sweden: Svenskt Tenn

Another catalyst for these "flower orgies" was the Austrian designer Josef Frank, who, after settling in Sweden in 1933, established an extremely productive partnership with Estrid Ericson at Svenskt Tenn. Picking up where he had left off in Vienna in the late 1920s, Frank created a large body of new designs, such as *Under Ekvatorn* (1941), featuring exotic flora in extraordinarily vibrant colours against a black background (fig. 3.46), as well as reviving some of his earlier patterns for Haus & Garten. Initially his patterns were block-printed, but later screen-printing was used. Frank's work brought about cross-fertilization between Austria, the established design superpower of the first quarter-century, and Sweden, the emergent design superpower of the next three decades.

One of the most interesting aspects of his career was his response to the environment in which he was living. Exploiting the *mille fleurs* formula he had developed in Austria, but responding to the stimulus of Scandinavian flora, his new patterns included *Svenska Vårblommor* (c.1935), depicting a meadow of Swedish spring flowers. While exiled in New York in 1942–6, Frank created *Manhattan*, in the form of an aerial plan. It was while here that the more surreal and fantastical qualities of his style were consolidated, prompted by his response to North America's flora and fauna. Using images derived from field manuals, he created patterns such as *California*, depicting flowers from the West Coast. *US Tree*, one of several Tree of Life patterns, featured a single continuous trunk with many branches, to which different specimen leaves were attached. *Vegetable Tree* (1943–5) (fig. 3.45) was even more remarkable, with its multitude of strange flowers, fruits, and vegetables. Plucked from his familiar surroundings, Frank let his imagination roam free, abandoning literal depiction and scientifically plausible groupings in favour of a more liberated and fanciful approach to design, as in *Brazil* (1943–5), juxtaposing a riotous array of fruits and flowers.

These late designs, although apparently traditional, were in fact very avant-garde. In the magazine *Svenska Hem* in 1943, Tyra Lundgren defined Frank's idiom as "The Modern Florid Style," and wrote of his designs: "Not only are they beautiful in colour and print but they also possess excellent quality as patterns *per se*. They have been composed with a rare knowledge of how patterns should be drawn in order to give an impression of imaginative wealth and a never-ending, captivating interplay of lines, while at the same time not unveiling the mechanics of the repetition so that they become neither banal nor too transparent."[28] On returning to Sweden, Frank continued to design patterns for Svenskt Tenn until 1950, and around 1947 created a group of wallpapers for Norrköpings.

Denmark: Marie Gudme Leth and Helga Foght

Just as Elsa Gullberg, Astrid Sampe, and Josef Frank brought Swedish printed fabrics to life during the 1930s, so Danish textiles were transformed by the inspirational contribution of Marie Gudme Leth. Because Denmark had no tradition in printed

Top Fig. 3.44
Ros och lilja screen-printed half linen furnishing fabric, designed by Gocken Jobs, produced by Jobs Handtryck, 1946, reprinted 1970s. Gocken Jobs, one of many Swedish designers influenced by Josef Frank, adopted the ploy of printing on a black background instead of customary white.

Above Fig. 3.45
Design for **Vegetable Tree***, Josef Frank, 1943–5.* This is one of a series of fantasy Tree of Life designs created by Josef Frank while in exile in New York. It was later produced as a screen-printed furnishing fabric by Svenskt Tenn following Frank's return to Sweden after the war.

textiles, Leth went to study at the Kunstgewerbeschule in Frankfurt in 1930. After returning to Denmark in 1931, she began to teach at the newly founded Kunsthåndværkskolen (School of Arts, Crafts, and Design) in Copenhagen and established a workshop producing block-printed fabrics. Finding this process too restrictive, however, she went back to Germany in 1934 to learn about screen-printing, and in 1935 set up Dansk Kattuntrykkeri (Danish Calico Printing Works). Contrary to commercial conventions, her patterns were often limited to two shades of the same colour, usually printed on unbleached or semi-bleached cotton or linen, or on rayon Vistra. Interestingly, though, Leth's new screen-printed patterns still resembled block-prints, and she adhered to her original design formulae, characterized by isolated silhouetted motifs. "A printed fabric should not be a painting," she asserted. "It should be a pleasant repetition of motives, a good division of the surface."[29]

"Brightness, homeliness, and humour characterize her prints, whether chameleons, frogs, cobras, or figures from Hans Andersen occupy the scene," observed Arne Karlsen and Anker Tiedemann.[30] Leth had spent three years in Java during the 1920s, and her memories of Indonesia and knowledge of batiks informed her unusual vocabulary and stylistic interpretation. The flora and fauna featured in designs such as *Orkidé* (1933), *Mexico* (1935), and *Kamæleon* (1937) certainly had an exotic Eastern flavour (fig. 3.47). The beguiling simplicity, clarity, and immediacy of her designs, and the importance of the pictorial element, invite comparison with Danish folk art. Her imagery was complex and subtle, however, as in *Landsby* (1936), which juxtaposed pastoral motifs of trees, cows, cottages, and windmills with industrial images of factories.

After leaving Dansk Kattuntrykkeri in 1940, Leth set up her own workshop. During the war she adopted a brighter palette to cheer people up. In the 1950s she abandoned pictorials and florals in favour of simplified abstract designs. These mainly took the form of dynamic, all-over patterns with small, closely repeated motifs in intense stimulating colours, such as *Medallion* (1955). They were produced until her workshop closed in 1963, and afterwards manufactured by C. Olesen until as late as the 1970s as part of the Cotil range, remaining enduringly popular.

Marie Gudme Leth's teaching inspired a generation of printed-textile designers in Denmark. One of her early pupils was Helga Foght, who took on the running of a screen-printing workshop, L.F. Foght, founded in 1932. Her early patterns included *Birch Trees* (1938), featuring two trees with drooping branches running in parallel along the full length of the fabric. During the war Foght abandoned large patterns in favour of more economical designs characterized by small, regular floral motifs arranged in neat rows, such as *Valmue* (1944). Some of these patterns were produced by NK in Sweden. After the war, Helga Foght's style changed again, and she adopted the bright colours and free-form, organic abstraction of "Contemporary" design.

Top Fig. 3.46
Under Ekvatorn *screen-printed linen furnishing fabric, designed by Josef Frank, 1941, printed by Ljungberg's Textiltryck for Svenskt Tenn, 1980s.* Josef Frank's extraordinary sense of colour distinguishes him from his contemporaries. This exotic *mille fleurs* pattern, "Under the Equator," provides an excuse for heightened effects.

Above Fig. 3.47
Kamaeleon *screen-printed linen, designed by Marie Gudme Leth, produced by Dansk Kattuntrykkeri, 1937.* Josef Frank's design (top) exploits a dazzling array of colours and the motifs are densely packed, whereas this pattern by Marie Gudme Leth is limited to two shades of green with generous spacing around each vignette.

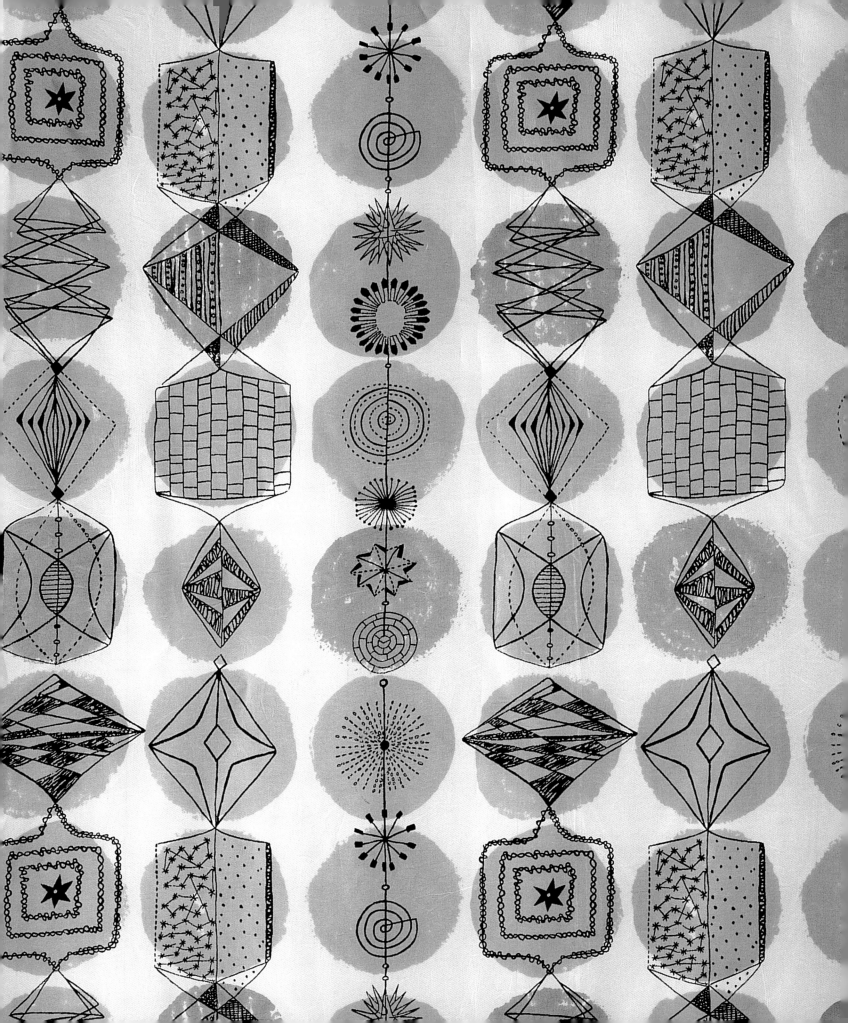

"Contemporary"

Attempts to downplay or even eliminate pattern within the home were confounded by the prolonged drabness of the war years. Afterwards, simply by way of reaction, there was renewed public appetite for colour and pattern. Textile and wallpaper design flourished for the following two decades. In the United States the fashion for coordinated fabrics and wallpapers took hold, prompting the emergence of dual-purpose firms. Post-war decorating fostered the increased use of wallpapers, particularly the fashion for contrasting designs – generally one loud, one quiet – on adjacent walls.

After six years of enforced inactivity, designers responded ebulliently to the freedom of the post-war era, creating dynamic and stimulating patterns inspired by art, architecture, and science (fig. 4.1). Springing up spontaneously in Europe and the United States, "Contemporary" textiles and wallpapers transformed modern interiors, and there was a surge of creativity on an international level. Forward-looking and optimistic, designers experimented fearlessly with new idioms, converting the hitherto conservative public to the progressive "Contemporary" style. Abstraction became the prevailing currency for both painters and pattern designers. Many artists designed textiles and wallpapers – some even set up their own companies – and designers were enthused by the works of Joan Miró, Paul Klee, Alexander Calder, and Jackson Pollock. After its initial youthful exuberance, "Contemporary" design became calmer and more consciously architectural in the late 1950s. Ambitious large-scale patterns, facilitated by screen-printing, were widely adopted for new buildings, while the mass market was enlivened by the trickle-down effect of the "Contemporary" style.

The war caused such a long break in production, and so many new designers emerged in the interim, that pattern design restarted completely afresh. "Where the pre-war moderns extolled boldness, simplicity, economy and logic, the critics today look for lightness, elegance and charm," observed Paul Reilly.[1] In 1953 James De Holden Stone of the Royal College of Art, London, placed textiles in three categories – "mobiles, doodles and spasms": "Recently designers took inspiration from an American art-form, the mobile, a sort of space-time genealogical tree which balances a family of balls, bars and melon-slices on a series of delicately interdependent

Opposite Fig. 4.1
Miscellany screen-printed acetate rayon taffeta furnishing fabric, designed by Lucienne Day, produced by British Celanese, 1952. The wiry structure of this composition, with its suggestion of sculpture, seed heads, and scientific models, typifies the new mood of visual inventiveness after the Second World War. Sharp colour contrasts, such as bright yellow and pale grey, were popular during the early 1950s.

Right Fig. 4.2
Fall screen-printed cotton crepe furnishing fabric, designed by Lucienne Day, produced by Edinburgh Weavers, 1952. After the war pattern designers explored a new vocabulary of skeletal plant forms, drawn in a delicate, spidery graphic style. Lucienne Day was a pioneer of this idiom.

arms. Today there is a growing obsession with the unrehearsed, the totally spontaneous. The expedient of blindfold drawing is producing marks, stains, smudges and other assaults on the paper. The designer with this indubitably free hand claims it is as much a part of nature as the glide of a snake or the track of wet pramwheels, and that being in this sense style-free it can never date."[2]

James De Holden Stone recognized that, although abstraction was all-pervasive, plants nevertheless still formed a key element in the post-war designer's vocabulary, newly reinterpreted in a sculptural, skeletal guise. "Artists still in revolt against the old-time floral have turned to frost-gripped trees, dry leaves, twigs, grasses, ferns, creepers. Emphasis will be less on flowers than on the total growth: stalks, thorns, leaves and tendrils will be given disproportionate attention, mostly in line, with colour an afterthought" (fig. 4.2).[3] Over the next seven years pattern design developed at a prodigious rate, becoming bolder and more textural as the decade progressed. At the end of the 1950s modern architecture, painting, and pattern design were more closely allied than at any time since the turn of the century.

Britain: Festival Pattern Group

By 1951 – the year of the Festival of Britain – the days of "make do and mend" were numbered, and the newly established Council of Industrial Design (CoID) set about stimulating activity in the field of pattern design. Scouting around for a new source of imagery appropriate to the atomic age, it hit upon the idea of X-ray crystallography, an idea first suggested by Dr Helen Megaw, a crystallographer from Girton College, Cambridge: "These crystal

structure diagrams had the discipline of exact repetitive symmetry," noted Mark Hartland Thomas, the CoID's chief industrial officer, "they were essentially modern because the technique that constructed them was quite recent, and yet, like all successful decoration of the past, they derived from nature, although it was nature at a submicroscopic scale not previously revealed."[4]

In 1949 the CoID invited a group of manufacturers to produce furnishings and accessories decorated with crystal structures for the Festival of Britain. Textiles were the largest component of the Festival Pattern Group, including printed and woven dress and furnishing fabrics, carpets, and lace, but the scheme also encompassed wallpapers, vinyls, plastic laminate, figured sheet glass, pierced sheet metal, ceramic tiles, and linoleum. The resulting products were illustrated in *The Souvenir Book of Crystal Designs*, and samples were displayed at the *South Bank Exhibition* and the *Exhibition of Science*, both in London.

Rather than bringing in "star" designers from outside the industry, the Festival Pattern Group provided opportunities for experimentation by in-house staff. At Warner, Marianne Straub created the remarkable *Surrey* fabric, an enlarged free-form organic pattern based on afwillite, woven from a mixture of wool, cotton, and rayon. S.M. Slade's smaller afwillite pattern, printed on rayon by British Celanese, was equally arresting (fig. 4.3). The screen-printed wallpapers designed by Robert Sevant and William Odell for John Line, based on insulin, afwillite, and boric acid, were also highly effective (fig. 4.4). H. Webster's machine-embroidered cotton-lace patterns for A.C. Gill provided a good example of the structure of the medium suiting the composition. Also memorable were the seven crisply detailed woven-silk fabrics created by Bernard Rowland for Vanners & Fennell. But although the public found the project intriguing from a scientific point of view, the concept was too literal to lead to a new school of design based on crystal structures. Instead, British pattern developed its own momentum during the 1950s, driven forward by the talents of free-thinking designers such as Lucienne Day and Jacqueline Groag.[5]

Britain: Ascher and Horrockses

During the 1940s there were fewer restrictions on the production of dress fabrics than of furnishing fabrics, and so innovation in pattern design was initially channelled into this area. The first injection of vitality came from Ascher (London) Ltd, founded by two Czech émigrés, Zika Ascher and Lida Ascher, in 1942. Fabrics were printed in their own workshop, mainly by screen-printing, but occasionally by block-printing, initially on rayon but later on silk and cotton. Most of the early patterns were by Lida Ascher and consisted of loosely painted spots, stripes, and checks, and simple rhythmic calligraphic sketches of flowers and plants. Other designers included Eric Stapler, who created miniaturized geometrics, and Gerald Wilde, who designed scribbly abstract patterns. The key to the appeal of Ascher's prints lay in the looseness and spontaneity of the markings and the freshness of the carefully chosen colours.

In 1946 Ascher embarked on an ambitious scheme to commission scarf designs, or "artist squares," from a large group of leading British and European painters and sculptors, including Alexander Calder, Jean Cocteau, Nicolas de Staël, Barbara Hepworth, Henri Matisse, Henry Moore, Ben Nicholson, John Piper, and Graham Sutherland. Matisse and Moore were also invited to design prints for silk and rayon dress fabrics, along with Felix Atlan, Cecil Beaton, Christian Bérard, Lucian Freud, Philippe Julian, Feliks Topolski, and Paule Vézelay. "The most successful designers are those who effortlessly express their own personality in their designs," said Zika Ascher.[6] Judged on this basis, Henry Moore's patterns, which featured miniaturized linear images from his sketchbooks, were the most effective, capturing all the nervous vigour and dynamism of his drawings (fig. 4.5). Ascher's dress fabrics were enormously popular, both with top French, British, and Italian couturiers, and the wider public, to whom they were made available through a subsidiary called Bourec, founded in 1946, which supplied budget dress firms such as Sambo. Although Ascher subsequently extended its portfolio to include plain silks and speciality woven fabrics, prints continued to form a key part of the firm's range, and it was later celebrated for its bold, painterly florals.

The reputation of Horrockses Fashions – founded in 1946 as a subsidiary of a large Preston-based textile manufacturer, Horrockses, Crewdson & Company – was also centred on the quality of its printed patterns. Horrockses specialized in high-quality printed

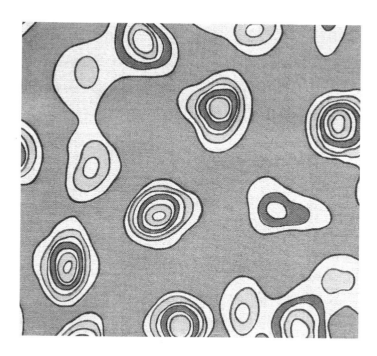

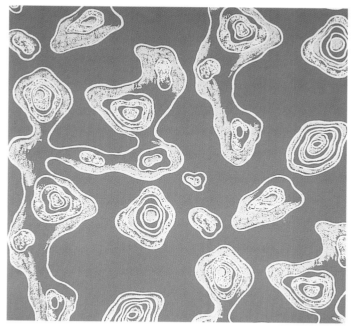

Top Fig. 4.3
Afwillite screen-printed rayon dress fabric, designed by S.M. Slade, produced by British Celanese, 1951. After the war a leading scientist suggested that X-ray crystallography diagrams might be used as the basis for textile and wallpaper patterns, an idea explored by the Festival Pattern Group.

Above Fig. 4.4
Afwillite screen-printed wallpaper, designed by William Odell, produced by John Line, 1951. Although they suggest advanced free-form organic abstraction, these two patterns were actually based on diagrams of the crystal structure of afwillite, a hydrated calcium silicate used in cement.

Right Fig. 4.5
Screen-printed rayon dress fabric, designed by Henry Moore, produced by Ascher, c.1945. Henry Moore was one of several leading artists who responded to Ascher's invitation to create patterns for scarves and dress fabrics after the war. This design is composed from images in his sketchbooks.

cotton dresses for day, evening, and leisure wear, and all its fabrics were custom-designed solely for the company's own use. Alastair Morton of Edinburgh Weavers played a key role in establishing the Horrockses style during the late 1940s, setting the trend for horizontally banded patterns, including linear abstracts and simple modern florals. Pat Albeck, who was recruited straight from the Royal College of Art and worked for Horrockses from 1953 to 1958, also had a decisive impact. From the late 1940s to the mid-1950s the firm produced several patterns created by artists, including William Gear, Eduardo Paolozzi, and Graham Sutherland.

Britain: Heal Fabrics and Lucienne Day

The major pattern-design success story of the 1950s in Britain was Heal Fabrics, which began life as Heal's Wholesale and Export, created in 1941 as a wartime trading subsidiary of the London furniture and furnishings store Heal & Son. After the war textiles became its main focus, and the name Heal Fabrics was adopted in 1958. A converter rather than a manufacturer, Heal Fabrics purchased patterns from freelance designers and used commission printers such as Bernard Wardle and Stead McAlpin to produce them. Initially they were roller-printed or hand screen-printed, with mechanized flatbed screen-printing adopted by 1959. Selling through Heal & Son and other outlets, Heal Fabrics became an influential force in home furnishings under the dynamic Tom Worthington, the firm's managing director from 1948 to 1971.

Heal's reputation for innovation was established during the late 1940s through collaborations with designers such as Helen Close,

Jane Edgar, Dorothy Lupton, Michael O'Connell, Helen Sampson, and Margaret Simeon. But it was the Festival of Britain in 1951 that confirmed Heal's growing reputation, acting as a showcase for Lucienne Day's revolutionary pattern *Calyx* (fig. 4.6), specially created at the designer's initiative for a room setting in the Homes and Gardens Pavilion designed by her husband, Robin Day. *Calyx* combined radical new abstract organic imagery with an arresting palette of acid and earthy tones. Lucienne Day, who had trained at the Royal College of Art from 1937 to 1940, went on to become the most successful and sought-after British pattern designer of the 1950s, creating around six designs per year for Heal's, and collaborating with a host of other British and European firms. Her clients included textile firms such as British Celanese, Cavendish Textiles, Edinburgh Weavers, Liberty and Mölnlycke; and wallpaper companies such as Cole & Son, John Line, Rasch and the Wall Paper Manufacturers Ltd (WPM). She also designed carpets for Tomkinson, I.&C. Steele and Wilton Royal, tea towels and table linen for Thomas Somerset, and ceramics for Rosenthal.

Inspired by the cartoons of Saul Steinberg, the paintings of Miró and Klee, Alexander Calder's mobiles, and the sculptures of Naum Gabo, Lucienne Day's patterns for Heal's were consistently imaginative and inventive. She was equally adept at creating stimulating abstracts such as *Ticker Tape*, witty figurative patterns such as *Spectators* (fig. 4.7), and wiry plant designs such as *Dandelion Clocks* (all 1953). Playful imagery, energetic rhythms, and adventurous use of colour were the key elements of her design vocabulary, and her patterns reflected a high level of

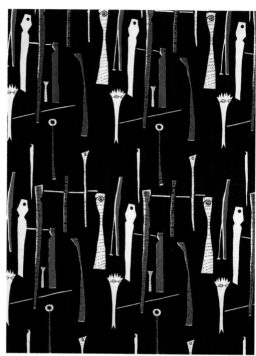

Far left Fig. 4.6
Calyx screen-printed linen furnishing fabric, designed by Lucienne Day, produced by Heal Fabrics, 1951. This innovative fabric, by Britain's leading post-war textile designer, triggered off a wave of "Contemporary" abstract organic patterns after it was showcased at the Festival of Britain in 1951.

Left Fig. 4.7
Spectators screen-printed cotton furnishing fabric, designed by Lucienne Day, produced by Heal Fabrics, 1953. The attenuated figures in this witty pattern recall the sculptures of Alberto Giacometti. The bespectacled individual with spiky hair embodies the playful, upbeat tone of the design.

artistic awareness in their compositions, colours, and repeats. Initially designed on a domestic scale, Day's patterns became bolder and more architectural over the course of the 1950s. Skeletal leaves and grasses were replaced by silhouetted trees, and narrow strips of colour expanded into half-width columns, as in *Sequoia* (1959) (fig. 4.8). Controlled textural effects formed the basis for second-generation "Contemporary" patterns such as *Ducatoon* (1959), demonstrating her belief that "Imaginative but modest patterns, perhaps purely textural in character, can take their place as an architectural component in the visual organisation of the interior."[7]

While Lucienne Day's designs dominated Heal's collections, Tom Worthington also commissioned an astonishingly wide range of other patterns. Particularly effective were those of Michael O'Connell, whose measured linear designs, such as *Segments* (1955) and *Modulus* (1958), were printed in sober tones. The artist Paule Vézelay also created calm, calculated patterns, characterized by flat, coloured motifs and tapering threads (fig. 4.9). Keenly aware of trends in contemporary art and their potential to cross-fertilize with textile design, Worthington also selected several Jackson Pollock-inspired abstract expressionist designs, including the painterly, bark-textured *Oak* by Dorothy Carr (fig. 4.10) and *Vineyard* by Harold Cohen (both 1958), the latter with dramatic splashed-paint effects. Also among Heal's designers during the 1950s were Paul Augener, Barbara Brown, Sylvia Chalmers, Gordon Dent, Hilda Durkin, T.A. Fennemore, Ellen Fricke, Dorothy Hall, Paul Gell, Rex Hayes, Denis Higbee, Hilaire Hiler, Fay Hillier,

Arthur Hull, Walter Kramer, Joan Ledingham, Françoise Lelong, June Lyon, Annette McClintock, Edwin Meayers, Mary Moran, Mary Morgan, Roger Nicholson, Dorothy Page, David Parsons, Sheila Pickersgill, Michael Poinsenet, Edward Pond, Eryl Price, Sylvia Priestley, Betty Middleton Sandford, Rana Stryck, Eve Swinstead-Smith, James Wade, Mary Warren, and Mary White.[8]

Britain: David Whitehead

After Heal's, Britain's most dynamic printed-textile company during the 1950s was David Whitehead, of Rawtenstall, Lancashire. Created in 1927 as a subsidiary of the Whitehead Group – founded in 1815 by three brothers, David, Peter, and Thomas Whitehead – it was given the task of designing and selling the Group's furnishing fabrics. In 1948 the architect Dr John Murray was appointed director, and he established the company's reputation at the forefront of "Contemporary" design. Murray's ambition was to democratize the avant-garde by making daring modern designs available on the mass market. Outlining his philosophy in an article entitled "The cheap need not be cheap-and-nasty," he wrote: "Much of the good design which is produced is confined to the higher price ranges, catering for the statistically insignificant wealthy class. My own firm, on the other hand, caters primarily for those vast sections of humanity in which the emphasis is on cheapness and serviceability."[9]

Launched in 1951, David Whitehead's Contemporary Prints consisted of vibrant, small-scale patterns roller-printed on low-cost spun rayon. The designers included two leading European émigrés,

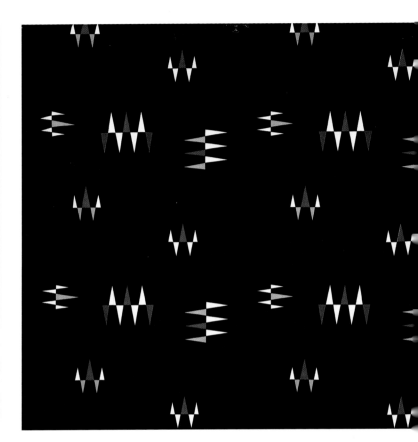

Above Fig. 4.8
Sequoia *screen-printed cotton crepe furnishing fabric, designed by Lucienne Day, produced by Heal Fabrics, 1959.* Towards the end of the 1950s textile designers became more architecturally aware and began to create larger-scale patterns suitable for floor-to-ceiling picture windows. The strongly vertical pattern on this fabric – shown here in two colourways, brown/white and yellow/white – is divided into two separate columns.

Above right Fig. 4.9
Pennons *screen-printed cotton furnishing fabric, designed by Paule Vézelay, produced by Heal Fabrics, 1958.* Paule Vézelay created a series of simple but striking abstract patterns for Heal Fabrics composed of flat shapes floating against a coloured ground, often dark.

Right Fig. 4.10
Oak *screen-printed cotton crepe furnishing fabric, designed by Dorothy Carr, produced by Heal Fabrics, 1958.* This abstract expressionist design shows the influence of Jackson Pollock, whose action paintings were admired by young British textile designers.

Marian Mahler and Jacqueline Groag, and two young British designers, Terence Conran and Roger Nicholson. Conran was still a student at the Central School when he sold his first design to David Whitehead in 1949. His doodle-like, irregular-grid design *Chequers* (1951) was displayed at the Festival of Britain and he continued to supply patterns to the company for several years, many in the wiry, sculptural "Contemporary" idiom. During the 1950s he also designed for fabrics for Gerald Holtom and Liberty, ceramics for Midwinter, and wallpapers for the WPM, as well as setting up Conran Fabrics, to which both he and his wife, Shirley Conran, contributed patterns. "Pattern fulfils two fundamental human needs in that it can be both stimulating and tranquilising," Terence Conran wrote in his book *Printed Textile Design* (1957).[10]

Austrian-born Marian Mahler, who had arrived in Britain in 1937 as Marianne Mahler, had already supplied designs to several leading firms before the war, some of which presaged the "Contemporary" idiom. During the early 1950s she created a series of lively, brightly coloured patterns for David Whitehead, some with cupped, crescent, boomerang, and tear-shaped motifs, others featuring window-like recesses framing tiny images of heads, birds, fish, and pots (fig. 4.11). Like Mahler, Czech-born Jacqueline Groag had trained at the Kunstgewerbeschule in Vienna during the 1920s, and some of her early designs were produced by the Wiener Werkstätte. An extremely inventive designer with a finely tuned colour sense, she was adept at constructing multiple layers of pattern (fig. 4.12). Groag's patterns for David Whitehead displayed a dynamic counterpoint between line and mass, with distant echoes of Paul Klee. "Few designers can move easily from abstract design to the representational, and produce equally good work in both disciplines," commented Misha Black in 1955.[11] In addition to her work for David Whitehead, Groag also designed printed textiles for Grafton, Haworth Fabrics, Gerald Holtom, John Lewis, Liberty, and Warner, plastic laminates for Warerite, carpets for Bond Worth, and wallpapers for the WPM.

Although John Murray left David Whitehead in 1952, he passed the reins into the capable hands of architect and painter Tom Mellor, design consultant from 1953 to 1960. Mellor himself contributed several patterns featuring typographical and architectural motifs, but his main achievement was to cultivate relationships with artists. In 1953 *The Ambassador* – an enlightened textile trade magazine run by Hans and Elsbeth Juda – organized the exhibition *Paintings into Textiles* at the Institute of Contemporary Art in London. Two firms subsequently produced patterns based on the paintings in the exhibition, Horrockses and David Whitehead. Whitehead's patterns varied in style depending on the medium of the original artwork, which ranged from Henry Moore's wax drawings with watercolour washes to Donald Hamilton Fraser's bold, expressionistic abstract oil paintings. Cawthra Mulock created ghostly figurative vignettes (fig. 4.13), Paule Vézelay produced subtle organic abstracts, J.D.H. Catleugh painted severe

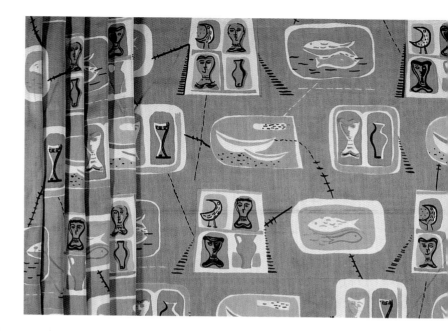

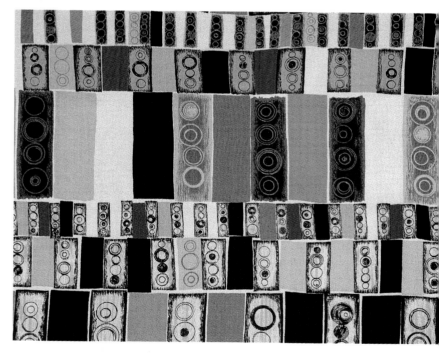

Top Fig. 4.11
Roller-printed cotton furnishing fabric, designed by Marian Mahler, produced by David Whitehead, 1952. After the war David Whitehead focused on well-designed, low-cost fabrics for the mass market. This light-hearted and accessible pattern was typical of the firm's "Contemporary" designs.

Above Fig. 4.12
Roller-printed rayon furnishing fabric, designed by Jacqueline Groag, produced by David Whitehead, 1953. Jacqueline Groag's Wiener Werkstätte roots are clearly evident in the shapes and composition of this lively, abstract pattern with its imaginative and stimulating colourway.

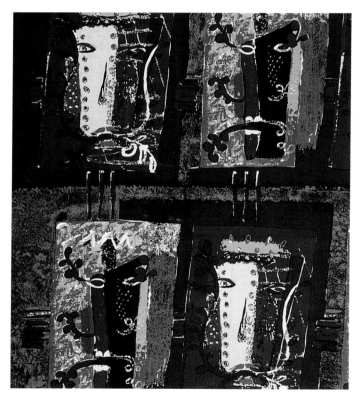

Top Fig. 4.13
Screen-printed cotton and rayon satin furnishing fabric, designed by Cawthra Mulock, produced by David Whitehead, c. 1953–4. Cawthra Mulock (top) and John Piper (bottom) both participated in an exhibition called *Paintings into Textiles* held at the Institute of Contemporary Art, in London, in 1953.

Above Fig. 4.14
Foliate Heads screen-printed cotton furnishing fabric, designed by John Piper, produced by David Whitehead, 1955. This pattern, depicting the mythical pagan figure the Green Man, was one of a series of John Piper designs produced by David Whitehead during the mid-1950s.

Top Fig. 4.15
Roller-printed cotton furnishing fabric, designed by Eduardo Paolozzi, produced by David Whitehead, 1952. Although best known as a sculptor, Eduardo Paolozzi taught textile design at the Central School during the 1950s. This random collage pattern is based on one of his screen-prints.

Above Fig. 4.16
Macrahanish screen-printed cotton furnishing fabric, designed by Robert Stewart, produced by Liberty, 1954. Robert Stewart contributed a series of lively "Contemporary" patterns to the Young Liberty collection. This zany design, with its wiry aesthetic, typifies the ebullience of the period.

geometrics, and William Scott's rhythmic composition suggested musical notation. John Piper's contributions included *Foliate Heads*, based on his stained-glass window design of the folkloric figure the Green Man (fig. 4.14).

Mellor also commissioned other artists independently, including Sandra Blow, Mitzi Cunliffe, Peter Kinley, Eduardo Paolozzi, and Louis Le Brocquy. Paolozzi, who taught textile design at the Central School, cited his influences as "primitive art, micro-zoology, the natural patterns formed by organic objects, and Picasso in all his periods."[12] His collage patterns, which had a refreshingly raw quality, were composed from scattered images of fossils, found objects, and sculptural components (fig. 4.15). Louis Le Brocquy, who taught textile design at the Royal College of Art, created a group of patterns featuring abstracted images of tiles, cobbles, and sickles. Inspired by a trip to Spain in 1956, these were marketed as the Iberia range. "Textile design has been feeding off its own body for too long," observed *The Ambassador*, which sponsored and documented his study visit. "Abstract design too often is merely derived from abstract design. The contrived texture and the playroom doodle are wearing a little thin."[13] Hand screen-printing was used for these more textural painterly patterns, although from 1957 costs were significantly reduced through the introduction of mechanized flatbed screen-printing.

The design studio of David Whitehead, which was responsible for converting these original artworks into patterns, also produced its own designs. Members of the studio during the 1950s included Anne Ashworth, Jack Bateman, Fred Peace, Stephen Richardson, and Derek Woodall. Other designers whose work was produced during this period included John Barker, Afro Basaldella, Eileen Bell, Gerald Downes, J. Feldman, Barbara Pile, Humphrey Spender, Robert Tierney, Mary White, and two Swedish designers, Lisa Grönwall and Maj Nilsson.

Britain: Liberty

Another firm infected with the fervour for "Contemporary" during the early post-war period was Liberty, which produced a range of furnishing fabrics from 1949 called Young Liberty. Lucienne Day, Terence Conran, and Jacqueline Groag all contributed patterns, but Liberty's most prolific designer during the early 1950s was Robert Stewart. A painter and textile designer, he was head of printed textiles at Glasgow School of Art from 1949 to 1978. Light-hearted figurative motifs were his speciality at Liberty, typified by *Masks* and *Macrahanish* (fig. 4.16) (both 1954). He also created engaging whimsical abstracts, such as *Raimoult* and *Applecross* (both 1954), featuring classic "Contemporary" devices such as stringing (fine lines linking motifs) and quartic and cupped shapes.

Colleen Farr also played a key role at Liberty during the 1950s, designing both dress and furnishing fabrics. Initially she worked freelance, but around 1952–3 she was invited to set up a design

studio at Liberty, a significant departure for the company, which had previously relied exclusively on bought-in textile designs. Farr remained head of the studio until 1962, winning much acclaim both for her own designs – such as *Atalanta*, which won a Cotton Board/House & Garden Award in 1961 – and for her buying policy. Among other designers whose work was produced by Liberty during the 1950s and early 1960s were Pat Albeck, Martin Bradley, Helen Dalby, Hilda Durkin, Gwenfred Jarvis, Janet Lacey, Anthony Levett-Prinsep, Annette McClintock, Althea McNish, Betty Middleton Sandford, H. Wardroper, and Mary White.

Britain: Edinburgh Weavers

During the war Edinburgh Weavers' design director, Alastair Morton, had taken time off to study hand weaving with Ethel Mairet at the Gospels workshop in Ditchling. After this he designed printed dress fabrics for Horrockses until activity picked up in the furnishing trade. Speaking of Edinburgh Weavers in 1946, he described it as "an experimental section where new ideas are developed."[14] As well as producing customized textiles for specific interiors, Edinburgh Weavers also marketed an "off-the-peg" range, initially designed mainly by Morton. An enthusiastic patron of modern design, he did all he could to support the profession, producing printed and woven textiles by, among others, Helen Dalby, Lucienne Day, Friedlinde di Colbertaldo Dinzl, Robert Dodd, Hilda Durkin, John Farleigh, David Gentleman, Fay Hillier (fig. 4.17), Marian Mahler, Peter McCulloch, Hugh McKinnon, Mary Oliver, Sylvia Priestley, Olive Sullivan, Robert Tierney, and Mary White.

Being a painter as well as a designer, Morton had a natural inclination to collaborate with artists as well as designers, and from the mid-1950s he focused much of his attention on an exclusive range of textiles designed by painters and sculptors. An early alliance with William Gear resulted in the bold printed abstract *Tropic* (1954). But forceful brushstrokes and robust compositions were more important to him than abstraction *per se*, and his main concerns were texture, contrast, and scale. The mural painter Hans Tisdall (formerly Aufseeser), a regular contributor since the 1930s, created dramatic designs with vigorous calligraphic brushstrokes, such as *Pheasant Moon* (1961). Another prominent artist-designer, Cliff Holden, was active in Britain as well as in Sweden, where he belonged to the Marstrand Designers group. Drawing on a wide range of idioms, from action painting to Oriental calligraphy, his designs included the printed *Aurora* and the woven *Manchu* (both 1959). The artist-photographer Humphrey Spender pursued an active career as a textile and wallpaper designer while teaching at the Royal College of Art from 1953 to 1975. He created textural woven abstracts such as *Inglewood* (1956) and a printed design inspired by stained-glass windows called *Minster* (1958).

Morton relished the challenge of converting an original artwork into a woven or printed image. According to his brother, Jocelyn Morton, he would spend weeks or months studying a painting

Above Fig. 4.17
Mithras screen-printed cotton furnishing
*fabric, designed by Fay Hillier, produced
by Edinburgh Weavers, 1960.* Edinburgh
Weavers pursued an ambitious agenda
in its approach to textile design,
commissioning bold, large-scale
printed and woven patterns from
leading artists and designers.

"before he was satisfied with the right weaves, the right yarns,
the best printing technique, the necessary blends of coloured yarns
to give a true interpretation."[15] The textural subtleties of William
Scott's paintings were masterfully reproduced in screen-printed
cottons, such as *Skara Brae* (1958), and in woollen tapestries,
such as *Skaill* (1960) (fig. 4.18). Morton's minute attention to detail
was particularly evident in *Adam* (1957), a complex cotton-and-
rayon jacquard tapestry evoking a collage by Keith Vaughan.
Other painters whose works were produced included Trevor Bates,
Cecil Collins, Stephan Knapp, Edward Middleditch, Ben Nicholson,
Alan Reynolds, Kenneth Rowntree, Joe Tilson, Victor Vasarely,
Scottie Wilson, and Leon Zack. Designs by sculptors, including
César Baldaccini, Geoffrey Clarke, Elisabeth Frink, and Marino
Marini, were also forcefully translated.

Alastair Morton's death in 1963, and the takeover of Morton
Sundour by Courtaulds, a major shareholder since 1935, marked
the end of an era. New printed fabrics by artists and designers
continued to be created for several years, and *Legend*, based on
a painting by Alan Reynolds, won a Design Centre Award in 1965.
But although Edinburgh Weavers continued in operation until the
end of the 1960s, the visionary character of the company gradually
ebbed away.

Britain: Hull Traders

Just as Edinburgh Weavers was reaching its zenith, Hull Traders
was founded in 1957 by Tristram Hull, with ambitious artistic
aspirations for printed textiles. The enterprise got off to a dramatic
start through its collaboration with Eduardo Paolozzi and Nigel
Henderson. The two artists' work was boldly experimental and
aggressively textural – the equivalent of Brutalism in contemporary
architecture. Their own business, Hammer Prints, which produced
idiosyncratic textiles and wallpapers such as *Cowcumber* and *Porto
Bello* (1958), was later absorbed into Hull Traders. Among other
early designers were Shirley Craven (later appointed colour and
design consultant), John Drummond, Althea McNish, Richard
Spelling, and John Wright. Drummond's theatrical classical frieze
patterns, although flowing against the tide of mainstream design,
had parallels with the WPM's Palladio wallpapers.

Britain: Tibor

European émigrés, who came to Britain in large numbers during
the 1930s, exerted a significant impact on the country's textile
industry. One of the most significant was Hungarian-born Tibor
Reich, who arrived in 1937 after studying at the Vienna School
of Textiles. Further training at the University of Leeds, where
he experimented with colour, texture, and yarns using dobby
and jacquard looms, consolidated his Bauhaus-inspired approach
to weaving. In 1945 Reich established Tibor Ltd at Clifford Mill,
near Stratford-upon-Avon, Warwickshire, winning early renown
for his jacquard-woven, deep-textured weaves, first created in 1949.
Over the next three decades the company was acclaimed for its

customized woven fabrics and wall hangings for public and commercial buildings, upholstery fabrics for cars, ships, and airlines, and domestic furnishing fabrics.

Although chiefly known for his woven textiles, Reich developed a keen interest in pattern design, his main contribution being his "textureprints," a range of screen-printed textiles introduced in 1954. Early designs, such as *Raw Coral* (1954), were characterized by bold, gestural effects. For his printed and woven Fotexur range of 1957, however, Reich used isolated photographic details of organic materials such as bark, cracked earth, and stone walls, as a basis for a series of positive or negative patterns. By arranging the repeated image in different formations, he created a variety of textural effects. *Flamingo*, a printed pattern based on a photograph of straw, won a Design Centre Award in 1957 (fig. 4.19). Other Fotexur designs included *Mantua* (1958), a jacquard-woven fabric incorporating gold Lurex, and *Lubiana* (1959), a printed fabric resembling a knotted fishing net. Reich applied the same principle to the decoration of other furnishings, including wallpaper, plastic laminates, carpets, ceramics, and tiles. "Mr Reich has discovered a new *way of seeing* nature," enthused Michael Farr.[16] In 1960 Reich launched the Colatomic range, featuring a textural abstract called *Atomic*, printed in fourteen colourways. According to the designer: "The purpose of pattern in printed textiles should be expression of flow and rhythm which will move sympathetically with its surroundings, distribution of colour areas, and to give visual pleasure and tranquillity on the one hand, and interest and thrill on the other."[17]

Britain: Cole & Son and John Line

In 1945 the exhibition *Historical and British Wallpapers* was held at the Suffolk Galleries in London, featuring a display of speculative patterns for wallpapers by leading artists and designers. Although very few designs were actually put into production – apart from an abstract pattern by Graham Sutherland block-printed by Cole & Son – the exhibition whetted the British public's appetite for patterned wall coverings. In 1946 Cole & Son used the *Britain Can Make It* exhibition to relaunch the block-printed Bardfield Papers designed by John Aldridge and Edward Bawden. In 1951 Cole became one of the first manufacturers in the country to venture into the field of "Contemporary" wallpapers, when it screen-printed two designs by Lucienne Day, *Stella* and *Diabolo*, for room settings shown at the Festival of Britain.

John Line's Limited Editions collection, featuring block-printed and screen-printed patterns by leading artists and designers, was also launched at the Festival of Britain. Contributors to this collection included Armfield-Passano, Lucienne Day, Bruce Hollingsworth, Jacqueline Groag, Olga Lehmann, Arnold Lever, Donald Melbourne, Bianca Minns, John Minton, William Odell, Sylvia Priestley, Henry Skeen, and Mary Storr. One of the most striking patterns in the collection was Sylvia Priestley's *Early Bird*,

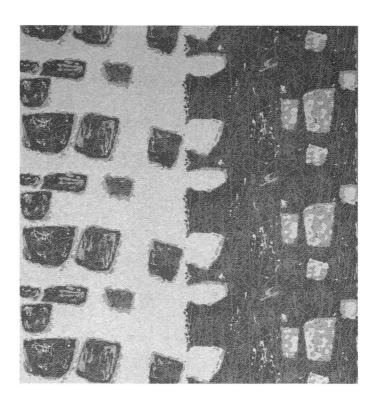

Top Fig. 4.18
Skaill woven wool tapestry furnishing fabric, designed by William Scott, produced by Edinburgh Weavers, 1960. Many of the designs produced at Edinburgh Weavers were based on original paintings. In woven fabrics, yarns and weaves were carefully chosen to evoke texture and depth.

Above Fig. 4.19
Flamingo screen-printed cotton furnishing fabric, designed by Tibor Reich, produced by Tibor, 1957. This design was created by a process known as Fotexur, in which an isolated detail from a photograph of organic materials – in this case straw – was used as the template for a repeat pattern.

Right Fig. 4.20
Gyro screen-printed wallpaper, designed by June Lyon, produced by John Line, c.1953. This sculptural wallpaper was used in the departure lounge at London Airport, designed by Frederick Gibberd. The furniture and furnishings were selected by June Lyon, who also created this pattern.

featuring ungainly, long-legged birds against a striped Regency ground. Also memorable was *Orpheus*, a linear pattern of string instruments by Arnold Lever, formerly chief scarf designer at Jacqmar, but by this time manager of his own dress fabric firm.

John Line continued to produce "Contemporary" ranges throughout the decade, alongside more traditional designs. "The well equipped factory existing as the core of a large merchant house provides the foundations of a policy ideally suited to the introduction of at least a proportion of designs of an advanced and experimental nature," observed *Design* magazine in 1956.[18] The company was fortunate in employing two very accomplished staff designers, William Odell and Henry Skeen, but it also purchased many patterns from freelance designers, notably Daphne Barder, Els Calvetti, Barbara Hirsch, and June Lyon (fig. 4.20). The wood engraver and illustrator John Farleigh also created a special collection for John Line in 1956.

Britain: Wall Paper Manufacturers Ltd

Galvanized into action by the Festival, the Wall Paper Manufacturers Ltd (WPM) embarked on a sustained initiative to promote "Contemporary" design, issuing four collections of the Architects' Book of One Hundred Wallpapers between 1952 and 1958. This series brought together a selection of modern machine-printed patterns produced by various branches of the WPM, marketed under the trade name Crown, and included patterns by high-calibre designers such as Robert and Roger Nicholson and Lucienne Day. "Dots, stripes, geometric patterns, abstract symbols, formalized plant motifs – all on a small scale; these are the characteristics of a type of design which is associated with the word 'contemporary,'" wrote John E. Blake of this range in 1955.[19]

The driving force behind the Architects' Books collections came from the progressive Lightbown Aspinall branch of the WPM, which was run by two brothers, managing director Richard Busby and design director Guy Busby. Subsequently they engineered an even more ground-breaking scheme, Palladio, featuring ambitious designs by top-ranking British designers. Whereas the Architects' Books were collated from wallpapers already in production, thereby reflecting prevailing trends, the Palladio ranges were specially commissioned, thus actively stimulating new creative ideas. The other crucial difference was that the Architects' Books contained machine-printed wallpapers with domestic-sized patterns, while the Palladio collections were hand screen-printed on a larger scale. "The restrictions which the silk screen imposes on the artist are negligible compared with traditional block or roller methods," noted John E. Blake. "Freedom of drawing and scale, richness of texture and colour can be achieved."[20] The Palladio range was specifically targeted at architects, and the name was deliberately chosen to convey grandeur of aspiration. Most of the designs were intended for large public and commercial buildings, although some were suitable for domestic interiors: "Placed on a single wall at the end of a room, in a niche by the chimney breast, or at the head of the stairs, such designs could be treated as focal points rather than as a background to other furnishings," noted Blake.[21]

Palladio designers were chosen by Richard and Guy Busby, working closely with Roger Nicholson. A painter turned pattern designer who played a key role in styling the first six Palladio collections, Nicholson was appointed professor of textiles at the Royal College of Art in 1958. As well as designing textiles for David Whitehead and wallpapers for the WPM, he was also closely involved with the Cotton Board's Colour Design and Style Centre in Manchester, designing exhibitions and graphics in partnership with his brother, Robert Nicholson. The Nicholsons made a substantial contribution to the first three Palladio collections, and their work was singled out by *Design* in 1957 for the "ebullient pleasure in their freedom to use large motifs with a rich painterly sense of texture and tone."[22] Among other contributors to the first three collections were William Belcher, Peter Devenish, Mary Frame, Julius Frank, David Gentleman, Elizabeth Griffiths, Walter Hoyle, Edward Hughes, Vibeke Kraus, Audrey Levy, Frank Martin, Peter Shuttleworth, Eric Thomas, Edward Veevers, Fritz Werthmüller, and F. Williams-Gobeaux.

From the outset the Palladio range was extremely varied in subject matter, tone, and style. Patterns ranged from modest geometrics, such as *Toccata* (1955), to the giant roundels of *Corolla* (1955). Architectural motifs and historical allusions were a recurrent feature, notably in Robert Nicholson's *Colonnade* (fig. 4.21) and *Columns* (1955). The painter Walter Hoyle cast a new slant on heraldry in *Unicorn* (1958), while the illustrator David Gentleman was inspired by French *toiles de Jouy* in *Andalusia* (1958). Early Palladio collections contained a high proportion of pictorial designs. *Locomotion* (1958) by Roger Nicholson depicted vintage transport, while *Bistro* (1955) evoked foreign holidays. Contemporary art was another potent force, manifested in the sculptural forms of Edward Hughes's *Bassuto* (1955) and Robert Nicholson's spiky *Avenue* (1955). The fashion for abstraction prompted geometric patterns such as Peter Shuttleworth's *Kaleidoscope* (1958) (fig. 4.22), and textural, speckled designs such as Robert Nicholson's *Brackley Weave* (1955).

By the time of the third Palladio collection in 1958, the concept was fully matured. It was in this group of designs that Audrey Levy, a gifted graduate of the Royal College of Art, emerged as a major contributor. Levy had already distinguished herself in Palladio 2 with her skeletal leaf pattern *Tracery* and her wiry chintz *Phantom Rose*. For Palladio 3 she created ambitious painterly murals such as *Maze* and *Treescape*, as well as smaller, textural patterns such as *Pebble*. Frank Martin's *Java*, with its spiky black

Top Fig. 4.21
Colonnade *screen-printed wallpaper, designed by Robert Nicholson, produced by the Lightbown Aspinall branch of the WPM, 1955. This design was created for the first Palladio collection, an ambitious, imaginative, and stylish range of hand screen-printed wallpapers intended mainly for architects.*

Above Fig. 4.22
Kaleidoscope *screen-printed wallpaper, designed by Peter Shuttleworth, produced by the Lightbown Aspinall branch of the WPM, 1958. Peter Shuttleworth worked as a staff designer at Lightbown Aspinall from 1946 to 1981. This stimulating abstract pattern was created for the Palladio 3 collection.*

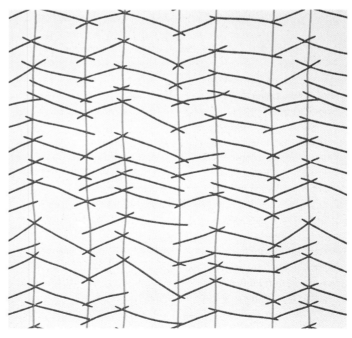

Top Fig. 4.23
Pannus *screen-printed wallpaper,* *designed by Humphrey Spender, produced* *by the Lightbown Aspinall branch of* *the WPM, 1960.* The pattern on this wallpaper is on a massive scale. It formed part of the Palladio Magnus 2 collection, intended primarily for public and commercial buildings.

Above Fig. 4.24
Portal *surface-printed wallpaper,* *designed by Terence Conran, produced* *by the Lightbown Aspinall branch of* *the WPM, 1960.* The machine-printed Palladio Modus range extended the upmarket Palladio aesthetic to lower-cost wallpapers conceived on a smaller domestic scale, such as this design.

Top Fig. 4.25
Impress *screen-printed wallpaper,* *designed by Edward Veevers, produced* *by the Lightbown Aspinall branch of* *the WPM, 1958.* The modest scale of this wallpaper made it suitable for both domestic and public buildings. Distressed, patinated, textural effects were popular at this time.

Above Fig. 4.26
Reed Screen *surface-printed wallpaper,* *designed by Cliff Holden, produced by* *Lightbown Aspinall branch of the WPM,* *1960.* This pattern from the Palladio Modus collection perpetuates the linear aesthetic associated with the "Contemporary" style, but in a simpler, pared-down form.

bamboos, was assertively sculptural. Edward Veevers produced more recessive tactile patterns, including *Impress* (fig. 4.25).

The main Palladio ranges were supplemented by two satellite collections – Palladio Magnus (1959–60) and Palladio Modus (1960), both complementing and reinforcing different aspects of the central architectural theme. Palladio Magnus consisted of extra-large patterns, its name reflecting the scale and confidence of the designs. Palladio Magnus 1 (1959) featured some patterns by experienced designers such as Terence Conran, and others by wallpaper novices such as the architects Alison and Peter Smithson. All the designs were abstract and many were flat geometrics. Titles such as *Directus*, *Digitus*, *Orbis*, and *Structure* proclaimed their conceptual basis. Palladio Magnus 2 (1960) offered greater variety, and included a combination of abstract and representational patterns by Pat Albeck, John Drummond, Cliff Holden, Edward Hughes, Audrey Levy, Roger Nicholson, Ann Reason, Humphrey Spender, Kristina Vaughan-Jones, and Edward Veevers. Spender's outsize geometrics *Clarion* and *Pannus* combined circles and blocks of flat, bright colour with dark, textured grounds (fig. 4.23). By contrast, Cliff Holden's leafy *Arcadia* and Pat Albeck's crisp *Sunflower* offered relief from the intimidation of hardcore Modernism.

Palladio Modus (1960) successfully mimicked the aesthetic of the main Palladio range, but with cheaper, smaller-scale, machine-printed patterns. Named designers were used as a strong selling point, and included Terence Conran, Lucienne Day, and Jacqueline Groag. Other designs were by José Bonnet, Cliff Holden (fig. 4.26), William Gear, Elizabeth Gould, Joyce Storey, and Fritz Werthmüller. Some patterns in this collection looked back to earlier "Contemporary" idioms, such as Jacqueline Groag's *Precious Stones*, with its playful balloon motifs, and Terence Conran's *Portal*, with its decorative architectural devices (fig. 4.24). More forward-looking was the rugged, painterly expressionism of William Gear's *Palette* and José Bonnet's *Textra*.

United States: Textiles

In 1940 the Museum of Modern Art (MoMA) in New York had organized a competition on the theme of Organic Design. The fabrics shown in the subsequent exhibition – by designers such as Dan Cooper and Antonin Raymond – stimulated interest in pattern and raised awareness about the relationship between textiles and interior design. In 1956 another exhibition at MoMA, *Textiles USA*, confirmed that over the previous fifteen years a revolution had occurred. Before the war the United States had been a design pioneer, but now it was a design superpower. "It is difficult to explain the velocity with which design exploded out of the dim war years," reflected the textile designer Jack Lenor Larsen in 1983.[23]

The achievements of American post-war furniture designers are well documented, but the revolution in pattern design between 1945 and 1960, although of equal magnitude, has yet to be fully appreciated. It was not led by established textile and wallpaper companies, whose output remained fairly conservative during this period, but instead the main avenues for creativity were numerous newly established, small, design-led firms. In 1952 Alvin Lustig reflected: "Most of the large producers of drapery and upholstery fabrics had little understanding, and often little sympathy, for the principles inherent in modern design. Added to this they were usually unable to visualize any potential market for such fabrics, and left the development of this new field to small and usually inexperienced firms and individuals. Turning away from the lush and expensive brocades, satins and silks so beloved by the traditional interior decorator and so well supplied by the large fabric manufacturers, the modern designers explored, discovered and exploited modest kinds of utility and industrial cloths never before thought appropriate for modern design. These modest fabrics as a background for printed designs gave an air of freshness of colour and design that could not be achieved with the more traditional materials."[24]

The minimal investment needed to produce hand screen-printed textiles and wallpapers made starting a business relatively inexpensive. Many new firms worked closely with architects, creating customized designs for specific interiors. The more their work was seen, the greater the demand, leading to larger-scale production using commission printers, and increasing sales through showrooms and shops. Close aesthetic correspondences developed between pattern design and contemporary art and architecture. "The sharp, clean forms of a crisp geometry that characterize modern architecture and some modern paintings have influenced some designs," wrote Alvin Lustig, who also pointed out the influence of physics and engineering. "Technology, the electron microscope, aerial photography, the delicate tracery of steel in tension – all these have had their share in developing patterns."[25]

United States: Angelo Testa

Although these new companies were scattered all over the United States, Chicago, renowned for the quality of its art education, spawned a particularly lively cluster, including Angelo Testa, Ben Rose, Elenhank, and the wallpaper firm Denst & Soderlund. Angelo Testa studied painting and sculpture during the early 1940s at the newly established Chicago Institute of Design. Having created his first printed textiles while still a student, he was led by his growing interest in pattern design to establish Angelo Testa & Company in 1947, producing hand screen-printed fabrics for architects. The company expanded rapidly as he began to win large contracts and opened a shop. Testa also designed woven textiles, and supplied patterns on a freelance basis to companies such as Cohn-Hall-Marx, Forster, Greeff, Knoll, and Schumacher.

Drawing on his skills as a sculptor and painter, Testa pioneered an accessible abstract style (figs. 4.28 and 4.29). "The textile designer

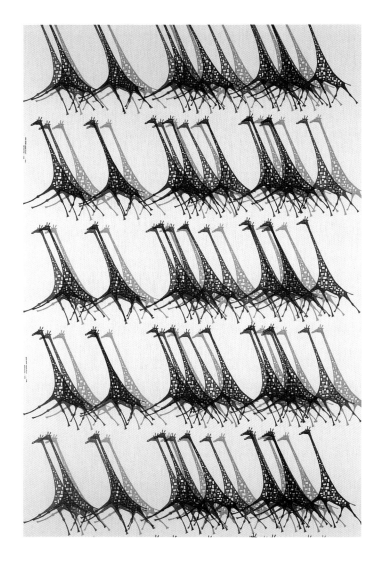

must start with a piece of plain fabric in mind. He must determine what the function of this fabric is and what justification he has for putting a design on it. He needs to experiment with line, form, texture, and colour, keeping in mind the monotony of most prints. A feeling of clarity and spaciousness must be introduced into his designs," he advised.[26] Applying a sculptural approach to pattern, and using limited colours, he explained that: "By the use of thick and thin lines, combinations of solid and outline forms, a freer articulation of positive and negative space is brought into play. By the use of pure linear elements, undreamed of vibrations and effects are created which, when properly controlled, are made subtle enough to reveal beautiful and exciting space experiences."[27] Although ideally suited to the austere rectilinearity of modern buildings, Testa's patterns displayed a lightness of touch that made them accessible to a wider market. Rigorous, yet relaxed, they influenced a whole school of American pattern-making.

United States: Ben Rose

Another artist turned designer was Ben Rose, who studied painting at the School of the Art Institute of Chicago from 1939 to 1941. In 1946 he set up Ben Rose, Inc., using the same equipment to hand screen-print both textiles and wallpapers. Collaborating from 1947 with the interior designer Helen Stern, Rose was fêted by the design cognoscenti, receiving numerous Good Design Awards from MoMA and the American Institute of Decorators (AID). In 1953 he opened a showroom in the Chicago Merchandise Mart, and the company continued to expand over the next fifteen years, employing around fifty staff by 1967.

Ben Rose's patterns epitomized the buoyancy and optimism of the post-war period. More varied in their imagery and colouring than those of Testa, although still strongly linear in style, they drew freely on abstracted motifs from art, science, and the natural world (fig. 4.30). An early pattern, *Hole in Stocking* (1946), employed biomorphic sculptural motifs. Thickly drawn, meandering lines were a feature of other designs from the late 1940s, including *Chinese Clouds*. Abstracted images from nature formed the basis for *Oak Leaves* and *Bird's Nest*. *Groves* (1955) was more lyrical, depicting bands of stylized trees (fig. 4.31). Some patterns featured everyday objects such as paper clips and keyholes, while others, such as *Scan* and *Schematics*, explored rhythm and space. A wallpaper called *Interlace* suggested fibres under a microscope, while another, *Time Capsule*, evoked the geodesic domes of the maverick architect Buckminster Fuller. Bubbling with wit and energy, puns remained a common feature of Rose's designs of the following decade, as in *Girafters* (1965), with its architectonic galloping giraffes (fig. 4.27).

United States: Elenhank

Many of the individuals who set up their own companies came from art or architecture backgrounds. Elenhank Designers, Inc. was a husband-and-wife team of the architect Henry Kluck and the artist Eleanor Kluck, Elenhank being a composite of their nicknames,

Above Fig. 4.27
Girafters *screen-printed modacrylic and rayon furnishing fabric, designed by Ben Rose, 1965, reprinted by Ben Rose, Inc., 1988. Although from the mid-1960s, this pattern conveys the essence of the witty and engaging style pioneered by Ben Rose during the late 1940s.*

Opposite top Fig. 4.28
Labyrinth *screen-printed cotton satin furnishing fabric, designed by Angelo Testa, 1942, produced by Angelo Testa & Co., c.1947. The sculptor and painter Angelo Testa developed a new vocabulary of abstract pattern-making during the early post-war period. His work particularly appealed to architects, and inspired other pattern designers.*

Opposite bottom Fig. 4.29
Skyscrapers *screen-printed cotton furnishing fabric, designed by Angelo Testa, 1942, produced by Angelo Testa & Co., c.1947. In this pattern Angelo Testa experimented with line, rhythm, form, colour, and texture to create a restrained but stimulating abstract design.*

Elen and Hank. Their earliest textiles, created in 1946, were lino-printed using blocks designed and cut by Eleanor Kluck. She worked independently for a couple of years, before entering into partnership with Henry in 1948. That year they announced: "We are concerned with meeting the fabric and design requirements of contemporary architects and interior designers, and with introducing a new vocabulary of fabric expressions."[28]

During the early years Elenhank produced witty pictorial and abstract repeat patterns for coordinated textiles and wallpapers. *Stone to Stainless* (1954), featuring outline drawings of vintage cutlery, and *Vertebrates* (1954), showing cartoon animals, were typical of their work from this period. Other designs included *Buttony Net*, composed of small discs linked by fine lines, and *Aerielle*, a criss-crossing wire pattern printed on fibreglass (both 1954). Elenhank switched to screen-printing during the mid-1950s, and later the company's designs grew in seriousness and scale. In 1951 the Klucks had developed the technique of "random prints," in which large motifs were block-printed at random across several widths of fabric or wallpaper. Out of this grew "mural prints," large screen-printed patterns that flowed across curtains and walls (fig. 4.32). Sometimes the designers exploited the fluidity of draped fabrics to create patterns that expanded or contracted, as in *Radiance* (1971), which mutated from ovals to circles. Much of their later work was inspired by nature, particularly the landscape of northern Indiana, and often took a stylized or abstracted form.

United States: Adler-Schnee Associates

Working along similar lines to Ben Rose, but based in Detroit, was German-born Ruth Adler Schnee. As a child, she was given drawing lessons by Paul Klee, a family friend, and after emigrating to the United States in 1939, she studied at Rhode Island School of Design and the Cranbrook Academy of Art, near Detroit, Michigan, completing a master's degree in architectural design in 1946. In 1947 she established a design studio in Detroit, and the following year she and her husband, Edward Schnee, set up Adler-Schnee Associates to hand screen-print her fabrics.

From the outset a light-hearted, witty tone and a delicate, wiry graphic style were adopted, and early designs included *Pits and Pods*, *Slits and Slats*, and *Bugs in Booby Trap* (1947) (fig. 4.35). The lasting influence of Klee was apparent in designs such as *Strings and Things* and *Seedy Weeds* (1953–4) (fig. 4.33), while echoes of Alexander Calder's mobiles and wire sculptures were clearly discernible in the linear doodles of *Wireworks* (1949) and the flat, organic segments of *Germination* (1954). Although often amusing, Adler's designs were by no means frivolous, and she was adept at transforming physical objects into abstract forms. With their stimulating vocabulary and dynamic rhythms, her printed fabrics functioned particularly well in an architectural context. Adler-Schnee Associates was extremely successful during the late 1940s and 1950s, and the company's work was sold through eight

Right top Fig. 4.30
Earthforms *screen-printed modacrylic and rayon furnishing fabric, designed by Ben Rose, 1967, reprinted by Ben Rose, Inc., 1988.* Ben Rose was skilled at abstracting imagery from the natural world. Here fine lines and coloured bands suggest geological strata.

Right bottom Fig. 4.31
Groves *screen-printed modacrylic and rayon furnishing fabric, designed by Ben Rose, 1955, reprinted by Ben Rose, Inc., 1988.* In this design silhouettes of leafless trees are transformed into abstract textural patterns. Sliced into strips, the pattern assumes an architectural quality.

Far right top Fig. 4.32
Skyline *screen-printed linen panel, designed by Eleanor and Hank Kluck, produced by Elenhank Designers, Inc., 1958.* Elenhank specialized in customized large-scale fabric and wallpaper mural prints for specific interiors. These were initially block-printed but later screen-printed.

Far right bottom Fig. 4.33
Seedy Weeds *screen-printed cotton furnishing fabric, designed by Ruth Adler Schnee, produced by Adler-Schnee Associates, 1953-4.* The influence of Paul Klee is evident in the linearity of this pattern. Its witty title reflects the playfulness of Ruth Adler Schnee's approach to design.

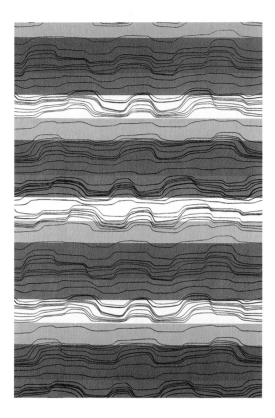

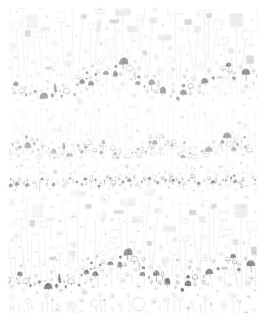

showrooms across the country and an Adler-Schnee shop in Detroit, with new designs being produced until the early 1960s.

United States: Laverne Originals

New York-based Laverne Originals (later Laverne International) was another firm that had huge success during the 1950s. It grew out of a partnership between two painters, Erwine and Estelle Laverne, who met at the Art Students League in 1934. Although they worked together from this time, it was not until 1942 that Laverne Originals was created. Erwine Laverne had won early renown for his faux-marble decorative paintings, and the aim of the partnership, which initially specialized in wallpaper, was to integrate the fine and applied arts. From 1942 both textiles and wallpaper were produced, complemented by contemporary furniture. At first hand screen-printing was the main technique used, but machine-printing was later adopted for popular lines.

Successful early ranges included the sumptuous Marbalia fabrics and wallpapers simulating marble and wood-grain effects. Designed by Erwine Laverne in 1948, they were described at the time as "design, colour and form in fluid motion – a visual music."[29] Dramatic Marbalia murals remained a key element of the Lavernes' output until the company closed in the mid-1960s. "Although the work grows out of their life together, neither partner dominates the other, and each has his own specialities and distinct manner of working," noted a commentator in 1949.[30] In general, Erwine Laverne favoured decorative textural abstraction, while Estelle Laverne's patterns ranged from Modernist geometrics, such as *Squared Circle*, to modern interpretations of folk art, as in the Amish-inspired *Pennsylvania Dutch*, to figurative patterns such as the Matisse-inspired *Fun to Run* (1948) (fig. 4.34). "Much of Estelle Laverne's work has proceeded from her intense interest in expressing symbolically the relations she feels between human beings and their aspirations," noted the same writer.[31]

Fun to Run was part of the Contempora Series, which marked a new departure for the Lavernes. They now began to commission patterns for textiles and wallpapers from leading artists, architects, and designers, including Alexander Calder, Gyorgy Kepes, Ray Komai, Ross Littell, Alvin Lustig, and Oscar Niemeyer. *Splotchy* and *Calder #1* (1949) by Alexander Calder were irreverent and amusing. The expressive linear motifs of *Masks* (fig. 4.36) and *The Big Catch* (1948) by Ray Komai, and *Incantation* (1948) by Alvin Lustig, with its primitive pictographs (fig. 4.37), defined the spidery, graphic style of the early post-war years. Lustig commented of the Lavernes: "Designers themselves, they have placed an emphasis upon creative freedom which they extend to any artists they employ."[32]

Laverne Originals flourished during the late 1940s and 1950s, and its geometric and organic abstract fabrics, such as *Fluctuation* (1949) and *Trapeze* (1953), were widely praised. Coordinated textiles and wallpapers included abstracts such as *Incandescence*

Top Fig. 4.34
Fun to Run *screen-printed rayon and gold foil furnishing fabric, designed by Estelle Laverne, produced by Laverne Originals, 1948.* This unusual figurative pattern, inspired by a painting by Henri Matisse, was issued by Laverne Originals as part of the company's Contempora Series.

Above Fig. 4.35
Bugs in Booby Trap *screen-printed cotton furnishing fabric, designed by Ruth Adler Schnee, produced by Adler-Schnee Associates, 1947.* The wiry lines in this pattern resemble the legs of "Contemporary" furniture, while the shapes bring to mind the mobiles of Alexander Calder.

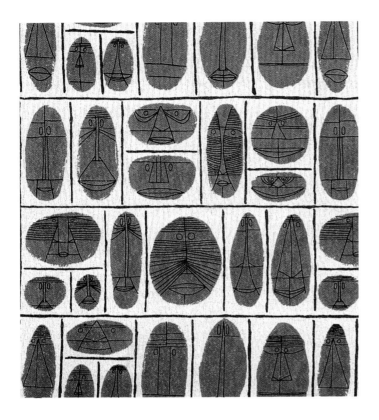

and *Scintillation*, as well as figurative patterns such as *Harlequin Holiday*. Some of the firm's wallpapers were more idiosyncratic, however, such as *Curtain Call*, depicting vintage newspaper advertisements, and its Documentary Prints, decorated with images of snakeskin and zebra stripes. By 1952 Laverne Originals had branches in Los Angeles and San Francisco, and a stunning showroom – more like an art gallery – in New York. Although the business was forced to close in 1964 owing to the ill health of Estelle Laverne, some of its classic lines remained in production through other companies for many years.

United States: Knoll and Herman Miller

Inspired by the positive design climate in the United States after the war, two progressive furniture manufacturers, Knoll, founded in 1937, and Herman Miller, founded in 1923, established their own textile divisions. Although their primary purpose was to supply woven upholstery fabrics for their furniture, printed textiles became an important component of both ranges. Knoll Textiles was established in 1947, initially with Marianne Strengell as consultant. Printed textiles were produced from the outset, and a two-way exchange was set up with Nordiska Kompaniet in Sweden. From 1949 to 1955 Hungarian-born Eszter Haraszty was director of textiles, a brilliant colourist who created the legendary *Knoll Stripe* (1950), as well as spidery patterns such as *Tracy* and *Fibra* (fig. 4.38) (both 1953). Knoll also produced abstract patterns such as *Diamonds* (1954) by Albert Herbert, *Criss-Cross* (1959) by Ross Littell, *Chinese Coins* by Noemi Raymond, *Campagna* by Angelo Testa, and *Kontiki* by Ingetoft. Haraszty's successor was her former assistant Suzanne Huguenin, head of textiles from 1955 to 1963. Although mainly concerned with woven textiles, she also designed printed patterns such as the enlarged herringbone design *Peru* (1963).

Herman Miller's textile division was established in 1952, with the inspired choice of Alexander Girard as its director. After training as an architect in Europe during the 1920s, Girard settled in the United States in 1932. In 1949 he designed and co-curated *An Exhibition for Modern Living* at the Detroit Institute of Arts, which included one of his earliest printed furnishing fabrics. Girard was an enthusiastic collector of folk art, which greatly influenced his use of colour. His fabrics for Herman Miller, created between 1952 and 1973, were some of the most progressive of the era. With their graphic directness and intensity, even early patterns such as *Quatrefoil* (1954) were prescient of the 1960s. Recognizing the importance of sensory and tactile stimulation in design, Girard characterized his proactive approach to pattern as "aesthetic functionalism." He believed strongly that "The design of a fabric must be an integral part of the fabric and not a superficial application. Fabric design is not easel painting or illustrating. It has its own specific desirable qualities and limitations."[33]

Most of Girard's patterns were abstract, composed of either simple linear motifs, as in *Lines* (1952) and *Names* (1957), or flat shapes, as in *Rain* (1953). The number of different motifs he used in a pattern was strictly limited, and repeats were as simple as possible, as in *Mikado* (1954), a Japanese-inspired geometric chrysanthemum design. Girard favoured warm colours such as red, yellow, blue, and magenta, which, when juxtaposed or overlapped, as in *Ribbons* and *Feathers* (both 1957), created effects of great richness and sensuality (fig. 4.39). Although they were abstract, Girard's designs often carried cultural resonances. *Ribbons* recalled folk-dance costumes and maypoles, for example, while *Feathers* evoked the royal ceremonial cloaks of the Incas of Peru. Stripes and checks, produced in a palette of unparalleled diversity, also formed a key element in his repertoire. "My approach to the design of fabrics, printed or woven, is to make available to the consumer a vocabulary of inter-related types," Girard explained. "The types vary in weight, woven texture, printed 'texture,' scale of pattern, yarn content and, of course, colour. Where patterns repeat I have made every effort to absorb the repeat in the pattern in such a way as to allow the pattern to 'flow' without obvious breaks or insistent repetition motifs."[34]

Girard also designed two groups of wallpapers for Herman Miller, in 1952 and 1957. Quieter in tone than his textiles, they consisted mainly of small, geometric motifs in single colours, as in *Double Triangles* (1952) and *Trispot* (1957), although sometimes the effects were dynamic, as in the optically stimulating *Facets* (1952). Several wallpapers were versions of his textiles, sometimes in miniaturized form, as in *Lines* (1952). Representational patterns included *Alphabet*, composed of rows of capital letters and numbers, and *Retrospective*, a linear, abstracted Italian cityscape (both 1952).

United States: Schiffer Prints

Designers of the calibre of Alexander Girard were few and far between. Other companies were obliged to cast their net more widely. "The more usual approach has been to build up a collection by various personalities with *names* in the field or in closely related areas," noted Alvin Lustig in 1952.[35] Lustig singled out the Stimulus Collection, produced by Schiffer Prints from 1949, as the most outstanding "name" collection. Established by Milton Schiffer in 1945, Schiffer Prints was a division of Mil-Art Company, Inc. Needing a new initiative to revitalize the company's fortunes after the war, Schiffer invited a number of architects, designers, and painters to create designs for printed fabrics, some of which were later modified as wallpapers. "There was not a professional fabric designer in the group, but nevertheless a distinguished collection was established," observed Lustig.[36]

The collection included designs by the artists Salvador Dalí and Ray Eames; the architects Bernard Rudofsky, Oliver Lundquist, and Abel Sorensen; and the furniture designers Paul McCobb, George Nelson, and Edward Wormley. Ray Eames contributed *Cross Patch*, with its miniaturized cross-braced panels, and *Sea Things*, featuring line drawings of starfish, seaweed, and octopuses.

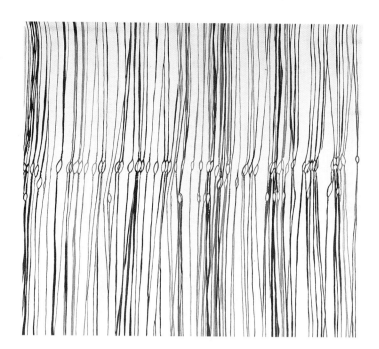

Top Fig. 4.38
Fibra screen-printed linen furnishing fabric, designed by Eszter Haraszty, produced by Knoll Textiles, 1953. Colour is employed sparingly in this apparently casual but carefully calculated design depicting the wire heddles through which the warp is threaded on a loom.

Above Fig. 4.39
Feathers screen-printed cotton and linen furnishing fabric, designed by Alexander Girard, produced by Herman Miller, 1957. The apparent simplicity of this pattern, composed of a single, repeated, overlapping motif, belies the sophistication of the composition and its translucent colouring.

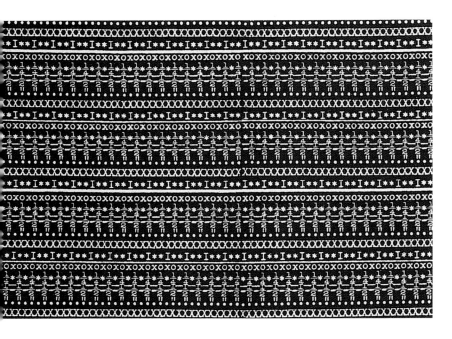

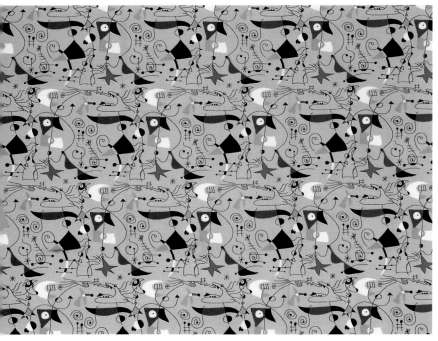

Bernard Rudofsky created patterns from rows of typewritten letters, numbers, and symbols, including *Si Non* and *Fractions* (fig. 4.40). Edward Wormley's *Trees* was composed of giant, overlapping silhouettes of leafless trees, resembling a mural. Paul McCobb's *Buoys* was an inventive abstract conjured up from mundane objects.

United States: Fuller Fabrics and Associated American Artists

Two other firms who produced "name" collections during the 1950s were Fuller Fabrics, Inc. and Associated American Artists. Fuller Fabrics, founded by Daniel B. Fuller in 1933, specialized in fabrics for women's sportswear. Although not generally associated with modern design, its Modern Master Print series of 1955 featured patterns inspired by the work of major internationally renowned artists, including Marc Chagall, Raoul Dufy, Fernand Léger, Joan Miró, and Pablo Picasso. The patterns, which were loosely adapted from their paintings, drawings, and prints by the Fuller design studio, were issued under licence. Most consisted of one or two small motifs arranged in standard repeats, and the artist whose work translated best to this format was Léger, whose patterns included *The Circus* and *Formes en Couleurs*. Miró's work was also successfully miniaturized in designs such as *Dancing Figures* and *Women and Birds* (fig. 4.41), but pocket-sized versions of works of art by Picasso, Dufy, and Chagall failed to capture the magic of the originals. The collection was actively promoted through a line of resort wear created by leading American fashion designers such as Clare McCardell.

During the late 1940s the design division of Associated American Artists embarked on a mission to disseminate the work of its members to the mass market via ceramics, graphics, textiles, and wallpapers. This resulted in the Signature Fabrics collections, which included printed apparel fabrics marketed by M. Lowenstein & Sons, Inc. from 1952, and three collections of furnishing fabrics produced by Riverdale Fabrics in 1952–3. The scheme was stylistically eclectic because of the sheer volume of contributors, among whom were Laura Jean Allen, Arnold Blanch, Roger Chaplin, Piero Dorazio, John Fucci, John Hull, Ilonka Karasz, Doris Lee, Howard Low, Gabor Peterdi, Louise Phillips, Raman Prats, Albert John Pucci, Anton Refrigier, Joe Richards, and Tom Vroman.

United States: Konwiser and L. Anton Maix

Design-aware commercial companies such as Konwiser and L. Anton Maix also produced high-quality screen-printed textiles during the 1950s. Konwiser drew on an impressive team of designers that included Joe Bascom, Matt Kahn, and Sara Provan (fig. 4.42). Provan specialized in painterly abstracts composed of overlapping irregular planes of colour, their titles often suggestive of music, such as *Cadenza*, *Capriccio*, and *Largo* (1954). L. Anton Maix was an entrepreneur who, although not a designer himself, was active in promoting and merchandising modern textile design. His collections, although they were not as coherent as those of

Top Fig. 4.40
Fractions screen-printed cotton furnishing fabric, designed by Bernard Rudofsky, produced by Schiffer Prints, c.1949. Produced as part of the Stimulus Collection, this pattern – one of a series – demonstrates what the architect Bernard Rudofsky described as his "typewriter art."

Above Fig. 4.41
Women and Birds printed cotton dress fabric, after Joan Miró, produced by Fuller Fabrics, c.1955–6. Created as part of the Modern Master Print series, produced under licence from leading international artists, this small-scale dress print draws on motifs derived from the paintings of Joan Miró.

designer-controlled companies, set high standards and were consistently innovative. Designers were credited by name, and noteworthy contributors included Olga Lee Baughman, Serge Chermayeff, Pierre Kleykamp, Elsie Krummeck, Alvin Lustig, Paul McCobb, Erik Nitsche (fig. 4.43), Paul Rand, Joel Robinson, Don Smith, and Paul Thiry. Imagery varied from the scientific to the jocular. In 1954 a group of patterns explored different aspects of geometry: Joel Robinson's *Ovals* featured overlapping circles; Pierre Kleykamp's *Infinity* was constructed from hexagons; and Olga Baughman's *Infinity* was composed of a mesh of diamonds and fine stringing. Other patterns were lighter in tone, such as *Kites and Mites*, a playful stick-figure design by Paul McCobb.

United States: Greeff and Schumacher

Large companies, such as Cheney Brothers, Schumacher, and Greeff Fabrics, the latter founded by Theodore Greeff in 1933, tended to be much more cautious and eclectic in their design policies. Virginia Nepodal, an in-house designer at Cheney Brothers during the 1940s, who transferred to the newly merged Cheney, Greeff & Co. during the early 1950s, worked in an accessible modern style, creating patterns such as *Mushrooms*, *Sanderlings*, and *Seeds* (all 1951). Subsequently, as design director of Greeff Fabrics from 1952 to 1985, Nepodal was responsible for the styling of both textiles and wallpapers, where she juggled the dual requirements of "Contemporary" and traditional design. Greeff had pioneered the introduction of elaborate themed collections, intended for the high-end interior decorator trade, since the early 1940s, featuring patterns by designers such as Marion Dorn, John Little, Dan Rasmassen, and Dagmar Wilson. These continued to form a key element of the company's repertoire, along with period ranges, such as *American Legacy*.

During the 1930s and 1940s Schumacher had begun to draw more heavily on the work of American designers, including Donald Deskey, Dorothy Draper, Ilonka Karasz, Ruth Reeves, and Joseph Urban, instead of relying exclusively on European design. The company began producing wallpapers in 1938, and introduced coordinated textiles and wallpapers the following year. After the war, modern design was embraced to a greater degree through patterns by Mariska Karasz, Raymond Loewy, Vera Neumann, Chris Ranes, Noemi Raymond, and Ken White Associates. Schumacher's showcase range was *The Taliesin Line* (1956), an extensive collection of coordinated textiles and wallpapers by the veteran architect Frank Lloyd Wright. Created at the end of Wright's working life, these abstract-geometric patterns harked back to an aesthetic originally pioneered several decades earlier.

United States: Vera Neumann

More genuinely "Contemporary" were the stylized nature studies created for Schumacher between around 1946 and 1967 by Vera Neumann, such as *Happy Leaves* (1950) and *San Marino* (c.1960) (fig. 4.44), many produced as matching textiles and wallpapers.

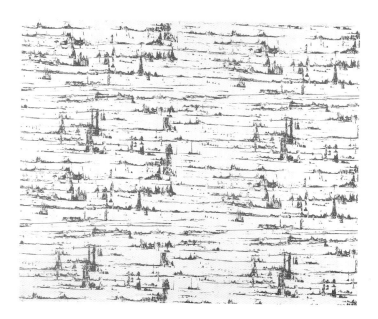

Top Fig. 4.42
Vista screen-printed cotton furnishing fabric, designed by Sara Provan, produced by Konwiser, c.1956. Sara Provan excelled in loose, painterly, textural abstract designs, often with a strong rhythmic dimension suggestive of music. This pattern evokes pulses on a scanner.

Above Fig. 4.43
Ditto screen-printed cotton furnishing fabric, designed by Erik Nitsche, produced by L. Anton Maix, c.1956. Designers experimented with many forms of abstraction during the 1950s. This clever optical pattern consists of variously sized dots in black on white and white on black.

Above Fig. 4.44
*San Marino screen-printed linen,
designed by Vera Neumann, produced
by F. Schumacher & Co., c.1960.*
Whereas advanced abstract designs
only ever appealed to a minority taste,
the stylized flower and foliage patterns
of the accomplished Vera Neumann
proved extremely popular.

Neumann, whose work was marketed under the name Vera, was the most successful and well-known American pattern designer of the post-war period. In 1946 she and her husband, George Neumann, set up Printex, producing machine screen-printed scarves and table linen on an industrial scale. Incredibly prolific, Vera Neumann also supplied patterns to several other scarf, bedding, and furnishing companies, including Scalamandré Silks and Greeff.

United States: United Wallpaper

The years 1945–70 marked a high point in American wallpapers in terms of quantity of production and quality of design. The renewed interest in wallpapers was directly linked to the rapid expansion of the suburbs. As Joanne Kosuda-Warner explains: "Wallpapering was an easy way to personalize the interior of a new tract house, and wallpaper manufacturers redesigned their lines to work with post-war floor plans and the new suburban lifestyle: bold patterns paired with textures to coordinate 'living-dining areas,' murals to provide the illusion of a view where none existed, and 'conversationals' to spark up one wall and avoid the expense of papering all four."[37]

Huge corporations such as Imperial Paper and United Wallpaper dominated the industry during this period. Stylistically promiscuous, their vast ranges, mainly surface-printed, included a bewildering mixture of traditional and "Contemporary" designs. One way for manufacturers to give their wallpapers an instant "Contemporary" feel was to exploit the ready-made vocabulary of modern art, as in the Masterpiece Interiors collection (1954) by United Wallpaper. The company also produced a collection of lightly embossed and printed wallpapers called Weaves (1947), "from Exclusive Hand-Loom Originals" by Dorothy Liebes.

United States: Katzenbach & Warren

Having pioneered a creative approach to wallpaper during the 1930s, Katzenbach & Warren became increasingly ambitious during the early post-war period. In 1948 the company produced a limited-edition collection of Mural Scrolls, screen-printed on canvas, designed by four leading artists, Alexander Calder, Henri Matisse, Roberto Matta, and Joan Miró. At the same time it also commissioned work from an impressive group of designers, including Dorr Bothwell, Franz Boueb, Christofanetti, Marion Dorn, E. Helen Dunbar, Frank Eckenroth, Franklin Hughes, William Justema, Ilonka Karasz, Tammis Keefe, Bob Lee, Zue Martin, Yves-Jean Piqué, June Platt, Victor Proetz, James Reynolds, Charles Smith, Ellen Stuart, Isabel Whitney, and Porter Woodruff. The company's achievements were showcased in a touring exhibition called *Modern Wallpaper*, devoted exclusively to its collections, organized by the American Federation of Arts in 1948.

James Reynolds had worked with Katzenbach & Warren since the early 1930s, transferring his skills as a mural painter to the design of dramatic and imposing wallpapers. An expert on Renaissance and Baroque architecture, he frequently incorporated historical references into his patterns. Marion Dorn began to collaborate with Katzenbach & Warren after she returned to the United States from Britain in 1940. Adapting her design vocabulary to suit the more opulent interiors market in her own country, she abandoned organic abstraction in favour of thematic pictorialism. "Wallpaper mirrors the Nostalgia of the person choosing it," she remarked in 1952. "Its design vision stands between the observer and the stark wall, thereby striking the mood of the room and revealing the temperament of the owner."[38]

William Justema believed that "the whole vocabulary of design is the polka dot, which elongated, becomes line; line multiplied becomes stripe, and intersecting becomes plaid."[39] Typical of his designs was the swirling combed pattern *Mirage*, part of the Sculptured Wallcoverings range, which used moulded plastics to create low-relief effects. This, and printed patterns such as *Web*, demonstrated his belief that there were two ways to create patterns: by starting from nature and abstracting it, or by starting with elements of abstraction and working back toward nature. A highly original and distinctive designer, Justema went on to create full-blown Op patterns for the Stamford Wallpaper Co. in 1967.

One of the most admired Katzenbach & Warren designers of the early post-war years was Hungarian-born Ilonka Karasz. After spending several years in Java, she emigrated to the United States, where she initially practised as a batik artist. Drawing on her skills as an illustrator, she created pictorial and abstract designs in a neat, linear style, sometimes produced as negative white-line prints. Subjects included still lifes, architectural vistas, and landscapes, some of the latter produced as large-scale scenics. *Wisconsin*, although nominally depicting farms and fields, resembled a patchwork quilt. Her large architectural murals, such as the collection called the Mezzotone Papers (1948) – described in publicity as "narrative scenic decoration of movement and humour" – resembled theatrical backdrops (fig. 4.47). Karasz avoided full-scale *trompe l'oeil* effects, however, believing that "design should be two-dimensional rather than three and that it must stay on the surface, neither creating depth nor coming forward in space."[40]

In 1951 Lois and William Katzenbach published *The Practical Book of American Wallpapers*, which featured designs by Paul Bry, Xenia Cage, Diana Gilmour, Elizabeth B. Hulbert, Neville Hussey, Leoda Miller, Elizabeth Mitchell, Roy Requa, Lanette Scheeline, Leslie Sherman, Lin Tissot, and Jacqueline Tompkins. The painter Peter Todd Mitchell, who specialized in illusionistic, Neo-Romantic designs tinged with surrealism, also supplied patterns during the 1950s, and Katzenbach & Warren continued to produce innovative collections for the rest of the decade. Particularly notable was American Futures (1954), which featured interesting tonal patterns, some with watery, collage-like effects such as *Emperor's Gold Fish* (fig. 4.46). Patterns were printed using the newly developed

photogravure process, in which designs were etched photochemically on to metal cylinders. Their subject matter included stone walls, magnified leaves, and fish, as well as abstract designs.

United States: Piazza Prints

After the war many small independent firms producing hand screen-printed wallpapers sprang up around the country. Some, such as New York-based James Seeman Studios, founded in 1946, specialized in large murals and scenics. Others, such as Gene McDonald, Inc., produced stylized and abstract patterns on a domestic scale. Many moved freely between wallpapers and textiles.

Among the new companies was Piazza Prints, founded in New York in 1946, which produced a group of highly entertaining pictorial designs by the cartoonist and graphic designer Saul Steinberg, drawn in his distinctive quirky, mischievous style. The cleverness and wittiness of these patterns, such as *Views in Paris* (1946) (fig. 4.45), appealed to a broad audience, and Steinberg's casual, doodle-like graphics were extremely influential. Steinberg later collaborated with Patterson Fabrics and Greeff, and his doodle-like graphics proved lastingly influential. Working in a similarly whimsical vein was John Rombola, who designed cartoon-like wallpapers during the 1960s for Harben Papers, another small New York firm (fig. 4.48).

United States: Denst & Soderlund

The most progressive of the new wallpaper companies established after the war was Chicago-based Denst & Soderlund, founded in 1947 by Jack Denst and Donald Soderlund, both of whom had trained at the Chicago Institute of Design. In 1952 Denst & Soderlund produced a collection of simple, linear, two-colour screen-printed wallpapers in the "Contemporary" style, including small-scale repeat patterns such as *Talisman* (fig. 4.49) and larger, single-image patterns such as *Dandelion*. *Deep Water*, which featured interlocking fish motifs, was designed by Clarence Hawking, a graphic artist who joined the company in 1951. *The Broken Ladder*, designed by Jack Denst, was composed from irregular, knobbly lines. Later in the decade Denst & Soderlund collaborated with the maverick British illustrator Roland Emett, as well as producing the Translation One collection of coordinated wallpapers and textiles by Ted Ramsay.

De-luxe, large-scale wallpapers and murals became the company's speciality later in the decade, designed to exploit the artistic potential of screen-printing. The Serigraph 30 collection reflected the unbridled eclecticism of American taste in interior decoration. Patterns ranged from *La Corrida*, designed by Clarence Hawking and showing Picassoesque vignettes of bullfighters, to *Weathervanes*, a whimsical and cartoon-like design by Donald Soderlund. Intense lyrical nature studies were one of Jack Denst's specialities, and the Mural Collection Volume 9 included *The Common*, a design featuring giant silhouettes of plants and grasses, extending the full width and height of the wall.

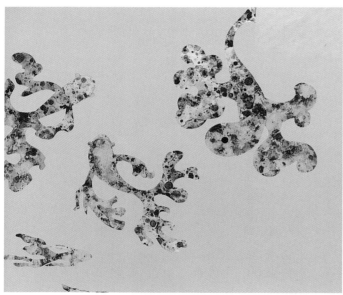

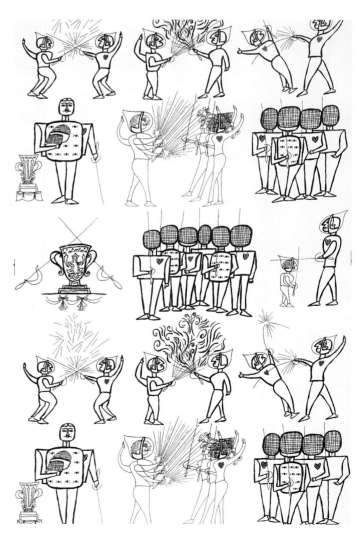

Top Fig. 4.45
Views in Paris screen-printed wallpaper, designed by Saul Steinberg, produced by Piazza Prints, 1946. Before joining New Yorker magazine in 1941, the Russian-born cartoonist Saul Steinberg studied architecture in Milan during the 1930s, an interest reflected in this design.

Above Fig. 4.46
Emperor's Gold Fish photogravure-printed wallpaper, produced by Katzenbach & Warren, 1954. The unusual textures in this pattern, part of the American Futures collection, arise from the adoption of the new photogravure printing process.

Above right Fig. 4.47
Arabian Nights mezzotone-printed wallpaper, designed by Ilonka Karasz, produced by Katzenbach & Warren, 1948. Produced as part of the Mezzotone Papers, this illusionistic mural wallpaper is illustrated in situ as part of a theatrical, playful, fantasy interior.

Right Fig. 4.48
Fencers screen-printed wallpaper, designed by John Rombola, produced by Harben Papers, 1968. The mood of frivolity introduced into American wallpapers by Saul Steinberg after the war was perpetuated by John Rombola two decades later.

Sweden: Nordiska Kompaniet

The creative seeds sewn by Astrid Sampe at Nordiska Kompaniet Textilkammare (NK Textile Design Studio) before and during the war bore fruit during the 1950s – an astonishingly bountiful era for pattern design. The passion for wild flowers was overtaken by an enthusiasm for abstraction, and Sampe entered her "Mondrianist" phase, producing series of serene abstract-geometric designs. Between 1954 and 1959 she created an impressive group of highly sophisticated, minimalist patterns, including *Lazy Lines*, *Modulor*, *Thermidor*, *Toros*, and *Windy Way*, characterized by vertical stripes pierced at intervals by rhythmic diagonals or arrowheads (fig. 4.50). Minute attention was paid to colour, and the graduated tones of *Windy Way* demonstrated Sampe's mastery of the colour spectrum. "I think a printed pattern should be architectural," she said. "This means that the design should have a basic feeling of either horizontals or verticals or both. Designs should be neat and precise; the broken surface of the hanging cloth will give all the necessary freedom."[41] "Order is liberty" was another of Sampe's maxims, and it was by adopting a systematic approach to design that she created her most inspired patterns.

As well as refining her own designs, Sampe commissioned a large body of work from other designers – some from textile specialists, some from other disciplines – including Carl-Axel Acking, Stig Anker, Ann-Marie Elvius, Ulla Ericson, Gunilla Hörberg, and Bjørn Wiinblad. Keen to push the medium forward, she encouraged designers to express their individuality, often to dramatic effect, as in the frenetic paint splatters of Ynge Gamlin's *Törnrosa* (1954) (fig. 4.51) and the airy spirals of *Looping* (1959) (fig. 4.52) by Lars and Gunilla Johansson. Humour was not forgotten, however, and formed a key feature of Hans Krondahl's *Spefåglar* (1959), with its giant gawky birds, and Stig Lindberg's *Fruktlåda* (1947), depicting slices through fruit, complete with roots and worms (fig. 4.53).

Much of NK's work was experimental, such as the *Photoprint in Focus* exhibition of 1954, which drew on the pioneering research of Arthur Siegel at the Chicago Institute of Design. This featured textiles printed with ghostly images abstracted from photographs, as well as a series of photograms (images created directly on the photographic plate, bypassing the camera). Some designs were extremely dramatic, particularly Sune Sundahl's *Stockholm by Night* and the Spontanism action paintings created by Astrid Sampe (fig. 4.54) and the art critic Ulf Hård af Segerstad. Other designs were quieter and more lyrical, such as *Pipes* by S.D. Bellander, *Strings* by Gunnar Jonson, and *Krattan* by G. Sorvik.

Keen to promote crossover between different disciplines, Sampe "curated" the ambitious Signed Textiles collection in 1954, to which leading Scandinavian artists, architects, and designers contributed. The most unusual participant was the nuclear scientist The Svedberg, who composed a pattern called *Atomics* showing electron configurations and the deflection of charged particles in magnetic

Top Fig. 4.49
Talisman screen-printed wallpaper, produced by Denst & Soderlund, 1952. Recessive in colouring but imaginative in subject matter, this crisply drawn linear pattern in the "Contemporary" style typifies Denst & Soderlund's fresh approach to wallpaper design during the early 1950s.

Above Fig. 4.50
Lazy Lines screen-printed cotton furnishing fabric, designed by Astrid Sampe, printed by Ljungbergs Textiltryck for Nordiska Kompaniet, 1954. Astrid Sampe's fascination with the relationship between textiles and modern architecture is clearly evident in this minimalist striped pattern.

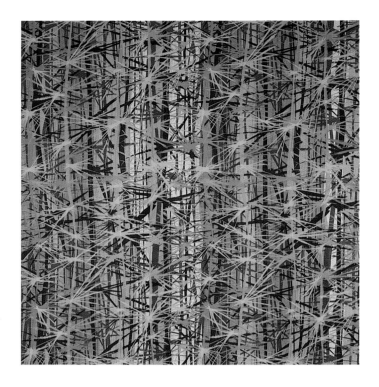

fields. The three architectural contributors, Alvar Aalto, Bengt Lindroos, and Sven Markelius, all favoured pure geometric patterns. Markelius, who had already designed the dazzling *Pythagoras* in 1952, now created *Set Square*, one of a series of variations on a theme (fig. 4.55). Other contributors included the graphic designers Olle Eksell and Anders Beckman, and the artists Olle Baertling, Olle Bonniér, Stellan Mörner, and Karl-Axel Pehrsson, mostly Concretists from the Swedish school of free abstract painting. What was striking about this visionary collection was the imposing scale of the patterns and the bold originality of the compositions, as in *Smoke* by Anders Beckman (fig. 4.56) and *Positiv-Negativ* by Olle Bonniér (fig. 4.57), both refreshingly direct and free. Stellan Mörner's *Comedy Goes* was upbeat and polychrome, whereas Olle Baertling's *Margot* and *Denise* used minimal colour for maximum impact.

Inez Svensson worked briefly in the NK studio during the early 1950s, and other staff designers included Louise Carling and Marianne Nilsson. Sampe's assistant from 1954 to 1960, Nilsson contributed a restrained but stylish group of geometric designs. The most important designer at NK during the first half of the 1950s, however, was Finnish-born Viola Gråsten. Gråsten had moved to Sweden in 1945 and originally joined the studio as a designer of traditional Scandinavian long-pile *rya* rugs. Later she crossed over into printed fabrics, making an extremely original contribution to the range. Free-spirited in her approach to pattern, she combined irregular organic and geometric elements with blazing colours. Dynamic serrated patterns such as *Oomph* (1952) (fig. 4.58) and *Revy* (1954), composed from rings or squares of small triangles, became her signature device. She also designed loose grid patterns with multicoloured squares, such as *Raff*, *Pic Up*, and *Festivo*, and diamond patterns such as *Boogi*, *Delicado* and *Harlekina*, their titles reflecting their upbeat mood.

Sweden: Mölnlycke

In 1956 Viola Gråsten was appointed head of fashion textiles at Mölnlycke, founded in 1849, although her association with NK was perpetuated subsequently through an arrangement whereby some of her designs for Mölnlycke were produced exclusively for NK. Her arrival, along with the appointment in 1957 of Inez Svensson as artistic director at Borås Wäfveri, founded in 1870, was a turning point in the Swedish textile industry. Mölnlycke's first professional designer had been the versatile textile artist Edna Martin, who joined the firm during the early 1940s. At this date Mölnlycke specialized in florals, but in 1951 it produced its first modern abstract printed pattern, *Arches* by Lars-Erik Falk, which won first prize in a Nordic design competition. Gråsten added further impetus to Mölnlycke's modernizing endeavours, and the company went on to produce an adventurous and stimulating range of patterns.

Although many patterns were abstract, the collection also encompassed stylized fruit and flower designs such as Lena

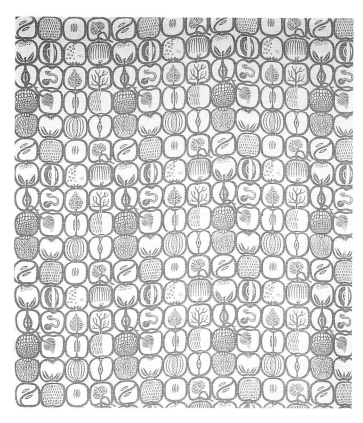

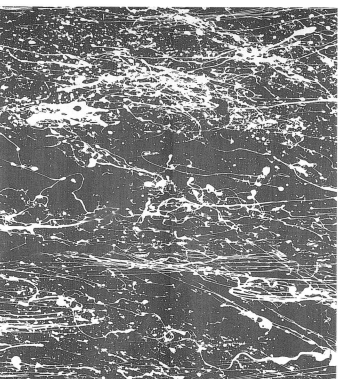

Opposite top Fig. 4.51
Törnrosa screen-printed cotton furnishing fabric, designed by Ynge Gamlin, printed by Ljungbergs Textiltryck for Nordiska Kompaniet, 1954. This dynamic abstract expressionist pattern formed part of the Signed Textiles collection by leading artists, architects, and designers.

Opposite bottom Fig. 4.52
Looping screen-printed fibreglass furnishing fabric, designed by Lars and Gunilla Johansson, produced by Nordiska Kompaniet, 1959. The two columns in this pattern extend the full width of the fabric. An illusion of shifting perspective is created by variation in the thickness of the lines.

Above left Fig. 4.53
Fruktlåda screen-printed cotton furnishing fabric, designed by Stig Lindberg, printed by Ljungbergs Textiltryck for Nordiska Kompaniet. The pronounced organic trends in post-war design are forcefully but amusingly expressed in this ingenious pattern by Stig Lindberg.

Left Fig. 4.54
Spontanism I photo-printed cotton furnishing fabric, designed by Astrid Sampe, printed by Stigens Fabriker for Nordiska Kompaniet, 1954. Keen to explore new technology, Astrid Sampe created this abstract expressionist photogram for the exhibition *Photoprint in Focus* of the same year.

Above Fig. 4.55
Prisma screen-printed linen furnishing fabric, designed by Sven Markelius, produced by Nordiska Kompaniet, c.1958. This subtle geometric pattern was designed by one of Sweden's leading architects, Sven Markelius, whose fabrics for NK were also marketed under licence by Knoll Textiles in the United States.

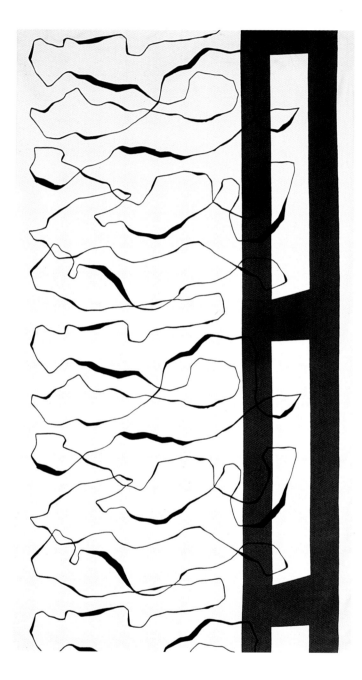

Above Fig. 4.56
Smoke *screen-printed cotton furnishing fabric, designed by Anders Beckman, printed by Ljungbergs Textiltryck for Nordiska Kompaniet, 1954.* This dramatic full-width design was created for the Signed Textiles collection.

Above right Fig. 4.57
Positiv-Negativ *screen-printed linen furnishing fabric, designed by Olle*

Bonniér, printed by Ljungbergs Textiltryck for Nordiska Kompaniet, 1954. A bold abstract designed for Signed Textiles.

Right Fig. 4.58
Oomph *screen-printed cotton furnishing fabric, designed by Viola Gråsten, printed by Ljungbergs Textiltryck for Nordiska Kompaniet, 1952, reprinted 1979.* The composition and colouring of Viola Gråsten's patterns are highly distinctive.

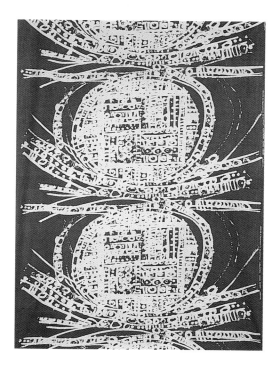

Far left Fig. 4.59
Allegro screen-printed linen furnishing fabric, designed by Annika Malmström, produced by Mölnlycke, 1960. Created with contemporary architecture in mind, this imposing sculptural pattern, by one of Sweden's leading post-war textile designers, extends the full width of the fabric.

Left Fig. 4.60
Betula screen-printed cotton furnishing fabric, designed by Viola Gråsten, produced by Mölnlycke for Nordiska Kompaniet, 1958. Dramatic and architectural in scale, but light and feathery in effect, this full-width design was one of a series by Viola Gråsten inspired by trees.

Trägårdh-Eklund's best-selling *Pomona* (1958). Annika Malmström, a talented and prolific freelance designer, created some of her work for Mölnlycke around this time. Her patterns included unusual interpretations of plant forms, such as *Curbita* (1959), as well as monumental, brooding, textural abstracts such as *Allegro* (1960) (fig. 4.59). Gråsten's own patterns included simple designs with coloured stripes, such as *Pastellrand* (1958), and the explosive circular *Meteor* (1959). She also created an intense and memorable series of tree patterns, including *Betula* (1958), composed of a fine mesh of branches (fig. 4.60), *Trädet* (1963), featuring a massive trunk, and *Hassel* (c.1958–9), with its shower of tiny leaves.

Sweden: Stobo

Other Swedish companies with artistic aspirations included Claes Håkansson, which produced designs by Brita and Lennart Svefors; and Sven Hultberg Textiltryckeri, which collaborated with Per Beckman and Mari Simmulson.But the most progressive new firm of the decade was Stobo, established by Sven Ericsson as a subsidiary of Stockholms Bomullsspinneri in 1954. Under the artistic direction of the fashion designer Göta Trägårdh, Stobo injected a new streak of vitality into Swedish design, using machine screen-printing to produce affordable, well-designed dress and furnishing fabrics. In 1939 Göta Trägårdh and Anders Beckman had co-founded the Beckmans School of Design, specializing in graphics and fashion design, and many of its graduates went on to become successful textile designers. Working alongside Trägårdh at Stobo during the mid-1950s was Inez Svensson, who excelled in stark geometrics such as *Kally* (1955). Trägårdh's own approach was radical and ground-breaking. Her earliest designs included a

drip pattern called *Planeta* and the scribbly, expressionist *Japan I* (fig. 4.61) (both 1954). Even when depicting flowers, as in *Invitation* (1958), she adopted a wiry, sculptural aesthetic (fig. 4.62).

The patterns that Trägårdh commissioned were often equally unconventional and uncompromising, many of them abstract, with brooding black elements, as in *Fagelbur* (1958) by Al Eklund (fig. 4.63). Eklund was a textile specialist, as were two other Stobo designers, Annika Malmström and Ulla Ericson. Other contributors came from a variety of backgrounds, and included Harry Booström, Ulla-Britt Carlsson, Olle Eksell, Age Faith-Ell, Lars-Erik Falk, Lars Gynning, Roland Kempe, Ture Lidström, Pierre Olofsson, Märta Olsson, Karl-Axel Pehrsson, Märit Persson, and Nisse Skoog. Some artists were completely new to the medium, and all were encouraged to take a free-spirited approach. Ultimately the company was ahead of its time, however, and it closed in the mid-1960s.

Denmark: Helga Foght, Ruth Hull, L.F. Foght, and Unika Vaev

Reflecting on the development of Danish textiles, a contemporary observer noted: "The representative designs of the Thirties, and the flower orgies of the Forties, were followed in the Fifties by strict geometrical patterns with rich colour effects achieved by overprinting."[42] Three of those who adopted the new idiom were Arne Jacobsen, Marie Gudme Leth, and Helga Foght, who now made a virtue out of overtly repetitive patterns printed in a limited range of colours. Abandoning small, regimented plant motifs in favour of abstraction, Helga Foght's post-war patterns were sometimes organic, as in *Fuga* (1950) (fig. 4.64), sometimes

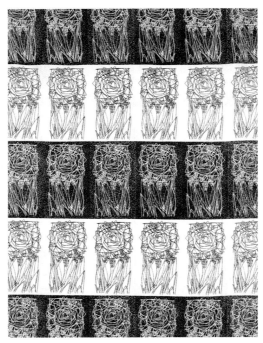

Above Fig. 4.61
Japan I screen-printed cotton furnishing fabric, designed by Göta Trägårdh, originally produced by Stobo, 1954, reprinted by Borås Wäfveri, 1984. Many Swedish designers favoured the graphic austerity of black and white during the 1950s. Here pattern is reduced to a giant scribble.

Above centre Fig. 4.62
Invitation screen-printed cotton furnishing fabric, designed by Göta Trägårdh, produced by Stobo, 1958. Göta Trägårdh had her finger on the pulse of international design in the post-war period. The scratchy lines of this pattern suggest dry-point engraving.

Above far right Fig. 4.63
Fågelbur screen-printed linen furnishing fabric, designed by Al Eklund, produced by Stobo, 1958. The birdcage referred to in the title of this pattern is evoked by the wiriness of the composition. The coarse texture of the linen on which it is printed complements the aesthetic of the design.

Opposite top left Fig. 4.64
Fuga screen-printed cotton furnishing fabric, designed and produced by Helga Foght, 1950. The overlaid motifs in this pattern suggest the free-form organic shapes of contemporary sculpture. Exhibited at the Milan Triennale in 1951, this fabric reflects the cross-fertilization between art and design.

Opposite top right Fig. 4.65
Congo screen-printed cotton furnishing fabric, designed by Ingetoft, produced by L.F. Foght, 1954. Inspired by the grid of streets on a city plan, this pattern characterizes the austere geometric designs of Ingetoft, often featuring white lines on a dark ground.

Opposite bottom right Fig. 4.66
Keramik screen-printed furnishing fabric, designed by Axel Salto, produced by L.F. Foght, 1950. Axel Salto worked as a ceramics designer at the Royal Copenhagen Porcelain Factory. This textile is decorated with images of his idiosyncratic knobbly and spiky organic pots.

painterly and textural, as in *Bark* and *Wood* (both 1958). Also active during the 1950s was Ruth Hull, a textile artist who had established her own workshop in 1935. Specializing in one-off fabrics produced by a combination of dyeing, screen-printing, and painting, she created bold, painterly abstracts with irregular colouring, as well as designing production patterns for Mölnlycke and Unika Vaev.

Restrained linear abstraction became the dominant aesthetic of post-war Danish textiles, epitomized by the patterns of Inge Toft, who had trained with Helga Foght. Taking the professional name Ingetoft, she screen-printed some of her own textiles, while others were produced commercially by L.F. Foght. Characterized by measured white-line patterns on dark-coloured grounds, as in *Metro* (1956), Ingetoft's patterns had a strong graphic identity. The grid-like *Congo* (1954) was specifically inspired by a street map (fig. 4.65). L.F. Foght also produced textiles by several other talented designers, notably Gudrun Stig Aagaard, Axel Salto, William Scharff, and Preben Vangaard. Axel Salto, a ceramic artist at the Royal Copenhagen Porcelain Factory, created a series of highly idiosyncratic patterns from 1944, some of which featured images of his knobbly pots, as in *Keramik* (1950) (fig. 4.66). Other patterns were intensely biological, such as *Levende Sten* (1950), depicting sprouting plant forms. Gudrun Stig Aagaard created powerful flowing contour patterns such as *Lianas* (1951) and *Mohamed* (1953), some produced by L.F. Foght, others printed in her own studio, established in 1928. The tradition of artists printing their own work remained strong in Denmark. Two other accomplished practitioners, both pupils of Marie Gudme Leth, were Dorte Raaschou and Rolf Middelboe.

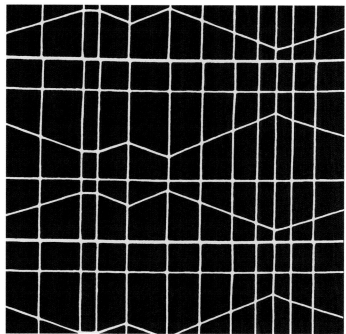

Rolf Middelboe also designed printed textiles for Unika Vaev, a progressive firm specializing in avant-garde rugs, carpets, and furnishing fabrics, owned by Percy von Halling-Koch. Originally trained as a graphic designer, Middelboe specialized in patterns composed of overlapping abstract motifs, such as *Juvel* (1956), where pure colours were contrasted with blended tones. These were intended primarily as works of art, and variants were often produced as wall hangings, such as the wheel-like *Unisol* (1957). The motifs in Middelboe's compositions were often positioned at the edge of the fabric, as in the leaf pattern *Blade* (1955). Another radical artist associated with Unika Vaev during the 1950s was Gunnar Aagaard Andersen, a painter and sculptor enthused by abstract expressionism. His patterns included the striking typographic design *Kronik* (1956), composed of jumbled, truncated lettering, and a series of exuberant action paintings, including *Doodlepoint* and *Doodledash* (both 1956).

Finland: Tampella and Artek

After the Second World War many Finnish textile artists devoted themselves to the production of tapestries and *rya* rugs. Dora Jung, one of Finland's most accomplished weavers, also designed machine-woven linen damasks for Tampella from 1956 to 1972. Her spindly, linear patterns such as *X-tra* (1956) and *Linenplay* (1957) had a similar aesthetic to "Contemporary" fabrics abroad. Printed textiles did not become properly established in Finland until the 1930s, however, following the establishment of Helsingin Taidevärjäämö (Helsinki Art Dyeworks) in 1926. Eva Taimi, its chief designer from 1937 to 1947, specialized in naïve floral designs. Kaj Franck, better known as a ceramics and glass designer,

Above Fig. 4.67
Putkinotko screen-printed cotton
furnishing fabric, designed by Maija
Isola, originally produced by Printex,
1957, reprinted by Marimekko, 2001.
This pattern, with its overlapping
cow parsley silhouettes, makes brilliant
use of the screen-printing process in
the layering of motifs.

also contributed patterns between 1940 and 1945. Printed fabrics were also produced during the 1930s by Artek, Alvar Aalto's furniture company, including stylized florals designed by Aino Aalto. After the war a monochrome abstract idiom was adopted in designs by Alvar Aalto and his second wife, Elissa Aalto.

Finland: Printex and Marimekko

The company that put Finnish printed textiles firmly on the map, however, was Marimekko, which opened up fruitful new avenues for pattern design by exploring the dynamics between furnishing fabrics and dress. Marimekko began life in 1951 as a subsidiary of Printex Oy, established by Viljo Ratia two years earlier to produce hand screen-printed fabrics. Marimekko, which means "a dress for Mary," was the brainchild of Ratia's wife, Armi, and its purpose was to produce clothes using fabrics supplied by Printex. The two companies, which were intimately allied from the start, merged in 1966, when the name Printex was finally dropped in favour of Marimekko. Armi Ratia, who had trained as a textile designer, contributed several early patterns, such as *Faruk* and *Brickstone* (both 1952), although her main role was marketing. During the 1950s most of the patterns were created by two young designers, Maija Isola and Vuokko Eskolin-Nurmesniemi. Maija Isola, who specialized in furnishing fabrics, joined Printex in 1949, fresh from the School of Applied Art in Helsinki, and remained with the company for the rest of her career. Vuokko Eskolin-Nurmesniemi, who originally trained in ceramics, worked for the two companies from 1953 to 1960, designing dress fabrics and fashion for Marimekko and furnishing fabrics for Printex.

From the outset there was considerable cross-fertilization between the two parts of the company, which shared the same ethos and aesthetic. Bucking the trend for tight-fitting tailored fashions and floral prints, Vuokko Eskolin-Nurmesniemi's frocks were loose, even tent-like, with the emphasis on abstract patterns and daring colour combinations. Her furnishing fabrics, such as *Tibet* (1952) and *Rötti* (1954), were characterized by striped patterns of extreme simplicity. They were printed in just two or three colours, but in daring colourways such as maroon and olive, and new composite colours were created where stripes overlapped. This device, which ingeniously overcame the problem of poor printing registration, became a distinctive feature of the Marimekko look, and was also used on *Piccolo* (1954), a pattern with narrow stripes used for Eskolin-Nurmesniemi's classic Everyboy shirts (1956).

Maija Isola, an instinctive pattern designer, experimented during the 1950s with a wide variety of different idioms. Some of her designs were detailed and delicate, such as *Putkinotko* (1957), featuring silhouettes of cow parsley (fig. 4.67), while others were pared down and monumental, as in the large, faceted circles of *Citrus* and *Stones* (both 1956). She also created jolly nursery patterns, such as *Circus* (1956), which showed lions and elephants in striped tents. In 1960 Isola designed a series of patterns inspired by Slovakian folk art, in which broad coloured stripes were overlaid with intricate lacy filigrees. She continued to explore this unusual vein of symbolism during the 1960s alongside her increasingly gigantic abstract patterns.

Scandinavia: Norrköpings, Duro, Vallø, Dahls, and Pihlgren-Ritola

Paralleling the emergence of Swedish, Danish, and Finnish printed textiles, the hitherto undistinguished Scandinavian wallpaper industry rapidly gained confidence during the post-war years. The Swedish firm Norrköpings Tapetfabrik took the lead during the 1930s and 1940s, commissioning patterns from designers such as Josef Frank and Elias Svedberg. Cross-fertilization from textiles was apparent initially in the prevalence of scattered floral motifs. In 1953 the Swedish design magazine *Form* held a wallpaper competition, and the winning pattern, *Slån*, a molecular two-colour abstract by Gerd Göran, was later produced by Norrköpings.

After the war another Swedish firm, Duro, founded in 1930 by Lennart Norström, produced low-key but imaginative abstract patterns by designers such as Carl-Axel Acking, B.B. Bräger, Viola Gråsten, Sven Hesselgren, and Harold Molander. Other progressive firms in Sweden during the 1950s included Kalmar Nya Tapetfabrik and Ljungqvists Tapetfabrik, the second of which worked with Sigvaard Bernadotte. The Swedish designer Folke Sundberg, who specialized in minimalist linear abstracts, collaborated with companies such as Engblads in Sweden (fig. 4.68) and Vallø Tapetfabrik in Norway. Vallø also commissioned a pattern during the early 1950s from the British designer Lucienne Day.

The most high-profile Scandinavian wallpaper designer was the Danish architect Bent Karlby, who collaborated with various companies in different countries after the war. In Sweden he worked with Göteborgs Tapetfabrik, while in Denmark he produced a stimulating group of designs for Dahls Tapetfabrik, ranging from botanical studies such as *Flora Danica* and *Haelderne* (both 1951), to mesh-like abstracts such as *Expansion* (1956). In 1946 Karlby won an American Institute of Decorators wallpaper competition, and the following decade two American companies, Schumacher and Wall Trends, produced his designs. Dahls also collaborated with other leading Danish artists and designers. Their Kunstner Tapet collection (1959–60) was particularly impressive, featuring patterns by major figures such as Acton Bjørn, Preben Dahlström (fig. 4.69), Nanna and Jørgen Ditzel, Ruth Hull, Ingetoft, Arne Jacobsen, Grete Jalk, Tove and Edvard Kindt Larsen, and Rolf Middelboe. Middelboe also designed wallpapers for Danske Tapetfabrikker, while Nanna and Jørgen Ditzel and Gunnar Aagaard Andersen collaborated with Rodia Tapetfabrik.

Even in Finland, hitherto rather backward in the field of wallpapers, the Pihlgren-Ritola company initiated a collection of artist-designed wallpapers in 1958. Contributors included the ceramicists Birger

Above Fig. 4.68
Alle screen-printed wallpaper, designed by Folke Sundberg, produced by Engblads Tapetfabrik, 1953. Scandinavian wallpapers tended to be quieter and more consciously repetitive than their British, European, and American counterparts. The subtle colouring and recessive pattern on this Swedish example are characteristic of the post-war Scandinavian genre as a whole.

Kaipiainen and Rut Bryk, the glass designer Tapio Wirkkala, the lighting designer Lisa Johansson-Pape, the furniture designers Antti Nurmesniemi and Olof Ottelin, the fashion designer Vuokko Eskolin-Nurmesniemi, and the silversmith Börje Rajalin. Complementing its own textiles, Artek also produced a range of minimalist wallpapers designed by Elissa Aalto, including the pattern *H55*, created for a major exhibition of Scandinavian design shown in Hälsingborg, in Sweden, in 1955.

Germany: Stuttgarter Gardinenfabrik, Pausa, Weberei Frittlingen, Alber & Co., and Storck

Art-inspired abstraction was embraced by many German textile companies during the 1950s. Margret Hildebrand, the most accomplished and versatile German pattern designer of the decade, began her long-term alliance with Stuttgarter Gardinenfabrik, founded in 1934, while still a student in 1936. Two years later she was appointed head of the design studio. Originally based in Stuttgart, the company relocated to Herrenberg after the war, and Hildebrand resumed her post as design director during the late 1940s. Her early post-war designs included stylized leaf and tree patterns such as *Empel* (1950) (fig. 4.70) and *Como* (1951). Moving effortlessly between representational and abstract idioms, she also designed controlled geometric patterns such as *Cadiz-10* (1952) and *Baku* (1955) and freer collages such as *Tunis* (1952) and *Mirolo* (1954). Hildebrand also designed ceramic patterns for Rosenthal, as well as being extremely influential in her capacity as professor of textiles at the Hochschule für Bildende Künste in Hamburg from 1956.

Stuttgarter Gardinenfabrik, which also produced designs by Heidi Bernstiel-Munsche and Gisela Thiele, emerged as one of the most confident design-led companies of the 1950s, along with Pausa AG of Mössingen, founded in 1911. Pausa, who had begun screen-printing textiles in 1932, collaborated after the war with designers such as Willi Baumeister, Eberhard Glatzer, Elsbeth Kupferoth, Walter Matysiak, Anton Stankowski, and Vuokko Eskolin-Nurmesniemi. Willi Baumeister was a painter, graphic designer, and theatre designer, whose patterns included unstructured abstracts such as *Montabaur* (1954–5). Scribbles, dots, and free-form shapes characterized the patterns of Elsbeth Kupferoth, such as *Espace* (1954), a playful organic, linear homage to Miró (fig. 4.71). Kupferoth, who had studied at the Textil- und Modeschule in Berlin from 1937 to 1941, also designed coordinated textile and wallpaper ranges for the Stuttgart firm Emtex, including an abstract expressionist pattern called *Sylvana*. In 1956 she established her own company, Textilfirma Kupferoth-Drucke, with her husband, Heinz-Joachim Kupferoth.

The artist Cuno Fischer, who designed printed textiles for Gesellschaft für Elbersdrucke and Weberei Frittlingen, Alber & Co., was another designer whose patterns frequently echoed the aesthetics of contemporary painting and sculpture. The influence

of Miró was clearly apparent in *Gotica* (1955), a white-line pattern on a black background with primary-colour highlights, produced by Weberei Frittlingen, Alber & Co. Music-inspired rhythmic abstraction was another source of ideas, and is reflected in *Blues* (1955), a printed design for Weberei Frittlingen (fig. 4.72), and *Swing*, a woven pattern for Riedlinger Möbelstoffweberei. More measured in tone were the designs of Elisabeth Kadow, who specialized in restrained striped linear abstract patterns, produced by Storck Gebrüder. Storck also collaborated with students from the Werkkunstschule in nearby Krefeld.

Germany: Rasch

In 1949 Rasch relaunched its low-key textural Bauhaus range of wallpapers featuring several new designs by Werner Schriefers with new colouring by Hinnerk Scheper. However, Emil Rasch, the owner of the firm, realized that after the prolonged austerity of the 1940s many consumers were thirsting for pattern. From 1950, therefore, he began to commission a new body of work in more expressive and decorative idioms. In 1939 Rasch had launched its Wiener Künstler-Tapeten, featuring patterns by the veteran Austrian architect Josef Hoffmann, as well as two younger designers, Tea Ernst and Maria May. Some of these designs were reissued in 1950, along with new patterns, as part of the Rasch-Künstler-Tapetenkollektion, which also included designs by Fritz August Breuhaus, Ruth Geyer-Raack, Margret Hildebrand, Ilse Kleinschmidt, Hans Schwippert, and Shinkichi Tajiri. As with her printed textiles, Margret Hildebrand's organic and skeletal leaf and twig patterns characterized the positive, upbeat tone of the post-war era (fig. 4.73). Shinkichi Tajiri, a young Japanese-American sculptor and painter who worked for Rasch during the 1950s in exchange for a student scholarship, took an offbeat approach to wallpaper, creating patterns ranging from *Louisiana*, depicting silhouettes of trees in a forest, to *Paris*, a colourful bird's-eye view of landmarks in the French capital. Because the collection was surface-printed by machine, this made it reasonably priced.

Encouraged by the success of this collection, Emil Rasch invited other leading European artists and designers to contribute to the range, which mushroomed over the next few years, culminating in an exhibition at the Städtischen Museum in Osnabrück called *Künstlerisches Schaffen – Industrielles Gestalten* (Creative Art – Industrial Design) in 1956. By this date Rasch was producing wallpapers by fifty freelance practitioners from ten countries, and among the contributors were Bele Bachem, Klaus Bendixen, Sigvaard Bernadotte, Arnold Bode, Letizia Cerio, Salvador Dalí, Lucienne Day, Jean de Botton, Christiaan de Moor, Cuno Fischer, Hein Heckroth, Irene Kowaliska-Wegner, Sibylle Kringel, Elsbeth Kupferoth, Arthur Langlet, Alfred Mahlau, Brigitte Mitchell-Arnthal, Bruno Munari, Raymond Peynet, Imre Reiner, Bernard Schultze, Renée Sintenis, Adriano Spilimbergo, and Friedrich Vordemberge-Gildewart. The patterns were highly eclectic, reflecting the varied backgrounds of the contributors, and included

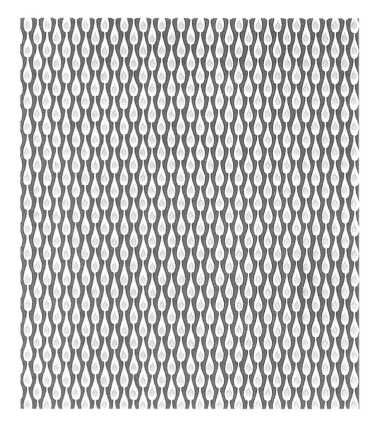

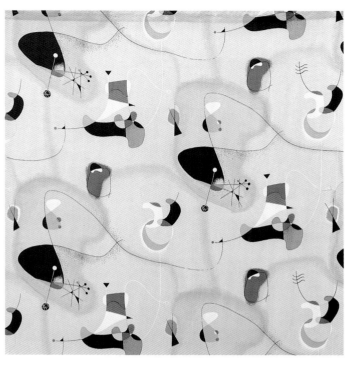

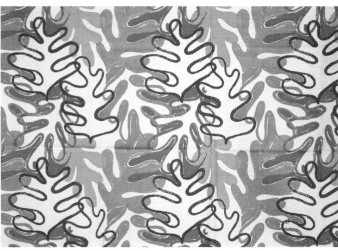

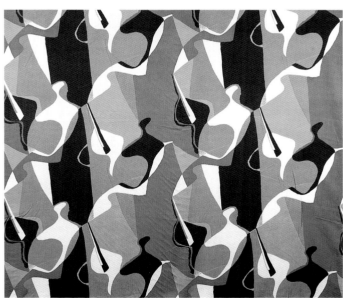

Top Fig. 4.69
Ljus I Flaske block-printed wallpaper, designed by Preben Dahlström, produced by Dahls Tapetfabrik, 1956. Dahls, the most progressive manufacturer of wallpaper in Denmark during the 1950s, favoured low-key abstraction. The title of this pattern means "light in bottles."

Above Fig. 4.70
Empel screen-printed cotton furnishing fabric, designed by Margret Hildebrand, produced by Stuttgarter Gardinenfabrik, 1950. Informality was an important feature of design during the 1950s. This pattern, with its fluid shapes and vibrant colours, captures the buoyant mood of the period.

Top Fig. 4.71
Espace screen-printed rayon furnishing fabric, designed by Elsbeth Kupferoth, produced by Pausa, 1954. Contemporary art exerted a powerful influence on textiles and wallpapers after the war. The paintings of Joan Miró were clearly a direct source of inspiration for this design.

Above Fig. 4.72
Blues screen-printed cotton furnishing fabric, designed by Cuno Fischer, produced by Weberei Frittlingen, Alber & Co., 1955. The lingering influence of Cubism shaped this design, which evokes musicians in a band. Underlying the composition is a pattern of broad vertical stripes.

Top Fig. 4.73
Nachsommer *surface-printed wallpaper,*
designed by Margret Hildebrand,
produced by Rasch, 1950. This
wallpaper formed part of Rasch's
acclaimed artists' collection. Margret
Hildebrand, the leading German
pattern designer of the period,
excelled at stylized nature studies.

Above Fig. 4.74
I Cirri *screen-printed cotton satin*
furnishing fabric, designed by Giò
Pomodoro, produced by J.S.A. Busto
Arsizio, 1957. The winner of a Gran
Premio award at the Milan Triennale
in 1957, this fractured textural abstract,
evoking broken clouds, was designed
by a leading sculptor.

Top Fig. 4.75
Concetto Spaziale *screen-printed cotton*
furnishing fabric, designed by Lucio
Fontana, produced by J.S.A. Busto
Arsizio, 1954. Closely mirroring the
relief effects of the artist's pierced and
slashed canvases, this pattern reflects
the intimate relationship between art
and design in post-war Italy.

Above Fig. 4.76
Notizie No. 5 *printed silk, originally*
designed by Piero Fornasetti, 1950,
produced by Fuggerhaus, 1978. Working
independently of mainstream design
trends, Piero Fornasetti created
timeless surreal *trompe l'oeil* patterns
using printed ephemera from his
extensive archive.

abstract, figurative, narrative, and floral designs, many whimsical and light-hearted in tone. Cuno Fischer and Salvador Dalí took a painterly approach, while Arnold Bode, Lucienne Day, and Bruno Munari explored minimalist abstract vocabularies. A group of young German artists calling themselves Junger Westen (Young West) designed playful modern abstracts for the Künstler Tapeten, and in 1956–7 they created their own collection for Rasch.

Germany: Marburger, Pickhardt & Siebert, and Rheinische Tapetenfabrik

Another German wallpaper company that embraced modern design after the war was Marburger Tapetenfabrik. Originally created as a wholesale merchant in 1845, Marburger became a manufacturer in 1879. Elsbeth Kupferoth, who also designed wallpapers for Bammental, Emtex, and Rasch, created an exclusive range for the company called Collektion Elsbeth Kupferoth. Her work was also marketed as part of Marburger's Neue Form collections of advanced abstract designs, subsequently overseen by Professor Kurt Franz. The factory also collaborated with students from the Werkakademie at Kassel, who supplied patterns for the Neue Wohnung collection under the direction of Hans Leistikow.

Pickhardt & Siebert of Gummersbach also pinned its flag to the mast of "Contemporary" design, excelling in wiry, rhythmic patterns. The company's designers included Georg Hempel, and it also produced patterns by students from the Folkwangschule in Essen. Links between specialist technical schools and the textile and wallpaper industry abounded in Germany during the 1950s, an enduring legacy of the Bauhaus. Bammental (Gebr. Ditzel) teamed up with the Staatliche Kunstschule in Bremen, for example, while a collaboration between the Rheinische Tapetenfabrik and Gerhard Kadow's students at the Werkkunstschule at Krefeld led to an exciting collection in 1953. This featured both whimsical figurative patterns and progressive abstract designs such as *Medium*, composed of clustered dots, and *Reigen*, which suggested a radiating wheel.

Italy: J.S.A. Busto Arsizio and M.I.T.A. di M.A. Ponis

The direct involvement of artists in textile design was very much an international phenomenon during the 1950s. The newly established Italian company J.S.A. Busto Arsizio, founded in 1948 by Luigi Grampa, entered into the fray with gusto, producing screen-printed transcriptions of avant-garde paintings by artists, sculptors and architects, including Gianni Dova, Lucio Fontana, Giò Pavesi, Giò Pomodoro, Giò Ponti, Enrico Prampolini, Ettore Sottsass, Gigi Tessari, and Piero Zuffi. Flamboyant in character and uninhibited in style, many designs made bold use of colour and painterly effects, as in *Spago* (1957) by Gigi Tessari, with its overlapping orange, red, green, and purple flags. Rich textural abstraction was a key feature of many designs, such as *I Cirri* (1957) by Giò Pomodoro, with its broken slits of fragmented pattern

(fig. 4.74). *Cosmico* (1957) by Gianni Dova, an explosive action painting, demonstrated the theory of Spazialismo, the dynamic Italian version of abstract expressionism. The originator of this movement was Lucio Fontana, who created the mesmerizing *Concetto Spaziale* (1954) (fig. 4.75). Closely paralleling his pierced and slashed canvases, this design, which featured rings of tiny craters casting extended shadows, was arguably the most memorable pattern in the range. Not surprisingly, *Concetto Spaziale* was one of several fabrics by J.S.A. Busto Arsizio that won medals at the Milan Triennale in 1957, another being *Fuma di Londra*, a fractured textural abstract by the British designer Daphne Barder.

Another Italian company that produced artists' designs was M.I.T.A. di M.A. Ponis. Its output included tachist abstracts such as *Ormeggio* (1951) by Enrico Paulucci, as well as large screen-printed wall hangings by Eugenio Carmi. Milan-based Manifatture Tessuti Stampati was similarly progressive, producing bold, painterly printed textiles by Gianni Dova and Roberto Sambonet.

Italy: Piero Fornasetti

Not everyone in Italy was convinced of the merits of abstraction, however. Piero Fornasetti countered prevailing artistic trends with his minutely detailed figurative and architectural patterns. The architect Giò Ponti, with whom he frequently collaborated, said of his work in 1962: "In our age of pronounced distrust of decoration, Fornasetti happily reveals its importance."[43] A compulsive collector of printed ephemera, Fornasetti drew on images from his compendious archive to adorn the surfaces of a variety of domestic objects, produced and sold under his own name. His oeuvre was vast, encompassing textiles and wallpapers, ceramics and furniture, as well as accessories such as wastepaper bins and umbrella stands. *Ultime Notizie* (1950), a printed silk fabric decorated with butterflies and flowers scattered on scraps of newspaper, typified his eclectic approach to surface pattern and his fascination with surreal, *trompe l'oeil* effects (fig. 4.76).

Because Fornasetti created his patterns by recycling "borrowed" graphic images, his designs do not fit into any convenient stylistic or chronological category. "I believe neither in periods nor in dates," said Fornasetti. "I refuse to define the value of an object in terms of its era."[44] Self-conscious and theatrical, he revelled in the artificiality of what he was creating. Although his vocabulary was historical, his witty reinterpretation of material culture positioned him firmly in the 20th century. A precursor of Pop Art, Fornasetti was a fully-fledged Post-Modernist decades before the term was even invented. Eduardo Paolozzi, an early admirer of his work, commented in 1957: "I admire the overall approach to design of Piero Fornasetti, who rattles through every subject as an inspiration, proving that interpretation counts for more than inspiration."[45] Although a maverick and a non-conformist, Fornasetti nevertheless made a significant contribution to "Contemporary" pattern design.

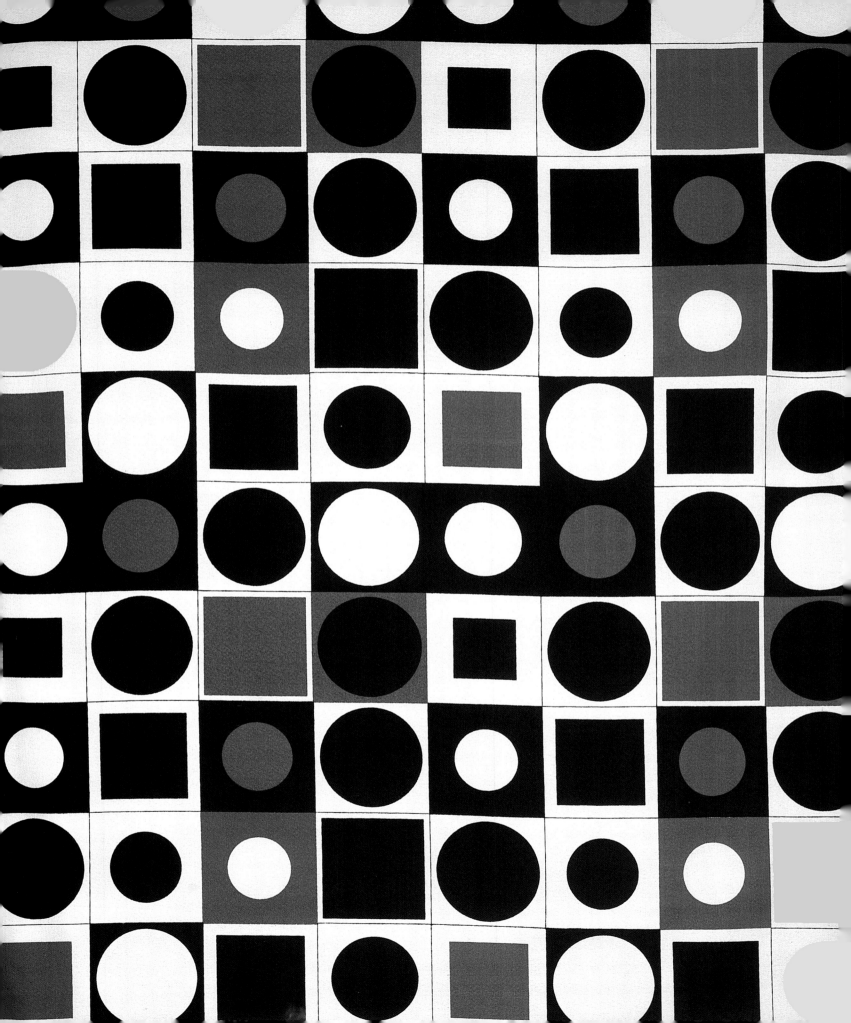

Op, Pop, and Psychedelia

Emboldened by the airy, open spaces of modern interiors, textile and wallpaper designers during the 1960s created furnishing patterns that were increasingly forceful. "I like big work, abstracts and modern florals, the bigger and sloshier, the happier I am," announced the textile designer Tessa Hagity in 1963.[1] Until this time Alexander Calder and Jackson Pollock had been the prevailing idols, but as soon as Bridget Riley and Victor Vasarely came on the scene, everything changed. Suddenly mobiles, doodles, and spasms were out, and circles, squares, and chevrons were in (fig. 5.1). During the mid-1960s geometry ruled, and discs of every description – rings, targets, spirals – dominated pattern design. "The Swinging Sixties, when it happened, did not really start until 1965, but then with an amazing crash of influences that was simply bewildering," recalled the textile and wallpaper designer Edward Pond.[2]

Op Art and Pop Art were key influences. Pop flattened patterns and Op distorted them, adding a stimulating new dimension to pattern design. During the second half of the decade there was a reaction against the excessive objectivity of abstraction. Flower power was immortalized in the craze for flat florals, while psychedelia prompted pattern meltdown, bringing a new intensity and mind-expanding freedom to colour and composition. Countering these futuristic impulses came successive waves of historical revivalism, first the swirls of Art Nouveau, followed by the sunbursts of Art Deco, while hippy wanderlust triggered a growing interest in ethnic patterns. "This year's sources of inspiration are diverse: the Orient, the Odeon and the *Yellow Submarine*," observed Elizabeth Good in 1969.[3]

During the 1960s Britain experienced an explosion of creativity in pattern design. The Carnaby Street "look" transformed not only fashion and graphics, but also textiles, wallpapers, and accessories. Wallpapers flourished in particular, and the 1960s marked the apotheosis of the remarkable Palladio range in Britain and the launch of United DeSoto's astonishing Bravo collection in the United States. In American textiles, Jack Lenor Larsen pioneered a unique programme of eclecticism, and from Finland the exuberant all-conquering Marimekko burst on to the international scene. "In the 60s there was still the sense of our being *design driven*," Larsen remarked forty years later. "Nowadays, when the whole world seems to be market-driven, the 60s were a Good Time, indeed."[4]

Opposite Fig. 5.1
Reciprocation *screen-printed cotton furnishing fabric, designed by Barbara Brown, produced by Heal Fabrics, 1963.* Barbara Brown was one of many young designers during the early 1960s who abandoned loose, painterly abstract expressionism in favour of hard-edged geometric abstraction. Although limited to variations on two shapes and colours, this Op-inspired pattern is extremely dynamic.

Top Fig. 5.2
Lokki *screen-printed cotton furnishing fabric, designed by Maija Isola, produced by Marimekko, 1961.* Maija Isola revolutionized design with her simple, bold, flat patterns, printed on a dramatic scale. The design, whose title means "seagull," evokes the lapping of waves and the flapping of birds' wings.

Above Fig. 5.3
Melooni *screen-printed cotton furnishing fabric, designed by Maija Isola, produced by Marimekko, 1963.* Marimekko fabrics were originally hand screen-printed, and adjacent colours were designed to overlap. Here the giant, melon-shaped target motifs extend the full width of the fabric.

Top Fig. 5.4
Unikko *screen-printed cotton furnishing fabric, designed by Maija Isola, produced by Marimekko, 1964.* This huge, exploded poppy pattern embodies the unbridled design confidence of the mid-1960s, and presages the ebullience and sizzling colours of the flower power era.

Above Fig. 5.5
Screen-printed cotton furnishing fabric, designed by Vuokko Eskolin-Nurmesniemi, produced by Vuokko, 1968. Vuokko Eskolin-Nurmesniemi originally designed for Marimekko before establishing her own company. Large-scale graphic patterns, often in black and white, became her speciality.

Finland: Marimekko

"The Finns' pet textile is printed cotton," wrote Anna Liisa Ahmavaara in 1970. "It walks to meet you in the street, hangs at windows, and upholsters suites."[5] Finnish printed textiles, championed by the charismatic Marimekko, were the big success story of the 1960s, emerging from obscurity to become the most celebrated pattern phenomenon of the decade. Armi Ratia, who ran Marimekko, had a genius for publicity, establishing the company as a leading Finnish brand. The 1960s marked a creative high point for Marimekko, when many of its most adventurous designs were created, printed in vibrant colours on robust cotton cloth. Remarkably, the company relied on hand screen-printing throughout this period, resisting the introduction of rotary screen-printing until the 1970s.

Marrying furnishing fabrics with fashion, Marimekko's larger-than-life patterns and fearless use of colour epitomized the creative openness of the 1960s. A new generation of large-scale patterns for dress fabric patterns was introduced during this period, typified by the magnified ovals of *Lens* (1966) by Kaarina Kellomäki. The doyenne of Marimekko dresses was Annika Rimala, chief fashion designer from 1959 to 1982. Trained in graphics, she designed dramatic patterns, including the scalloped *Laine* (1965) and the giant, scrolling *Oasis* (1966). She also created the cape-like dresses in which these fabrics were so cleverly used.

Maija Isola's furnishing fabrics – precursors of the bold, flat, simple, extra-large effects of 1970s "supergraphics" – were even more daring in colour and scale. Two patterns from 1961 signalled a new era: *Lokki* (fig. 5.2), with its giant undulations, and *Silkkikuikka*, meaning "Great Crested Grebe," with its tripartite coloured bands. Throughout the decade Isola created a string of confident and inspiring fluid abstract designs that combined extreme simplicity of form with striking purity of colour. Mark Rothko's "colour field" paintings may have been subliminal influences, but Isola's designs were graphic rather than painterly, and the idiom she pioneered grew spontaneously out of the medium of screen-printed cloth. Patterns such as *Melooni* (1963) (fig. 5.3) and *Kaivo* (1965) (cover), with their stacked, concentric ovals, and *Siren* (1964), with its broad, snaking stripe, were conceived as continuous vertical repeats, all the more powerful when viewed in long lengths. Rhythm was crucial to Isola's aesthetic, as in the slithering *Gabriel* and the horizontal tentacles of *Albatrossi*.

Isola's patterns embodied all the key elements of 1960s iconography, as well as presaging future trends. Moving seamlessly from ethnic (*Tamara*, 1960) to Op (*Jonah*, 1961) to Pop (*Love, Love, Love*, 1967), she also explored flower power (*Unikko*, 1964) (fig. 5.4), psychedelia (*Emperor's Crown*, 1966), and Space Age design (*Milky Way*, 1969). Her joyful, stimulating designs provide a fascinating reflection of the zeitgeist – free-spirited and forward-looking.

Finland: Vuokko and Metsovaara

Vuokko Eskolin-Nurmesniemi, one of Marimekko's chief designers during the 1950s, established her own company, Vuokko Oy, in 1964. Alongside ready-to-wear fashion, she specialized in dual-purpose dress and furnishing fabrics, screen-printed with simple but dramatic patterns. Circular motifs, sometimes radiating outwards, sometimes collapsing inwards, were a recurrent feature of her patterns, and the launch collection featured the swirling whirlpool design *Pyörre* (1964). Strongly linear and rhythmic, her patterns exerted a forceful graphic impact and were usually limited to a single colour, often black on white (fig. 5.5). "I don't mind when others call me a purist," she reflected. "There are two sides to me: the very clean Vuokko and the fantasy Vuokko. I prefer the clean me. If you are too complicated no-one understands you."[6]

Another high-profile Finnish textile designer who ran her own company was Marjatta Metsovaara, the founder of Metsovaara Oy (later Metsovaara, Van Havere) in 1954. During the 1960s her speciality was rich, textural, brightly coloured woven furnishing fabrics, including flat weaves, pile fabrics, tweeds, and embossed jacquards, produced in integrated, colour-coordinated ranges. Experimenting freely with natural and man-made fibres, Metsovaara produced textiles that were both visual and tactile. Her patterned jacquards included abstracts, ethnics, and florals, the last exemplified by the Primavera range (1967).

Finland: Finlayson-Forssa, Helenius, and Tampella

Marimekko gave a tremendous boost to other Finnish textile manufacturers. Finlayson-Forssa, founded by James Finlayson in 1920 and merged with Forssa in 1934, produced some printed furnishing fabrics by Marimekko's Annika Rimala during the late 1960s, as well as recruiting Pirkko Hammarberg, Helena Perheentupa, and Mirja Tissari to its in-house team. Helenius Oy, a go-ahead firm established in 1960 by Erkki Helenius, was also clearly inspired by Marimekko. Its designers included Rislakki-Aarnio-Blomqvist, Ulla Härkönen, Lissa Keikkilä, Keta Procopé, and Anita Wangel. During the late 1960s Helenius Oy produced patterns featuring blown-up photographs of landscapes and natural phenomena. Another company specializing in bold printed cottons was Porin Puuvilla, founded in 1898, where Timo Sarpaneva was artistic director from 1955 to 1965. He was succeeded by Raili Konttinen, whose highly productive alliance with the company continued into the 1970s.

Tampella, founded as the Tampere Flax and Iron Industry in 1856, produced an inspiring range of printed furnishing fabrics during the 1960s, drawing on the talents of designers such as Olli Mäki and Marjatta Metsovaara. Metsovaara's patterns from the latter part of the decade included both exuberant stylized florals such as *Windflower* and lively colourful rhythmic abstracts such as *Lava*. Tampella's most remarkable collaboration, however, was with Timo Sarpaneva, who developed the radical Ambiente range between

1964 and 1969 (fig. 5.6). Described by the firm as "Shade Prints," these fabrics, decorated with fluid swirled and trailed patterns, were "hand-painted" by robot automation, sometimes on both sides. Initially produced at Tampella's Lapinniemi factory, the Ambiente range was subsequently also manufactured by Finlayson-Forssa, Tampella's sister company.

Although best known as a glass designer, Timo Sarpaneva originally trained as a graphic designer, and taught textile design at the Central School of Industrial Design in Helsinki from 1953 to 1957. During his time at Porin Puuvilla, he also designed printed textiles for PMK, a joint marketing organization servicing Tampella and Finlayson-Forssa. Later, while collaborating with the Swedish company Kinnasand, where he acted as artistic director from 1964 to 1972, he created some remarkably dynamic jacquard-woven Op designs (fig. 5.7).

Sweden: Almedahls

Like their Finnish counterparts, Swedish designers experimented with dramatic full-width patterns during the early 1960s. This trend was reflected in several designs produced by Almedahls, a company founded in 1846 that had previously specialized in woven table linen, but which branched out into printed tablecloths, tea towels, and furnishing fabrics during the 1950s. *Ljung* (1959) by Louise Carling, depicting huge, wiry clumps of heather, and *Flykt* (1962) by Lisa Grönwall, suggesting an abstracted flock of birds (fig. 5.8), were both in this idiom. Later Almedahls worked with Astrid Sampe, head of Nordiska Kompaniet Textilkammare (NK Textile Design Studio), who had already collaborated with the company since 1955 on the Linenline range of table linen. During the mid-1960s Sampe created a startlingly original group of printed patterns, including giant, cartoon-style abstracts and Carnaby Street florals, totally different in character to her earlier, minimalist designs. The rippling Op pattern *Versailles* (1965) and the giant stamen design *Flora Suecana* (1970) represented an unexpected late twist in Sampe's consistently surprising career (fig. 5.10).

Sweden: Mölnlycke, Borås Wäfveri, and KF Interior

Viola Gråsten remained at Mölnlycke (latterly Mölnlycke-Tuppen) until 1973, although the company struggled to maintain its identity after being taken over by Borås Wäfveri in 1966. Gråsten's later patterns, such as *Kardborre* (1965), suggest the influence of Indian and Op design (fig. 5.9). During the 1960s, however, a new generation of pattern designers emerged on the Swedish textile scene. Many gravitated towards Borås Wäfveri, where the open-minded Inez Svensson was art director from 1957 to 1969. Hedvig Hedqvist, head of design at KF Interior (the furnishings division of the Swedish Cooperative Society) from 1967 to 1975, was also extremely receptive to innovation, producing radical designs by Birgitta Hahn and Carl Johan De Geer. Although he was not trained as a textile designer, De Geer displayed a natural talent for

Top Fig. 5.6
Bolero *machine-printed cotton furnishing fabric, designed by Timo Sarpaneva, produced by Tampella, 1968.* The fluid psychedelic patterns in Timo Sarpaneva's revolutionary Ambiente range were "hand-painted" by robot automation. The fabrics could be decorated on both sides.

Above Fig. 5.7
Glan *woven cotton, rayon, and linen furnishing fabric, designed by Timo Sarpaneva, produced by Kinnasand, c. 1966.* Equally adept at 2D and 3D design, Timo Sarpaneva crossed freely between glass and textiles. This woven pattern merges two contemporary idioms, Op and psychedelia.

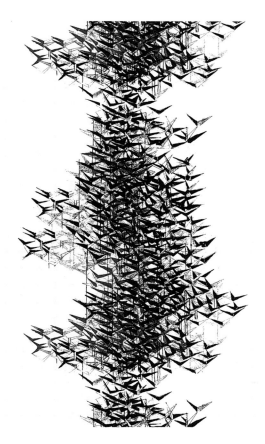

Top Fig. 5.8
Flykt screen-printed cotton furnishing fabric, designed by Lisa Grönwall, produced by Almedahls, 1962. Lisa Grönwall was a member of an Anglo-Swedish design trio called Marstrand Designers, founded in 1959 with Maj Nilsson and Cliff Holden. The group practised internationally.

Above Fig. 5.9
Kardborre screen-printed linen furnishing fabric, designed by Viola Grästen, produced by Mölnlycke, 1965. During the 1960s a wide variety of styles were absorbed into the creative melting pot. The influences of both Op Art and Indian textiles can be detected in this pattern.

Top Fig. 5.10
Flora Suecana screen-printed polyester and linen furnishing fabric, designed by Astrid Sampe, produced by Almedahls, 1970. Also known as *Santa Cruz*, this exotic, large-scale pattern, suggesting giant stamens, illustrates the continued inventiveness and adventurousness of Astrid Sampe.

Above Fig. 5.11
Brooklyn screen-printed cotton furnishing fabric, designed by Inez Svensson, produced by Borås Wäfveri, 1961. Inez Svensson, a major figure in Swedish textiles since the 1960s, excelled in striped patterns, creating innumerable subtle and inspiring variations on this theme.

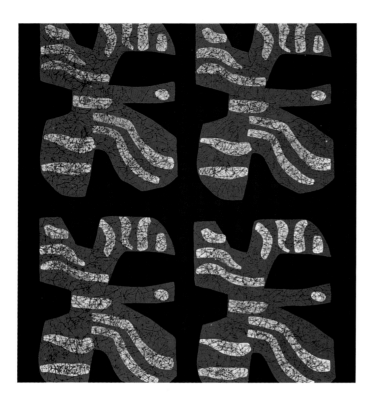

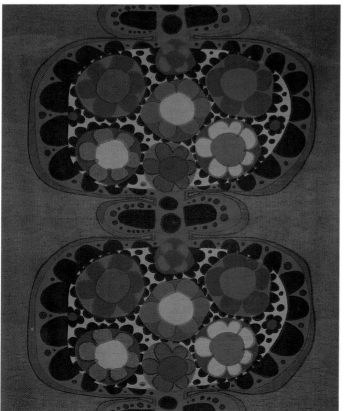

pattern-making in his printed fabrics for the Fontessa workshop during the mid-1960s. His idiosyncratic style and wayward vocabulary always set his patterns apart from the mainstream.

In her own patterns for Borås Wäfveri, Inez Svensson favoured a strongly graphic, reductivist approach, typified by disciplined architectural designs such as *Brooklyn* (1961), which was composed of coloured bands overlaid with fine black stripes (fig. 5.11), and *Tivoli* (1961), featuring large circular motifs on alternating white and coloured squares. Later she introduced a range of basic, no-nonsense striped fabrics, such as *Camelot* (1965), which were highly sophisticated and yet consciously under-designed. "All the problems that occur when you're dealing with writing come up again in pattern making," explained Svensson, "the importance of spaces, the tensions and contrasts between different surfaces, how the shapes bunch together, having to divide the pattern image evenly over the surface."[7] In 1965 she was joined at Borås Wäfveri by Sven Fristedt, who had previously created stunning dress fabrics for Katja of Sweden (Sweden's answer to Mary Quant). Fristedt immediately made his mark with the pattern *Oppo* (1966), composed of jumbled fragments of target motifs, spots, and zebra stripes. Later he designed a series of dazzling Op florals and lively scrolling Pop patterns, printed in vivid colours, especially yellow and green.

Among other designers whose work was produced by Borås Wäfveri during the late 1950s and the 1960s were Gunila Axén, Vuokko Eskolin-Nurmesniemi, Lisa Gustafsson, Lotta Hagerman, Birgitta Hahn, Hans Krondahl, Kerstin Persson, Saini Salonen, Thea Turner, Ritwa Wahlström, and Helene Wedel. Hans Krondahl, a leading textile artist with a parallel interest in production design, created bold, colourful collage patterns resembling his textile hangings. Some, such as *Captain Cook* (1968), featured large, irregular appliqué-like motifs with the authentic craquelure of wax-resist batiks (fig. 5.12). Saini Salonen's fantastical bulbous compositions, suggesting giant insect antennae and exotic flowers, were a remarkable feature of Borås Wäfveri's output during the late 1960s (fig. 5.13).

Birgitta Hahn's "neo-simple" poppy pattern *Vallmo* (1968) (fig. 5.14), produced by Borås Wäfveri from 1970, was a classic of hippy chic. Gunila Axén's *Moln*, depicting flat, white clouds against a bright-blue sky, was even more disarmingly simple (fig. 5.15). Initially produced by Borås Wäfveri in 1967, and later by KF Interior, it sold in huge quantities during the 1970s, becoming an icon of Swedish design. Several of Axén's subsequent patterns for Borås Wäfveri featured single "primitive" motifs, such as lions or geese, repeated *ad infinitum*. Radical in their gaucheness, these patterns paved the way for the formation of the Tio-Gruppen (Ten Swedish Designers), an artist-led collective established in 1970.

Denmark: Unika Vaev

Unika Vaev's reputation as the most adventurous textile company in Denmark was confirmed in 1960 when it began to produce a

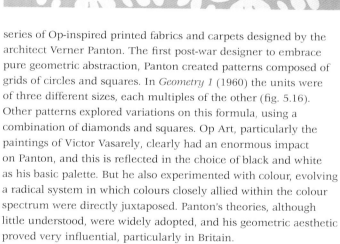

series of Op-inspired printed fabrics and carpets designed by the architect Verner Panton. The first post-war designer to embrace pure geometric abstraction, Panton created patterns composed of grids of circles and squares. In *Geometry 1* (1960) the units were of three different sizes, each multiples of the other (fig. 5.16). Other patterns explored variations on this formula, using a combination of diamonds and squares. Op Art, particularly the paintings of Victor Vasarely, clearly had an enormous impact on Panton, and this is reflected in the choice of black and white as his basic palette. But he also experimented with colour, evolving a radical system in which colours closely allied within the colour spectrum were directly juxtaposed. Panton's theories, although little understood, were widely adopted, and his geometric aesthetic proved very influential, particularly in Britain.

Britain: Textiles

In 1963 *The Ambassador* noted: "Enlightened post-war British art education and a new direction from industry is now bearing fruit with a crop of young designers whose work has given British textiles a fresh impetus. Their imaginative fantasy finds epic qualities in everyday objects: advertising, graffiti, child-art, the wide and small screen, all the paraphernalia of modern living. In this they have much in common with 'pop' art; a sentimental sardonic and positive expression of our time."[8] The 1960s was a schizophrenic period for British textiles, at once buzzing and depressing. The industry was awash with lively young designers fresh out of art school, and many companies enthusiastically embraced modern design. In Manchester the Cotton Board's

Opposite top Fig. 5.12
Captain Cook stencilled wax-resist cotton furnishing fabric, designed by Hans Krondahl, produced by Borås Wäfveri, 1968. A long-standing fascination with batik prompted the Swedish textile artist Hans Krondahl to collaborate with Borås Wäfveri on a collection of richly coloured, stencilled wax-resist patterns.

Opposite bottom Fig. 5.13
Mykerö screen-printed cotton furnishing fabric, designed by Saini Salonen, produced by Borås Wäfveri, 1967. Flower power meets psychedelia in this vibrant flat floral pattern. The use of heightened colours of the same intensity was a distinctive feature of the period.

Above left Fig. 5.14
Vallmo screen-printed cotton, designed by Birgitta Hahn, 1968, produced by Borås Wäfveri, 1970. Birgitta Hahn sought to introduce a pared-down "neo-simple" aesthetic into Swedish printed textiles at the end of the 1960s. This poppy design was her calling card.

Above Fig. 5.15
Moln screen-printed cotton, designed by Gunila Axén, produced by Borås Wäfveri, 1967. Well ahead of its time when it first appeared, this disingenuously naïve cloud pattern did not become a commercial success until it was reintroduced by KF Interior in the 1970s.

Top Fig. 5.16
Geometry 1 wool carpet and screen-printed cotton furnishing fabric, designed by Verner Panton, produced by Unika Vaev, 1960. The impact of Verner Panton's Op-inspired textiles – seen here in an installation in Zurich in 1961, along with his furniture for Plus-linje – was arresting.

Above Fig. 5.17
Decor screen-printed cotton satin furnishing fabric, designed by Barbara Brown, produced by Heal Fabrics, 1967. Heal Fabrics adopted an uncompromisingly modern approach to pattern during the 1960s spurred on by Barbara Brown, its most adventurous designer.

Colour Design and Style Centre worked tirelessly to promote links between designers and manufacturers, mounting a series of inspirational exhibitions. *The Ambassador* likewise took a highly creative and proactive approach to the marketing of British textiles.[9]

Meanwhile the infrastructure of the country's textile industry was rapidly collapsing, mainly because of cut-price foreign competition. Exports plummeted and imports escalated, prompting mergers such as that between the once-powerful Calico Printers Association (CPA) and Tootal in 1968. Another destabilizing factor was the shift from cotton to synthetics, which radically altered the balance of commercial power and strengthened competition from the United States. The rise of synthetics-led Courtaulds prompted dramatic upheavals, such as the takeover of Morton Sundour in 1963. Many of the most successful printed furnishing textile companies at this time were, in fact, converters rather than manufacturers. This was how Heal Fabrics, Fidelis, and Cavendish Textiles (part of the John Lewis Partnership) operated, and eventually this was the direction in which other firms, such as Warner, opted to go. Companies with a manufacturing base, such as David Whitehead, struggled to survive. The 1960s ended on a gloomy note, with many firms closing. And, despite its heroic achievements, the Colour Design and Style Centre was shut down abruptly in 1969.

Britain: Heal Fabrics

Having established its design supremacy during the 1950s, Heal Fabrics moved up another gear during the 1960s, thriving under the confident leadership of Tom Worthington, "the most brilliant and dynamic impresario/converter in the business."[10] Lucienne Day, the company's foremost post-war designer, continued to produce outstanding patterns. Among these were textural prints such as *Cadenza* (1961), collage botanicals such as *Rock Rose* (1961), ingenious geometrics such as *Dovetail* (1965), flat florals such as *Pennycress* (1966), and futuristic abstracts such as *Helix* (1970). These designs alone would have assured the company's reputation, but as well as buying patterns from Day, and other well-established designers, including Friedlinde di Colbertaldo Dinzl and the artist Paule Vézelay, Worthington built up relationships with successive generations of young art-school graduates.

Mixing tried-and-tested talent with regular infusions of new blood proved a highly successful formula, since it allowed top designers to be informally "retained" at the same time as new faces were nurtured. Working with more designers than any company since the Wiener Werkstätte, the far-sighted Tom Worthington – "the eminence anything but grise of Heal Fabrics"[11] – put an astonishing range of textiles into production during the 1960s, averaging thirty each year. His adventurous approach was lauded in an article in *The Ambassador* in April 1966 entitled "Hip Hip Heals!": "Stimulating, encouraging, prodding and persevering in his search for designers, he produces each season a collection which draws on talent from both recognised and new sources. To young designers

Left Fig. 5.18
Automation screen-printed cotton crepe
furnishing fabric, designed by Barbara
Brown, produced by Heal Fabrics, 1970.
Barbara Brown began to explore three-
dimensional effects in some of her
later patterns. This design was part of
a series inspired by technical drawings.

Heal's spells hope, and many established textile design names got their first chance under the Worthington wing."

Barbara Brown, Heal's most high-profile designer at this time, began supplying designs in 1958 after studying at the Royal College of Art. Her earliest patterns were rather mannered and painterly, and it was only after embracing the discipline of pure geometry that she found her true design identity (fig. 5.1). *Recurrence* (1962), with its column of discs in squares, signalled transformation. Other patterns, such as *Piazza* and *Colonnade* (both 1964), drew on the same vocabulary but varied the dynamic and modified the alignment and scale. Brown's ability to work on a massive scale suited the architectural aspirations of the period (fig. 5.17). In later designs, such as *Expansion* (1966) and *Frequency* (1969), she experimented with optical distortions. Three-dimensional geometry was explored in ingenious *trompe l'oeil* patterns, including *Construction* (1966) and *Complex* (1967), complete with false perspective. This trend culminated in a series of giant, quasi-mechanistic designs suggesting magnified images of huge springs and wheels, such as *Spiral* (1969) and *Automation* (1970) (fig. 5.18). According to *Design* magazine, "Miss Brown says quite firmly that she never consciously designs with either fashion or the commercial market in mind, but works more like a painter, in that her designs – all of which have a characteristic three-dimensional quality – evolve and develop over a period of time. Earlier designs were clearly influenced by geological studies, the current ones by technical drawings."[12]

Equally adventurous was Doreen Dyall, whose early forte was textural abstracts such as the subtle *Cumulus* (1961). However, when design veered in a different direction, she switched to outsize geometrics, creating severe patterns, including *Alternation* and *Repetition* (both 1962). Dyall continued exploring different strains of abstraction for the rest of the decade, sometimes treating the cloth as a canvas, as in the painterly *Composition* (1964), but at other times taking a more controlled graphic approach, as in the exploded, cartoon-like *Creation* (1968) (fig. 5.19). Another prominent designer for Heal Fabrics was Jyoti Bhomik, a graphic designer trained at the Central School (fig. 5.21). Bhomik combined Indian-inspired motifs with a Carnaby Street palette, creating Anglo-Asian patterns with a lively Pop flavour, such as *Indian Summer* (1966) and *Persian Garden* (1968). Peter Hall was another regular contributor, skilled in reducing natural forms to their simplest, flattest elements. Designs such as *Petrus* (fig. 5.20) and *Tivoli* (both 1967) had an organic-psychedelic character, overlaid with hints of Art Deco and Art Nouveau. Haydon Williams, who joined the design team towards the end of the decade, created patterns that were similarly arresting and topical. In *Extension* and *Suspension* (both 1968) he converted the dazzling effects of Op paintings into fluid, workable textile designs (fig. 5.23).

The standard of design at Heal Fabrics was exceptionally high, and many designers made memorable contributions. Landmark patterns included *Sunflowers* (1962) by Howard Carter, marking the culmination of a vogue for giant botanicals that had begun

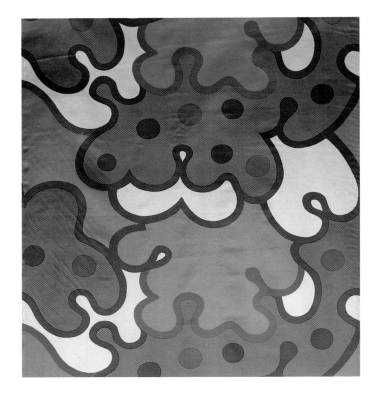

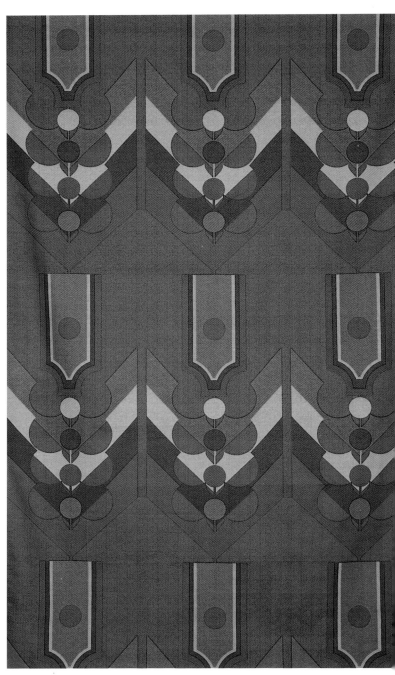

Top Fig. 5.19
Creation *screen-printed cotton satin furnishing fabric, designed by Doreen Dyall, produced by Heal Fabrics, 1968.* Doreen Dyall mined many veins of abstraction in her patterns over the course of the decade. The melted forms and cartoon style of this design typify the late 1960s.

Above Fig. 5.20
Petrus *screen-printed cotton crepe furnishing fabric, designed by Peter Hall, produced by Heal Fabrics, 1967.* This large-scale pattern, which extends the full width of the fabric, has a similar aesthetic to contemporary animated films such as the Beatles' *Yellow Submarine* of the following year.

Above Fig. 5.21
Insignia *screen-printed cotton crepe furnishing fabric, designed by Jyoti Bhomik, produced by Heal Fabrics, 1970.* Jyoti Bhomik originally trained as a graphic designer, which explains the visual clarity of this pattern. Hot colours played a central role in his decorative palette.

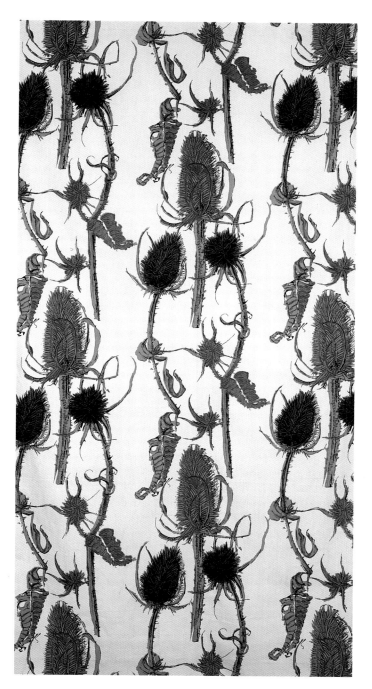

Above Fig. 5.22

Teasle *screen-printed cotton furnishing fabric, designed by Jane Daniels, produced by Heal Fabrics, 1960.* Magnified botanical designs were popular at the start of the 1960s, and this is a particularly masterly example. The spiky plant forms mirror the sculpture of the period.

Top Fig. 5.23

Suspension *screen-printed cotton furnishing fabric, designed by Haydon Williams, produced by Heal Fabrics, 1968.* Op Art provided a great stimulus to designers throughout the 1960s. The logic of this pattern would have seemed more apparent when the fabric was viewed in folds.

Above Fig. 5.24

Tobago *screen-printed cotton crepe furnishing fabric, designed by Althea McNish, produced by Heal Fabrics, 1961.* At the start of the 1960s loose, painterly abstraction dominated pattern design. Althea McNish excelled in this genre, and her patterns were suffused by radiant colour.

with designs such as *Teasle* (1960) by Jane Daniels (fig. 5.22). Also popular at the start of the decade were grainy, graduated abstracts such as Nicola Wood's *Vibration* (1962), and expressionistic florals such as *Flora Bella* (1960) by Robert Dodd, with its virtuoso daubs and trickles of paint, and *Tobago* (1961) by Althea McNish (fig. 5.24). McNish, who collaborated with many leading firms, including Cavendish Textiles, Danasco, Hull Traders, Liberty, and the WPM, was one of the most successful designers of the period. Born in Trinidad, she settled in Britain in 1951 and initially trained as an architect and graphic designer before studying textiles at the Central School and the Royal College of Art. In her dazzling, impressionistic florals, pattern dissolved in a sea of blazing, saturated colours.

Circle motifs were all-pervasive at Heal Fabrics, from the giant fragmenting orbs of Fay Hillier's *Corona* (1961) to the quartic rings of Mo Sullivan's *Catena* (1964), to the flat discs of Peter McCulloch's *Project* (1968). Offset circles formed the basis of Evelyn Brooks's striking black-and-white pattern *Impact* (1965), created at the height of Op mania. Hard on the heels of Op came flower power and psychedelia, both combined in Colleen Farr's cartoon-style *Cloister* (1968). The heady, late-1960s design cocktail was further intensified by liberal injections of Art Nouveau and Art Deco revivalism, the latter reflected in the ziggurats of Cathryn Netherwood's *Spectrum* (1970). Orientalism, another potent theme, surfaced in patterns such as the Persian-inspired *Trellis* (1968) by Robert Dodd. Dodd, who ran a joint studio with his wife Fay Hillier, worked for many leading firms, including Edinburgh Weavers, Mackinnon & Jenkins, Sanderson, Bernard Wardle, David Whitehead, and Mölnlycke in Sweden, in which country he had trained for a time. In 1965 his work was featured alongside that of Barbara Brown and Shirley Craven in a high-profile exhibition at the Whitworth Art Gallery in Manchester.

The roll-call of designers at Heal Fabrics was very impressive, numbering over eighty individuals during the 1960s alone. A significant number of European designers contributed patterns, and in 1964 a German branch, Heal Textil GmbH, was established. New contributors who fed into Heal's over the course of the decade included Liv Arveson, David Bartle, Wolfgang Bauer, Giorgio Bay, Robert Birch, Wolfgang Buller, Pamela Colledge, Henrietta Coster, Susan Crook, Gay Dulley, Hamdi El Attar, Colleen Farr, Anne Fehlow, Sigrid Fettel, Frederick Fuchs, Natalie Gibson, David Green, Michael Griffin, Beth Hall, Mary Harper, Michael Hatjoullis, Judith Henderson, Cliff Holden, Hansjürgen Holzer, Caroline Irving, Richard Jarvis, Kristina Vaughan Jones, Hans Juda, Ruth Kaye, Brian Knight, Colin Lacey, Janet Lacey, Monica Lorentzen, Joan McFetrich, John Miles, James Morgan, Regina Moritz-Evers, Maj Nilsson, Ann Ogle, Carola and Daniel Olsen, Evelyn Pauker, Barbara Payze, Barbara Pegg, Peter Perritt, John Plumb, Zandra Rhodes, Dorothy Smith, Margit Steiner, Annikki and Ilmari Tapiovaara, Janet Taylor, Arno Thöner, Tiny van Alphen,

D. van Golden, Isabel Watson, and John Wright. Realizing that experimentation represented a sound investment, Tom Worthington reflected in 1968: "It may take a year or longer for a really advanced design to start selling. And sometimes an avant-garde design – although not selling itself – can gain so much publicity it will help create a market for similar designs."[13] His retirement in 1971 marked the end of an era. No company has since come near to equalling the achievements of Heal Fabrics in the field of modern printed pattern design.

Britain: Hull Traders

Heal's closest rival in artistic terms was Hull Traders, whose fabrics – marketed under the name Time Present – were wholly committed to a contemporary aesthetic. Shirley Craven, who joined the company as design and colour consultant in 1960 after studying at the Royal College of Art, was chief designer, and a director from 1963. With the support of the managing director, Peter Neubert, Craven refined the firm's design policy, while retaining its original experimental edge. Initially based at Willesden, in London, Hull Traders relocated its factory to Trawden, Lancashire, in 1961, where fabrics were hand screen-printed using mainly pigment dyes. Pigment dyes, which float on the surface rather than penetrate the cloth, were simpler to process than vat dyes. As *Design* noted in 1963: "The choice of dyestuff and processing technique are appropriate to the scale and nature of the firm's business, which is to produce short runs of forward-looking and experimental designs."[14] Although the firm doubled in size, employing twenty-seven people by 1969, it was small compared with most other textile manufacturers, which allowed it greater flexibility. Shirley Craven kept a close eye on production, ensuring that designers' intentions with regard to texture and colour were respected in the printed cloth.

Craven herself flowered as a designer during the 1960s, winning a string of Design Centre Awards. Early designs, such as *Le Bosquet* (1959), were loose and textural, although gradually her patterns took on greater definition. *Pasco* (1962) suggested overlaid scraps of tissue paper, while *Redland* (1963) was composed of torn coloured strips. *Shape* and *Division* (fig. 5.28) (both 1964) combined the boldness of abstract painting with the flatness of collage, and were printed in intense colours on a dramatic scale. After a brief foray into pure geometric patterns, spontaneity broke out again in the unruly *Five* (1966) (fig. 5.27) and *Simple Solar* (1967), composed of overlapping, striated, cloud-shaped forms. *Design* noted in 1968: "Shirley Craven says that she usually works out her ideas not just as two-dimensional textiles but in a series of related designs. Thus, *Simple Solar* and *Five* were developed side by side with drawings, paintings, and experiments in three-dimensional ideas."[15]

Given a completely free hand in choosing the rest of the company's range, Craven adopted an extremely adventurous buying policy. "Textiles should be an artistic field, not just a

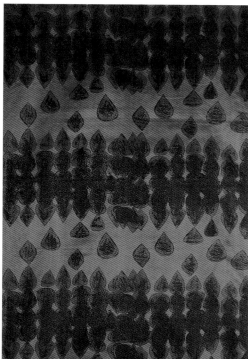

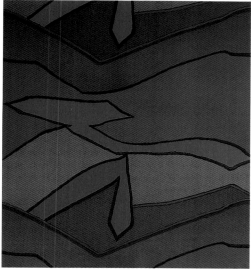

Far left top Fig. 5.25
Metropolis screen-printed cotton satin *furnishing fabric, designed by Mea Angerer, produced by Hull Traders, 1962.* Operating on a smaller scale than Heal Fabrics, but pursuing equally rigorous design standards, Hull Traders produced some of the most progressive patterns of the decade.

Far left bottom Fig. 5.26
Struan screen-printed cotton satin *furnishing fabric, designed by Peter McCulloch, produced by Hull Traders, 1962.* Taste in colour was extremely adventurous during the 1960s. The combination of pink and red in this fabric would not have seemed extraordinary at the time.

Top left Fig. 5.27
Five screen-printed linen and cotton *furnishing fabric, designed by Shirley Craven, produced by Hull Traders, 1966.* Shirley Craven was the creative driving force behind Hull Traders. This unusual crayon-like pattern, and the collage-style *Division* (centre left), both won Design Centre Awards.

Centre left Fig. 5.28
Division screen-printed cotton satin *furnishing fabric, designed by Shirley Craven, produced by Hull Traders, 1964.* Exploiting Hull Traders' expertise in hand screen-printing, this pattern sets up a striking contrast between sombre, dark colours and a streak of bright red.

Bottom left Fig. 5.29
Sigma screen-printed cotton satin *furnishing fabric, designed by Elizabeth Armstrong, produced by Hull Traders, 1962.* Named after a Greek letter, this pattern is composed of a single, repeated, horizontal, S-shaped motif, printed in three alternating colours.

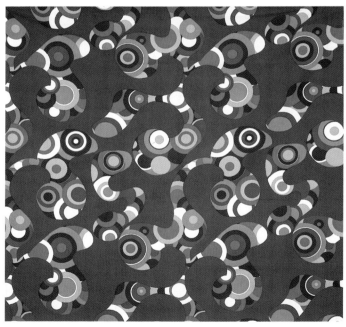

commercial transaction," she believed.[16] Fearless experimental abstraction was the norm, as reflected in Peter Perritt's free painterly *Pintura* and Mea Angerer's brooding sculptural *Metropolis* (fig. 5.25) (both 1962). Even florals were clothed in the guise of abstract expressionism in the intense sensuous designs of Althea McNish. *Struan* (1962) and *Cruachan* (1963), both by the talented Scottish designer Peter McCulloch, featured dramatic, irregular surges of matter (fig. 5.26). Elizabeth Armstrong's *Sigma* (1962), a scintillating pattern composed of overlapping S-shaped motifs, won a Cotton Board Design Award (fig. 5.29), as did Michael Taylor's *Queen of Spain* (1963), with its clustered, pod-shaped forms (fig. 0.3).

Many of Hull Traders' designers collaborated with Heal Fabrics, and there were strong cross-currents between the two companies. Each, however, projected its own distinctive character, Hull Traders being more committed to pure abstraction and less interested in passing trends. When prevailing fashion was embraced, as with Op Art, this was given a fresh interpretation. "The designer's attitude should be flexible, constantly exploring," said Humphrey Spender, a leading artist-designer who supplied patterns to several major firms, including Hull Traders, while teaching at the Royal College of Art.[17] The company's visionary nature shone through in its remarkable collections. Other contributors included Richard Allen, Joao Artur, Margaret Cannon, Dorothy Carr, Trevor Coleman, Susan Dewick, Roger Dickinson, John Drummond, Doreen Dyall, Derek Ellwood, Olive Fisher, Natalie Gibson, Linda Harper, Ivon and John Hitchens, Bernard Holdaway, Cliff Holden, Flavia Irwin, Guy Irwin, Roger Limbrick, Alexander MacIntyre, Kathleen May, Hugh McKinnon, James Morgan, Maj Nilsson, Ann Ogle, Robert Smyth, Robert Tierney, Molly White, and Susan Williams-Ellis. New patterns by Shirley Craven continued to appear until around 1973. Later, however, Hull Traders lost its creative momentum. In 1980 the company was taken over by Badehome, and two years later it was closed.

Britain: Warner

During the 1950s Warner's printed fabrics collection had been somewhat eclectic owing to the high proportion of bought-in designs. Later, however, greater coherence was achieved by narrowing down the number of different sources and building a strong in-house studio team. John Wright supplied designs during the early 1960s, along with Friedlinde di Colbertaldo Dinzl, a high-profile Italian freelance designer, who was a regular contributor for several years. Adept at modifying her style to suit prevailing trends, Dinzl created painterly abstracts such as *Sequence* (1963), Art Nouveau Revival designs such as *Mucha* (1962) and *Bernhardt* (1964), and psychedelic paisleys such as *Pavlova* (1967), the latter inspired by an early 18th-century Spanish brocade (fig. 5.30).

Following the model of its American sister company, Greeff Fabrics, Warner introduced themed collections in 1965. Created mainly by staff designers, including Jennifer Lowndes (1959–67),

Top Fig. 5.30
Pavlova screen-printed cotton furnishing fabric, designed by Friedlinde de Colbertaldo Dinzl, produced by Warner & Sons, 1967. Although inspired by an 18th-century Spanish brocade, this pattern bears the stylistic hallmarks of the late 1960s, particularly its psychedelic colouring.

Above Fig. 5.31
Delores screen-printed cotton furnishing fabric, designed by Eddie Squires, produced by Warner & Sons, 1965. The baubles in this pattern – produced as part of the Theme on the Thirties Collection – vaguely allude to Art Deco, while the melted scrolls appear to evoke Art Nouveau.

Sue Palmer (1967–71), and Eddie Squires (1963–93), Warner's Studio Collections marked a radical departure in the mid-1960s. Even at the end of the decade a commentator remarked that the company's "of-this-moment colours and patterns still come as a surprise to those in whom the idea of Warner's predominantly traditional fabrics is well entrenched."[18] The charismatic Eddie Squires exerted a decisive influence. "After the first few years here I was given a free hand," he later recalled. "It's never been anything but refreshing."[19] An instinctive iconoclast, Squires openly raided historical and ethnic sources as a vehicle for youth-orientated Pop design. *Soumak* from the Caspian Sea Collection (1965), for example, was inspired by a carpet in the Victoria & Albert Museum, while in Theme on the Thirties (1965) his plaything was Art Deco, long before the style returned to mainstream fashion. This collection included the glorious, bubbly *Delores*, which combined Pop target motifs with jazzy retro-scrolls (fig. 5.31).

The Accent on Pattern Collection (1966) was Warner's design manifesto, featuring playful Pop interpretations of historical genres in the simplified, flat, Carnaby Street style. Squires contributed the Moorish-style *Geometric* and the Celtic-inspired *Interlace*, while Jennifer Lowndes designed a Greek Revival pattern, *Volute*. The Pharaoh Collection (1967) took Egyptian revivalism as its starting point, and featured exuberant patterns, including *Karnak* by Jennifer Lowndes and *Thebes* by Sue Palmer, both inspired by Owen Jones's *Grammar of Ornament*. Countering this light-hearted historicism was a series of futuristic ranges. The Programmed Pattern Collection (1967) was particularly daring in its style and subject matter, featuring a series of designs by Squires inspired by computers and electrical circuitry. *Colourtron*, which depicted an integrated silicon circuit, took its name from a device used in colour television sets. *Circuit* was based on a printed copper-foil circuit, and *Univac*, named after an American digital computer, was based on a computer-drawn map (fig. 5.32). The Stereoscopic Collection (1968) was more tongue-in-cheek, marrying pointillist imagery with allusions to Op Art. This included *Archway* by Eddie Squires, with radiating ziggurat motifs that paid homage to 1930s cinema architecture, and *Isometric* (1968) by Sue Palmer, inspired by opticians' colour charts (fig. 5.33).

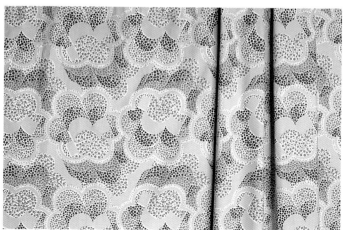

Palmer and Squires shared a keen interest in Pop Art, particularly Andy Warhol's prints and the paintings of Roy Lichtenstein. The disintegrated dots of enlarged silk-screen prints clearly influenced the Stereoscopic Collection, and were also prominent in Palmer's *Space Walk* (1969), an arresting mirrored composition of astronauts, with exaggerated dotted shading. This design, along with Squires's *Lunar Rocket* (1969), was created to celebrate *Apollo 11*'s landing on the moon. Although hand-drawn, *Lunar Rocket* was photographic in its detail, paving the way for the use of actual photographs in textiles during the 1970s. The composition, which juxtaposed views of the earth and moon with the rocket in full thrust, was completely unparalleled at the time.

Top Fig. 5.32
Univac *screen-printed cotton furnishing fabric, designed by Eddie Squires, produced by Warner & Sons, 1967.* Part of the Programmed Pattern Collection, this futuristic design was inspired by a computer-generated image. The pattern's name was derived from an American digital computer.

Above Fig. 5.33
Isometric *screen-printed cotton furnishing fabric, designed by Sue Palmer, produced by Warner & Sons, 1968.* This extraordinary pointillist floral pattern, inspired by opticians' colour charts, formed part of Warner's Stereoscopic Collection, which was influenced by both Op Art and Pop Art.

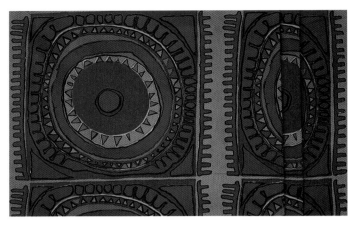

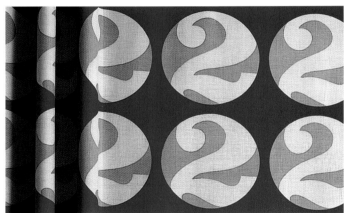

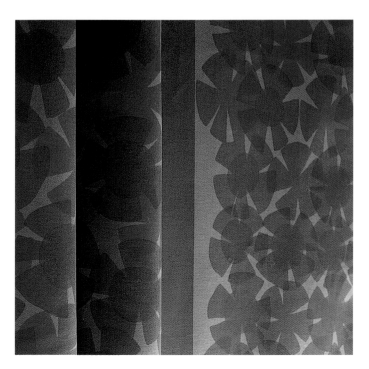

Top left Fig. 5.34
Jackanapes screen-printed furnishing fabric, designed by Juliet Glynn Smith, produced by Conran Fabrics, 1966. With its crisply drawn motifs and bright colours, this eye-catching nursery fabric recalls the style of illustration popular in children's books of the period.

Centre left Fig. 5.35
Graphic 2 screen-printed cotton furnishing fabric, designed by the Ryman-Conran Studio, produced by Conran Fabrics, 1970. Like many British companies during the Swinging Sixties, Conran Fabrics pitched its designs at the buoyant and affluent youth market.

Bottom left Fig. 5.36
Abberley screen-printed cotton satin furnishing fabric, designed by Ann Sutton, produced by London Seventy, 1964. Winner of a Cotton Board Award in 1964, this flat floral was described in advertisements as "a fresh, original idea with a subtle blending of colour."

Top right Fig. 5.37
Negus screen-printed cotton furnishing fabric, designed by Sigrid Quemby, produced by Fidelis Furnishing Fabrics, 1964. Design magazine noted of the recently established Fidelis in May 1965 that the colours of its fabrics were "very much in line with young modern tastes."

Above Fig. 5.38
Age of Kings screen-printed cotton satin furnishing fabric, designed by Pamela Kay, produced by Tibor, 1964. The title of this pattern alludes to Shakespeare's history plays, and the design was originally created for the Shakespeare Centre in Stratford-upon-Avon, Warwickshire, where Tibor was based.

Britain: Conran Fabrics

Another company that enthusiastically embraced the aesthetics of Pop was Conran Fabrics, led by the textile designer turned entrepreneur Terence Conran. Offering a variety of printed and woven fabrics – some imported, others home-produced – the company targeted both the architect-led contract field and the domestic market, exploiting Conran's new store Habitat, opened in 1964, to bypass conservative retailers. Lively printed cottons and linens, targeted at the youth market, were its speciality, and three young designers with their finger on the pulse of contemporary youth culture were Gillian Farr, Natalie Gibson, and Juliet Glynn Smith. Gillian Farr designed *Gilliflower* and *Master Tuggie* (both 1964). Natalie Gibson created patterns such as *Shimmy* and *Happy Dreams* (both 1967). Juliet Glynn Smith designed a series of striking patterns, including the ravishing *Prince of Quince* (1965) and the lively *Lollipop* and *Jackanapes* (fig. 5.34) (both 1966). Among other contributors were Russell Greenslade and Elizabeth Rayton, and at the end of the decade the Ryman-Conran studio created *Graphic* (1970), a series of number-based patterns that explored typographic motifs (fig. 5.35).

Britain: Danasco, London Seventy, and Mary Oliver Textiles

The healthiness of the market for printed textiles during the 1960s prompted the formation of several new companies in Britain. Danasco Fabrics, founded in 1960, was an offshoot of the wholesale import company, Danasco, established by Paul Glitre in 1955. Originally Danasco had imported textiles by the Swedish firm Mölnlycke into Britain as part of its package of Scandinavian furniture and furnishings. Subsequently, however, it commissioned patterns from British, French, Danish, and Finnish designers, including Natalie Gibson, Douglas Hamilton, Danny Harrison, Maija Isola, Françoise Lelong, Althea McNish, Rayne Walker, Isabel Watson, and John Wright. "In this first collection I intend to follow the simplicity and style of the Scandinavian fabrics and also to introduce new trends in design and, more particularly, in colour," announced Paul Glitre in 1961.[20] The fabrics were manufactured in Britain, and Danasco also later marketed Timo Sarpaneva's Ambiente collection under licence in Britain. Later, in 1970, after a break in production of six years, Danasco launched a new collection featuring designs by Althea McNish and the American designer Mary Bloch.

One of the most striking patterns produced by Danasco was *My Love* (1963) by Natalie Gibson, featuring giant hearts. Another new company that successfully tapped into the mood of the Swinging Sixties was London Seventy, which produced printed fabrics by Evelyn Pauker and Ann Sutton. Later renowned as a textile artist, Sutton created the highly successful pattern *Abberley* (1964), decorated with wheel-shaped flower heads in the Carnaby Street style (fig. 5.36). Op and ethnic patterns later became equally common idioms in British textiles. When the designer Mary Oliver

established Mary Oliver Textiles as a subsidiary of Donald Brothers in 1967, her first collection included two abstract-geometric patterns inspired by the Middle East, *Jerusalem* and *Jericho*.

Britain: Fidelis, Tamesa, and Tibor

One of Britain's most high-profile start-up companies was Fidelis Furnishing Fabrics, active from 1961 and run by J.P. Mavrogordato, with Mo Sullivan as colour consultant. Specializing in medium-price screen-printed textiles, Fidelis acted as a converter, producing modish geometric and ethnic patterns by freelance designers such as Nadia Czapla, Natalie Gibson, Josephine Patten, Sigrid Quemby, Hilary Rosenthal, Anthony Sharp, Grace Sullivan, Robert Tierney, Shelagh Wakely, and John Wright. Sigrid Quemby, who was half Norwegian, began designing for the firm in 1964, creating a group of patterns featuring the ubiquitous circle motif, including *Corona*, *Omega*, *Orbit*, and *Negus* (fig. 5.37). Shelagh Wakely's *Minar* (1966) was a psychedelic-Moorish design, while John Wright's *Fancy Pansy* (1969) was a Carnaby Street Pop floral. In 1969 Fidelis collaborated with Courtaulds to produce a range of designs screen-printed on the dye-resistant acetate fabric Dicel. Among these was *Perilandra*, a high-Pop design by Nicola Wood, drawn in the cartoon style of the Beatles' film *Yellow Submarine*.

But this kind of fashion-led approach did not suit everyone, and some companies, such as Tamesa Fabrics, made a point of offering an alternative to the prevailing Pop styles. Tamesa was established in 1964 by Isabel Tisdall, formerly head of Edinburgh Weavers' London showroom. Although chiefly concerned with textural woven textiles – mainly designed by Frank Davies and Marianne Straub and woven at Warner – Tamesa also produced a selection of printed furnishing fabrics. Unusual for the restraint and subtlety of their patterns and colouring, early designs included the quasi-heraldic *Golden Lions* (1965) and the flat floral *Ortensia* (1966). Working chiefly with the contract market, Tamesa went against prevailing trends by not naming its pattern designers, preferring to build a reputation for the company rather than for individuals. However, many prints were, in fact, created by Isabel Tisdall's husband, Hans Tisdall (formerly Aufseeser), who had enjoyed a distinguished career as a textile designer since the 1930s, working with Edinburgh Weavers for many years.

Woven fabrics for the contract market were also the main focus of Tibor during the 1960s, although new printed fabrics continued to be issued throughout the decade. In 1964 Tibor was commissioned to produce a group of printed hangings for the Shakespeare Centre in Stratford-upon-Avon, prompting a striking printed furnishing fabric called *Age of Kings* (1964) by Pamela Kay, featuring etiolated figures evoking characters from Shakespeare's history plays (fig. 5.38). Tibor's patterns became increasingly eclectic over the course of the 1960s. In 1965 the company embraced the "pressed flower" look, and the following year it launched T21, a diverse collection produced to celebrate its twenty-first birthday. Patterns ranged

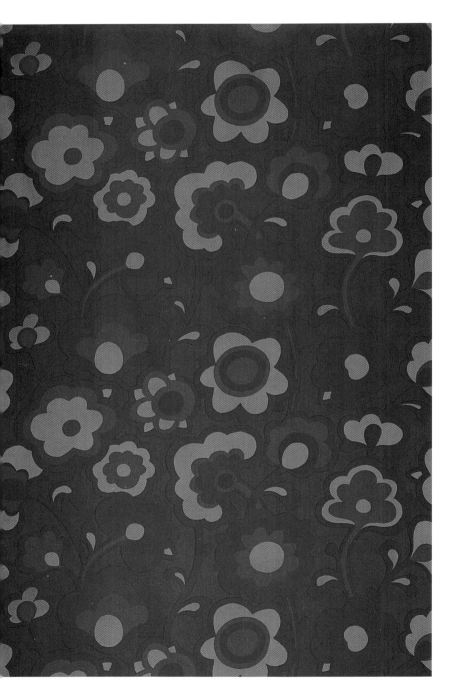

Jupiter screen-printed cotton furnishing fabric, designed by Isabel Colquhoun, produced by Simpson & Godlee, 1966. Produced as part of the modish Constellation range, this vibrant, uninhibited, Pop-inspired flat floral is printed in five different shades of red and pink.

from *Adiscos*, composed of half and quarter circles, to a folk art-inspired design called *Anna*, in which the designer, Tibor Reich himself, returned to his Hungarian roots.

Britain: Turnbull & Stockdale, Simpson & Godlee, and David Hicks

Modern design was embraced by firms of all complexions during the 1960s. Turnbull & Stockdale's Futura collection (1963) signified the company's new-found interest in progressive abstraction, featuring ambitious, large-scale, painterly designs by John Blackburn, Hilda Durkin, and June Locke. Simpson & Godlee, whose textiles were marketed under the Bevis trade name, launched its Royal College of Art range in 1963, with designs by three young graduates, Valerie Gough, Julie Hodgess, and Adrianne Leman. The following year the firm collaborated with the WPM to produce a range of fabrics coordinated with the second Palladio Mondo wallpaper collection, including crisp mini-botanicals by Pat Albeck. In 1966 it launched the Constellation range, featuring designs by Peter Perritt and Isabel Colquhoun exploring the vocabulary of Op and Pop. Perritt designed *Orion* and *Saturn*, the latter composed of dissected circles. *Jupiter*, a sizzling flat floral by Colquhoun, was perfectly in tune with the flower power era (fig. 5.39).

During the 1960s even the upper classes could tap into their own, slightly sanitized version of the Carnaby Street "look" through the coordinated carpets and fabrics of the interior designer David Hicks. In 1965 Hicks designed a group of four printed textiles, *Turkish Tulip*, *Daisy Daisy*, *Seeds*, and *Edward*, for the wholesale company Goods and Chattels. Later he created a range of crisp, repetitive patterns with echoes of Gothic Revival and chinoiserie for Burrows Textiles, specially designed to complement the period interiors of his wealthy clients.

Britain: John Lewis Partnership and Pat Albeck

One of the most active retailers of modern textiles over the past half century has been the John Lewis Partnership, also a producer under the trade name Jonelle. Among its subsidiaries are Cavendish Textiles, founded in 1929, converters of dress and furnishing fabrics, and Stead McAlpin, a textile-printing company based in Carlisle. During the late 1940s John Lewis collaborated with designers such as Jacqueline Groag and Margaret Simeon. Another early post-war contributor was Lucienne Day, who continued to supply occasional patterns for dress and furnishing fabrics until 1975. Also active during the 1960s was John Lewis Overseas, a subsidiary responsible for exporting furnishing fabrics, which commissioned patterns from designers such as Tessa Hagity, Danny Harrison, Thalia Perceval, and Sheila Yale.

A leading designer closely associated with John Lewis from the 1960s was Pat Albeck, who designed numerous printed textiles, including the best-selling dress fabric *Daisy Chain* (1964), as well as bed linen and tea towels. After training at the Royal College of

Art from 1950 to 1953, Albeck was employed as a dress fabric designer by Horrockses until 1958. On becoming freelance she collaborated with numerous companies, designing furnishing fabrics for David Whitehead, Grafton, and Sanderson, dress prints for Liberty and Tootal, bed linen for Finlay, wallpapers for Sanderson and the WPM, and tea towels for the National Trust. Albeck's neatly structured florals were lively and engaging, providing a reassuring antidote to the otherwise excessive "artiness" of the period. Her status as one of the most successful and highly regarded freelance pattern designers of the 1960s was confirmed in 1969 by her book *Printed Textiles*, which offered advice and guidance to textile students and recent graduates.

Britain: Bernard Wardle

During the 1960s British textiles were distinguished not only by innovative design, but also by high-quality cloth and superb printing. Particularly outstanding in this respect was Bernard Wardle, based at Chinley, near Stockport, Cheshire, which acted as commission printers for converters such as Heal's, as well as producing its own ranges. Wardle's fabrics were printed with colourfast vat dyes, introduced into the industry during the second half of the 1950s as a replacement for chrome dyes. During the following decade translucent colours were favoured at Wardle, overlaid like watercolours to produce rich, luminous effects.

Wardle's design director from 1962 to 1965 was Edward Pond, who from 1958 had been chief designer at the firm's Everflex branch in north Wales, where he designed the award-winning Harlequin range of vinyl-coated textiles and wall coverings. Pond's printed fabrics included a grainy Piperesque design called *Cathedrals* and *Leirion* (both 1962), the latter featuring silhouettes of attenuated flowers. He also commissioned patterns from freelance designers, including Robert Dodd, Colleen Farr, Natalie Gibson, Janet Taylor, and Elizabeth Tuff. Before leaving to take up the post of design director at the WPM, Pond commissioned the 6/65 Crescendo Collection, featuring patterns such as *Toxophilite* by Natalie Gibson, a bold, circle-based abstract design (fig. 5.40).

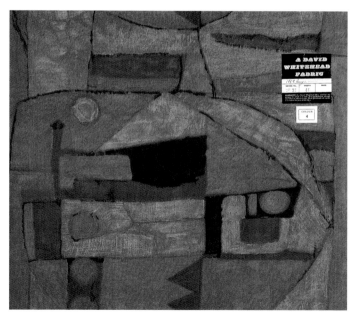

Britain: David Whitehead

After the golden era of design at David Whitehead during the 1950s, the firm's progress was more erratic during the 1960s. Nevertheless, many interesting patterns were produced at intervals by freelance designers, including Pat Albeck, Helen Dalby, Jane Daniels, Friedlinde di Colbertaldo Dinzl, Robert Dodd, Tessa Hagity, Pamela Kay, and Barbara Payze. Painterly effects were a feature of the early 1960s, and a broad range of architectural, floral, and figurative imagery was explored. During the late 1960s there was a surge of artistic activity after Whitehead's chief designer, George Butler, decided to revive the ideas behind the 1953 Paintings into Textiles scheme. This initiative, known as the Living Art Collection, began in 1967 with the translation of works by two Irish artists, George Campbell and John Pakenham, and culminated in an exhibition in

Top Fig. 5.40
Toxophilite screen-printed cotton furnishing fabric, designed by Natalie Gibson, produced by Bernard Wardle, 1965. During the 1960s target patterns, such as this design in Wardle's youth-orientated Crescendo Collection, became a symbol of modernity.

Above Fig. 5.41
Sun God screen-printed rayon satin furnishing fabric, designed by Padraig MacMiadhachain, produced by David Whitehead, 1969. This textural abstract was part of the Living Art Collection, which translated paintings by leading artists into printed textiles.

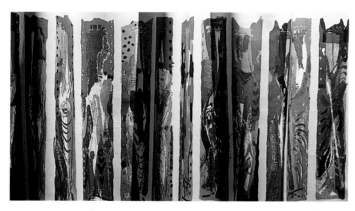

Top Fig. 5.42
Bye, Bye Blackbird screen-printed cotton furnishing fabric, designed by Robert Holmes, produced by Sanderson, 1967. This pattern was created as part of the Odeon Collection, an Art Deco Revival range, although it reveals more about the colour preferences and graphic style of the 1960s.

Above Fig. 5.43
Arundel screen-printed cotton satin furnishing fabric, designed by John Piper, produced by Sanderson, 1960. Having recently designed the stained glass for Sanderson's new showroom, John Piper created this evocative pattern for the company's prestigious Centenary Collection in 1960.

1969 that also included designs based on paintings by Roy Britton, David Brooke, Merrick Hansel, Padraig MacMiadhachain (fig. 5.41), and John Piper. All the patterns were uncompromisingly abstract, and many were in scorching desert hues. Sadly, the Living Art Collection proved to be David Whitehead's creative swansong. In 1970 the company was swallowed up by the Lonhro conglomerate, bringing its twenty-year programme of design innovation to an untimely end.

Britain: Sanderson

As well as producing designs by its in-house studio, Sanderson had always bought in a proportion of its patterns, and after the war a number of ranges were sold under licence from foreign companies such as J.S.A. Busto Arsizio in Italy and Schumacher in the United States. This policy of purchasing designs from abroad was promoted as a glamorous feature of Sanderson's identity through the suave "Our Man" advertisement campaigns during the early 1960s: "Our Man flies in. With him, a batch of designs for Sanderson fabrics and wallpapers… The more he travels, the wider and the more exciting the Sanderson range becomes."[21] European textile designers in the company's repertoire at this date included Walter Krauer, Elsbeth Kupferoth, Bente Lorenz, Lois Persio, Wanda Wistrich, and Leo Wollner.

In 1960 Sanderson launched its prestigious Centenary Collection, which included an exotic, large-scale fantasy botanical called *Dream Flower* by Helen Dalby, and a group of patterns by John Piper, including *Arundel* (fig. 5.43), *Chiesa della Salute*, and *Northern Cathedral*. Piper's designs, which echoed the rich colours of his watercolours and stained glass, were later supplemented by the best-selling pattern *Stones of Bath* (1962). Having already worked with accomplished freelance designers such as John Drummond during the 1950s, Sanderson continued to cherry-pick from the wealth of talent on offer in its subsequent textile collections, producing patterns by Margaret Cannon, Friedlinde di Colbertaldo Dinzl, Robert Dodd, Doreen Dyall, Christine Risley, and Anthony Sharp. During the second half of the decade attempts were made to attract the growing youth market through patterns such as *Pop Baroque* (1967) by David Vaughan, the Art Nouveau-inspired *Floppy Poppy* (1967) by Diana and Derek Collard, and Pat Albeck's *The Secret Garden* (1970), the latter described as having "a touch of hippie art about it in the finely detailed profusion of flowers."[22] Pat Etheridge, who had recently joined the in-house studio, contributed to the Young Sanderson range in 1966, and produced a string of lively, colourful, and commercially successful Pop florals during the late 1960s, working alongside other young designers, including Ronaele Jones and Robert Holmes. The Art Deco Revival Odeon Collection (1967), created by Etheridge and Holmes, marked Sanderson's most ambitious attempt to update its image. Infused with pop styling and psychedelic colours, the collection evoked the spirit of 1930s Hollywood through patterns such as *Top Hat*, *Sunset Boulevard*, and *Bye Bye Blackbird* (fig. 5.42).

Sanderson's Centenary Collection (1960) also contained wallpapers, including bought-in designs by Raymond Loewy, Giò Ponti, and Frank Lloyd Wright, as well as newly commissioned patterns from Jupp Dernbach-Mayen, Jacqueline Groag, and Humphrey Spender, and competition-winning designs by Peggy Angus and Gordon Crook. Some of these hand screen-printed wallpapers were subsequently incorporated in Sanderson's machine-printed Tempora collection (1960), which was praised by Paul Reilly, director of the Council of Industrial Design, as an "act of faith in the imaginative designs of our own times."[23]

When the fashion for coordinated furnishings spread to Britain from the United States, not surprisingly it was Sanderson, with its parallel textile and wallpaper operations, which took the lead. Its Triad collections, produced every two years from 1962, proved enormously successful, and it was only in 1981 that these were replaced by the more diverse Options range. The first Triad collection consisted of sixty-eight machine-printed patterned wallpapers, each with a matching textile and a plain companion wallpaper. Although the collection was dominated by small-scale florals, some modern designs were included, and later collections reflected other fashions, such as the vogue for ethnic design. Hedging its bets between traditional and modern, Sanderson, under the design direction of George Lowe, took a deliberately hybrid approach to design. "At any one time, Sanderson's has thousands of different designs and colourways available for buyers to choose from," noted *The Ambassador* in 1968. "These range from traditional florals and figurative patterns, through the revival William Morris to the highly stylised, brightly coloured modern designs, which reflect the London fashion scene."[24]

Sanderson had been producing block-printed William Morris wallpapers since 1927, using the original wood blocks inherited from Jeffrey & Co., but during the 1960s coordinated Morris fabrics were also introduced, complemented by the Allan Vigers range. Modified and re-coloured in the Sanderson studio by designers such as Pat Etheridge and the colourist Esme Bosc, the Morris designs were adapted for screen-printing and machine production, to make them more widely accessible. "Revamped in rich contemporary colours, the William Morris collections have dominated fashions and furnishings for the past five years," noted *The Ambassador* in 1968.[25] At the end of the decade, exploiting the Victorian revivalism that was now in full swing, Sanderson launched Tempo – The Young Sanderson Set (1969), a collection of inexpensive washable wallpapers in which contemporary fashions were melded with Art Nouveau.

Britain: ICI

The Wall Paper Manufacturers Ltd (WPM), of which Sanderson formed a part, had dominated the industry since the start of the century. From 1961, however, the WPM's supremacy was challenged by ICI, whose Vymura wallpapers were launched that year. Vinyl

Above Fig. 5.44
Avignon vinyl wallpaper, designed by Sue Faulkner, produced by ICI, 1971. ICI's Vymura wallpapers were extremely popular during the late 1960s and the early 1970s. Cool, geometric abstracts and blazing historical-revival patterns both formed part of the company's wide-ranging design repertoire at this time.

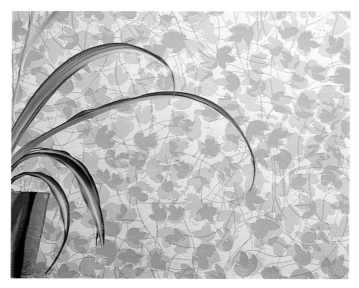

Top Fig. 5.45
Cotswold screen-printed wallpaper,
designed by Audrey Levy, produced by
the Lightbown Aspinall branch of the
WPM, 1960. Produced as part of the
Palladio 4 collection, this pattern
exploits the textural subtlety and depth
of colour that are distinctive qualities
of hand screen-printing.

Above Fig. 5.46
Trifoliate screen-printed wallpaper,
designed by Cliff Holden, produced by the
Lightbown Aspinall branch of the WPM,
1961. Although the large repeats of
many Palladio wallpapers limited their
use in the home, this delicate pattern
from Palladio 5 was domestic in
composition and scale.

wall coverings, although more expensive than conventional wallpapers, became extremely popular during the 1960s, particularly for kitchens and bathrooms, because of their durability and washability. Advertisements described Vymura as "Handsome – Resilient – Aloof – with as many lives as a cat."[26] By 1969 ICI had won more than half of the home market and was exporting to more than thirty countries.

Initially developed at ICI's Leathercloth Division, but later transferred to the Paints Division, the Vymura range was styled by Robin Gregson-Brown, who joined ICI in 1960, straight from the Royal College of Art. Vymura exploited the new technique of photogravure (an updated version of engraved roller-printing in which photochemical processes are used to etch intaglio patterns on metal rollers). Flat patterns later gave way to lightly embossed relief effects. In 1969 *Design* praised Vymura's "subtle gradations of tone" and "unusual light-reflecting textures."[27] Painterly abstracts were favoured initially, as in *Bamboo* by Carol Williams, followed later by geometric designs. Of the group of three patterns given a Design Centre Award in 1969, *Solitaire* by Pat Turnbull was composed of diamond motifs; *Gemini* by Sue Faulkner was a complex check pattern; and *Tempo* by Robin Gregson-Brown was a bold vertical, undulating design. Shortly afterwards, however, Victorian revivalism kicked in, and Vymura took on a more liberated psychedelic character (fig. 5.44).

Britain: John Line, Shand Kydd, and Hayward & Son

Vymura prompted the introduction of vinyl wall coverings by several other manufacturers, including John Line's Balarex range (1963), Commercial Plastics' Craymuir (1965), and the WPM's Crown Vinyls (1966). John Line also followed Sanderson's lead by tapping into the vogue for the revival of Victorian and Art Nouveau designs. The company's Epoch Collection (1964) included a whiplash floral called *Solvay*, referring to the Hôtel Solvay in Brussels, a masterpiece of Belgian Art Nouveau by Victor Horta.

John Line and Shand Kydd, after merging in 1958, were both absorbed into the WPM in 1961. Subsequently John Line's upmarket modern hand screen-printed Folio collections were transferred to Shand Kydd, where they were produced alongside Shand Kydd's machine-printed Focus collections, launched in 1964. Artistically ambitious, as well as technically innovative, Focus exploited both photogravure and flexographic printing (a new form of surface roller-printing using low-relief rubber rollers). The translucent inks used in these two processes, as well as producing wallpapers that were sharper and finer than traditional surface-printed designs, also enabled colours to be overlaid.

While the machine-printed Focus collections were geared towards a mass audience, the hand-printed Folio range was more upmarket and had larger patterns. Although the two collections were stylistically similar in some respects, their differing production methods meant that, in terms of tone, texture, and colour, they were quite distinct. Henry Skeen, a John Line staff designer, had significant input into the Focus ranges, as did Donald Melbourne. Adept at transforming the avant-garde into the mainstream, Melbourne spent his entire career working for Shand Kydd, rising to become design director. Several other designers associated with the two firms also contributed to both ranges, including Harry Cadney, John Harbour, James Heath, William Odell, and Joyce Storey. Freelance designers were also widely used for both collections, many concurrently active in textiles. Folio featured designs by, among others, Robert Dodd, Cliff Holden, Carola and Daniel Olsen, Fritz Werthmüller, and John Wright, while Focus included patterns by Mea Angerer, José Bonnet, Dorothy Evans, Michael Griffin, Tessa Hagity, Deryck Healey, Fay Hillier, and Evelyn Pauker.

Hayward & Son, another company in the WPM portfolio, had earlier printed Tibor Reich's experimental Fotexur wallpapers in 1957. During the early 1960s the company produced radical hand screen-printed abstracts, targeted at architects and interior designers, which were marketed alongside the WPM's Palladio ranges. Hayward & Son's Spring Collection of 1963, featuring bold patterns such as *Circles* by Mea Angerer, was the subject of a special exhibition at the WPM's Architects Showroom.

Britain: WPM

Although the 1960s was an extremely creative period for British wallpaper design, dramatic restructuring left the industry lastingly destabilized. In 1963 the Monopolies Commission decided that the WPM's restrictive trading practices were not in the public interest, and decreed that the organization should be broken up. Thrown into disarray, the WPM was taken over by the Reed Paper Group in 1965, and during the next ten years Reed International (as Reed later became) oversaw its gradual dismantlement.

In 1964 the WPM established its Central Design Studio, with Deryck Healey as studio head. The following year Edward Pond was appointed design director at the WPM, and production of the prestigious Palladio ranges was transferred from Lightbown Aspinall to Sanderson. Remarkably, despite all these radical changes, the WPM's bold adventure in pattern design continued unabated for several years. Five Palladio collections were created between 1960 and 1969, along with two Palladio Mondo collections in 1962 and 1964, and Crown's Scene Collection in 1966. The machine-printed Palladio Mondo collections, featuring small textural, geometric, and foliate motifs, marked a natural progression from the earlier Modus range. *Design* welcomed the initiative, saying: "Although British wallpapers have made a unique contribution to modern design, the innovations and outstanding success have on the whole been confined to screen prints, while machine printed ranges have tended to remain stereotyped and pedestrian. Now, however, the Lightbown Aspinall branch of the

Top Fig. 5.47
Lubi-Lu screen-printed wallpaper, designed by Pat Albeck, produced by Sanderson, 1966. This design from Palladio 7, the first Palladio collection to be produced by Sanderson rather than Lightbown Aspinall, is by the textile designer Pat Albeck, who excelled in neat, stylized florals.

Above Fig. 5.48
Chantilly screen-printed wallpaper, designed by Robert Dodd, produced by Sanderson, 1968. Part of the Palladio 8 collection, this design illustrates how floral motifs were flattened and geometricized during the mid-1960s. The title alludes to French medieval *mille fleurs* tapestries.

Top Fig. 5.49
Concord screen-printed wallpaper, designed by Michael Hatjoullis, produced by Sanderson, 1966. The Palladio 7 collection, created at the height of Op Art mania, featured several patterns with distorting effects. Op resonances were strongest in black-and-white patterns such as this.

Above Fig. 5.50
Berkley screen-printed wallpaper, designed by Edward Pond, produced by Sanderson, 1968. Edward Pond was the art director for the Palladio 8 collection. Printed in modish silver, this flamboyant, large-scale pattern presents a futuristic Pop interpretation of the Greek Revival style.

WPM, which helped to pioneer screen printing in wallpapers, has issued a range of progressive new machine prints which should meet a real need."[28] Selected by Lightbown Aspinall's design director, Guy Busby, and design consultant, Roger Nicholson, the collection featured patterns by Palladio stalwarts such as William James, Audrey Levy, Edward Veevers, and Fritz Werthmüller. The success of the pocket-sized Palladio formula prompted a follow-up, Palladio Mondo II in 1964. Pat Albeck's distinctive crisp botanicals were a feature of both collections, while the prevailing fascination with geometry was reflected in a plethora of circle and triangle patterns. Tapping into the fashion for coordinated furnishings, Simpson & Godlee produced a range of printed fabrics to complement the second collection.

The Palladio 4, 5, and 6 collections were also collated by Guy Busby and Roger Nicholson and produced at Lightbown Aspinall. Nicholson himself continued to supply patterns, and other designers included Bettina, Howard Carter, Lisa Grönwall, William James, Robert Nicholson, Eric Thomas, Rayne Walker, and Fritz Werthmüller. Some, such as Peter Shuttleworth, a staff designer at Lightbown Aspinall from 1946 to 1981, had contributed to earlier Palladio ranges. Others, such as Althea McNish, had recently graduated from the Royal College of Art and were also designing for progressive textile firms.

As with the earlier Palladio collections, abstraction was but one of many idioms. Palladio 4 (1960) contained Edward Hughes's nostalgic pastoral *Wealden Hill* and several stylized plant patterns, including the skeletal and silhouetted leaves of Edward Veevers's *Folia* and Joyce Storey's *Bracken*. Even within the field of abstraction, there were a number of diverse styles, ranging from Ronnie Thomas's bespattered *Stalasso* to Audrey Levy's rich, textural *Cotswold* (fig. 5.45). Palladio 5 (1961) contained the lyrical *Trifoliate* by Cliff Holden, with its delicately tinted overlapping leaves (fig. 5.46), and Pat Albeck's *Juliette*, which featured minutely delineated plants. Grainy textural effects were the basis for both Peter Hall's *Gradua* and Humphrey Spender's *Salamander*, although other patterns were in sharper focus, such as Audrey Levy's *Universe*.

Palladio 6 (1963) reflected the growing eclecticism of design, juxtaposing ethnic, historical, and contemporary styles. Patience Gray made a Pop assault on classicism in *Baroque*, while Margaret Cannon gave Moorish design a contemporary makeover in *Valencia* and *Alhambra*. Deryck Healey's *Lamina* overlaid emergent hard-edged geometric forms with the receding fashion for distressed textural effects. *Formula* and *Quadrille* by Edward Veevers, both based on square grids, demonstrated the increasing dominance of pure geometry, an aesthetic embraced unreservedly by Natalie Gibson in the kaleidoscopic *Zeus*. The boldest pattern in the collection was Brian Knight's *Ancora*, featuring circles composed of diamond motifs floating on a triangulated ground, which paved the way for full-blown Op.

Palladio 7 (1966), styled by Deryck Healey, was the first collection to be created at the WPM's Central Design Studio, and the first to be manufactured by Sanderson. It drew on patterns from three different sources: first, freelance designers (Pat Albeck, Helen Dalby, Colleen Farr, Edward Gilbert, Peter Hall, Cliff Holden, Brian Knight, Althea McNish, Tania Midgeley, Carola and Daniel Olsen, and Humphrey Spender); secondly, guest designers (Tessa Hagity and Mo Sullivan); and thirdly, studio designers (Ann Berwick, Kay Ferrier, Michael Hatjoullis, Deryck Healey, and Rosemary Newson). Op mania – which was at its height when Palladio 7 appeared – was reflected in dazzling patterns such as *Domino* by Humphrey Spender, with its transmuting dots. Geometric forms, chopped up and reconstituted in new arrangements, were another Op formula, as in *Tambourine* by Brian Knight. Other designers took regular geometric patterns but distorted them, as in *Concord* by Michael Hatjoullis (fig. 5.49). Deryck Healey created a series of complex, multi-layered Op patterns, including *Stereo* and *Rondeau*. *Sphere*, co-designed by Healey and Rosemary Newson, featured overlapping circles superimposed on a striped ground. At the other end of the spectrum, Pat Albeck created several gems in the Pop floral genre, such as *Arabella* and *Lubi-Lu* (fig. 5.47), while *Geranium* by Colleen Farr hinted at the rising tide of Morris mania.

Crown's Scene Collection (1966), which was coordinated by Edward Pond at the Central Design Studio, featured machine-printed vinyl wallpapers aimed at a younger audience. Some designs contained distinct echoes of Palladio, such as a striking black-and-white Op design by Deryck Healey, whereas others embraced full-blown Pop idioms, notably a cartoon psychedelic pattern by Evelyn Erlbeck. Pond believed that: "The best designers are always part of a collection, and collections are at their best when planned. In this way, the best individual characteristics of designers can be used to advantage, as in casting the actors in a play."[29] Palladio 8 (1968), the first Palladio range to be stage-managed by Pond, contained thirty-eight designs by twenty-two designers. In addition to Pond himself, new contributors included David Bartle, Ann Berwick, Susan Burgess-James, Judith Cash, Inge Cordsen, Ann Cotton, Robert Dodd, Evelyn Erlbeck, Tony Fraser, John Halton, Zandra Rhodes, Eddie Squires, Jeremy Talbot, Sandra Watts, and Erica Willis.

The impending fragmentation of design at this time was reflected in Palladio 8. Excess was a recurrent theme, as in the giant cartoon squiggles of *Ida* by Judith Cash. *Compendium* by Rosemary Newson (fig. 5.51) and *Gambit* by Deryck Healey (fig. 5.52) combined the legacy of Op with the high-voltage colours of psychedelia. Several designers freely ransacked Islamic and Celtic idioms, and historical revivalism surfaced in many exuberant guises. *Chantilly* by Robert Dodd embodied witty references to medieval *mille fleurs* tapestries (fig. 5.48); *Pomona* by Erica Willis contained stylistic allusions to Toulouse Lautrec's posters; *Ziggurat* by Margaret Cannon was a celebration of Art Deco (fig. 5.53); *Tournament* by Deidre Baker

Top Fig. 5.51
Compendium *screen-printed wallpaper, designed by Rosemary Newson, produced by Sanderson, 1968.* Part of the Palladio 8 collection, this pattern exploited the ubiquitous circle motif, sliced up and reconstituted into an Op-inspired design.

Centre Fig. 5.52
Gambit *screen-printed wallpaper, designed by Deryck Healey, produced by Sanderson, 1968.* Originally head of the WPM's Central Design Studio, Deryck Healey later established a major international textile design consultancy.

Above Fig. 5.53
Ziggurat *screen-printed wallpaper, designed by Margaret Cannon, produced by Sanderson, 1968.* This pattern from the Palladio 8 collection heralded the official arrival of Art Deco revivalism.

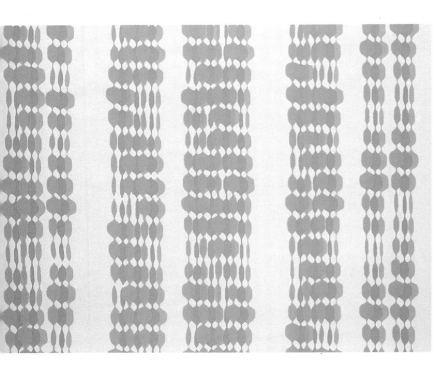

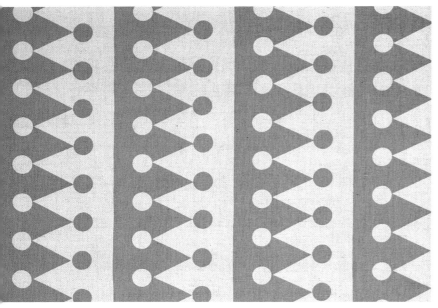

Top Fig. 5.54
Meteoric screen-printed vinyl wallpaper, designed by Ben Rose, produced by Ben Rose, Inc., 1965–9. While still adhering to aspects of the "Contemporary" style established during the early post-war years, Ben Rose adapted his later patterns to suit the more sophisticated tastes of the 1960s consumer.

Above Fig. 5.55
Palio 6 screen-printed cotton and linen furnishing fabric, designed by Alexander Girard, produced by Herman Miller, 1964. The dark and light elements of this ingenious positive-negative pattern – part of a collection inspired by Italian heraldic banners – are an exact duplicate of each other.

was a Carnaby Street "Gothick" medley; and the silver *Berkley* by Edward Pond was a Space Age take on Greek Revival (fig. 5.50).

Reflecting on the achievements of the Palladio ranges, Edward Pond later concluded: "For twenty years, from 1955 to 1975, these collections moved through tachism, Op art, Pop art, 'new' art nouveau, decorative romanticism, and a few styles that never quite 'made it.' Palladio, along with Heal Fabrics, were without doubt the greatest incentives to the creative ingenuity of British designers during the period."[30]

United States: Greeff and Ben Rose

After an astonishingly creative fifteen-year period following the Second World War, some of the forward momentum in American design began to slip away during the 1960s. Sensing a shift in the decorative climate, mainstream manufacturers reverted to traditional genres. Blowsy English chintzes in souped-up colours became big business during this period, imported by staunchly conservative firms such as Scalamandré Silks, founded in 1926. Greeff's American Legacy II collection (1962) typified prevailing trends, but Virginia Nepodal, the company's design director, also promoted accessible, modern, upbeat textile and wallpaper designs.

Significantly, two of the most adventurous post-war designers in the United States, Ruth Adler Schnee and Angelo Testa, both stopped creating patterns at the start of the 1960s. Although Ben Rose continued in operation, attention was increasingly focused on the contract market, where the main demand was for woven textiles. In 1964 he launched the Skyline collection of coordinated textiles and vinyl wall coverings, including *Caissons*, *Monolithic*, and *Mullions*, based entirely on squares and stripes. Rose's printed fabrics and wallpapers for the domestic market, although somewhat more restrained than those created during the early post-war period, were still characterful and expressive. Stylized flat florals, such as the wallpaper *Flower Fence* (1965–9), marked a new departure. Measured abstract designs generally prevailed, however, among them *Earthforms* (1967), a banded textile suggesting geological strata (fig. 4.30), and *Nairobi* (1965–9), a wallpaper evoking rows of octagonal tiles. Linear motifs with a wiry sculptural feel remained a key part of his aesthetic, as in the towering cages of *Zambezie* (1965–9). This wallpaper, along with others, such as *Meteoric* (1965–9), which suggested strings of beads (fig. 5.54), had a pronounced vertical emphasis. Although not architectural, these compositions reflected the designer's awareness of the needs of modern interiors. Occasionally the maverick side of Rose's character resurfaced, as in the ebullient printed textile *Girafters* (1965) (fig. 4.27) and the Pop Victorian wallpaper *Penny Candy* (1965–9), composed of line drawings of storage jars overlaid with multicoloured sweets.

While the rise of the contract market fostered greater anonymity and seriousness in design, patterns produced for the domestic market were often extremely exuberant, humorous, and upbeat. "The 1960s was a period of the new Establishment, of the rise of contract design, of the International Style," reflected Jack Lenor Larsen. "We saw, too, a schizophrenic split between a youth-oriented, free-wheeling residential market and the growing contract market, staid and Establishment in its point of view."[31]

United States: Knoll and Herman Miller

Similar reductivist trends were evident at Knoll, where Suzanne Huguenin designed woven striped patterns such as *Linea* (1962). Two years later, when Knoll launched its Casement Collection, the emphasis was on texture and translucency rather than pattern. Alexander Girard continued his heroic commitment to design innovation at Herman Miller, although even here simple woven checked and striped fabrics were in the ascendant, and the range of printed patterns was much narrower than before. The decade began on an upbeat note with two flat florals, *April* and *Flores*, and an amusing lettering design, *Alphabet* (all 1960). *Printstripe* and *Tristripe* marked a change of direction the following year, in turn countered by the zigzag-striped *Jagged* (1962). The high point of the decade was Girard's Palio collection (1964), inspired by the emblematic banners and flags at the Palio horse race held each year in Siena, Italy (fig. 5.55). The Palio collection consisted of eight patterns exploring variations on a theme. A variety of motifs resembling combs, fringes, flames, spikes, chequerboards, and coronets were vertically aligned in parallel bands, presented as positive-negative images. Overtly graphic in character, Palio marked a significant departure in terms of imagery, structure, and scale.

Love (1967), designed by Girard at the height of the Summer of Love, was a lively typographic pattern that featured the word "love" in various languages. Significantly, this was the last year in which any new printed patterns by Girard were issued, although his Environmental Enrichment Panels, intended to enliven Herman Miller's Action Office 2 furniture system, appeared in 1972. These were printed on cotton or linen, and some, such as *International Love Heart*, related to his earlier repeat patterns. Others, such as *Circle Sections*, contained bold new abstract or figurative designs.

United States: Boris Kroll

After growing in prominence during the 1950s and 1960s, Boris Kroll Fabrics eventually became one of the largest textile manufacturers in the United States. A self-taught weaver, Kroll began practising as a freelance textile designer in 1932. In 1946 he established Boris Kroll Fabrics, and he also ran Boris Kroll Prints from 1950 to 1979. In his Caribbean and Mediterranean collections of the 1950s, he experimented with rich woven colours and textures. During the 1960s he developed his trademark jacquard-woven geometrics, composed of a jigsaw of triangles and squares. Produced in an intense cocktail of colours, such as pink, red, and orange, they were also translated into printed designs. Kroll believed that "the fabric designer must understand fibre and colour,

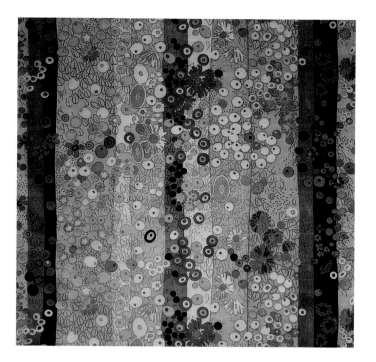

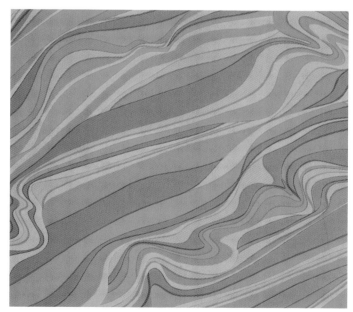

Top Fig. 5.56
Primavera *screen-printed cotton velvet furnishing fabric, designed by Don Wight, produced by Jack Lenor Larsen, Inc., 1961.* Produced as part of Larsen's Palette '61 collection, this sumptuous fabric has echoes of both Japanese stencilled textiles and the paintings of Gustav Klimt.

Above Fig. 5.57
Bojangles *screen-printed Caprolan textured stretch nylon bonded to polyester foam, produced by Jack Lenor Larsen International, 1967.* Designed to upholster the sculptural organic furniture of the period, the Butterfly Collection featured fluid patterns that could literally stretch with the fabric.

Top Fig. 5.58
Screen-printed furnishing fabric, designed by Marcelle Tolkoff, produced by Tiger Things, c.1965–7. Catering to the youth market, Marcelle Tolkoff's company, Tiger Things, produced furnishing fabrics and accessories decorated with patterns inspired by flower power and psychedelic designs.

Above Fig. 5.59
***April** screen-printed vinyl wallpaper, designed by Jack Denst, produced by Jack Denst Designs, Inc., 1963.* Jack Denst preferred the translucency of pure pigments to chalky, clay-based inks. The results are shown to great effect in this luminous multi-layered screen-printed pattern.

and *then* he is qualified to approach surface."[32] Woven fabrics with overprinted images were one of his specialities, such as *Bahama* (1965), a stylized leaf pattern screen-printed on a figured wood-grain ground. "My integrity of design can only be achieved because I have complete control over every phase of the manufacture of my fabrics," Kroll asserted.[33]

United States: Jack Lenor Larsen

The most dynamic force in American textiles during the 1960s was Jack Lenor Larsen, whose imaginative and energetic approach to both woven and printed textiles made him the dominant figure of the period. Larsen originally studied architecture and furniture but later switched to weaving, studying at the Cranbrook Academy of Art with Marianne Strengell. In 1952, inspired by the example of Dorothy Liebes, he established a studio in New York where he experimented with innovative weaves and novel combinations of yarns. This led him to found Jack Lenor Larsen, Inc. in 1953 in order to manufacture his designs, and in 1958 he teamed up with Win Anderson to create the Larsen Design Studio.

Screen-printed fabrics were produced from 1954. Influential early designs included *Midsummer* (1956), a stylized floral described by Larsen as "a sort of marriage between Tiffany and Matisse."[34] A few years later his firm caused a sensation with its unashamedly rich, decadent Palette '61 collection. Don Wight's *Primavera* (1961) (fig. 5.56), adorned with clusters of small flower heads scattered over a striped ground, was particularly intoxicating, recalling the Secessionist paintings of Gustav Klimt. Sensuous printed velvets remained a key component of the Larsen repertoire for many years, ranging from the exotic floral mosaic *Samarkand* (1968) to the photographic realism of *Pansy* (1970).

Larsen's wide-ranging ethnographic and historical interests energized the company's output, starting with the Andean Collection (1956) and the Indonesian Collection (1959), and continuing with the African Collection (1963). Inspired by textiles from all over the world – particularly pre-Columbian textiles from the Andes and resist-dyed fabrics from Africa and Asia – Larsen used ideas from other cultures as catalysts for stimulating modern designs. "I have grown by appreciating a broad range of cultures and design," he explained.[35] As a weaver, he believed strongly that patterns should be designed as an integral component of the fabric. In 1965 he launched the Baedeker Collection, which, in addition to several batiks, included a flocked polyester voile casement fabric called *Marmara*, and a reversible jacquard-woven cotton called *Hellespoint*. These two fabrics, which complemented each other, were decorated with patterns of swirling, eddying lines. Commentators noted correspondences with Op Art – all the rage in New York at the time, after a major exhibition entitled *The Responsive Eye* – and observed: "A free-wheeling exuberance has taken over with patterns on fabrics which are eclectic with rhythm and colour."[36] Larsen subsequently launched the Butterfly Collection (1967), a

Left Fig. 5.60
Where It's At machine screen-printed wallpaper, designed and produced by United DeSoto, 1968. This pattern, from the youth-orientated Bravo collection, "samples" graphics from teenage magazines. In order to heighten the colours, fluorescent pigments were added to the company's standard range of inks.

remarkable group of psychedelic patterns printed on stretch rayon. These upholstery fabrics for sculptural foam furniture featured free-flowing, organic patterns that were intentionally fluid, in order to counter the effect of distortion. *Labyrinth* and *Momentum* were suggestive of animal markings, while *Bojangles* (fig. 5.57) and *Firebird* were evocative of Art Nouveau. "[Larsen] recognizes fabric as a tactile, visual, sensitive element in today's society," observed Mildred Constantine. "He is constantly aware of its relationship to people, to their bodies, and to the environment."[37]

United States: Tiger Fabrics

Although full-blown psychedelia of this type was rare in American furnishing textiles, the Italian fashion designer Pucci was enormously popular at this date, and his patterns had a major effect on apparel fabrics. The screen-printed silks of Tzaims Luksus reflected his influence, as did both the colourful dress fabrics of Eileen Mislove for H.M. Kolbe and Marcelle Tolkoff's zingy patterns for Tiger Fabrics and Tiger Things. Tolkoff had initially worked as a stylist and publicist for Fuller Fabrics. In 1959 she and her husband, Daniel Tolkoff, established Tiger Fabrics, Inc.

as a converter of printed apparel fabrics, mainly for cotton sportswear. Tiger Things was formed about five years later and produced psychedelic furnishing fabrics (fig. 5.58), along with accessories such as aprons, printed with upbeat flat floral designs.

United States: Jack Denst

Wallpapers emerged as an extremely exciting medium for American pattern design during the 1960s, and the most adventurous firm of the decade was Jack Denst Designs, Inc. (previously Denst & Soderlund). Clarence Hawking, one of the company's chief designers, summarized its philosophy in 1966, saying: "We, at Denst, take an awareness of the past and present and use this to create a design that is a distinctive, significant artistic statement."[38] Ambitious murals continued to form an important feature of the firm's output – as in the giant sun mural *Hyperion* from the Environment 15 collection (1966) – often influenced by trends in graphics and contemporary art. "Wallpaper design is more than making a living," announced Jack Denst. "I am concerned with the beauty of art and its effect on our civilization."[39] Nature and landscape were recurrent themes in his

Above Fig. 5.61
L.B. Jawbreakers *screen-printed Mylar-coated wallpaper, designed and produced by Blue River Handprints, Inc., 1967–71.* Mylar, a polyester film with a shiny silver finish, was adopted as a ground for screen-printed wallpapers. The psychedelic pattern used here is similarly futuristic.

Opposite Fig. 5.62
Screen-printed silk velvet cape from the Vivara collection, designed and produced by Emilio Pucci, 1966. In the Op-inspired Vivara collection Pucci incorporated a compendium of popular 1960s leitmotifs: squares, chevrons, and circles contrast with the melted ovals and undulating waves.

designs, which were often given lyrical titles. A floor-to-ceiling, full-wall design of leafless trees was called *Beyond the path – you can see the sky* (1966), and later he designed a stylized landscape entitled *A gentle pleasure roaming in Indiana* (c.1968).

Denst was rightly proud of his firm's pioneering achievements in colour printing, particularly his use of pure pigments instead of traditional clay-based inks, resulting in colours of unusual luminosity and depth (fig. 5.59). "If we were to have listened to our printers and considered the limitations of the silk screen process, we should still be doing designs that would be served just as well through machine prints," he explained.[40] Denst's innovations culminated in an impressive collection of large repeat wallpapers called Dialogue 16 (1969). His penchant for witty and provocative titles reached a high point in this range, which included *A Dialogue of History and Contemporary Man*, juxtaposing silhouettes of skyscrapers with gothic arches, and *Jack Frost – You Rascal*, depicting giant ice patterns with a hint of Jugendstil. Art Nouveau influenced the looping ribbon pattern *Who is Julia*, while the Op-inspired *Point of Discussion* featured large, striped, colliding discs. "The Mystic, the architect, and even the couturière are among the improbable but pervading spirits of this collection," said Denst, "each inspiring my hand to turn to the exotic, the cool contemporary, or the glossy 'patent leather' look. A literal panorama of designs in extravagant colours, this collection contains my personal message of conviction that pattern has returned to all four walls."[41]

United States: United DeSoto

Novelty wallpapers had existed since the late 19th century, but it was in the 1960s that this area of the market really exploded. In 1966 United Wallpaper produced its Feminique collection, which included comic and film-linked wallpapers featuring characters such as Superman, Batman, and James Bond. One of the largest American manufacturers, the Chicago-based United Wallpaper – a division of DeSoto Chemical Coatings – was later renamed United DeSoto. During the late 1960s, under the design direction of William Sefton, it entered an astonishingly fertile and confident phase. "Modern tastes have given us the freedom to include exciting new patterns and to step up the wattage on the colours," said Sefton. "Our goal is to design wallcoverings for all types of home decorators. We try to come up with new twists on colonial patterns for the New England homemaker, op arts for the swingers, flocks for those with plush tastes, children's designs – new and exciting patterns for every type of personality and decor."[42]

United DeSoto scored its biggest success of the decade with Bravo, a free-wheeling Pop collection subtitled "Young Ideas for the New Generation," which caused a sensation in 1968. "From nearly every viewpoint the line was a revolution in itself," noted *Wallpaper & Wallcoverings* magazine. "It was a machine print line that appealed to hand-print oriented consumers. Designs were big, bold and, most important, *young*. Not only were designs big but they were printed in the brightest, newest colours. The secret was that they were the first manufacturer to add fluorescent pigments to their regular paint pigments, noticeably intensifying the colours."[43] Technically ingenious, the collection included everything from "wet look" finishes simulating patent leather to electrostatically applied acrylic flocks. Bravo's Space Age shiny silver foils were particularly innovative, especially those using Mylar (a polyester film produced by Dupont as a spin-off from the NASA space programme) as a background for printed patterns.

Bravo was designed by United DeSoto's in-house team, which included Willie Alexander, David Beskid, Russel Des Enfants, Stephen Fania, Richard Hoffman, and Raymond Woessner. Irreverence and fun were the keynotes of the collection, which cocked a snook at good taste and the establishment. *Doctor Livingston I Presume*, an outrageous flocked Op pattern featuring massed leopards and tigers, characterized the spirit of iconoclasm. Another outrageous design was *Secretarial Pool*, a Pop photo-collage composed of jumbled engravings of Victorian female nudes. *Where It's At* made a direct assault on teenagers through its arresting magazine-style graphics (fig. 5.60). *Dead End* was composed of traffic signs, and other patterns featured large directional "black" arrows on "wet look" or metallic grounds. Op was celebrated in *Way Out*, a large design featuring black and white stripes with giant, button-like indentations. Carnaby Street and flower power were the genres quoted in *Pick-A-Dilly*, a flat floral in pulsating colours. *Be-Dazzled* was a Pucciesque paisley printed on silver, and *Strip-Strap* featured a medley of psychedelic borders.

"The growing youth market has set the trend toward bold way-out designs," announced United DeSoto, "but Bravo's smashing sales record indicates there is an increasing interest in such patterns with the 'young at heart' as well."[44] Through promotional booklets such as *Wallcoverings and You* (1969), the company encouraged consumers to be more adventurous and liberal in their use of wallpapers, applying them to ceilings and furniture as well as walls. Bravo's success stimulated other companies to launch assertively upbeat collections. Among these was Blue River, whose Hand Prints Vol.1 (1967–71) contained silver mylar and vinyl-coated patent effects (fig. 5.61). Woodson Wallpapers, which specialized in hand screen-printed coordinated fabrics and wallpapers, produced psychedelic paisleys, including *Malabar* and *Carnival*, in 1968–9. These patterns not only reflected the prevailing interest in Victorian and ethnic design, but also highlighted the American love affair with Pucci.

Italy: Pucci

The Italian aristocrat Emilio Pucci began his career in 1948 as a designer of sportswear, but soon expanded into the wider field of fashion casuals. Although based in Florence, he established close links with American manufacturers and retailers, and Pucci soon became a leading brand in the United States. Printed patterns were

a key element of the company's garments and accessories from the 1950s, all designed by Pucci himself. Printed on cotton, silk, silk jersey, and later synthetics, early designs were strongly Mediterranean, featuring eclectic classical and Sicilian motifs.

Dubbed the "Prince of Prints," Pucci exerted a huge influence that spilled out from fashion to furnishings during the 1960s, and his colours and patterns became more and more intense. Reflecting diverse influences from Op to psychedelia, his designs became increasingly abstract over the course of the decade, although representational motifs never completely disappeared. During this period Pucci's sources became more global, inspired by his travels to Indonesia, India, Africa, and South America. His range of products burgeoned during the mid-1960s, encompassing ties and tights, handbags and towels. "These were the years in which Puccimania filled the headlines of American magazines and newspapers," recalled Katell le Bourhis. "Pucci prints were the most widely copied fashion phenomenon in the United States."[45]

Two collections, Vivara (1965–6) (fig. 5.62) and Paggio (1966), marked a high point, juxtaposing modules of vibrant organic and geometric patterns, printed either in hot yellows, pinks, and oranges or Mediterranean purples, blues, and greens. Patterns were often composed on the diagonal with intricate, winding structures, and some designs, such as *Portici*, were melted and fluid. After the Vivace collection (1967), however, fashion changed dramatically. Daring futurism was dropped in favour of limp romanticism, and during the early 1970s the market for Pucci prints collapsed.

Ruralism, Revivalism, and Giganticism

It is customary to write off the 1970s as the decade that design forgot, but in reality it was more of a mixed bag. The oil crisis of 1973, and the ensuing global recession, had a huge impact on the textile and wallpaper industries, prompting the closure of many firms and the dramatic shrinking of huge conglomerates. The buoyancy and confidence of the post-war years were replaced by insecurity and doubt. This, in turn, undermined confidence in design, inhibiting innovation and risk-taking in favour of safe solutions. "Does our age have a style?" asked the Swedish design magazine *Form* in 1977, reflecting the degree to which confidence had been eroded by the collapse of Sweden's textile industry. In Britain the economic situation was even more dire. Huge swathes of the manufacturing sector were decimated – production in the textile industry dropped by 50 percent between 1972 and 1982 – and this had a serious effect on the careers of pattern designers.

In terms of style, however, the 1970s was, like any other period, part of a continuing cycle of reaction and counter-reaction. Design momentum did not stop with the onset of recession, but was simply redirected into different channels. Some of these avenues were still overtly futuristic, exaggerating and embellishing Space Age phenomena such as Op and Pop. But others were openly reactionary, and hard-core Modernism was increasingly rejected in favour of soft-focus ruralism and nostalgia. Economic instability, social unrest, and growing concern about the environment all intensified the impulse towards escapism, as consumers sought to establish a cosy domestic retreat in an increasingly disquieting world. "In the 1970s – the beige decade – we saw the popularization and exploitation of the 'natural' looks," observed Jack Lenor Larsen. "Eclecticism was rampant, and so was a nostalgia strangely new, and the erasing of many of the barriers between modern and traditional design."[1]

Many of the issues that came to a head during the 1970s had, in fact, been welling up throughout the previous decade. Revivalism, active since the mid-1960s, was intensified during the 1970s.

Opposite Fig. 6.1
Sågblad screen-printed cotton furnishing fabric, designed by Ingela Håkansson, printed by Borås Wäfveri for the Tio-Gruppen, 1977. During the 1970s the members of Sweden's Tio-Gruppen revitalized pattern design with their brightly coloured, graphically direct fabrics and wallpapers. This design, whose title means "saw-blade," was featured in the group's influential Black/White collection. Black backgrounds are rare in printed furnishing fabrics, although, as this example demonstrates, they can be used to striking effect.

Originally a playful exercise, part of a process of re-evaluation, it later became more cynical, exploited as a lucrative commercial formula. It culminated in the so-called "document" collections – designs based on period textiles and wallpapers held in museum or company archives – which slowed the momentum in design. "Design leadership was fuzzy," noted Larsen. "Market focus, with increasingly important emphasis on best sellers, was on the minds of most designers and manufacturers."[2] Despite the general loss of nerve, however, there were some extremely positive initiatives, particularly in Sweden, where the revolutionary Tio-Gruppen was founded (figs. 6.1, 6.5, and 6.8), and in Germany, where the textile firm Stuttgarter Gardinenfabrik and the wallpaper company Marburger reasserted their commitment to progressive design.

Technical refinements, such as the widespread adoption of flexographic and photogravure printing in the wallpaper industry, had a major impact on furnishings, giving them a smoother and more standardized appearance. Similarly, in textiles, the idiosyncrasies of hand screen-printing were replaced by the predictability of fully mechanized rotary screen-printing, resulting in fabrics that, while technically perfect, were lacking in tactile expression. Printed patterns had to work much harder to make an impact, therefore, to counter the more polished finish of the medium. This may account for some of the design excesses of the 1970s – giganticism, revivalism and ruralism, to name but three.

Sweden: Tio-Gruppen

After the Second World War, Sweden had emerged as an international design superpower, with textiles central to its creative achievements. However, as the woven textile designer Age Faith-Ell observed regretfully: "At the end of the 1960s, our luck turned. There was a crisis in the textile industry. Many factories closed and many designers lost their jobs."[3] But even before the economic downturn textile designers were becoming increasingly dissatisfied with their lot, frustrated with the negative attitude of manufacturers and their cavalier approach when translating their patterns into cloth. One solution was to form collectives and to take control of the production of their own designs. Some rejected industry altogether and set up shared craft workshops, printing their own textiles by hand. The Stockholm-based Textilgruppen (Textile Group) had forty-four members, and also important was the Konstnärernas Kollektivverkstad (Artists' Collective Workshop), which opened in 1970, providing communal facilities. However, although such workshops provided a healthy avenue for experimentation, the fabrics were limited to short runs. For designers committed to mass production, it was the Tio-Gruppen (Ten Swedish Designers) that provided a viable alternative.

Formed in 1970 as a radical protest group, the Tio-Gruppen aimed to bypass the industry's stranglehold on design. Established at the initiative of Inez Svensson, formerly head of design at Borås Wäfveri, it brought together ten like-minded but creatively diverse individuals, some with experience in fashion and graphics as well as textile design. Apart from Svensson, the original members were Gunila Axén, Britt-Marie Christoffersson, Carl Johan De Geer, Susanne Grundell, Lotta Hagerman, Birgitta Hahn, Ingela Håkansson, Tom Hedqvist, and Tage Möller. The Tio-Gruppen's aim was to seize power from timid industrialists and repressive retailers, and to establish its own alternative design-led chain of supply. As artists, the group wanted to be free to innovate and to exert full control over the interpretation of their designs. Instead of taking jobs as in-house factory designers, or selling designs to the trade on a freelance basis, members arranged for their collections to be commission-printed in factories, but marketed under the Tio-Gruppen name. Henceforth Borås Wäfveri became the group's contractor rather than its client, and thus the normal designer-manufacturer relationship was inverted, with the designers in control. Direct action was the Tio-Gruppen's *modus operandi*. The group announced its formation and its early collections by means of manifesto-like posters and performance art-style exhibitions. Also taking direct responsibility for marketing, it opened a Tio-Gruppen shop in Stockholm in 1973.

Although created by ten very different individuals, Tio-Gruppen patterns had a coherence that made them immediately identifiable as part of a family group. Partly this arose out of an electrifying use of colour – typically bold primaries or intense secondaries – and partly from a startlingly direct graphic approach to textile design. Hahn believed there was a definite correlation between strong colour and upbeat mood. Within this framework each designer retained his or her own distinctive character. "We were very different from the beginning," recalled Lotta Hagerman, "but our fabric patterns gradually became closely linked."[4]

The first Tio-Gruppen collection, featuring one pattern by each designer, was launched in 1972. A truly startling debut, it included remarkable designs such as *Hundar* by Gunila Axén, depicting barking dogs with cartoon voice bubbles (fig. 6.2); *Kyoto* by Tom Hedqvist, a punchy design featuring stark bird symbols (fig. 6.3); and *Blixten* by Birgitta Hahn (fig. 6.4), with its diagonally cascading segments and flashes of lightning. Inez Svensson, who favoured pure geometry, created the optical design *Kuba*. Also in the abstract geometric idiom were the striped *Zip* by Susanne Grundell, the plaid *Sport* by Ingela Håkansson, and *Skvär* by Britt-Marie Christoffersson, resembling a patchwork of flags. Tage Möller created a stylized summer landscape called *Sommaräng*; Lotta Hagerman's *Angels* was a fanciful figurative design; and *Rendez-vous* by Carl Johan De Geer, with its intertwining plant forms, expressed his own brand of hippy folk art (fig. 6.8).

In 1973 the Tio-Gruppen issued its Basic collection, five ultra-simple patterns intended to complement its earlier range and typified by *Böljan* by Birgitta Hahn, which featured horizontal white wavy lines on a coloured ground. It also teamed up with

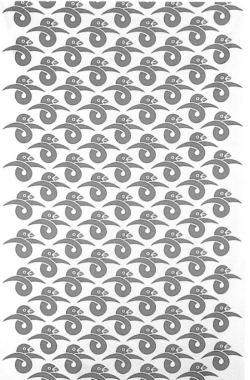

Far left top Fig. 6.2
Hundar screen-printed cotton furnishing fabric, designed by Gunila Axén, printed by Borås Wäfveri for the Tio-Gruppen, 1972. This cheeky pattern sums up the irreverent attitude of the Tio-Gruppen. With its launch collection the group promoted a ground-breaking new creative agenda.

Far left bottom Fig. 6.3
Kyoto screen-printed cotton furnishing fabric, designed by Tom Hedqvist, printed by Borås Wäfveri for the Tio-Gruppen, 1972. The Tio-Gruppen's ten designers came from diverse backgrounds. Tom Hedqvist's expertise in graphics is reflected in this punchy design.

Left top Fig. 6.4
Blixten screen-printed cotton furnishing fabric, designed by Birgitta Hahn, printed by Borås Wäfveri for the the Tio-Gruppen, 1972. This pattern, whose title means "flash," appeared in the Tio-Gruppen's launch collection. It illustrates Birgitta Hahn's skill in designing on the diagonal.

Left bottom Fig. 6.5
Bananasplit screen-printed cotton furnishing fabric, designed by Inez Svensson, printed by Borås Wäfveri for the Tio-Gruppen, 1979. In this playful crazy-paving pattern from the Jamaica collection, Inez Svensson broke with her customary practice of creating regular geometric designs.

Top Fig. 6.6
Dataros *screen-printed fibreglass furnishing fabric, designed by Astrid Sampe, printed by Ljungbergs Textiltryck for Nordiska Kompaniet, 1975.* This and *Datorcolonne* (above) were experimental patterns that arose out of a collaboration between veteran designer Astrid Sampe and the computer company IBM.

Above Fig. 6.7
Datorcolonne *screen-printed cotton furnishing fabric, designed by Astrid Sampe, 1975, reprinted by Ljungbergs Textiltryck, 1984.* Astrid Sampe's long-standing interest in technology led her to appreciate the potential of computers as a tool for pattern designers at an early date.

Duro, which issued two Tio-Gruppen wallpaper collections in 1973 and 1978. Although intended to complement the group's fabrics, the wallpapers were generally less assertive, with smaller motifs and a more restrained palette, as in Inez Svensson's pale-blue and white diagonal-striped *Uppåner* (1973). Light, airy, stylized nature patterns were also produced, such as the floral *Blombersä* (1973) by Birgitta Hahn and *Grass* (1978) by Susanne Grundell. "Original patterns have an incubation time of about two years," observed Duro's managing director, Nille Kjerstensson. "If a pattern is an immediate success it is a sign that it is a copy of something."[5]

The Tio-Gruppen's first thematic collection, Sea, appeared in 1975, featuring designs such as Carl Johan De Geer's *Flygfiskar*, a fantastical pattern of flying fish in blazing colours. The following year IKEA began to purchase Tio-Gruppen fabrics for tablecloths, bedspreads, and wall hangings. *Öar* by Gunila Axén, depicting jagged, hilly islands emerging from a spotted sea, was a runaway success. Striking for its black background, it paved the way for the Tio-Gruppen's Black/White collection (1977), consisting exclusively of coloured patterns printed on white or black. Ingela Håkansson's *Sågblad*, depicting floating coloured leaves on a black background, stood out (fig. 6.1). In the Jamaica collection (1979) the primary palette was supplemented by unusual shades of pea green and pale blue, and Inez Svensson broke away from her standard horizontals and verticals with a striped crazy-paving pattern called *Bananasplit* (fig. 6.5). By this date the group's aesthetic had struck a chord on an international level, signified by a special collection for IKEA in 1978. "The design world engaged in an unequal struggle with commercialism," observed Kerstin Wickman. "During these miserable seventies Ten Swedish Designers filled a vacuum."[6]

Sweden: Ljungbergs and Borås Wäfveri

Peter Condu was another designer who took control of the production of his textiles during the 1970s, collaborating with master printers Ljungbergs Textiltryck to produce his powerful graphic abstract designs. Ljungbergs also printed a remarkable group of patterns by Astrid Sampe for Nordiska Kompaniet, resulting from her collaboration with the computer firm IBM. In 1975, working with the IBM programmer Sten Kallin, she became one of the first textile designers in the world to create patterns using a computer. The arresting *Dataros* (fig. 6.6) and *Datorcolonne* (fig. 6.7), both originally printed on fibreglass, recalled complex Spirograph drawings and the fluctuations of seismographs.

Equally ambitious was the work of Sven Fristedt, whose remarkable run of creativity at Borås Wäfveri continued throughout the 1970s. At the start of the decade his designs were characterized by rippling, amorphous forms, evoking the freedom and fluidity of psychedelia, but magnified in scale. Some patterns, such as the wavy-striped *Stora Bält* (1970), were produced in dramatic black and white (fig. 6.9). Others, such as the ghostly *Frost* (1970), were printed in white on unbleached cloth. When Fristedt exploited colour, it was

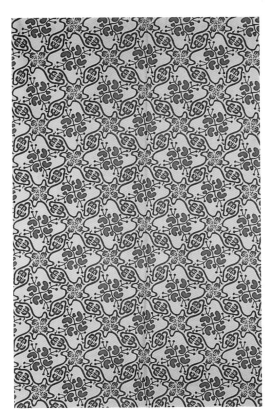

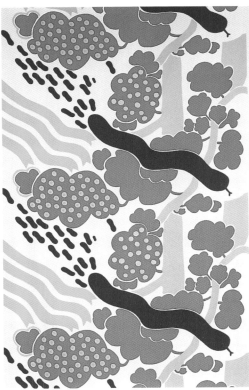

Far left top Fig. 6.8
Rendez-vous screen-printed cotton furnishing fabric, designed by Carl Johan De Geer, printed by Borås Wäfveri for the Tio-Gruppen, 1972. The idiosyncratic composition, colouring, and imagery of this pattern reflect the nonconformist approach of Carl Johan De Geer.

Far left bottom Fig. 6.9
Stora Bält screen-printed cotton furnishing fabric, designed by Sven Fristedt, produced by Borås Wäfveri, 1970. This was one of a series of dramatic, fluid, large-scale abstract patterns created by Sven Fristedt, some in black and white, others in white on off-white.

Left top Fig. 6.10
Jazz screen-printed cotton furnishing fabric, designed by Hans Krondahl, produced by Borås Wäfveri, 1968. Having originally developed these arresting collage-style patterns during the late 1960s, Hans Krondahl continued to refine this idiom during the early 1970s.

Left bottom Fig. 6.11
Paradis screen-printed cotton furnishing fabric, designed by Charlotte Lallerstedt, produced by KF Interior, 1971. KF Interior produced many innovative printed fabrics during the 1970s. This huge pattern, shown here at full width, depicts the serpent in the Garden of Eden.

Top Fig. 6.12
Gimmic screen-printed cotton furnishing fabric, designed by Louise Carling, produced by Almedahls, 1972. The giganticist propensities manifested internationally in pattern design during the early 1970s are reflected in this large-scale floral, printed in modish dark brown.

Above Fig. 6.13
Den glade bagarn screen-printed cotton furnishing fabric, designed by Anne-Marie Netterdag, produced by Alingsås Textiltryck, 1970s. Ruralist nostalgia became a potent force in design during the 1970s. In Sweden it surfaced in a spate of idyllic, cartoon-like depictions of villages.

in a pure, direct way, as in the tangled ribbons of *Ormen* (1972) and *Glada Blad* (1973), featuring white silhouetted leaves on a coloured ground. All his patterns were perversely irregular, defying conventional rhythms with clusters and surges of mass.

Other contributors at Borås Wäfveri during the 1970s included Lena Andersson, Mona Björk, Lena Boje, Teija Bruhn, Ingela Håkansson, Studio Hoff, Annika Malmström, Ateljé Miljö, Annica Nordlöf, and Marie-Louise Sjöblom. Hans Krondahl, by this time a seasoned contributor, continued to supply bold, colourful designs inspired by Matisse (fig. 6.10). Cut-out shapes also formed the basis for an inspirational group of patterns by Krondahl for Katja of Sweden between 1970 and 1975, printed by Alingsås on stretch fabrics.

Sweden: IKEA and KF Interior

Working alongside Sven Fristedt at Borås Wäfveri during the early 1970s was Vivianne Sjölin, whose appointment as head of textiles at IKEA in 1974 prompted many exciting commissions from Fristedt, Göta Trägårdh, the Tio-Gruppen, and others. Founded by Ingvar Kamprad in 1943, IKEA gradually evolved from wholesaler to manufacturer to retailer, opening its first store in Sweden in 1958 and expanding into Europe during the 1970s and the United States during the 1980s. Working with a network of manufacturers, IKEA originated and commissioned an extensive range of products, including furnishings, furniture, and accessories. Its role as a champion and popularizer of a distinctly Swedish aesthetic in textiles began during the late 1960s when it began to sell printed textiles by designers such as Birgitta Hahn, Sven Fristedt, and Göta Trägårdh. During the 1970s the company produced designs by, among others, Viola Gråsten, Annika Malmström, Anne-Marie Netterdag, and Inez Svensson, and at this time textiles accounted for a quarter of its total sales. Svensson's positive-negative striped patterns *Strix* and *Strax* (both 1972), became IKEA classics, embodying the simplicity and directness of Swedish design. Often IKEA established an arrangement with another company, such as Strömma, to supply particular designs on an exclusive basis, and in this way it tapped into the best of Swedish design at the same time as forging its own identity.

Hedvig Hedqvist, head of design at KF Interior from 1967 to 1975, played a similarly influential role, shaping public taste through the range of textiles she commissioned for the cooperative society's nationwide chain of shops. One of the first to appreciate the talents of non-conformist designers such as Carl Johan De Geer, Hedqvist put into production lively Pop patterns by Birgitta Hahn, Charlotte Lallerstedt (fig. 6.11), and Ulla Ericson. Later KF Interior produced several designs by Inez Svensson, including the multicoloured, horizontal-striped *Pensel* (1977), meaning "paintbrush," and the checked two-colour *Bistro* (1978). "These large chains of furnishing stores that spread across the country in the seventies, were, with their commissions, the salvation of textile designers in Sweden," observed Kerstin Wickman.[7]

Sweden: Nordiska Kompaniet, Almedahls, and Strömma

In 1971 Nordiska Kompaniet closed its pioneering Textile Design Studio, which was replaced by the more generalized NK Design Group, headed by textile designer Wanja Djanaieff. Djanaieff had made her mark with a classic neo-primitive pattern called *Swans* (1970) for Almedahls, where she previously worked. Almedahls continued to produce some adventurous patterns during the early 1970s, typified by *Gimmic* (1972), an exploded Pop floral by Louise Carling, printed in newly fashionable brown (fig. 6.12). Among other designers for the company were Lisa Bauer, M.L. Bjerhagen, Ulla Bodin, Susan Engel, Toni Hermansson, Jennifer Jade, and Peter Wide. "To begin with, the designs of the 70s were very much in the pop art vein," noted Inez Svensson. "But a few years later a tidal wave of Swedish summer motifs with a good pinch of rustic romanticism swept in over the textile industry. Suddenly we were awash in naivist landscapes, gingham checks, ticking stripes and cute small town idylls."⁸ Wanja Djanaieff's *Idyll* (1972) for NK, depicting a summer picnic table, typified the new trend. Another accomplished exponent of the "naivist" style was Anne-Marie Netterdag, who excelled in whimsical cartoon panoramas of Swedish villages, resembling illustrations from children's books, as in *Skillingaryd* for IKEA and *Den glade bagarn* for Alingsås (fig. 6.13).

Wanja Djanaieff was appointed head of design at Strömma in 1977, where her debut collection was the romantically named Tones of the Folk Song. Strömma, founded in 1832, emerged as the most progressive Swedish textile company during the 1970s, producing patterns by top designers such as Kerstin Boulogner, Annika Malmström, and Göta Trägårdh Continuing where she had left off at Stobo during the mid-1960s, Göta Trägårdh created a remarkable series of large-scale designs for public spaces, another spectacular episode in an inspirational career. *Monolog* (1971) was a stimulating black-and-white design in the melted Op idiom. *Ikaros* (1971), with its giant, overlapping, radiating sun-discs, suggested the magnified workings of a machine (fig. 6.14). Strömma pursued its independent course until 1992, when it was taken over by Borås Wäfveri.

Finland: Marimekko

Having weathered a financial crisis in 1968, Marimekko was reorganized and henceforth assumed a more pragmatic character. A large new factory was opened at Herttoniemi in 1973, and from this time most of the firm's furnishing fabrics were rotary screen-printed, and its range of products was broadened to include wallpapers, table linen, and duvet covers. Having pushed bold, fluid abstraction as far as it could go, Maija Isola's work became more eclectic in style and subject matter. Her enduring interest in folk art resurfaced in patterns such as *Fortune Teller*, composed of arcane dotted lines. Other designs ranged from lively flat florals such as *Peony* to giant Pop cartoons such as *Pepe* (both 1972). Colour remained the key to Marimekko's distinctive character, and designers were able to choose from over 2,500 tones. David Davies

Above Fig. 6.14

Ikaros screen-printed cotton furnishing fabric, designed by Göta Trägårdh, produced by Strömma, 1971. Although Modernist abstraction was gradually eclipsed during the 1970s, at the start of the decade it was still being vigorously upheld and masterfully expounded by Göta Trägårdh.

noted in 1975: "Marimekko designers have sole responsibility for deciding all aspects of their work; no division of interests exists. Pattern, colours and choice of colourways are all considered as inseparable designer responsibilities, indicating the degree of respect and confidence enjoyed by the design team."[9]

Other pattern designers at this date included Maija Lavonen, Ristomatti Ratia, and Pentti Rinta. Rinta, who joined Marimekko as a fashion designer in 1969, designed furnishing fabrics with dramatic abstract compositions, such as *Tempest* (1977). Towards the end of the decade his ideas became increasingly conceptual, culminating in surreal landscapes such as *Connection* (1979), showing ploughed fields and sky, and the contemplative Phenomena of Light collection (1980). Two new designers, both from Japan, injected a rather different character into Marimekko's second-generation designs. Katsuji Wakisaka, who had trained at the Kyoto School of Art and Design, worked at Marimekko from 1968 to 1976 (fig. 6.15). He scored an early hit with *Yume* (1969), a nursery print featuring primitive drawings of animals in an endearingly naïve style. Later he successfully translated this aesthetic into Marimekko's main textile range through patterns such as *Straw* (1970), depicting houses and trees on mound-shaped hills. Intense bright colours – particularly yellow, red, orange, green, and blue – were a feature of his designs, which ranged from bold abstracts, such as the giant coloured circle pattern *Onnimanni*, to the stylized oak leaf and acorn pattern *Sademetsa*. Wakisaka also created subtle textural designs, such as the sponged *Saxifrage* (1975), produced in sombre, dark colours as well as his trademark vibrant hues.

The second Japanese designer to join Marimekko was Fujiwo Ishimoto, in 1974. Originally trained as a commercial artist, he developed an approach to pattern that was graphic in its simplicity, painterly in its boldness, and calligraphic in its finesse. Dramatic full-width patterns such as the zigzagging *Jama* and the criss-crossing *Sumo* (both 1977) were created from enlarged brushstrokes, while at the other extreme were the delicate striations of *Taiga* (1979). Rather than producing individual designs, Ishimoto preferred to create integrated collections. The Mättäillä collection (1979), inspired by Finnish forests and bogs, contained spotted and tufted patterns such as *Rimpi* and *Vihma*, printed in dark, earthy colours on unbleached cloth. Similar textural effects, but more loosely structured, were evident in the random combed *Painokangas* (1980), meaning "gust of wind." Webs and meshes were another recurrent theme in Ishimoto's early compositions, typified by the gossamer-like cocoons of *Katve* (1980) (fig. 6.16).

Finland: Porin Puuvilla, Tampella, and Vuokko
Spurred on by Marimekko, the Finns excelled in "supergraphics." Raili Konttinen and Juhani Konttinen produced arresting abstracts for Porin Puuvilla, some in bright colours, some in stark black and white. In 1973 Porin Puuvilla merged with Finlayson-Forssa, whose designers included Kaarina Berglund, Eine Ekroos, and Uhra

Top Fig. 6.15
Bo Boo *screen-printed cotton furnishing fabric, designed by Katsuji Wakisaka, produced by Marimekko, 1975.* Marimekko's upbeat, colourful style was well suited to nursery prints. Katsuji Wakisaka also applied this naive primitive aesthetic to the company's main furnishing ranges.

Above Fig. 6.16
Katve *screen-printed cotton furnishing fabric, designed by Fujiwo Ishimoto, produced by Marimekko, 1980.* The arrival of Marimekko's second Japanese designer, Fujiwo Ishimoto, opened up new creative avenues, triggering off a wave of patterns exploring texture and line.

Simberg-Ehrström. Tampella continued confidently, producing striking colourful abstract designs such as *Enza* (1972–3) by Barbara Brenner. At Vuokko the patterns of Vuokko Eskolin-Nurmesniemi became increasingly minimalist during the mid-1970s. In *Plaani* (1976) the pattern was reduced to a single black line zigzagging from side to side across the full width of the white fabric. At the end of the decade Vuokko changed direction, creating designs from enlarged grainy black-and-white photographic images of people and fruit, such as *Myllynkivi* (c.1979) and *Hedelmä* (1980) (fig. 6.17).

Germany: Stuttgarter Gardinenfabrik and Fuggerhaus

Germany's receptiveness to modern printed textiles had prompted Heal Fabrics to establish a German subsidiary in 1964. Marimekko followed suit in 1975, and Knoll in 1979. Germany's showcase printed textile firm was Stuttgarter Gardinenfabrik, whose output was dominated by Antoinette de Boer. De Boer had trained at the Hochschule für Bildende Künste in Hamburg from 1957 to 1961, where she was taught by Margret Hildebrand. She subsequently joined Hildebrand as a designer at Stuttgarter Gardinenfabrik in 1962, and was appointed studio head in 1963 and artistic director in 1975. From 1973 she also ran her own company, De Boer Design, designing carpets and household textiles.

Working in a confident modern abstract idiom, De Boer produced a stream of masterful patterns for Stuttgarter Gardinenfabrik. *Zimba* (1969), composed of wavy horizontal bands in graduated colours, demonstrated the essence of her style, at once rhythmically stimulating and highly controlled (fig. 6.18). Manipulation of colour formed the basis for many patterns, such as *Sipri* (1972), featuring rows of parallel tubes in subtly changing hues. Playful optical devices also formed a key part of her repertoire, as in *Mahan* (1974–5), suggesting interwoven webbing, and *Rinde* (1980), evoking grained wood. Sometimes flat patterns were designed to suggest draped undulations, as in *Zazi* (1969), with its disjointed strips of chevrons and waves, and *Baribada* (1977), a stretched and condensed harlequin pattern. Adopting a softer palette, De Boer continued exploring new avenues of abstraction into the following decade. Rigorous standards were also upheld in the work of other designers at Stuttgarter Gardinenfabrik. The freelance designer Tina Hahn contributed patterns such as *Macon* (1979), consisting of fine coloured rings in pipe formations (fig. 6.19). Heidi Bernstiel-Munsche, who worked as an in-house designer from 1964 to 1980, created patterns such as *Iwu* (1974), composed of diminishing diagonal stripes fragmenting into chequers.

Another company where printed patterns flourished during the 1970s was Fuggerhaus, founded at Augsburg in 1954. Best known for its woven upholstery fabrics, Fuggerhaus commissioned an innovative range of printed textiles from Wolf Bauer during the late 1970s. A leading freelance designer who collaborated with Heal Fabrics, Knoll, and Pausa, Bauer had studied under Leo Wollner at

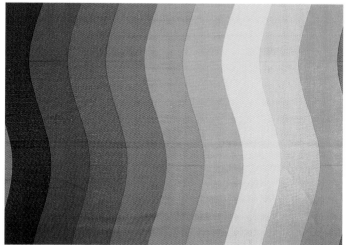

Top Fig. 6.17
Hedelmä *screen-printed cotton furnishing fabric, designed by Vuokko Eskolin-Nurmesniemi, produced by Vuokko, 1980.* Patterns exploiting photographs were a new phenomenon in the 1970s. Here the image has been artfully fragmented and distorted to increase its graphic impact.

Above Fig. 6.18
Zimba *screen-printed cotton and linen furnishing fabric, designed by Antoinette de Boer, produced by Stuttgarter Gardinenfabrik, 1969.* This colour spectrum pattern was a sophisticated precursor of some of the many textiles and wallpapers of the 1970s decorated with parallel coloured bands.

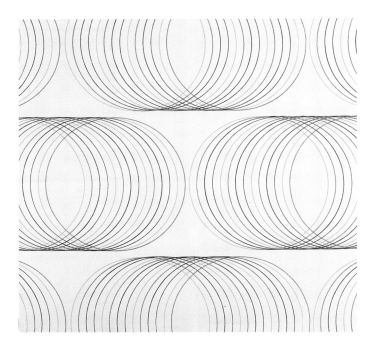

Top Fig. 6.19
Macon screen-printed cotton furnishing fabric, designed by Tina Hahn, produced by Stuttgarter Gardinenfabrik, 1979. Stuttgarter Gardinenfabrik retained its commitment to pure abstraction throughout the 1970s. Inspired colouring is the key to this memorable design.

Above Fig. 6.20
Decor 1 screen-printed cotton furnishing fabric, designed by Verner Panton, produced by Mira-X, 1969. This was one of the first patterns in an extended family of furnishing designs created by Panton for Mira-X. The graduated tones demonstrate his complex colour theories.

the Staatlichen Akademie der Bildende Künste in Stuttgart during the early 1960s. In the Articolor series (1978) he explored the visual impact of colour through diverse abstract idioms, ranging from tightly controlled geometric structures to fragmented and anarchic compositions.

Germany: Rasch, P. & S. International, and Marburger

The surge of creativity in German pattern design was also reflected in wallpapers. In 1973 Rasch produced Avan' Garde, a coordinated collection of printed fabrics and wallpapers designed by Klaus Dombrowski, composed of bold, colourful, large-scale abstract designs. Op Art and Pop Art were major sources of inspiration, and patterns included chevrons, targets, and interlocking coloured bands. Also launched the same year were two other progressive modern ranges, the Contempora and Künstler collections, featuring further designs by Dombrowski, along with others by Pat Albeck, Juliet Glynn Smith, Roger Limbrick, and Carola Olsen from Britain, and Wolf Bauer, Helmer Jehnert, and Peter Raacke from Germany. Giganticism was the keynote for all these collections, many of the pattern motifs being full-width. Another feature was flexibility: patterns designed to interlock in different ways and to run either horizontally or vertically, so that do-it-yourself murals could be created. However, towards the end of the decade fashions changed and gargantuan geometrics were replaced by the dense, discordant florals of the Jardin collection (1979).

In order to achieve stability during a time of economic turbulence, German wallpaper companies actively expanded their export markets. For example, Pickhardt and Siebert adopted the name P&S International, and the firm's Collection Duett (1975) was marketed in several European countries. With its huge patterns, dazzling compositions, and startling colours, this collection (subtitled The New Answer to Large Rooms) was the wallpaper equivalent of Glam Rock. Produced at the height of the trend for giganticism, it featured decadent exploded versions of Op, Pop, flower power, psychedelic, and Art Nouveau patterns. Instead of "tasteful" coordination, the wallpapers of Collection Duett gleefully celebrated the concept of pattern overkill.

Marburger had also explored daring forms of art-inspired abstraction in its Arte collection (1968-9), which featured expressive giant patterns by Brigitte Doeg with heightened colouring by Hilde Eitel. In 1972 it went one step further by collaborating with the Zurich Gallery to produce the Xartwall collection, featuring designs by leading European artists. Among the contributors to what was one of the most radical initiatives ever undertaken in the wallpaper industry were Otmar Alt, Getulio Alviani, Werner Berges, Niki de Saint Phalle, Allen Jones, Peter Phillips, Jean Tinguely, and Paul Wunderlich. Each pattern was highly idiosyncratic, and no limitations were placed on subject matter or style. Getulio Alviani's *Testura Grafica* used Op techniques to simulate a padded wall, while Jean Tinguely's *Vive La Liberté* juxtaposed scattered "found" images with crazy diagrams. Some artists adopted shock tactics to challenge conventional notions of decoration, as in Paul Wunderlich's *trompe l'oeil* pattern *Shadow Folds*, evoking the contours of female breasts. Xartwall was not only artistically ground-breaking but also technically innovative, incorporating special effects such as textured polyester foil in Peter Phillips's *Kenya* wallpaper. The most effective designs were those that exploited graphic devices, such as Werner Berges's *Beauty*, depicting a woman's head with coloured stripes (fig. 6.21). Otmar Alt's *Happy Cow* and Niki de Saint Phalle's *Nana* both featured giant cartoon-like animals and figures. Irreverence was the keynote. *Nana*, resembling Saint Phalle's jaunty, rumbustious sculptures, was printed in shocking pink.

Switzerland: Mira-X

During the early 1960s Verner Panton had played a key role in pushing forward the boundaries of colour theory and pattern design. In 1969 he teamed up with Mira-X, a Swiss firm whose textiles were printed by Pausa and Taunus in Germany, and with which he collaborated until 1985. A limited vocabulary of geometric forms, including triangles, squares, stripes, and circles, formed the basis for an extensive range of furnishing fabrics and carpets exploring diverse complex optical effects. Some of Panton's printed patterns were broken down to a minute level, resembling graph paper or scientific charts. Others were simpler and more direct, including broad, multicoloured stripes and concentric rings (fig. 6.20). Initially based on a system of twelve basic colours, consisting of three yellows, three reds, three blues, and three greens, Panton's palette was later expanded to encompass eighty-six related colours, including lighter pastels, darker bass tones, and what he called "spectral colours" and "naturals." "Our concept is to be able to combine, without any problem, colours of the same degree of strength and brightness," he explained.[10]

Netherlands: Ploeg

Traditionally the chief area of textile production in the Netherlands was linen damasks, and the country was not generally associated with printed textiles. From 1957, however, Weverij De Ploeg NV, which was originally founded as a cooperative weaving company in 1923, began to expand into this area, specializing in printed and woven fabrics in integrated colours. During the 1930s Ploeg had worked closely with the Bauhaus-trained weaver Otti Berger, and Modernism remained central to the company's ethos. Ulf Moritz designed for Ploeg during the 1960s, and in 1965 it produced a group of textural abstracts by two British designers, Janet Taylor, and John Wright. These were followed by bold, large-scale designs such as *Polaris* (1975) by Jeanne Schaap, evoking vintage Marimekko. Subsequently the Modernist idiom was resumed, however, and during the 1980s striped patterns, such as *Collino* (1982), created by the Ploeg Design Team, made up the core of the company's repertoire.

Above Fig. 6.21
Beauty *screen-printed wallpaper, designed by Werner Berges, produced by Marburger, 1972.* This extraordinary pattern, more like a rock album cover than a wallpaper, formed part of the Xartwall collection, a compilation of designs by leading European artists.

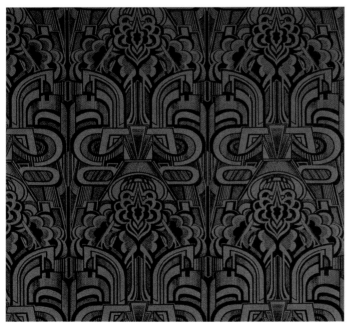

Top Fig. 6.22
Deco screen-printed wallpaper, designed
by Judith Cash, produced by Sanderson,
1971. Gaining momentum during the
late 1960s, the Art Deco Revival was
in full swing by the early 1970s. This
jazzy pattern from the Palladio 9
collection was printed in fashionable
silver and brown.

Above Fig. 6.23
Apollo screen-printed wallpaper, designed
by John Wilkinson, produced by
Sanderson, 1971. The eclectic patterns
that made up Palladio 9 reflected the
fragmentation of design during the
early 1970s. This wallpaper was an
Art Deco-inspired celebration of
Apollo 11's moon landing in 1969.

Britain: Sanderson wallpapers

The 1970s witnessed the dismemberment of the once-powerful
WPM, now drastically reduced in size and renamed Crown
Wallcoverings. Sanderson retained its separate identity, although
machine-printed wallpaper production was transferred to a Crown
factory at Gosport, Hampshire, during the early 1970s. Production
of block-printed and hand screen-printed wallpapers continued at
Sanderson's Perivale factory, and printed textiles were still produced
at its Uxbridge branch, where the main design studio for both
operations was now located. As the market for wallpapers declined,
however, the emphasis gradually shifted from wallpapers to fabrics.

The shift from Modernism to Revivalism that had begun in Britain
during the late 1960s reached fruition in the following decade. The
Palladio 9 wallpaper collection, produced by Sanderson in 1971,
signalled the end of the road for this showcase architect's range.
Markedly less coherent than the earlier collections, it reflected the
growing fragmentation of design through the clear divergence
between different trends. Styled by Edward Pond, it featured many
designers from the earlier ranges, along with Pat Etheridge from
the Sanderson studio, and new faces such as John Garnet, Clare
Hartley Jones, Peter Jones, Shelagh Wakely, and John Wilkinson.
Historical revivalism was a dominant theme of the collection.
Clare Hartley Jones's *Cranston* – referring to the chain of tearooms
decorated by Charles Rennie Mackintosh – was an overt homage to
the Glasgow School, although the choice of hot pinks and oranges
added a contemporary twist. In David Bartle's *Gandalf* the sinuous
lines of Art Nouveau were reheated and injected with "trippy"
colours (fig. 6.24). Art Deco was another favoured genre, its innate
exuberance appealing to the prevailing spirit of excess. *Deco* by
Judith Cash, with its jagged borders and shooting-star motifs, was
a full-throttle celebration of the Jazz Age (fig. 6.22), as was *Main
Street*, a giant radiating starburst pattern by John Wilkinson. Both
were produced in silver and gold. Art Deco Revival, couched in a
high-Pop idiom, was also the driving force behind John Garnet's
Broadway East and *Broadway West*, two complementary patterns
featuring skyscraper ziggurats and fountain motifs. Even Space
Age patterns, such as John Wilkinson's *Apollo*, were redolent with
streamlined Art Deco styling (fig. 6.23).

Shelagh Wakely's *Stereo One* and *Stereo Two*, composed of bands
of disjointed diagonal stripes, were produced in complementary
positive-negative colourways, for use on adjacent walls. These
designs displayed the legacy of Op Art, as did Edward Pond's
complex hexagonal *Zeppelin*. The decade's rampant eclecticism was
reflected in Tony Fraser's *Monte Carlo*, a sumptuous paisley, while
John Garnet's *Mata-Hari* used Islamic motifs. Both were printed
in decadent colours, combining turquoise, mauve, purple, and gold.
Sanderson's Pavilion (1973–4), a collection of vinyl wallpapers
coordinated by Edward Pond, also had strong ethnic overtones,
although patterns such as *Kasim*, *Pergola*, and *Sultan* were on a
much smaller scale and were treated rather more formulaically.

Sanderson had long been associated with the vogue for period design, and in 1974 it launched its upmarket Heritage collection, featuring hand block-printed and screen-printed designs by William Morris, C.F.A. Voysey, Owen Jones, and Lewis F. Day. Meanwhile the company's Triad collections of coordinated textiles and wallpapers met with continuing success, and from 1974 it adopted the American fashion of colour-coordinated patterns and stripes. Designs ranged from soft-focus florals to pepped-up Morris variants, to dainty, small-scale chintzes. "Big designs had had it by 73," noted Edward Pond. "Manufacturers and customers played safe as a need for security represented itself in chintzy cheerfulness and more and more small-scale co-ordination."[11]

Britain: ICI

ICI's Vymura range took on a rather decadent character during the early 1970s. Sizzling pink florals in a Pop version of the Victorian style, such as *Romany* by Pat Hopkins (1972), became popular, along with small-scale modular geometrics, such as *Checkpoint* (1972) by Sue Faulkner, produced in a Biba-inspired palette of turquoise, purple, and black. Black-and-white patterns, reflecting the combined influence of Aubrey Beardsley and Op Art, were also fashionable, and the two genres were melded in patterns such as *Barbarella* (1974), depicting black and white striped flowers in a heightened, dream-like style (fig. 6.25). In 1976 ICI won a Design Centre Award for its Studio One collection, its first range produced using rotary screen-printing. Styled by Sue Faulkner, the collection had pale brown, cream, and petrol blue as its predominant colours, and the patterns were mostly formal geometrics, such as *Piazza*, or trellis and interlace designs, such as *Plaza* and *Treillage*. Studio One was notable for offering the same patterns in three different sizes. "I wanted to give the customers the chance to be creative, to work out their own schemes without dictating to them," Faulkner explained.[12] By the end of the decade, however, a change of major direction was evident, as abstraction was abandoned in favour of miniaturized florals. In 1979, following the lead of Sanderson and Laura Ashley, ICI launched a range of coordinated printed fabrics and wallpapers called the Vymura Interior Designer collection, featuring small retro-florals such as *Etienne*.

Britain: Osborne & Little

In 1968 a new company was founded that set out to challenge the monopoly of the mainstream wallpaper industry. Osborne & Little, established by the designer Antony Little and his brother-in-law Peter Osborne, initially specialized in hand screen-printed wallpapers, produced in-house. Little had trained at Kingston School of Art during the early 1960s and then worked as a book illustrator and interior designer for five years, designing textiles and wallpapers for private clients. It was this experience that prompted him to establish his own firm.

Little's early designs included Pop-psychedelic flat florals such as *Oxeye Daisy* (1968), and metallic Op abstracts such as *Cul-de-Sac*

Top fig. 6.24
Gandalf screen-printed wallpaper, designed by David Bartle, produced by Sanderson, 1971. The title of this pattern refers to a character in *The Lord of the Rings.* Art Nouveau revivalism remained popular into the 1970s, latterly injected with more pronounced psychedelic overtones.

Above Fig. 6.25
Barbarella vinyl wallpaper, designed and produced by ICI, 1974. The influence of popular culture is reflected in the title of this wallpaper, taken from a cult science-fiction film. The pattern contains stylistic allusions to Op Art, although the floral imagery reflects the mounting tide of ruralism.

Top Fig. 6.26
(First three rolls, left to right) **Links**, **Parsley**, *and* **Willow** *flexo-printed wallpapers, produced by Osborne & Little, 1977.* Drawing on historical sources but reinterpreting them in a fresh modern idiom, Osborne & Little developed a range of practical small-scale wallpaper patterns in attractive colours.

Above Fig. 6.27
Sarah *flexo-printed wallpapers, designed by Linda Beard, produced by Coloroll, 1979.* Catering to the fashion for miniaturized florals, this pattern was part of Coloroll's highly successful Dolly Mixtures range. Designed for the mass market, it is illustrated here in three colourways.

(1971). Countering the prevailing trend towards giganticism, he pioneered the introduction of small, tightly organized patterns composed of interlocking modular units, arranged in a consciously repetitive manner. The neat disciplined patterns of Owen Jones were a key source of early inspiration, along with Islamic design, the latter reflected in the titles *Rabat*, *Minaret*, and *Koh-I-Nor* (all c.1968), part of a group of patterns that won a Design Centre Award in 1970. "Antony Little points out that his designs are mostly tradition-based," noted *Design* magazine at the time of the award. "Several are simplified versions of Islamic patterning, either for carpets or tapestries; others are reminiscent of Victorian tilework or Regency papers. These are transformed by fresh and original colour combinations, with many strong darkened primary colours."[13]

Other contributors to the Osborne & Little range during the late 1960s and 1970s included Linda Bruce, Collier Campbell, Edward Gilbert, Sara Gravestone, and Julie Hodgson, but as the company built up its own studio individual designers were no longer identified. Pop elements continued to resurface on occasion, as in a metallic vinyl wallpaper decorated with zebra motifs designed by Linda Bruce in 1975, and the self-consciously kitsch *Palm Trees* (1979) by Sara Gravestone. However, the general trend was towards informal formality, with tried-and-tested historical design formulae reinterpreted in a crisp, modern way (fig. 6.26). Coordinated printed fabrics, introduced in 1975, included designs such as *Pomegranate* by Antony Little, a leafy homage to William Morris. From 1976 most of Osborne & Little's wallpaper collections were mass-produced by flexographic printing (see below), an indication of the rapidity with which the company had penetrated the market.

Britain: Coloroll

Although it was expanding, Osborne & Little remained decidedly upmarket during the 1970s. More significant in the field of low-cost wallpapers was Coloroll, which rapidly captured the mass market over the next twenty years. The firm began life as a manufacturer of paper bags during the 1960s, but later diversified into wallpaper. Its success was based on its early adoption of flexographic printing, an economical, high-volume process in which low-relief rubber rollers were used in conjunction with solvent-based inks. Although Coloroll later became associated with derivative designs, particularly imitative versions of Laura Ashley, its early wallpapers were showcased at the Design Centre in 1969–70 – the ultimate design establishment accolade. In 1974 the company produced a lively collection designed by David Hicks, featuring South American ziggurat and Celtic knotwork patterns, in a somewhat unlikely alliance between a high-end designer and a low-end firm. Coloroll's breakthrough collection, Dolly Mixtures (1978), was designed by Linda Beard, and featured easily digestible, miniaturized floral motifs (fig. 6.27). Coordinated printed fabrics were later introduced, and these were successfully marketed through budget retail outlets. The driving force behind Coloroll's expansion was its art director, John Wilman, who later established his own company.

Britain: Textiles

"Britain's textile industry has always been characterized by a boom/slump business cycle," observed Bruce Clarke in 1979. "Today, many of the large inflexible manufacturers which evolved during the "sixties boom" are in a poor commercial state. Markets have been eroded and many of them have surplus production capacity. This is the reason behind recent plant closures and the diversification of investment into manufacturing abroad, or into the more profitable retail and service sectors."[14] Despite its remarkable achievements in pattern design, the British textile industry had been in steady decline since the start of the 20th century. Finally, during the 1970s, the axe fell. Between 1969 and 1976, 245,000 jobs were lost, reducing the workforce by 25 percent.

The printed textiles sector was also dramatically affected by the introduction of rotary screen-printing. "In the lifetime of the older generation of printers, the character of the business has altered radically," noted Jacquey Visick in 1978. "Small firms have gone to the wall or have been absorbed by larger companies. In order to survive, the industry is structured on such a scale as to make it more or less impossible for printer and first-time converter to make economic use of each other."[15] Those printed-textile manufacturers and converters who survived, however, had a wealth of design talent to draw on, although as the textile industry shrank in size it became increasingly difficult for designers to sell their work in Britain. The annual Texprint exhibitions (successor to the Cotton Board's Inprint exhibitions, held from 1964) increasingly attracted buyers from the United States, Japan, Germany, and Scandinavia. In 1977 Jack Lenor Larsen commented: "Perhaps it is not so surprising that an exhibition series of this calibre should come out of Britain. Britain has by far the best colleges with fabric design courses. Britain is training more designers better than any other countries. But more and more often it is English designs which set light to the fabric collections of the Continent and the US. The best work is being syphoned off."[16]

Britain: Heal Fabrics

Reflecting on the 1950s and 1960s, Howell Leadbeater wrote, "Year in, year out, Heal Fabrics under Tom Worthington's direction marketed as a standard range of products arresting original designs that hardly anyone else would dream of putting on the market, textiles that made Heal Fabrics a byword for originality and vitality in design and at the same time were a commercial success."[17] Although Worthington's retirement in 1971 marked the end of an era, the beacon of progressive design continued to be championed at Heal's for several years in the work of Barbara Brown. In *Ikebana* (1970) she incorporated flamboyant Japanese-inspired decorative elements within a bold graphic framework. Several patterns were composed of parallel coloured bands, such as the billowing, rhythmic *Galleria*. Fractured compositions were another recurrent theme, as in the fragmented *Tympany*. Musical analogies were a feature of many designs, including *Largo/Legato* (1973),

Above Fig. 6.28
Nimbus *screen-printed cotton satin furnishing fabric, designed by Jane Sandy, produced by Heal Fabrics, 1971.* Designed on the gigantic scale characteristic of the early 1970s, this quasi-surreal pattern combines photographic images of clouds with chunky *trompe l'oeil* cubes.

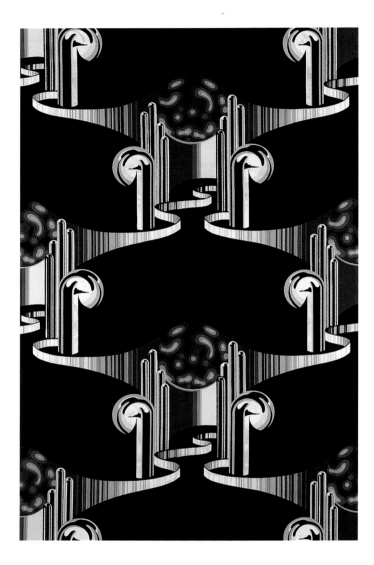

Above Fig. 6.29
Chrome City screen-printed cotton
furnishing fabric, designed by Sue Palmer,
produced by Warner, 1970. This
sophisticated pattern embodies an
interesting concoction of stylistic
influences. Its slick, airbrushed graphic
style derives from Pop Art; its melted
forms reflect the legacy of psychedelia;
and there are allusions to American
Art Deco in its celebration of
streamlined chrome. The black
background, monochrome colouring,
and oversize scale serve to intensify
these imposing effects.

Scherzo (1974), and *Counterpoint* (1976). Brown's work influenced
a whole school of pattern-making, and many designers emulated
her powerful gargantuan idiom, among them Hamdi El Attar, Anne
Fehlow, and Gabrielle Fountain (fig. 6.30). However, after Heal
Fabrics began to pitch more of its textiles at the contract market
during the mid-1970s, there was a noticeable toning down of effects.

Existing alliances were maintained with several designers from the
previous decade, including David Bartle, Jyoti Bhomik, Lucienne
Day, Doreen Dyall, Natalie Gibson, Peter Hall, James Morgan, Peter
McCulloch, and Haydon Williams. Many new designers were also
enlisted to the Heal's fold, such as Diane Bell, Neil Bradburn, Helen
Burns, Hazel Canning, Elizabeth Castell, Henri Delord, John Frith,
Julius Heller, Anne James, Karen Macdonald, Kathy Marry,
Adrienne Morag-Ferguson, Jack Prince, Annabel Ralphs, Evelyn
Redgrave, Grace Sullivan, and Marcella Tanzi.

The inspiration of Islamic design was particularly strong during the
early 1970s, reflected in hippy-influenced patterns such as Heather
Brown's *Alhambra* (1971). Textiles incorporating photographic
images, such as Jane Sandy's *Nimbus* (1971) (fig. 6.28), showing
clouds through a window, were a new departure. Later came
Kew (1974) and *Camelia* (1975) by Mary Oliver and *Rose* (1974) by
James Morgan, featuring blown-up photographs of flowers. As in
the work of the American artist Robert Rauschenberg, the grainy
dots of the enlarged photograph formed a key element of the
composition. In 1976 *Design* noted that Heal's had "consciously
gone away from geometrics to concentrate on the so-called 'softer'
designs."[18] In fabrics for the domestic market, ruralism became the
prevailing theme, typified by *Flowerfall* (1975) by Gillian Harding.
Country designs were all-pervasive during 1976–7, including
stylized landscape panoramas and pseudo-rustic patchwork designs
such as *Tuscany* (1977) by Jennie Foley. Although Heal Fabrics
continued producing imaginative designs for a few more years,
the visionary fervour began to ebb away, and in 1984 the company
was absorbed into the more generalized Heal Products Division.

Britain: Warner

During the 1970s Warner's printed textiles continued to grow and
develop under the dynamic direction of Eddie Squires, who was
promoted to chief designer in 1971. Ultra-traditional and ultra-
progressive designs were created in tandem throughout the decade,
with no apparent conflict between the two. In 1970, for example,
Sue Palmer created *Chrome City*, in which slick, advertising-style
airbrush graphics and Art Deco streamlining were seamlessly
combined (fig. 6.29). In 1982 Jane Lott noted that Warner had
managed to do three seemingly contradictory things at once:
"maintain a library of Victorian and Edwardian designs upon
which it can call for exact replicas for special orders; translate the
traditional British fabric motifs into contemporary language; and
nurture a streak which ensures that innovation is as much on the
minds of the company's five resident designers as is reproduction."[19]

Eddie Squires continued to create distinctive and highly sophisticated textile designs, although his main role now was originating and commissioning Warner's themed collections. The themes themselves provide a fascinating insight into the design psyche of the 1970s, mirroring key issues, fashions, and styles. At the start of the decade Squires was still preoccupied with Pop Art, and the Mineral Collection (1971) contained slickly drawn, hyper-real patterns, such as *Mineralogist* by Sue Palmer and his own design *Gemstones*. Sue Palmer's *Jewelled Sky* had a decidedly "trippy" quality, suggesting a veiled reference to the Beatles' song *Lucy in the Sky with Diamonds*. Hippy associations were also evident in the Springs of Wisdom Collection (1974), which contained the remarkable *Tree of Life* by Sue Palmer. More a philosophical treatise than a textile design, it presented a modern-day "alternative" interpretation of the universe, juxtaposing signs of the zodiac, images of the solar system, corona, radiolaria, and a double helix. *Last Supper*, a complex panel print by Eddie Squires, was similarly bizarre, incorporating Leonardo da Vinci's famous mural alongside images of the Garden of Eden and *Apollo 11*'s moon landing. Although too extreme to succeed commercially, the collection confirmed Warner's reputation for pushing forward the frontiers of textile design. "Things like that have a feedback that is understood within this company," noted Squires.[20]

A key difference between the 1960s and the 1970s was the attitude towards historical and ethnic sources, which shifted from playful to reverent. *Hamza's Pavilion*, from the Eastern Splendour Collection (1973), a minutely detailed pattern designed by Eddie Squires and Mike Quigley, based on an Indian miniature in the Victoria & Albert Museum, signified the change. The Ethnic Origins Collection (1977), containing patterns inspired by African, Indonesian, Moroccan, Turkish, and North American Indian textiles, also reflected a new spirit of respectfulness. This collection featured patterns by Graham Smith, a studio designer at Warner from 1974 to 1980. Gradually historical revivalism transmuted into "document" design. *Palace Birds*, by Sue Lewis and Eddie Squires, from the Pagodas and Palaces Collection (1977), was based on a 19th-century embroidery.

Other designers who contributed to the company's eclectic output during the 1970s included Vanessa Calver, Jenny Crowley, Sonja Dunthorne, David Exley, Chris Marriott, Mary Ratcliffe, and Eileen Vickery. David Exley, a characterful British designer based in San Francisco, created extravagant designs such as *Honey Combe*, *Zantha* (both 1974), and *Kentia* (1976). Chris Marriott contributed to the World of Flowers Collection (1975), featuring patterns based on original watercolours, such as *Anemone* and *Gladioli*.

Britain: David Richards, Jane Teale, Tarian, and Textra

The narrowing of opportunities for pattern designers in the textile industry prompted designer-entrepreneurs to establish their own companies. David Richards launched a collection of coordinated

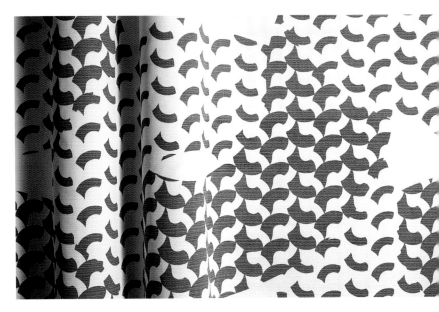

Top Fig. 6.30
Equilibrium and *Equilibrium 2* screen-printed furnishing fabrics, designed by Gabrielle Fountain, produced by Heal Fabrics, 1972. Created towards the end of the fashion for giant abstract geometric patterns, *Equilibrium* was produced in a second version on a smaller scale.

Above Fig. 6.31
Screen-printed cotton furnishing fabric, designed by David Richards, produced by David Richards Fabrics, 1971. This intriguing pattern, with its clusters of directional motifs, was part of a coordinated range of textiles and carpets created specifically for the contract market.

Top Fig. 6.32
Everglade screen-printed cotton
furnishing fabric, designed by Nicola
Wood, produced by Textra, 1972. Although
still couched in the late-Pop idiom, this
pattern hints at the emergence of the
new ruralist trends. Orange and red
recall the 1960s, while brown and
pastel pink herald the 1970s.

Above Fig. 6.33
Pebbledash wallpaper, produced by
Designers Guild, 1978. This pattern
formed part of the Geranium
collection, a collaboration between
Kaffe Fassett and Tricia Guild. The
recessive motifs and colouring signified
a reaction against the design excesses
of the late 1960s and early 1970s.

hand screen-printed furnishing fabrics and embossed nylon carpet tiles for the contract market in 1971, decorated with experimental abstract patterns (fig. 6.31). Jane Teale, who founded her own company in 1975, used commission printers to produce lush printed floral textiles that were extremely successful in the United States. After seven years at Heal Fabrics, Evelyn Redgrave set up Tarian Design in 1977, initially using commission printers in Germany. Her patterns included stylized plant silhouettes which tapped into the ruralist vogue, such as *Alpine*, as well as textural abstracts with a grittier, post-industrial aesthetic, such as *Shimono*.

One of the most high-profile companies of the 1970s was Textra Furnishing Fabrics, originally known as Mackinnon & Jenkins, founded by Malcolm Mackinnon and Richard Jenkins in 1963. Catering mainly to European and American markets, the firm specialized initially in woven fabrics, but from 1964 prints were added to the collection, which was marketed under the name Textra. Early pattern designers included Robert Dodd, Pamela Kay, and Peter McCulloch, and during the 1970s the company produced designs by David Bartle, Dorothy Carr, Raye Clements, Hamdi El Attar, Peter Hall, Paul Kilshaw, Peter Perritt, Kay Politowicz, Brigitta Ricke-Larsen, Nicola Wood, and Henri Delord of Garrault-Delord. Several of these designers also contributed to Heal Fabrics, which marketed Textra's fabrics on the Continent during the early years, and Textra's style marked a natural development from the progressive modern idiom pioneered by Heal's. Peter Perritt's *Monaco* (1970) was a broad-banded pattern in graduated colours. *Metropolis* (1973) by David Bartle, suggesting clusters of building blocks, was an abstract *trompe l'oeil* design with an Op dimension. Nicola Wood adopted a Pop formula in *Everglades* (1972), a cartoon landscape in hangover psychedelic colours (fig. 6.32). *Salad Days* (1973) by Kay Politowicz, with its heightened depiction of lettuce, eggs, and tomatoes, was also in the high-Pop vein.

Britain: Zandra Rhodes, Patrick Lloyd, Slick Brands, and OK Textiles

In 1974 the Victoria & Albert Museum mounted an exhibition called *The Fabric of Pop*, which highlighted the influence of Pop Art on textile design. The fashion designer Zandra Rhodes, who graduated from the Royal College of Art in 1964, was a pioneer in this field. In 1965 she established a printing studio with Alexander MacIntyre producing dress fabrics decorated with Pop motifs such as lipstick, teardrops, and teddy bears, with titles such as *Lipstick Print* and *I Love You Vanessa* (both 1968). Some of Rhodes's early furnishing patterns were produced by Heal Fabrics, and in 1973 she joined forces with interior designer Christopher Vane Percy to form a wholesale company called By the Yard by the Yard. The Pop idiom was further refined during the mid-1970s by a number of small, independent, fashion-led dress and furnishing fabric companies. Lloyd Johnson's *Soup Can* (1973) for Patrick Lloyd, and Christopher Snow's *Marilyn* (1974) for Slick Brands were both undisguised homages to Andy Warhol. OK Textiles, founded during the early 1970s by Sue Saunders and Jane Wealleans, produced screen-printed synthetic furnishing fabrics with ironic, over-the-top patterns that openly challenged the notion of good taste. *Cakes* depicted slices of green cake against a red-and-white gingham tablecloth while *Raspberry Lips* (both 1973) featured a woman's hand with red fingernails holding a raspberry to a pair of lips.

Britain: Designers Guild

Paralleling the rise of Osborne & Little, but from the starting point of textiles, was the interior design company Designers Guild, founded in 1970 by Tricia and Robin Guild. The opening of a shop on London's King's Road in 1972 prompted the introduction of a collection of fabrics called Village, based on traditional Indian block-printed textiles, re-coloured by Tricia Guild and Chris Halsey to suit the British market and screen-printed in Britain. Wallpapers were added shortly afterwards, initially hand-printed but later machine-printed. Patterns such as *Quetzalcoatl* (1973) reflected ethnic influences of a bolder and more adventurous kind, while other designs were overtly playful, such as *Cabbage White* (1974) by Sheila Reeves, featuring Pop flowers bursting out from a fish-scale ground.

From the mid-1970s Designers Guild became associated with painterly florals, many designed by Tricia Guild herself, such as *Poppy Vase* (1977). *Geranium* (1976), featuring overlapping geranium leaves, marked her first collaboration with knitwear designer Kaffe Fassett, and its soft palette of creamy orange and chalky green was characteristic of this period. *Pebbledash* (1978), a wallpaper depicting scattered pebbles and shells in white outline against a monochrome ground (fig. 6.33), and *Peasweed* (1979), a printed textile with an all-over, organic design, typified the company's patterns of the late 1970s in being gently stimulating and modest in scale. The Watercolour collection (1979) – so-called because the designs were executed in watercolour rather than gouache – paved the way for a decade of limpid pastel effects. Printed using nickel-coated Galvano screens, which allowed for greater tonal subtlety, *Paper Roses* (the best-selling design from this collection) was an all-over floral in muted tones.

Britain: Laura Ashley

Although pattern design manifested itself in many different guises during the 1970s, for most people the decade is indelibly associated with Laura Ashley. Summing up the nature of her appeal after twenty-five years of hard-core Modernism, Iain Gale and Susan Irvine commented: "Laura Ashley was a romantic, a sentimentalist, a traditionalist. Unashamed of her taste for nostalgia, she brought poetry and fantasy back into ordinary domestic life, liberating design from chrome, plastics and man-made fibres."[21] Just as the forward-looking "Contemporary" style could not have happened without the catalyst of wartime deprivation, so the Laura Ashley phenomenon arose from a backlash against the artificiality and

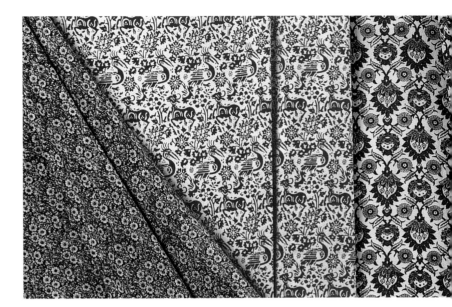

Top Fig. 6.34
Screen-printed furnishing fabrics, designed and produced by Laura Ashley, 1972. These three prints were among the earliest furnishing fabrics manufactured by Laura Ashley. Small, quasi-historical patterns such as these were refreshing after a decade of extravagant futuristic designs.

Above left and right Fig. 6.35
Wild Clematis screen-printed furnishing fabric and wallpaper, designed and produced by Laura Ashley, c.1975. Coordinated textiles and wallpapers printed in complementary positive-negative colours proved incredibly popular. *Wild Clematis* remained in production until the early 1990s.

Right Fig. 6.36
Bauhaus roller-printed cotton furnishing fabric, designed by Susan Collier and Sarah Campbell, produced by Liberty, 1972. This design, adapted from a tapestry woven by Gunta Stölzl at the Bauhaus, paved the way for a new era of intense, vibrant, all-over pattern-making by Collier Campbell.

Far right Fig. 6.37
Honey Bunny screen-printed polyester and cotton furnishing fabric, designed by Carlton Varney, produced by F. Schumacher & Co., 1972. This entertaining pattern, featured in the Dorothy Draper Collection, reflected the lighter, Pop-orientated side of American pattern design.

excess of the 1960s. With her nostalgic evocation of a mythical golden age and her soft-focused vision of the countryside, she offered instant escape from the harsh realities of the urban environment. "Laura Ashley brought the country back to the city, allowing every home to recapture at least a visual reminder of a rustic dream that may never have existed in reality, but which will continue to provide an enchanting escape from the imperfections of the present," observed Gale and Irvine.[22]

In 1955, at the height of the fashion for "Contemporary" design, the Victoria & Albert Museum organized an exhibition in conjunction with the Colour Design and Style Centre called *English Chintz: Two Centuries of Changing Taste.* The roots of the Laura Ashley phenomenon lie in the re-evaluation of chintz triggered off by this exhibition, an interest which continued to swell during the 1960s in tandem with Op and Pop, and which finally burst forth and captured the market in the 1970s. Bernard and Laura Ashley had begun producing screen-printed scarves on a small scale as early as 1953, initially using equipment constructed and operated by Bernard Ashley. Their first company, Ashley-Mountney Limited (Mountney being Laura's maiden name), was established in 1954, mainly producing furnishing fabrics designed by Bernard Ashley. The runaway success of a tea towel printed with a Victorian theatre playbill prompted Laura Ashley to start researching other historical print sources for patterns, produced from 1957 under the name Laura Ashley Limited. Originally based in London, then Kent, the Ashleys subsequently moved to Wales, establishing a factory at Carno, Montgomeryshire, in 1961. In addition to tea towels, accessories such as aprons, oven gloves, and napkins

formed the mainstay of production during the early years, all made using their own printed cloth. Gradually they developed a wider range of garments and, after they opened a shop in South Kensington in 1968, the fashion side of the business quickly took off. During the 1970s the company mushroomed despite the recession, and by the end of the decade there were over seventy Laura Ashley shops around the world. By this time, in addition to its main clothing range, the company was producing coordinated furnishings fabrics and wallpapers, the latter launched in 1972. Mechanical flatbed screen-printing was now used for the textiles, while the wallpapers were produced by rotary screen-printing.

Largely self-taught, Laura Ashley created a winning formula by adapting motifs from a variety of historical and vernacular sources, drawing on both artefacts in museums and her own growing collection of reference material (fig. 6.34). Early 19th-century pattern books containing printed cotton dress fabrics were a major source of inspiration, along with patchwork quilts, end papers, and ceramic motifs. Miniaturized floral sprigs and twining plant motifs formed the basis for many of her early patterns, which were delicate and feminine in character. As the company grew, other designers were recruited, notably Brian Jones, who played a key role during the 1970s and was highly skilled at transforming historical prints into successful textile designs. Some patterns had a vaguely gothic or chinoiserie flavour, incorporating simplified images of lions and birds. Flower and leaf-based designs predominated, however, with seductive rustic names such as *Wild Clematis* (c.1975) (fig. 6.35). The earliest furnishing fabrics were printed in monochrome, often "reversed out" in light on dark.

Matching furnishing fabrics and wallpapers, offered in positive-negative colourways, were a distinctive feature of the Laura Ashley "look," produced in colours such as sage green and plum. These features, combined with the small scale and delicacy of the patterns, were the key to the firm's commercial success. During the second half of the 1970s greater formality crept into the range, and simple geometric patterns appeared, printed in pairs of colours, such as navy and maroon. By this time, textiles and wallpapers could be coordinated by colour as well as design, the simplicity of the patterns facilitating the coordination of different elements. Although loosely "historical," these early patterns were quite distinct from the more elaborate and self-conscious "period" designs that followed.

Britain: Collier Campbell and Liberty

Ironically, one of the few companies to offer an alternative to the all-conquering Laura Ashley style during the 1970s was Liberty, a firm more commonly associated with historical revivalism through its Voysey, Morris, and Silver Studio reissues. The driving force behind this renaissance was two sisters, Susan Collier and Sarah Campbell, who later formed their own company, Collier Campbell. Largely self-taught as a designer, Susan Collier learned the tools of the trade from Pat Albeck, and in 1961 began supplying patterns to Liberty of London Prints. Working at first as a freelance and then from 1968 on a retainer, Collier initially specialized in floral dress prints for the ever-popular Tana Lawn range, and subsequently created designs for Liberty's famous scarves. In 1971, on being appointed Design and Colour Consultant for Liberty, she assumed responsibility for the company's entire range of dress and furnishing textiles, and embarked on a mission to revitalize its designs. *Bauhaus* (1972), a bold, colourful abstract based on a design by the Bauhaus weaver Gunta Stölzl, marked a significant turning point, paving the way for a vibrant new aesthetic (fig. 6.36). "Collier forced people to sit up and notice that Liberty's was changing gear," commented Jacquey Visick in 1975.[23]

In 1968 Collier began to collaborate with her sister, Sarah Campbell, who had studied painting and graphics at Chelsea School of Art. Campbell became a retained designer for Liberty in 1971, and henceforth Collier and Campbell worked together as a team. The fabrics were printed until 1973 at Liberty's printworks at Merton Abbey, south London, and subsequently by commission printers such as Stead McAlpin. A range of wallpapers, first produced for Liberty's centenary in 1975, was screen-printed by Osborne & Little. Collier Campbell also supplied wallpaper designs to Osborne & Little's own ranges in 1974–5.

Adopting an all-or-nothing approach to design, Collier Campbell pioneered an intense, all-over style of pattern-making in which almost every inch of the ground was covered with stimulating motifs. Their work exuded an infectious *joie de vivre*, and they were equally adept at creating exotic ethnics such as the Persian-inspired

Karabag, zingy abstracts such as the Op herringbone *Derebend* (both 1974), or casual florals like the Country Garden range (1976).

Drawing on her previous experience in designing dress prints, Collier's early floral furnishing fabrics, with their eruptions of foliage and flowers, were like magnified versions of Tana Lawn. Gradually, though, as Collier Campbell responded to the larger furnishing fabric format, their patterns became freer and more overtly painterly, and they explored a richer abstract vocabulary of pulsating rhythms and saturated colours. Inspired and stimulated by the whole world of textile history, they produced work that contained echoes of many other genres, from ikats to quilts.

The new school of pattern-making that Collier Campbell originated at Liberty proved extremely popular. But because their work was marketed anonymously, the designers were not credited. Frustrated at the company's refusal to acknowledge their designs personally, Susan Collier left in 1977. Two years later she and Campbell established themselves as designer converters under the name Collier Campbell Ltd. This gave them direct control over production and marketing, and enabled them to reach a wider audience through collaborations with mass-market retailers such as Habitat, for which they created special ranges throughout the 1980s.

United States: Schumacher and Jack Lenor Larsen

Even at the height of the "Contemporary" fervour of the 1950s, many American firms had continued to cater to the conservative tastes of the decorator market. By the end of the 1970s "document" collections based on historic designs held in archives and museums were becoming increasingly popular. However, some firms, such as Schumacher and Greeff, continued to produce some modern designs. Carlton Warney's exuberant, Pop-inspired *Honey Bunny* (1972) (fig. 6.37) for Schumacher is a good example of a pattern reflecting the flavour of its time.

Two firms who "kept the faith" in the 1970s were Jack Lenor Larsen and Knoll. Well established yet still resolutely non-establishment, Larsen concentrated mainly on woven fabrics for the contract market, while continuing to produce innovative printed textiles. The company's jacquard-woven fabrics ranged from geometrics such as *Doublecheck* (1978), to florals such as *Pictograph* (1978), to ethnic patterns such as *Turkoman* (1978). Larsen believed that "Pattern – whether integral or applied, geometric or figurative – is the visual configuration of a cloth; it is not a 'design' on cloth."[24] A collaboration with the painter Richard Landis resulted in the remarkable *Landis Polychrome* (1970), a woven double cloth with an ingenious geometric pattern in a ravishing shifting palette. "Of all fabric structure, double cloths are my favourites," Larsen remarked. "I love the visual pun of their interlacing."[25]

Katsuji Wakisaka, previously at Marimekko, joined the Larsen Design Studio in 1977. Other designers of printed textiles included

Right Fig. 6.38
Extra Hollow Ground *screen-printed cotton furnishing fabric, designed by Frances Butler, produced by Goodstuffs, 1977.* This illusory three-dimensional abstract, with its ingenious pattern, was inspired by bathroom tiling.

Below Fig. 6.39
On The Scene *screen-printed vinyl wallpaper mural, designed and produced by James Seeman Studios, Inc., 1971.* This pattern, featured in a collection called Kaleidoscope – Murals and Supergraphics for Contemporary Walls, consisted of five panels designed to cover an entire wall.

Far right top Fig. 6.40
To the Point *screen-printed vinyl wallpaper, designed and produced by Perceptive Concepts, Inc., early 1970s.* Giganticism was rife in American wallpapers during the early 1970s. These huge arrowheads extend the full width of this "feature" wallpaper.

Far right bottom Fig. 6.41
Life Savers *screen-printed vinyl wallpaper, designed by Alan Buchsbaum, produced by Norton Blumenthal, Inc., c.1971.* Wallpaper was pushed to its limits in terms of physical scale and graphic audacity during the "big is beautiful" era of the early 1970s.

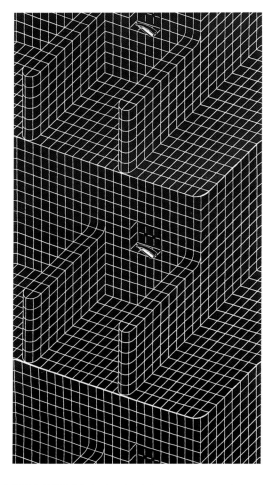

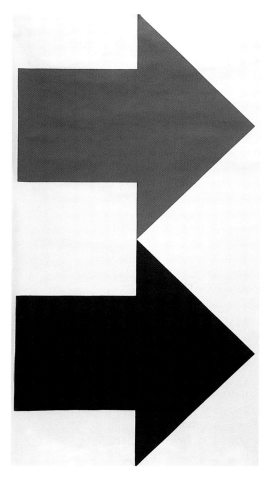

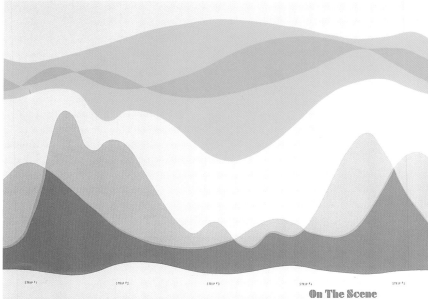

June Groff, Wendy Klein, Jack Prince, Don Wight, and Jack Lenor Larsen himself. Wendy Klein's *Evenstar* (1972), suggesting a knotted textile wall hanging, reflected Larsen's passion for Art Fabrics. Flat, stylized landscapes composed of overlapping diagonals, such as *Hills of Home* (1971) and *Shangri-La* (1976), were a Larsen Studio speciality of the period. While reflecting the fashion for ruralism, such patterns were rigorously composed.

United States: Knoll

Knoll's commitment to modern textiles remained strong, despite several changes of ownership, and Knoll Textiles became an autonomous unit within Knoll International in 1979. International activities were spearheaded from 1973 by the German designer Barbara Rodes, and at this time bold abstract prints became an important part of Knoll's range, particularly in Europe. In recognition of the firm's popularity in Germany, Stuttgart was chosen as the base for its European operations in 1975. Four years later a European subsidiary, Knoll Textilien, was created under the direction of Peter Seipelt, an accomplished Swiss woven textile designer. In order to appeal to the varied tastes of an international market, prints were commissioned from designers in various countries, including Anni Albers, Wolf Bauer, Lynne Crosbee, Christa Häusler-Goltz, Marc Held, Alexandre Mimoglou, Francisco Reichardt, Nob and Non Utsumi, and Gretl and Leo Wollner.

United States: Goodstuffs and David Exley

Outside the confines of the mainstream contract market, American pattern design was often characterized by wayward exaggeration. New firms established during the 1970s were inspired not by Modernism but by Pop Art, and their main aim was to create arresting patterns that stopped you in your tracks. Goodstuffs Hand-Printed, a short-lived enterprise run from 1972 to 1979 by the graphic designer Frances Butler in Berkeley, California, specialized in screen-printed "fabric graphics"[26] that were intellectually and visually provocative. Black-and-white Op patterns were married with photo-realism to produce heightened decorative effects with intentionally disconcerting results. A typically bizarre design was *Beast in the Jungle* (1972) – its title derived from a Henry James novel – featuring two giant tigers, one hyper-real, the other a deconstructed ghostly reflection striding towards a female figure lying on the ground drinking tea. Similarly unconventional was *Extra Hollow Ground* (1977), a black-and-white *trompe l'oeil* puzzle inspired by bathroom tiling (fig. 6.38).

The West Coast seemed to foster an "alternative" approach to pattern design during the 1970s and 1980s. Surreal imagery, presented in a slick, commercial, graphic style, also formed the basis of fabrics by the San Francisco-based British designer David Exley. Patterns such as *Cat and Tinned Eye* (1972), which showed a human eye inside a can of sardines, were deliberately shocking in a Daliesque way.

United States: Norton Blumenthal, Perceptive Concepts, and James Seeman

The early 1970s was also the era of the "statement" wallpaper, and several American companies adopted extreme ploys to capture public attention. Supergraphics were all the rage at this date, exemplified by designs such as *To the Point* by Perceptive Concepts, featuring giant arrowheads extending the full width of the wallpaper (fig. 6.40). "Big is Beautiful" seems to have been the motto for many pattern designers during the early 1970s. The modest geometrics of the 1960s were exploded on to such a huge scale that they appeared to be literally bursting out of the confines of the wallpaper medium. Alan Buchsbaum's *Chopped Herringbone* (1971) for Norton Blumenthal, with its exploded herringbone pattern, emphasized the idea of magnification. Another Buchsbaum pattern, *Life Savers* (c.1971), featured giant rings spilling off the edge of the roll (fig. 6.41).

The Americans had long displayed a penchant for the grandiose, which explains the continuing popularity of mural wallpapers. New York-based James Seeman Studios, Inc. had been catering to this market since its foundation in 1946. Displaying no particular allegiance to any one style, its murals reflected whatever trends were currently in vogue. In 1971 the firm produced the collection Kaleidoscope – Murals and Supergraphics for Contemporary Walls, featuring flat, fluid, undulating patterns, screen-printed in unusual colour combinations, with colours intensified in areas of pattern overlap. *On The Scene* suggested the irregular peaks and troughs of a mountain landscape (fig. 6.39), while *Il Mare* evoked the sea.

United States: Winfield Design Associates and Jack Denst

Even more decadent were the fantastical, oversized decorative murals conjured up by San Francisco-based Winfield Design Associates. Pitched at the liberated high-camp end of the interior decorator market, Winfield Spectaculars featured gigantic, sprawling Art Nouveau designs such as *Empyrea*, and magnified quartz patterns such as *Cyanin*. Winfield's designers, who included David Winfield Wilson and Ted Ramsay, also exploited materials such as foil and metallic pigments to create extravagant, glittering special effects.

Another firm infected by the prevailing spirit of excess was Jack Denst, whose collections became increasingly daring and technically audacious during the 1970s. During the previous decade Denst had pioneered the introduction of translucent pigments in place of traditional clay-based inks. By the 1970s his palette had grown to 1,000 colours, and he was experimenting with Space Age materials such as shiny polyester Mylar. Whereas other firms got carried away with special effects, however, Denst's work was redeemed by the unflagging cleverness of his designs. *Alimony*, from the Love Stories collection (1977), was printed with shiny dollar bills, emphasizing the link between visual ingenuity and verbal wit.

Post-Modernism, Document, and Digital Design

The textile and wallpaper industries were dramatically downsized during the 1980s, with the market increasingly controlled by a small number of profit-driven multinational firms. British companies, such as Crown Wallcoverings and Sanderson, were acquired by large American corporations, prompting a more reactionary policy towards design. In the light of such changes, and as a result of the prevailing fashion for retrospection, it became increasingly difficult for companies to maintain their creative individuality. Mainstream pattern design fell into the doldrums during the 1980s, bogged down in over-reliance on slick, formulaic "document" styles.

The deadlock was broken at intervals by initiatives such as the Memphis group in Italy, who revelled in high-voltage decorated surfaces. Post-Modernism also took hold in Britain, where Timney Fowler and English Eccentrics turned revivalism on its head. Focusing on fashion accessories rather than furnishings, Georgina von Etzdorf blazed a trail during the 1980s, mining eclectic new sources of inspiration. Today the fast-moving world of fashion is more likely to attract go-ahead young designers than the more conservative world of furnishings, and in recent years it is fashion fabric designers such as Eley Kishimoto and Rebecca Earley who have caused the biggest stir.

Wallpapers have become so recessive over the past two decades – a victim of taste timidity – that they risked slipping into oblivion. However, since the late 1990s there has been a minor flurry of activity in Britain as designers rediscover the pleasures of patterned walls. Printed furnishing fabrics continue to develop, if on a reduced scale. Seizing the initiative as designer-converters, Britain's Collier Campbell and Sweden's Tio-Gruppen enlivened the 1980s, sending

Opposite Fig. 7.1
Stora Skuggan screen-printed cotton furnishing fabric, designed by Gunnel Sahlin, produced by Kinnasand, 1998. Capitalizing on the prevailing interest in post-war design, some of the printed fabrics produced recently by the Swedish firm Kinnasand recall the aesthetics of the 1950s and 1960s, but in a pared-down, Neo-Modern style. Gunnel Sahlin trained as a textile designer, but also designs glass, and the motif on this fabric suggests a cross-section through a vessel.

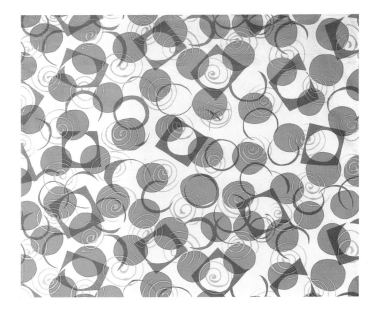

out creative ripples through the retail trade. Of late, the Swedish firm Kinnasand has carried the torch for modern furnishings, combining 1990s lifestyle awareness with a dash of Neo-Modern retro-styling (fig. 7.1). At the progressive end of the market, new technology is having an increasing impact on pattern design, fostering a new digital aesthetic and radically influencing materials and production processes. The Nuno Corporation in Japan has inspired the world with its commitment to technical innovation and its fearless approach to textile design.

United States: The Fabric Workshop

With the burgeoning art textiles movement in the United States, printed fabrics were harnessed as a vehicle for social and political comment, a new genre pioneered by Malcolm Clark Robertson. Using screen-printing, hand painting, and resist techniques, he created patterns exploring issues of racism and sexuality through jumbled contemporary and historical photographs. A new emphasis on textiles as an art form led to the creation of the Philadelphia-based Fabric Workshop, established by Marion Boulton Stroud in 1977 and still going strong today. Stroud believes that good artists should be able to express themselves in a wide range of media. Over the past twenty-five years several hundred invited artists, including painters, sculptors, architects, and craftspeople, have created more than 3,500 textiles at the Fabric Workshop. Its goal has been "to explore, to take liberties, to be a studio and laboratory of new design, unhampered by rules and precedents,"[1] with a secondary aim to teach textile design and printing, and to promote interest in textile art through exhibitions and educational activities.

High-profile contributors have included the painters Howard Hodgkin and Roy Lichtenstein, the performance artists Scott Burton and Robert Kushner, the sculptors Robert Morris and Louise Nevelson, the textile artists Lenore Tawney and Claire Zeisler, and the ceramicists Dorothy Hafner and Betty Woodman. Because each artist has pursued his or her own creative agenda, every fabric created at the Workshop is distinctive and personal in character. The majority have been produced in the form of wall hangings, garments, or accessories, such as the glass artist Dale Chihuly's calligraphic abstract expressionist scarves of 1989. Some practitioners have created designs that relate to their own speciality, such as Mineo Mizuno, who designed the *Peppers* tablecloth (1979) to coordinate with his ceramic tableware. However, while most contributors have co-opted the fabric as a vehicle for self-conscious artistic "statements," others have explored the concept of decoration through repeat patterns for lengths of printed fabric, such as the ceramicists Philip Maberry and Tony Costanzo. Maberry's *Four Seasons* (1982) drew on a vocabulary of circles and spirals (fig. 7.2), while Costanzo's *trompe l'oeil* pattern *Linoleum* (1980) simulated marbleized black-and-green floor tiles. From a practical point of view, it is artists such as Tina Girouard, who engaged with rhythm, structure, and repeats in her witty, multi-layered pattern *Animals* (1984), who have created the most effective and workable printed textiles (fig. 7.3).

Top Fig. 7.2
Four Seasons screen-printed cotton satin, designed by Philip Maberry, produced in collaboration with the Fabric Workshop and Museum, 1982. Promoting textiles as an art form, the Fabric Workshop has revived the art of hand screen-printing to produce short runs of artists' designs.

Above Fig. 7.3
Animals screen-printed cotton satin, designed by Tina Girouard, produced in collaboration with the Fabric Workshop and Museum, 1984. Fabric Workshop contributors come from many branches of the visual arts. Tina Girouard is a painter, sculptor, and performance artist.

United States: Venturi Scott Brown and Michael Graves

While most designs at the Fabric Workshop were only produced in limited runs, the exception was *Grandmother* (1983) by the architects Robert Venturi and Denise Scott Brown, a pastiche chintz printed with stylized roses in cloying pastel colours (fig. 7.4). Previously Venturi and Brown had designed a black-and-white mottled pattern called *Notebook*, an ironic inflation of the deliberately banal type of pattern found on lever-arch files. Created at the height of the fashion for Post-Modernism, *Grandmother* was hugely successful, and was also produced in the form of plastic laminate, used for the duo's spoof Queen Anne chair for Knoll.

Another Post-Modernist American architect inspired to try his hand at designing printed textiles was Michael Graves, although he opted to collaborate with a commercial firm, Sunar Hauserman. Graves's patterns, which were self-consciously ironic in their reference to historical decorative motifs, included *Scroll*, *Fret*, and *Tracery* (all 1981).

Italy: Studio Alchymia and Memphis

The patterns created by Venturi Scott Brown and Michael Graves in the United States relate closely to those of the Memphis group in Italy, who unleashed full-blown Post-Modernism on to an unsuspecting world in 1981. Memphis grew out of an earlier radical design collective called Studio Alchymia, founded in 1976 and spearheaded by the designer and journalist Alessandro Mendini. Mendini had been fostering an interest in pattern through his promotion of "Banal Design," which rejected the Miesian concept of "less is more" in favour of heightened surface decoration. His preoccupation with pattern was shared by Andrea Branzi, one of the chief protagonists behind the Centro Design Montefibre. During the late 1970s the Centro produced a series of publications called *Decorattivo*, described by Andrea Branzi as "a working handbook, a compendium of graphic information chosen to provide a basis and stimulus for the creative work of other professionals."[2] The main feature of these publications was eclectic compilations of images of 19th-century printed dress fabrics, chosen for their uninhibited approach to pattern design. "While textiles for interior decorating have concentrated on the shape of rooms and objects, relegating pattern design and decorative themes to a limited, secondary role, clothing fabrics have traditionally emphasized the importance of design, thus enriching it," Branzi explained.[3]

It was the images in *Decorattivo* that prompted the multi-talented architect and designer Ettore Sottsass to start designing patterned plastic laminates for Abet, his mottled *Bacterio* being one of several designs subsequently incorporated into his exuberant furniture for Memphis. The idea behind Memphis was to create furniture and furnishings which openly celebrated colour and decoration. In addition to Sottsass, the main pattern designers were George Sowden from Britain and the self-taught French designer Nathalie

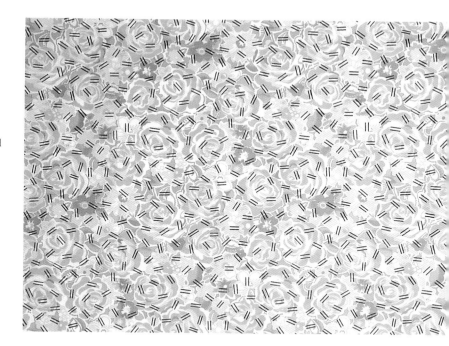

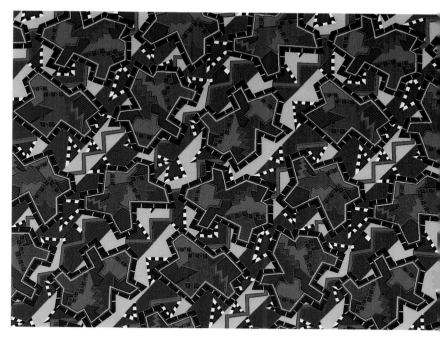

Top Fig. 7.4
Grandmother *screen-printed cotton, designed by Denise Scott Brown and Robert Venturi, produced by the Fabric Workshop, 1983.* In this Post-Modern pattern the aim of the architects was "to use ordinary and conventional elements in an extraordinary and unconventional way."

Above Fig. 7.5
Gabon *screen-printed cotton furnishing fabric, designed by Nathalie du Pasquier, printed by Rainbow for Memphis, 1982.* Rock music, comic books, and African textiles were just some of the eclectic inspirations that fed into this pattern, which was described by the designer as a "jerky dance."

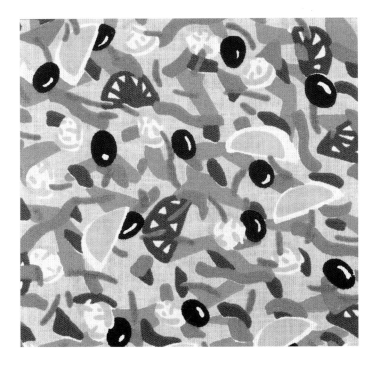

du Pasquier. Sowden's designs challenged pattern-making conventions with their dismembered compositions. *Quadro* (1983) consisted of jumbled cubes. Other designs were disrupted by snaking lines and intercepting amorphous forms. Whereas Sowden was primarily interested in pattern from the point of view of its transformative role on domestic objects, du Pasquier was interested in pattern itself, and had already begun designing for the Milan-based dress fabric company Rainbow Studio in 1980. Intense colours, irregular motifs, and frenetic, multi-layered compositions were the main characteristics of her patterns, which were deliberately overloaded with visual stimulation and brimming with energy. Her printed textiles for Memphis, dating from 1982, included *Gabon*, composed of chequered zigzags (fig. 7.5), *Zambia*, with its explosive starbursts, and *Zaire*, featuring jagged shapes within serrated cartouches. These titles point to African textiles as a key source of inspiration. The addition of cartoon graphics and artificial colours resulted in what the designer herself called an "ethnic-metropolitan" mix.[4]

Among the many spin-offs from Memphis were a group of designs commissioned from du Pasquier and Sowden by the British company Steeles Carpets, and ceramic tiles manufactured by Italian firm Cedit. Du Pasquier went on to pursue a highly successful career as a textile designer, creating patterns for numerous fashion companies, including Esprit, Fiorucci, Lorenz, Missoni, and Pink Dragon. She and Sowden also subsequently contributed to the Zeitwände collection of wallpapers produced by Rasch in 1992, featuring an ambitious group of patterns by leading Post-Modern designers, including Alessandro Mendini, Borek Sipek, Ettore Sottsass, and Matteo Thun.

Spain: Marieta

During the late 1970s and 1980s design also flourished in Barcelona, where the chief protagonist was the cartoonist Javier Mariscal. His cheeky graphic style, delight in colour and pattern-making, and frequent historical plundering, link his work to that of Memphis. In 1978 he was one of several artists invited to design textiles for Marieta Textil, a small experimental company established by Maria Cordoner in 1974. Deliberately irreverent in his choice of subject matter, Mariscal created playful printed and woven patterns in a loose, spontaneous, scribbly style, including *Ensaladilla* (1978), depicting abstracted salad motifs (fig. 7.6), and *Muchos Pesces* (1990), composed of jumbled fish. More recently Phillip Stanton has designed some lively printed textiles for Marieta featuring everyday objects such as domestic appliances.

France: Nobilis

Post-Modernism exerted a generally refreshing influence on European textiles, prompting some manufacturers to diversify from their primary allegiance to period design. In France the iconoclastic design group Robert le Héros, founded in 1986 by Corinne Helein, Christelle le Dean, Blandine Lelong, and Isabelle

Top Fig. 7.6
Ensaladilla screen-printed cotton furnishing fabric, designed by Javier Mariscal, produced by Marieta, 1978. The legacy of Pop Art is evident in this ironic, playful, Post-Modern pattern, which deflates design by co-opting a prosaic image of salad as the vehicle for a fabric.

Above Fig. 7.7
Il rêve à son tour surface-printed wallpaper, designed by Robert le Héros, produced by Nobilis, 1998. Robert le Héros are the *agents provocateurs* of contemporary French pattern design. Here the group's designers exploit the painting style of children to create a sophisticated *faux-naïf* wallpaper.

Rodier, have created several collections of textiles and wallpapers for Nobilis since the late 1980s. Their designs, which are quite unlike anything else currently on the market, often feature imagery derived from Gothic, Renaissance, and Baroque paintings and architecture, reinterpreted in a raw, "unfinished" way. Other designs are folksy and deliberately childlike (fig. 7.7).

Sweden: Tio-Gruppen

In 1980 the Tio-Gruppen (Ten Swedish Designers) celebrated its tenth birthday. From a design history perspective the group provides the vital link between late Modernist and early Post-Modern patterns. As Kerstin Wickman has noted in her recent book on the group, the Tio-Gruppen predated Memphis by a full decade, displaying a quintessentially Post-Modern attitude to pattern long before this surfaced in the rest of the design world. "Memphis may be wonderful, fresh and exciting, but we've not been inspired by them, we've been working this way for ten years," confirmed Inez Svensson, one of the group's chief protagonists, in 1984.[5]

During the 1980s the Tio-Gruppen created five stunning thematic collections, using tangible subjects as a vehicle for abstract effects, interpreted laterally rather than literally. The Play collection (1980), alluding to the Swedish Ballet's performances in Paris during the 1920s, demonstrated their confident approach to colour and pattern, featuring intensely stimulating designs such as *Intervall* by Susanne Grundell (fig. 7.8) and *Jazz* by Britt-Marie Christoffersson (fig. 7.9). The next two collections, Megaphone (1983) (fig. 7.10) and Signal (1985), were all about making a noise and demanding attention, while Metropolis (1986) was equally demonstrative, evoking the intensity of the urban experience in cities around the world. One of the patterns from Metropolis was *Buenos Aires* (1986) by Birgitta Hahn, full of dynamic cross currents and electric motifs (fig. 7.11). The Signal collection contained Tom Hedqvist's best-selling *Bongo*, with its spoof 1950s doodle motifs. The Tio-Gruppen also designed several collections of wallpapers for Duro during the 1980s, some with coordinated positive-negative fabrics. Elements of the group's textile patterns reappeared in their wallpapers, but shrunk in size and moderated in colour, as in Ingela Håkansson's *Stössel* (1981), meaning "hundreds and thousands," which is composed of scattered miniaturized candy-coloured straws.

Although the Tio-Gruppen gradually dwindled in size as various members left to pursue other commitments, eight new fabric collections were produced during the 1990s, along with accessories such as trays, bags, and plates. Since 1995 Ingela Håkansson, Birgitta Hahn, and Tom Hedqvist have made up the core group, although former members such as Carl Johan De Geer and Inez Svensson have contributed occasional patterns, along with guest designers such as Pontus Djanaieff and Anders Wenngren. The Tio-Gruppen aesthetic has remained remarkably stable over the years (fig. 0.2), and the former hippy-revolutionaries are now respected figures of Sweden's design establishment. "We have never worried

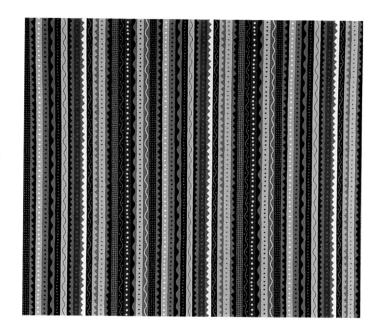

Top Fig. 7.8
Intervall screen-printed cotton furnishing fabric, designed by Susanne Grundell, printed by Borås Wäfveri for the Tio-Gruppen, 1980. It is often assumed that the high-velocity patterns of the Tio-Gruppen were inspired by the Memphis design group, whereas, in fact, they predate them by a decade.

Above Fig. 7.9
Jazz screen-printed cotton furnishing fabric, designed by Britt-Marie Christoffersson, printed by Borås Wäfveri for the Tio-Gruppen, 1980. These two colour-coordinated patterns formed part of the Play collection, inspired by the performances given by the Swedish Ballet in Paris during the 1920s.

Top Fig. 7.10

Megafon *screen-printed cotton furnishing fabric, designed by Gunila Axén, printed by Borås Wäfveri for the Tio-Gruppen, 1983.* The title pattern from the Megaphone collection, this "loud" design exudes energy with its splintered composition and unashamedly exuberant palette.

Above Fig. 7.11

Buenos Aires *screen-printed cotton furnishing fabric, designed by Birgitta Hahn, printed by Borås Wäfveri for the Tio-Gruppen, 1986.* The spiky motifs, red background, and criss-crossing structure of this pattern from the Metropolis collection combine to produce a highly charged effect.

about being opportunistically tasteful and contemporary. Right from the beginning we determined never to speculate about taste. We have done what we believe in ourselves."[6]

Sweden: KF Interior, Almedahls, and Borås Wäfveri

"The outlook appears promising for Swedish textile design in the 80s," prophesied Inez Svensson in 1984; "companies have realized their responsibilities and are concentrating heavily on building up and strengthening their design departments."[7] One of the companies Svensson was referring to was KF Interior, where Birgitta Löfdahl commissioned innovative modern furnishing fabrics and accessories by designers such as Mikael Löfström. At Almedahls, Ulla Bodin was appointed design director, and designers for the firm during the past two decades have included Eva Best, Anna Lena Emdén, Susan Engel, and Peter Wide. Textural painterly abstract landscapes were Bodin's speciality during the 1980s, while Emdén excelled in primitive "ruralist" patterns in primary colours.

At Borås Wäfveri, Sven Fristedt continued to create original, witty and stimulating patterns, including *Haväng* (1982), depicting grass and butterflies, which was sold in Britain under the title *Green, Green Grass of Home.* Inez Svensson also supplied patterns on a freelance basis, complementing her work for the Tio-Gruppen. In 1983 Göta Trägårdh created a dramatic group of wild, scribbly, and splattered patterns, including *Cosmos* and *Rapid*, recalling the abstract expressionist idiom of the 1950s, a stunning finale to a remarkable career. Borås Wäfveri also reprinted some of her earlier designs for Stobo, such as *Japan I* (4.61), originally produced in 1954. Such patterns triggered off a wider appreciation of Sweden's post-war textile heritage, prompting other companies, such as Almedahls and Ljungbergs, to reissue archive designs. At Ljungbergs, the glass designer Lena Bergström has introduced a sophisticated urban aesthetic, reflecting the minimalist Neo-Modern retro trends of the 1990s (fig. 7.12).

During the 1990s Borås Wäfveri, now better known as Borås Cotton Studio, has continued to produce attractive, cheerful, and upbeat printed fabrics by designers such as Mona Björk and Lena Cronholm. In 1999 it launched the Palestra collection designed by Maria Löw, a vibrant and dynamic contract range inspired by Swedish summer landscapes. Painterly florals form the centrepiece of the current Nordic Inspiration collection, designed by Fanny Aronsen on the theme of Scandinavian flowers.

Sweden: IKEA

The 1980s and 1990s witnessed the continued global expansion of IKEA. During this period the company exerted a huge international influence in promoting Swedish design, including printed textiles. "Their textile department is characterized by good Swedish design throughout, presented in a commendably clear and accessible manner," noted Inez Svensson in 1984.[8] In recent years IKEA has been one of the few places where consumers can buy affordable modern printed furnishing fabrics. "Our Scandinavian roots play an important role in our style of interior decoration," the company announced in its 1999 catalogue, which featured lively printed furnishing fabrics by the interior designer Mikael Löfström. IKEA's 2001 range included vibrant fabrics by Katarina Brieditis and Åsa Gray in rich, saturated colours, and a zingy collection of rugs, mats, and furnishing fabrics by the Tio-Gruppen, with whom it has collaborated over many years, both individually and collectively. The crucial link between textiles and IKEA's image was highlighted by a recent high-profile British television and poster advertising campaign urging consumers to "chuck out the chintz."

Sweden: Kinnasand

The most progressive company in Sweden at present is Kinnasand, although the company's youthful image is rather misleading as it actually dates back to 1873. Kinna was an important linen-weaving centre during the mid-19th century, and until the 1970s Kinnasand concentrated primarily on woven fabrics and carpets. The company's reputation for design dates back to the years following the Second World War, when it began to employ leading designers such as Age Faith-Ell. The Finnish designer Timo Sarpaneva was Kinnasand's artistic director from 1964 to 1972, and during the 1970s and early 1980s it numbered among its woven textile designers Annalisa Åhall, Ingrid Dessau, Gillian Marshall, and Barbro Petersson. During this period a minimalist geometric aesthetic prevailed. "My ultimate aim is trying to give vibrancy to what is simple," explained Dessau. "I often begin with complicated patterns, but I peel them away bit by bit."[9]

Kinnasand remained a family-owned company until 1987, when it was sold by Proventus to the investment group Art & Technology. By this time it had begun to produce printed textiles, collaborating with the artist Thomas Brolin, whose approach to pattern was refreshingly non-conformist. *Air* (1990) was a *trompe l'oeil* abstract featuring three-dimensional chevrons hovering over a marbled ground, while *Alakatt* (1990) depicted elongated, loping cat motifs (fig. 7.14). Other designers during the late 1980s included Ninna Bingman, Bernice Christoph, Lena Fransson, and Anna Severinsson. Christoph's *Tabasco* (1987), suggesting torn and crumpled coloured streamers (fig. 7.13), and Severinsson's woven fabric *Chili* (1987), with its Memphis-inspired pattern and fluorescent colours, both typified the more extrovert qualities of Kinnasand's output at this time.

Design and manufacturing are now divided between two Kinnasand factories, in Sweden and Germany, and the company employs an in-house design team as well as collaborating with freelance designers in both countries. Pattern designers during the late 1990s have included Anne Brand, Franziska Falke, Bettina Göttke-Krogmann, Carl Johan Hane, Noriko Hiroshige, Ulrica Hydman-Vallien, Vollrath Hopp, Kitty Kahane, Oskar Kollar, Christel Kurén,

Top Fig. 7.12
O-LIK screen-printed cotton furnishing fabric, designed by Lena Bergström, produced by Ljungbergs Textiltryck, 1992. Lena Bergström, the creator of this large-scale Neo-Modern pattern, is one of several designers who have crossed over between glass and textiles, two of Sweden's great design strengths.

Above Fig. 7.13
Tabasco screen-printed cotton furnishing fabric, designed by Bernice Christoph, printed by Ljungbergs Textiltryck for Kinnasand, 1987. Originally best known for its woven fabrics, Kinnasand established its reputation for imaginative modern printed textiles during the 1980s.

Above Fig. 7.14

Alakatt screen-printed cotton and linen furnishing fabric, designed by Thomas Brolin, printed by Ljungbergs Textiltryck for Kinnasand, 1990. Thomas Brolin, the designer of this idiosyncratic pattern, trained as a painter and sculptor. The fabric was hand screen-printed by Sweden's most celebrated printing firm.

Kristina Pihl, Caroline Ramberg, Gunnel Sahlin, Anna Salander, Inez Svensson, Sofia Thedvall, Gunilla Lagerhem Ullberg, and Liselotte Zetterlund. Several of the German designers are artists, notably Vollrath Hopp, who specializes in minimalist florals, and Oskar Kollar, whose patterns reproduce the expressive fluidity of his watercolours. Gunnel Sahlin and Ulrica Hydman-Vallien are both well-known Swedish glass designers, although Sahlin's original training was in textiles (fig. 7.1). Hydman-Vallien excels in colourful primitive florals, while Sahlin explores the Neo-Modern idiom.

Aiming its products at architects and style-conscious young professionals, Kinnasand has adopted an increasingly sophisticated approach to design in recent years. Its 1998 collection, Stockholm Rooms, included several patterns with a 1950s flavour, such as *Pampas* by veteran designer Inez Svensson and *Tegelbacken* by Carl Johan Hane (fig. 7.15). Christel Kurén's Cocktail series, composed of circles, rings, and squares, adopted a 1960s vocabulary, reinterpreted in a contemporary way. Kinnasand's use of colour is particularly inspiring, ranging from the subtle tones of Kristina Pihl's flower-head pattern *Kajsa* (1998), to the luminous, shifting richness of Anne Brand's patterns, *Spot*, *Peak*, and *Patch* (all 1999) (fig. 7.16). Pure, singing colours are the main focal point of Kinnasand's 2001 collection, which includes simple geometrics such as the horizontally banded *Mega* by Caroline Ramberg and the rectangular grid-pattern *Maria* by Gunilla Lagerhem Ullberg.

Finland: Peterzens and Tampella

"There is a feeling of confidence and vitality in the Finnish textile trade, backed up by growing export figures," noted Penny Sparke in 1982. "It is an inspiring phenomenon and one which should make other countries feel that furnishing fabrics need not be the dull or discreetly neutral backcloth to life that they so often are."[10] In addition to Marimekko, Sparke singled out Finlayson, Tampella, and Peterzens Oy as sources of innovation. Peterzens, founded in 1982, produced textural abstract patterns inspired by the Finnish landscape, created by a Scottish designer, Alex Ward.

Tampella's speciality during the early 1980s was strong, direct, colourful designs, many by Anneli Airikka-Lammi, its chief designer from 1981 to 1985. Winner of the Finnish Textile Artist of the Year award in 1982, Airikka-Lammi had previously designed for Finlayson and Helenius, and went on to join Kangastus in 1986. Her designs included *Seitti*, subtle and thread-like, and *Purje* (both 1980), featuring bold criss-crossing lines and large, overlapping circles in primary colours (fig. 7.17).

Finland: Marimekko

In 1985 Marimekko was bought by the Amer Group, and Kari Mattson, president of Marimekko, stated in 1986: "Marimekko's basic idea has been and still is to be different from the ordinary. However, designers will perhaps have to be in closer touch with actual realities: they are the interpreters of reality and cannot

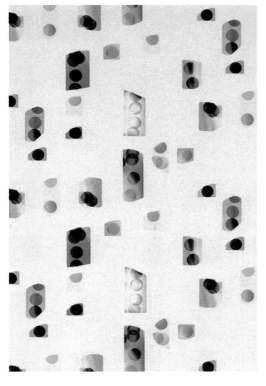

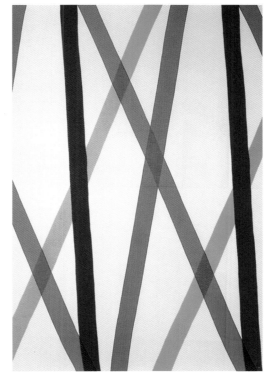

Above Fig. 7.15
Two screen-printed cotton and Kanecaron modacrylic furnishing fabrics, **Pampas** *(left) designed by Inez Svensson and* **Tegelbacken** *(right) designed by Carl Johan Hane, produced by Kinnasand, 1998.* Both of these designs are highly evocative of the 1950s, the decade when Inez Svensson began her career.

Far left Fig. 7.16
Spot *screen-printed polyester furnishing fabric, designed by Anne Brand, produced by Kinnasand, 1999.* Part of a series of patterns exploring subtle luminous watercolour effects, this design suggests both digital and painterly aesthetics at the same time.

Left Fig. 7.17
Purje *screen-printed cotton furnishing fabric, designed by Anneli Airikka-Lammi, produced by Tampella, 1980.* The primary colours in this fabric, which was clearly influenced by the bright Marimekko aesthetic of the 1970s, distinguish it from the palette of more recent designs.

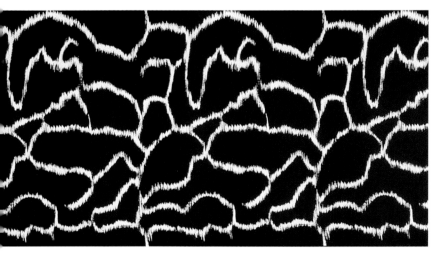

create in a vacuum."[11] Marimekko did not thrive under Amer's ownership, however, and in 1991 it was sold to Workidea Oy, owned by Kirsti Paakkanen, a former advertising agency executive, who has spent the past decade revitalizing the company. Despite its commercial ups and downs, Marimekko has consistently produced original new patterns throughout the 1980s and 1990s. Maija Isola continued to work for the firm until 1987, collaborating from 1980 with her daughter, Kristina Isola, who is still one of Marimekko's chief designers, along with Fujiwo Ishimoto. A key feature of Marimekko's current marketing policy is the reissue of classics from its fifty-year back catalogue, notably a large group of patterns from the 1950s and 1960s by Maija Isola.

Marimekko's most prolific and creative designer during the past two decades has been Fujiwo Ishimoto, who has created over 300 designs since joining the company in 1974. Combining his natural dexterity as an artist – evident in the scribbly *Oikkuja*, the calligraphic *Harha*, and the dramatic, painterly *Kuiskaus* (1982) – with a growing interest in the application of new technology, Ishimoto continues to create arresting new patterns, such as *Kierto* (2001), with its digital simulation of tie-dye effects. In the Maisema collection (1982) his imaginative response to the textures of the Finnish landscape was married with the changing colours of the seasons (fig. 7.18). Multicoloured, cross-hatched squares were loosely drawn in soft wax crayon, creating patterns of great subtlety and depth, resembling patchwork quilts. Chequerboard compositions also formed the basis for many of the designs in the Iso Karhu collection (1983), although these ikat-inspired patterns were more tonal than textural, as in *Karhusaari* (fig. 7.19).

Ishimoto's Sinitaivas collection (1986), featuring subtle speckled and graduated effects evoking the sky, signalled a further departure from formal structured compositions and clearly defined patterns. These trends were also reflected in the fluid marbled patterns of the Sydäntalvi collection (1985), in which colours were swirled together in a free and painterly way. Heightened textural effects evoking natural phenomena and plants remain a feature of Ishimoto's more recent work, as in *Humiseva* (1995), showing ghostly overlapping leaves. Ishimoto has proved himself to be highly flexible, complementing progressive abstracts with more accessible representational designs. "My foremost object is to design fabrics that are suitable for everyday use, fabrics that are not too 'artistic,'" he has stated. "The fabrics can (or should) of course be of high aesthetic quality, but they also have to be appropriate for practical use."[12]

Other Marimekko designers during the 1980s included Inka Kivalo, Irma Kukkasjärvi, Satu Montanari, Heikki Orvola, and Jatta Salonen, while among more recent contributors are Anna Danielsson, Antti Eklund, Stefan Lindfors, Robert Segal, and the cutting-edge graphic designer Marjaana Virta. Jatta Salonen, who specialized in florals, joined the company as a staff designer in 1983. Satu Montanari

Top Fig. 7.18
Maisema screen-printed cotton furnishing fabric, designed by Fujiwo Ishimoto, produced by Marimekko, 1982. Scribbly crayon effects evoke the shifting textures of the Finnish landscape in this pattern, produced in contrasting colourways to reflect summer's heat and winter's darkness.

Above Fig. 7.19
Karhusaari screen-printed cotton furnishing fabric, designed by Fujiwo Ishimoto, produced by Marimekko, 1983. This pattern formed part of the Iso Karhu collection, celebrating the life of the Finno-Ugrian peoples. The indistinct borders of the design were inspired by ikat textiles.

caused a stir during the mid-1980s with arresting *trompe l'oeil* printed patterns such as *Lucky Beetle*, *Sparks*, and *Hydrangea*, featuring magnified photographic images. Inka Kivalo created patterns such as *Artificial Flowers* (1987) and *Arvoitus* (1988), with a "distressed" background and expressionistic highlights that simulated the aesthetic of hand-painted textiles. The architect Antti Eklund designed a brightly coloured cartoon lizard pattern, *Lisko* (1995), which had a quirky Post-Modern appeal (fig. 7.21). Stefan Lindfors, the wild man of Finnish design, well known for his theatrical furniture and interiors, created the skeletal *Alaris* (1997), featuring a blown-up image of dragonfly wings (fig. 7.22). Several different versions were produced by manipulating the image on the computer. Similar techniques were used to modify the lettering that formed the basis of Lindfors's *Anakonda*, while *Alandia* (both 2000) was inspired by an aerial view of the archipelago between Finland and Sweden.

Denmark: Kvadrat

The effect of all this pattern-making activity in Sweden and Finland was to stimulate renewed interest in printed textiles in Denmark. Some were created by independent textile artists such as Else Kallesøe and Vibeke Riisberg – the latter a pioneer of computer-generated patterns for printed fashion and furnishing fabrics – while others were produced by the adventurous manufacturer Kvadrat, founded in 1966. The company's output was enlivened from 1977 by the work of the painter and graphic artist Finn Sködt, who designed vigorous, scribbly prints such as *Babylon* (1983), explosive constructivist designs such as *Cursiva* (1984) (fig. 7.20), and colourful structured wovens such as *Etruska* (1989). Sködt continued to design for Kvadrat during the 1990s, and other contributors over the past two decades have included Ole Kortzau, Ross Littell and Vibeke Riisberg.

Switzerland: Création Baumann

The reputation of Swiss companies such as Zurich-based Christian Fischbacher and Création Baumann of Langenthal has grown steadily in recent decades, and is based not only on design but also on commitment to rigorous production standards. Création Baumann, founded in 1886 as a linen-weaving mill, is still a family-run company. It controls every stage of manufacture at its state-of-the-art factory, with design largely undertaken as a group exercise by an in-house team. Previously associated during the 1960s with a restrained, functionalist Bauhaus aesthetic, Création Baumann began to adopt a livelier style during the 1980s with patterns such as *Scritto* (1988) by Arlette Balinari, a jacquard-woven double cloth inspired by graffiti. Understatement is still at the heart of the Baumann philosophy, exemplified by the subtle coordinated Neo-Modern printed and woven fabrics of the Uptown range from its recent Living collection (2001) (fig. 7.23). Création Baumann also markets an eye-catching range of thin, translucent, metallic sheer fabrics produced for the firm by the Swiss fashion textile company Jakob Schlaepfer & Co., including some cut-out fabrics featuring intriguing "deleted" patterns.

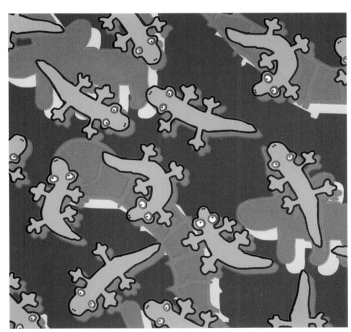

Top Fig. 7.20
Cursiva *screen-printed cotton furnishing fabric, designed by Finn Sködt, produced by Kvadrat, 1984.* Finn Sködt's prints for Kvadrat were among the strongest and most imaginative of the 1980s. This pattern appears to have been influenced by the Suprematist paintings of the Russian artist Kasimir Malevich.

Above Fig. 7.21
Lisko *screen-printed cotton furnishing fabric, designed by Antti Eklund, produced by Marimekko, 1995.* Bright colours reinforce the quirkiness of this pattern. The design is constructed in two layers, with small lizards scurrying on the surface and larger creatures lurking below.

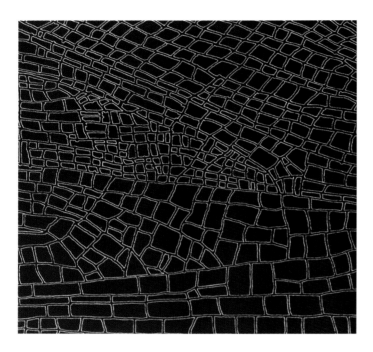

Britain: Colefax and Fowler

Having taken its cultural heritage for granted until the 1970s, Britain suddenly woke up during the 1980s to the wealth of history on its doorstep. The National Trust boomed, and with it came a wave of chintz mania and the craze for the "country house style." All at once the name Colefax and Fowler – the decorating firm established by Sibyl Colefax and John Fowler in 1938, catering to the rarefied needs of the aristocracy – was on everyone's lips. Initially acting purely as interior decorators, Colefax and Fowler rescued and preserved the slightly faded but genteel grandeur of the country house style, or "humble elegance" as it was described. It was not until 1960 that the company began to disseminate its aesthetic, acting first as distributors and later also as editors for a carefully selected range of *haute couture* period textiles and wallpapers. "I realised that we had some of the most beautiful documents ever in our archives," explained Tom Parr, the chairman, in 1994, "and it was time to produce them for the benefit of countless other people who shared our regard for those vital ingredients that furnish a house."[13] According to Jane Ducas, the essence of the Colefax and Fowler style lies in Fowler's unique colour palette, in which "offbeat, smudgy mezzotints, even drab black are a foil to pretty pastels or more vibrant hues (fig. 7.24)."[14] Colefax and Fowler flourished during the 1980s, greatly expanding and diversifying its portfolio. Today it controls a large sector of the international market, having acquired major firms from Britain (Jane Churchill, 1989), the United States (Cowtan & Tout, 1988; Larsen, 1997), and France (Manuel Canovas, 1998).

Spurred on by the success of Colefax and Fowler, historic companies such as G.P. & J. Baker and Warner realized they were sitting on a goldmine in the form of their company archives, which offered unlimited potential for ready-made "document" designs. In wallpapers, the ultimate "document" design firm is Cole & Son, which owns a huge collection of original printing blocks dating back to the 19th century. Museums also took advantage of the income-generating potential of their textile and wallpaper collections, and began to strike up licensing deals with companies catering to the heritage market. Soon almost the entire furnishings market, from the high end to the low end, was saturated with the all-pervasive country house style.

A large sector of the pattern-design profession is now devoted to the task of translating archive material into workable contemporary textiles and wallpapers. As Jane Ducas points out in relation to Colefax and Fowler, "the creative process of turning a document into a flawless furnishing item is lengthy. To achieve the right scale, balance and proportion, the ideal tone for the background, not to mention specific colours (let alone shadows and highlights) means months of toil for the studio."[15] Some designers specialize in creating new patterns with an authentic period feel, such as freelance designer Pat Etheridge, who has supplied hundreds of patterns to leading firms in Britain, Europe, Japan, and the United States over the past thirty years. Highly accomplished, yet almost completely "invisible" outside the profession, such designers are vital to the success of the furnishing trade.[16]

Britain: Laura Ashley

During the 1980s the simple rusticism of Laura Ashley's early style was gradually replaced by the grander decorative idiom of the country house look, and the company began to embrace a wider range of

Opposite left Fig. 7.22
Alaris *screen-printed cotton furnishing fabric, designed by Stefan Lindfors, produced by Marimekko, 1997.* Stefan Lindfors designed a series of patterns based on a computer-manipulated image of a dragonfly's wing. Here the veins are magnified; another variant shows the whole wing.

Opposite right Fig. 7.23
Dakota *screen-printed Trevira polyester voile furnishing fabric, designed and produced by Création Baumann, 2001.* Understatement is the keynote of many contemporary patterns. At first glance this looks like a striped fabric, but on closer inspection spidery doodles can be seen.

Left Fig. 7.24
Oakwood *surface-printed wallpaper, designed and produced by Colefax and Fowler, 2001.* This wallpaper, with its sinuous composition and mellow colouring, sums up the luxurious traditional appeal of Colefax and Fowler. Updated archive-based "document" designs are supplemented in the company's ranges by newly created patterns in period styles.

period styles. "Richer colours were used with greater daring and understanding," noted Iain Gale and Susan Irvine in their book *Laura Ashley Style* in 1986; "cotton, no longer a 'cottagey' fabric, was given greater sophistication with the application of prints on a larger scale and the introduction of chintz and a heavier weight cotton satin." Whereas the early patterns were light and informal, mainly used in kitchens, bathrooms, and bedrooms, the second generation of designs included more complex and formal patterns intended for lounges, dining rooms, and hallways.

The company continued to expand throughout the 1980s, turning public in 1985, the year of Laura Ashley's death. By the end of the decade there were 450 shops worldwide. Although the company suffered from market saturation during the 1990s, there is still a healthy market for Laura Ashley's period furnishings, although patterns now play a less prominent role in the appeal of its products as a whole and colours are more recessive.

Britain: Osborne & Little

"The relationship between old and new is one of interdependence," explained Antony Little in 1988. "For without the influence of the new, interior decoration would wither to a museum state, but equally, were it not for the firm foundation of classic design with its tried and tested virtues, innovation would have difficulty taking root."[17] Osborne & Little has grown into a major international public limited company over the past two decades, taking over Tamesa Fabrics in 1985 and subsequently acquiring distribution rights to Lorca, Nina Campbell, and Liberty Furnishings. Adopting a more robust and characterful approach to period design during the 1980s than most British firms – less blindly respectful, more

imaginative – Osborne & Little was not afraid to use striking motifs and strident colours, as in its coordinating *Arcadia* wallpaper and *Camellia Ribbon* fabric (1986). When the company tackled florals, it was in a no-holds-barred way, as in *Botanica* (c.1986), featuring panels of blowsy pink roses, a composite adaptation of two 19th-century archive designs. Striped patterns were also much bolder than the norm, often in rich colourways with jazzy embellishments, as in the upbeat Regatta range (1985).

Never a company to be pigeon-holed, Osborne & Little takes an open-minded approach, reflected in the consistent freshness of its output, and historical references tend to be lateral rather than literal. Antony Little's continued role as design director, heading a large studio team, underlies the company's confident and knowledgeable approach to design. "An important strength is a broad approach which explores diverse sources of inspiration. Ideas are found everywhere: the natural world, art, and architecture as well as archival documents and historical sources. Spontaneously and often wittily interpreted, they form just some of the many eclectic images represented in a vast array of patterns and colourings (fig. 7.25)."[18] Most designs are created in-house, but on occasion the company has collaborated with outside designers, such as the fashion designer Zandra Rhodes during the 1980s, whose self-consciously theatrical fabrics perfectly complemented its own style.

Britain: Designers Guild

Building on the success of its Watercolour collection (1979), Designers Guild continued, during the early 1980s, to develop and refine its distinctive painterly approach to floral textiles through patterns such as *Anemone* (1983) (fig. 7.27). While most patterns

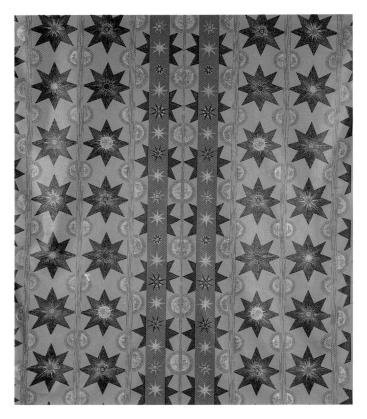

Top Fig. 7.25
Coronata screen-printed glazed cotton furnishing fabric, designed and produced by Osborne & Little, 1988. Osborne & Little's patterns often combine historical allusions with contemporary resonances, as in this vibrantly coloured pattern from the Renaissance-inspired Romagna collection.

Above Fig. 7.26
Tracer screen-printed cotton furnishing fabric, designed by Michael Heindorff, produced by Designers Guild, 1992. Part of the Still Life collection, this pattern is outstanding for the delicacy and luminosity of its colouring and the subtlety of its suffused, watercolour-like effects.

Top Fig. 7.27
Anemone screen-printed cotton satin furnishing fabric, designed by Tricia Guild, produced by Designers Guild, 1983. Tricia Guild's approach to furnishings is strongly colour-led and overtly painterly. This floral, produced in a colourway called sapphire, is typical of her early style.

Above Fig. 7.28
Côte d'Azur (left) and Havana (right) screen-printed cotton furnishing fabric, designed by Collier Campbell, produced by Fischbacher, 1983. These patterns were part of the Six Views collection, which won a Design Centre Award in 1984. *Côte d'Azur* was inspired by the paintings of Matisse.

are created by the in-house studio under the direction of Tricia Guild, regular collaborations with outside artists have been a continued feature of Designers Guild ranges. In 1986 the artist Howard Hodgkin created a group of giant tulip patterns, while the potter Janice Tchalenko designed the lush, colour-rich Waterleaf collection. Tchalenko's patterns transposed the rich glazes of her ceramics into printed cloth via her watercolour paintings. Exquisite subtle, watery effects were also the basis for the luminous patterns of artist Michael Heindorff in the Still Life collection (1992) (fig. 7.26). In 1994 Tricia Guild renewed her collaboration with the knitwear designer Kaffe Fassett through the Kaffe's Pots collection.

In 1983 the Angles collection was launched, featuring bold, painterly abstracts such as *Plane*, *Pyramid*, and *Outline*. However, although Designers Guild has retained its contemporary edge, the company has explored a broader design vocabulary since the mid-1980s. Ethnic influences, particularly from India and Morocco, have become increasingly dominant, and period sources, especially French and Italian, have also been absorbed. Tricia Guild cites gardens and travel as her main sources of inspiration, and a relaxed, sensuous approach lies at the heart of her aesthetic. Current designs for textiles are simpler and more direct, with greater emphasis on texture and pure colour, and in recent years a fearless palette of orange, turquoise, and bright pink has replaced the creamy pastel tones of earlier times.

By 1998 there were more than 2,500 fabrics and 700 wallpapers in the Designers Guild catalogue, including silks, jacquards, tapestries, velvets, and linens, as well as printed cottons. Today an extensive selection of plains, checks, and stripes complement the trademark florals, and the company also acts as a distributor for imaginative new furnishings by William Yeoward and Emily Todhunter. Catering to British, European, and international markets, Designers Guild has grown rapidly since the early 1990s. Tricia Guild is chairman and creative director, and since 1986 her brother, Simon Jeffrey, has been chief executive. A guru in the world of interior design, Tricia Guild has published a string of influential and popular books, including *Tricia Guild's New Soft Furnishings* (1990) and *Tricia Guild on Colour* (1992).

Britain: Collier Campbell

Although period designs dominated the interiors market during the 1980s, Collier Campbell offered a refreshing alternative. Having established themselves as designer-converters in 1979, Susan Collier and Sarah Campbell produced a stream of intoxicating patterns during the 1980s, using colour to enliven their rich, painterly designs. Particularly successful was their much-lauded Six Views collection (1983), printed in Britain by Standfast for the Swiss firm Christian Fischbacher. This won a Design Centre Award in 1984, and its seductive palette and dynamic all-over patterns led Carol Doye to praise it in *Design* magazine as "one of the most adventurous ranges to have been produced for at least ten years"

(fig. 7.28).[19] The best seller from the collection was *Côte d'Azur*, with its evocative tapestry of palm trees, balconies, and vivid blue skies, painted in a fluid, uninhibited style suggestive of Dufy or Matisse. *Havana*, with its multicoloured, zigzagging ribbons, was a celebration of pure, unadulterated pattern-making, abstraction in an accessible and stimulating guise. *Kasbah* and *Spice Route*, with their geometric compositions and earthy, reddish-brown colours, hinted at ethnic sources, while *Water Meadow* and *Romany* were described at the time as looking "as if they've just been plucked from the casement windows of a thatched cottage."[20]

Collier Campbell's twice-yearly fabric collections and annual wallpaper collections for Habitat from 1980 to 1992 further popularized the firm's distinctive style. Visually rich, structurally dynamic, and saturated in colour, its patterns were positive, life-affirming, and celebratory. Post-Modernism did not enter into the equation, and there was no hint of irony in the work. Working anonymously, Collier Campbell have also designed furnishing fabrics and wallpapers for Marks & Spencer, and bed linen for numerous companies, including John Lewis, ITC in France, and Trois Suisses in Switzerland. Since the mid-1990s the company has concentrated on design rather than production, working mainly with American firms. In recent years Collier Campbell's main clients in the United States have included Martex and J.P. Stevens for bed linen, Imperial Wallcoverings for wallpapers, and P. Kaufmann for printed fabrics. "Good design should be available to everybody," asserted Susan Collier in 1981. "It costs just as much to draw, engrave and colour a bad design as it does a good one."[21]

Britain: Timney Fowler

Another British success story was Timney Fowler, established in 1980 as a partnership between two graduates of the Royal College of Art, the artist Sue Timney and the textile and graphic designer Grahame Fowler. The catalyst for Timney Fowler's rapid expansion was the overwhelming success of the company's Neo-Classical collection of furnishing fabrics, launched in 1983 at its newly opened London shop (fig. 7.29). Drawing on a pool of "borrowed" engravings of classical statues and architectural features, the collection featured dramatic patterns such as *Columns* and more playful designs such as *Roman Heads*. These designs worked on more than one level, satisfying the interior decorator market with their imposing historical imagery, while at the same time fuelling the fashion for Post-Modernism with their ironic and playful sampling of historical "ready-mades." Some patterns were "straight," whereas others were wittily deconstructed, as in the collapsing architectural fragments of *Fallen Angel* (1986). On a more basic level, the crisply delineated black-on-white or white-on-black patterns made a striking impact through the boldness and clarity of their graphic effects. Timney Fowler's work helped to popularize a more witty and ironic approach to period design. The obvious parallels with the work of Piero Fornasetti fuelled a resurgence of interest in the Italian designer.

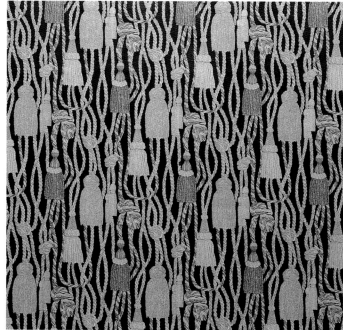

Top Fig. 7.29
Statues screen-printed cotton satin furnishing fabric, designed by Sue Timney and Grahame Fowler, produced by Timney Fowler, c.1984–5. Timney Fowler's Neo-Classical collection, with its "sampled" engravings of sculptures and architectural features, satisfies both period and Post-Modern tastes.

Above Fig. 7.30
Hands screen-printed and discharge-dyed silk dress fabric, designed by Helen Littman, 1984, produced by English Eccentrics, 1986. Palmistry diagrams, Keith Haring's graffiti art, and Gustav Klimt's Tree of Life spirals are juxtaposed in this eclectic design.

Above right Fig. 7.31
London Tassels screen-printed glazed cotton, designed by Mandy Martin, produced by Warner, 1987–8. This pattern panders to the fashion for luxurious country house furnishings at the same time as wittily subverting it.

A limited company since 1985, Timney Fowler now produces complementary wallpapers and accessories alongside its printed textiles, while the Timney Fowler Design Studio (created as a subsidiary in 1993) designs a wide range of products for other manufacturers. Historical sources still form Timney Fowler's core vocabulary, broadened during the 1990s to include Renaissance paintings and 18th-century garden ornaments and clocks. Recently classical architecture and sculpture have been arranged in more structured compositions, as in the grids and bands of *Dancing Colonnades* and *Porticos*. Although still centred around a black-and-white palette, some designs are produced with coloured backgrounds, and the current Pompeian and Aesthetic collections are printed in significantly brighter tones.

Britain: Zoffany and Warner

Over the past two decades the British textile and wallpaper industry has remained very volatile, with older firms such as G.P. & J. Baker, Cole & Son, Sanderson, and Warner repeatedly destabilized by changes of ownership. After being sold to its American partner, Greeff Fabrics, in 1970, Warner (renamed Warner Fabrics in 1987) changed hands three times during the 1970s and 1980s. In 2001 it was sold to Turnell & Gigon by Walker Greenback, its owner since 1994. Warner is now managed by Zoffany, a British wallpaper company founded in 1984, specializing in museum-based "document" designs. In 1987 Zoffany expanded into textiles, and it has recently collaborated with the National Trust on a range of country house archive designs.

Despite all this disruption, Warner maintained its design identity throughout the 1980s, under the direction of Eddie Squires until his retirement in 1993. "The only way to go is to raise design standards all the time. To level off to the middle-of-the-road would be disaster," Warner's marketing director observed astutely in 1982.[22] At this date three themed collections were produced annually, and with 50 percent of Warner's income generated from exports, Squires recognized the need to cater to the tastes of an essentially conservative market. Adopting a positive, but subtly subversive, approach to period design, he oversaw collections which, while focusing on historical themes, allowed designers scope for imaginative digressions. A good example was *Flower Dance* (1986) by Melanie Greaves, a chintz with striped overlay, produced in an overtly contemporary palette. Squires himself continued to demonstrate his own decidedly offbeat character through patterns such as *Microchip and Vine*, from the Studio collection (1982), which juxtaposed electrical circuitry with floral motifs. Later he designed *Capriccio* (1986), resembling pixelated images on a television screen.

In the Stately Homes collection (1982), Squires included faux-marble patterns such as *Marble Hall* and *trompe l'oeil* designs such as *Flamestitch*, as an ironic Post-Modern commentary on the vogue for the country house style. Fabrics simulating the appearance of other materials were also the basis for *Panache* by Anne White from the Designers Choice collection (1984). Another witty aside on the mania for period textiles, this pattern depicted a crumpled length of striped silk (fig. 7.32). The use of historical furnishings as a source of imagery for printed patterns was also the basis for *London Tassels* (1987) by Mandy Martin, depicting an overabundance of *passementerie* (fig. 7.31). Some of Alex Fenner's designs, such as *Pearl Drop Stripe* (1986), also contained *trompe l'oeil* motifs. Others drew on historical motifs such as paisley patterns, reinterpreted in a detached Post-Modern way. Marc Camille Chaimowicz, Agathe Charlot, Graham Cracker, Susan Craney, Mike Quigley, Mark Rochester, Corinne Samios, and Catriona Terris also contributed to Warner's output around this time.

In 1983 Warner collaborated with the artist Howard Hodgkin on a group of fabrics for an Arts Council exhibition entitled *Four Rooms*, shown at Liberty in 1984. The decorative effects of Hodgkin's paintings translated remarkably well into printed patterns. Designs such as *Water* and *Autograph*, the latter suggestive of animal markings, retained the character of the artist's brushstrokes. Always on the lookout for new design talent, Eddie Squires kept a close eye on emerging textile graduates. Among his discoveries were Cressida Bell, who created a lively floral called *Exotic Tulip* (1986), and Neil Bottle, who contributed to the Architextural collection (1993) (fig. 7.33). Both were designer-makers producing short runs of fashion and furnishing fabrics. Bottle specialized in one-off silk wall hangings decorated with printing, painting, and stencilling. His Warner patterns, including *Accademia* and *Galleria*, featured "borrowed" architectural and botanical imagery, against a background of distressed decorative effects.

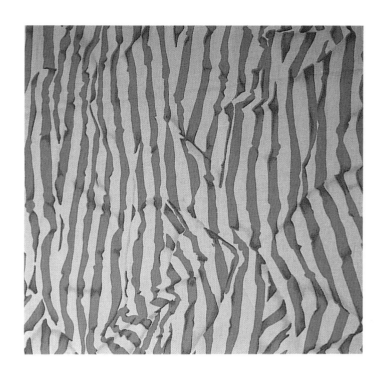

Top Fig. 7.32
Panache *screen-printed glazed cotton, designed by Anne White, produced by Warner, 1984.* Although t*rompe l'oeil* patterns have a venerable pedigree in the history of interior decoration, this design is particularly audacious, and takes on an ironic dimension in the context of the Post-Modern era.

Above Fig. 7.33
Accademia *screen-printed cotton furnishing fabric, designed by Neil Bottle, produced by Warner, 1993.* Architectural drawings and sculptural features provide the starting point for this design, notable for its complex multi-layered composition. It formed part of the ingenious Architextural collection.

Britain: Timorous Beasties

Eddie Squires also commissioned patterns from Timorous Beasties, a Glasgow-based design duo founded by Paul Simmons and Alistair McAuley in 1990. Timorous Beasties has subsequently concentrated on its own collections of screen-printed textiles and wallpapers, produced to order in short runs. The group's early designs were extremely decadent, in a consciously ironic Post-Modern way. In *Grand Acanthus* for Warner's Architextural range (1993), Paul Simmons combined scrolling acanthus leaves with Gothic tracery, artificially heightened with biological vigour. *Large Eel* (1992), designed by Simmons for Timorous Beasties, drew on engravings from a Victorian encyclopedia, juxtaposed in a bizarre arrangement and pumped full of lurid colour (fig. 7.34).

Wit remains a key factor in the work of Timorous Beasties, typified by patterns such as *Force Ten* (1998), where a weather chart is the starting point for a swirling abstract design (fig. 7.35). A variant of this pattern, *Isobar*, forms part of a new range of wallpapers, along with *Circuit* (both 2001), depicting an electrical circuit board. Most patterns are produced as both textiles and wallpapers, and the current range includes both sumptuous Baroque designs such as *Rose* and *Thistle*, and Neo-Modern minimalist retro patterns such as *Aviator* and *Bullet* (both 2000).

Britain: The Cloth and English Eccentrics

Because opportunities to design modern furnishing fabrics and wallpapers for large companies diminished so rapidly during the 1980s, designers with a penchant for pattern had to find other avenues. The main beneficiary has been fashion, and one of the most energetic pattern-led companies of the 1980s was a short-lived textile and fashion label called The Cloth, which was in business from 1983 to 1987. Founded by four graduates of the Royal College of Art – David Band, Brian Bolger, Helen Manning, and Fraser Taylor – the company supplied prints to leading fashion designers and high-street stores, as well as producing its own garment collections. The Cloth's patterns, although printed, gave the suggestion of hand painting, and were characterized by loose, sketchy doodles and daubed, painterly marks.

Another designer whose printed patterns electrified the British fashion scene during the 1980s was Helen Littman, the creative force behind English Eccentrics. After graduating in textiles from Camberwell School of Art in 1977, Littman, who now works under the name Helen David, co-founded English Eccentrics in 1982 with her sister, Judy Littman, who had trained as a painter, and Claire Angel, a fashion designer. During the mid to late 1980s the partnership produced a series of highly stimulating print-led fashion collections, with titles such as Mad Dogs and Englishmen (1983) and Spirit of the Forest (1988). Later the emphasis shifted to printed scarves and garments decorated with scarf-related feature prints, and since 1996, when the company was renamed Helen David English Eccentrics, it has focused on women's fashion.

Offbeat, maverick, and quintessentially British, Littman's early printed patterns were extravagantly decorative, in an ironic, knowing way. Often inspired by foreign travel or artefacts in museums, although sometimes prompted by current issues, her approach to design was characterized by an irreverent Post-Modern sensibility. Drawing on a highly eclectic but carefully chosen range of historical and contemporary imagery, ranging from Roman mosaics to Victorian phrenological busts, Littman created intricate jigsaws from jumbled fragments of "borrowed" decorative motifs. "Fragmentation allows my work to reflect the weight of my own cultural luggage which inevitably colours my perception of other civilizations," she wrote in 1992.[23] In *Hands* (1984) she juxtaposed palmistry diagrams with graffiti art (fig. 7.30), while *Faces* (1987) consisted of myriad rows of "sampled" historical heads, ranging from Arcimboldo to Medusa to Picasso. Although diagrammatic line engravings formed the basis for many of the designs, colour was also important, and the scarves were printed on silk using vivid, translucent acid dyes.

Britain: Georgina von Etzdorf

Now a leading international fashion accessories brand, Georgina von Etzdorf was originally established as a small textile-printing workshop in Wiltshire in 1978. Officially constituted in 1981, the company is still run today by its three original partners, Jonathan Docherty, Martin Simcock, and Georgina von Etzdorf, with Etzdorf as artistic director. She and Simcock had studied textile design together at Camberwell School of Art during the mid-1970s, while Docherty studied industrial design at the Central School. Although scarves have always formed the mainstay of the company's output, production has also encompassed garments such as pyjamas, ties, and gloves, as well as furnishing accessories such as cushions and wall hangings.

Dynamism was the key to Etzdorf's vivacious early patterns, which were full of vigorous, darting movement, as in *Star Wars* (1981) with its shooting stars, and *Dragons* (1984), which featured rippling, fringed dragon tails. "When we started, the feel of fabrics was terribly static, with no flow or rhythm," the designer recalled. "We wanted to create a seamlessness and fluidity which, rather than act as an interesting distraction, would take the eye on a journey."[24] Avoiding conventional subjects, Etzdorf explored astronomical and architectural imagery in patterns such as *Neptune* (1985) and *Metropolis* (1991), evolving a highly personal abstract style.

Created in watercolour, gouache, and chalk, Etzdorf's designs are overtly painterly, with unorthodox diagonal and horizontal compositions and cleverly disguised repeats. "I am vehement about the quality of something created by hand," she explains. "That is what gives the work its vitality and movement."[25] Vivid, non-standard colours and adventurous colour combinations play a key role in her designs. Because the company undertakes its own

Opposite top Fig. 7.34
Large Eel screen-printed cotton velvet furnishing fabric, designed by Paul Simmons, produced by Timorous Beasties, 1992. The design group Timorous Beasties has broken away from the commercial mainstream by producing its own nonconformist fabrics and wallpapers. This highly charged textile, with its bizarre imagery and extravagant colouring, asserts that patterns should be seen and heard.

Opposite bottom Fig.7.35
Force Ten screen-printed linen furnishing fabric, designed by Paul Simmons, produced by Timorous Beasties, 1998. By tackling pattern design from an unusual angle (often humorous), Timorous Beasties has come up with some imaginative solutions, such as this design inspired by a weather chart.

Above Fig. 7.36
Jupiter screen-printed silk crêpe de chine scarf fabric, designed and produced by Georgina von Etzdorf, 1987. "I believe it is colour that draws people to our work, not an intellectual process," says Georgina von Etzdorf. "The senses have always been my form of expression."

Top Fig. 7.37
Hawthorn *flexo-printed wallpaper, designed and produced by Neisha Crosland, 1999.* This pattern was part of the first collection of wallpapers by the textile designer Neisha Crosland. Her rhythmically stimulating designs, printed in soft, chalky colours, explore a vocabulary of stylized organic forms.

Above Fig. 7.38
Nudes *flexo-printed wallpaper, designed by Emily Todhunter, produced by the Paint & Paper Library, 1998.* Figurative patterns in wallpaper are extremely rare. This design works brilliantly, however, because of the calligraphic minimalism of the abstracted figures and the subtle palette.

Top Fig. 7.39
Scattered Pins *heat photogram-printed polyester microfibre dress fabric, designed and produced by Rebecca Earley, 1995.* The pattern on this one-off heat photogram-printed fabric was made by pressing pins into synthetic microfibre with a heated plate. It was commissioned by the Icelandic singer Björk.

Above Fig. 7.40
Red Flash *screen-printed wallpaper, designed by Mark Eley and Wakako Kishimoto, produced by Eley Kishimoto, 2001.* This swirling Neo-Op wallpaper, which bucks the trend towards recessive patterns, was originally conceived as a high-fashion catwalk dress fabric.

printing, Etzdorf is able to exert full control over the translation of her artwork into cloth. In order to achieve the desired painterly effects, dyes are sometimes applied to the screen using a brush rather than a squeegee, as in *Jupiter* (1987) (fig. 7.36). Over the years Etzdorf's fabrics have become more textural and tactile, with printed velvets being introduced in 1985 and devorés (velvets partly burnt with acid to create relief effects) in 1993. Patterns became somewhat simpler and calmer during the 1990s, although Etzdorf's work remains highly sensual and stimulating, in both the choice of fabrics and the nature of the printed designs.

Britain: Nigel Atkinson and Neisha Crosland

The boundary between high fashion and upmarket furnishings has become increasingly blurred in recent years, and it is not uncommon to find designers crossing over between different fields. After studying printed textiles at Winchester School of Art, Nigel Atkinson established a workshop in 1987 where he carried out pioneering experiments in the field of printed fashion fabrics using a process called Expandex. By printing the fabrics on the reverse with heat-reactive dyes, then baking them, he moulded the fabrics into remarkable sculptural relief patterns, such as *Sea Anemone* (1989). Such effects were clearly as relevant to furnishings as to fashion, and after launching an accessories range in 1994 (since supplemented by his own fashion label), the designer founded Nigel Atkinson Interior Textiles in 1997.

Neisha Crosland began producing scarves and fashion fabrics under her own label from 1994, and more recently has crossed over into furnishing fabrics and wallpapers. Her first collection of wallpapers, launched in 1999, featured elegant, abstracted, scrolling, organic patterns such as *Anemone* (fig. 0.1) and *Hawthorn* (fig. 7.37), printed in a distinctive palette of soft neutrals combined with muted darker tones. Her third collection (2001) includes subtle, delicate, abstract patterns inspired by granite, quail's eggs, and moiré. Crosland's distributor is the Paint & Paper Library, originally established in 1996 as a specialist paint supplier. Since 1998 the firm has diversified into wallpapers, and as well as marketing Crosland's work, it also produces collections by the interior designer Emily Todhunter and the company's founder, David Oliver. Todhunter's patterns include the cursive linear design *Nudes* (1998) (fig. 7.38), while Oliver's most successful design is *Liberation* (1999), a minimalist geometric abstract inspired by the layout of blocks of newspaper text.

Britain: Rebecca Earley and Eley Kishimoto

Highlighting the importance of experimental textiles in contemporary British fashion, the curators of the recent British Council exhibition *Fabric of Fashion* noted: "Fabrics allow designers greater freedom to explore a wider range of issues than those offered simply through the conventions of style and silhouette. Using a range of materials as their starting point, they seek to re-examine not just the appearance and construction of clothes,

but other concerns too, from environmental and political issues to personal and philosophical ideas."[26] Spearheading the movement are designers such as Rebecca Earley, a graduate of Central St Martin's, who established her own label, B. Earley, in 1993. Earley specializes in fabrics and scarves printed by heat-photogram, decorated with patterns resembling X-rays. The luminous, ghostly, one-off prints are created by pressing objects on to polyester microfibre or synthetic fleece using a heated plate. Source materials include lace, plants and pins, prompting witty patterns such as *Scattered Pins* (fig. 7.39) and *Pin Stripe* (both 1995).

Pattern is also central to the work of Eley Kishimoto, a husband-and-wife fashion team established by Mark Eley and Japanese-born Wakako Kishimoto in 1992. The duo specialize in printed textiles, which they use in their own fashion collections, as well as supplying other designers, including Hussein Chalayan and Alexander McQueen. Demonstrating no particular allegiance to any one style, and often juxtaposing elements from different genres, Eley Kishimoto's patterns are intrinsically eclectic, sometimes incorporating ironic references to floral chintzes, at other times exploring uncompromisingly abstract effects. In 2001 they transferred two dress fabric patterns on to wallpaper: the faux-Art Deco *Landscape* and the optically disturbing *Red Flash* (fig. 7.40). "We're not afraid of colour or pattern," Eley confirms.[27]

Britain: Designer Makers and Design Studios

Over the past two decades many textile graduates who might previously have pursued a career in industry have been diverted into the burgeoning field of art textiles, as in the case of Jasia Szerszynska, whose screen-printed wall hangings inspired by 1950s textiles attracted widespread attention during the late 1980s. Marta Moia also won acclaim during the mid-1980s for her loose, casual florals with fluid, painterly outlines (fig. 7.41), while Rodney Moorhouse, the founder of Moorhouse Associates, was more daringly experimental. His patterns ranged from arresting abstracts such as *Rainbone*, a vibrant colour-spectrum chevron design, to the prosaic *Potato* (1984) (fig. 7.42), depicting portions of chips wrapped in newspaper. However, for most designer-makers since the mid-1980s, the printing process is just the starting point for further hand-painted decoration, and they are not aiming for standardization either of colours or patterns. Victoria Richards, for example, produces short runs of printed silk for her own fashion accessories range, exploring a painterly, abstract vocabulary and drawing on a rich palette of unique customized colours.

Some textile artists also "moonlight" as pattern designers, although this is not widely known because very few textile and wallpaper manufacturers currently identify their designers. Sally Greaves-Lord, internationally celebrated for her arresting one-off discharge-printed and painted silk banners, also sells designs through First Eleven Studio, a leading British textile design group. The group represents the still successful, but almost completely anonymous,

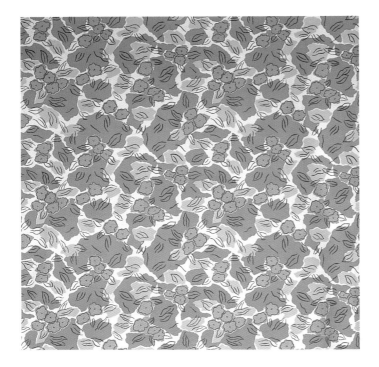

Top Fig. 7.41
Small Flowers *screen-printed cotton furnishing fabric, designed and produced by Marta Moia, c.1985.* Since the mid-1980s designer-makers who hand screen-print their own fabrics in limited quantities have frequently injected fresh ideas into the British pattern-making scene.

Bottom Fig. 7.42
Potato *screen-printed cotton satin furnishing fabric, designed by Rodney Moorhouse, produced by Moorhouse Associates, c.1984.* Designer-makers are able to experiment in ways that are impossible for freelance, studio, or company designers, as demonstrated by this offbeat pattern.

face of contemporary pattern design in Britain. Founded in 1986 by Jenny Frean, who had previously run Jenny Frean & Associates, First Eleven Studio consists of eleven designers specializing in various branches of textiles, including print, weave, and embroidery, who supply designs to leading international manufacturers and retailers. Up to 40 percent of the group's designs are currently sold in the United States. British clients include John Lewis, Monkwell, and Mary Fox Linton, while European customers have included IKEA, Kinnasand, Manuel Canovas, Pierre Frey, Rubelli, and Nya Nordiska (an innovative Swedish-inspired textile company based at Dannenberg in northern Germany). Whereas many design practices specialize in period designs, First Eleven Studio is renowned within the profession for its contemporary approach.

Britain: Tracy Kendall, Jocelyn Warner, and Deborah Bowness

Since the early 1990s a new generation of designer-makers has emerged with even greater confidence and commercial awareness than their predecessors. In recent years a number of pattern designers have switched from textiles to wallpaper, prompting a minor revival in this neglected field. Tracy Kendall, who screen-prints giant photographic images of cutlery, feathers, and dandelions on to wallpaper, was one of the first to cross over. Kendall's approach is similar to that of Jocelyn Warner, whose Larger Than Life collection (1999) features enlarged images of leaves and flowers, manipulated on the computer to simplify their form (fig. 7.43). Printed in simple column repeats, they can be hung in rows or used as single banner strips.

Deborah Bowness also uses large-scale photographic images as the basis for her wallpapers, but her designs, which incorporate details of everyday interiors, are tailored to the interests of individual clients. "Voyeurism and humour are combined with domestic and nostalgic images to create ready-made backdrops for living," she explains.[28] Her approach typifies the ironic detachment and playfulness of many young British designers.

Britain: Santos & Adolfsdóttir, Elenbach, and James Bullen

Entrepreneurialism has flourished in British pattern design since the 1990s, and many small-scale designer-producers now exist, catering, often by choice, to niche markets, creating custom-designed furnishings for individual clients. Santos & Adolfsdóttir is a husband-and-wife partnership consisting of Leo Santos-Shaw and Margrét Adolfsdóttir. They met while studying printed textiles at Middlesex Polytechnic in 1988, and have subsequently specialized in experimental furnishing textiles. Using custom-dyed natural and synthetic fabrics, including silk, velvet, and polyester-polyamide, they print some of their textiles with surface patterns. Other designs exploit blade or laser cutting and multi-layering to create novel textures and three-dimensional effects. Printed designs range from rows of digital numbers (fig. 7.44) to displaced honeycomb patterns. Their work reflects a keen interest in post-war art and design, reinterpreted with a forward-looking twist.

Until recently textiles and wallpapers were designed on a drawing board, but today computers are playing an increasingly central role, revolutionizing printed surface patterns. Early computers were huge, expensive, cumbersome pieces of equipment, and although computer-aided design (CAD) was explored in the textile industry during the 1970s, the main role of computers initially was as a tool for transferring technical data from the designer to the machine. Knitted textiles was the first area in which computers were successfully applied, followed by jacquard weaving and machine embroidery.[29] It is only since the 1990s, with the rapid advances in hardware and software, that surface-pattern designers have been able to harness the full potential of computers. In recent years new technology has fostered a more independent approach among young designers, many of whom are now exploring the potential of digital printing to produce short runs of textiles and wallpapers. Sir Bernard Ashley, the co-founder of Laura Ashley, was so excited by this process that in 2000 he came out of retirement to establish a new company, Elenbach, producing digitally printed furnishing fabrics designed by himself, his daughter Emma Ashley, his granddaughter Lily Ashley, and Linda Bruce.

One of the most exciting new technology-led pattern design companies is James Bullen Design Ltd (formerly Bullen.Pijja), founded by James Bullen in 1998. Bullen won immediate acclaim for his Trompe L'Oeil Illusionary Prints Collection (1998), a startling range of designs simulating pierced, slashed, buttoned, and folded fabrics (fig.7.46). Originally developed for fabrics, the patterns have since been applied to a wide range of furnishings, including plastic laminates and wallpapers. Although faux patterns have an ancient pedigree in the history of decorative art, Bullen's "virtual textures" have a strange, eerie beauty. He uses computers to crop and stretch isolated details from scanned photographs, altering the balance of light and dark, and the resulting designs are either digitally or rotary-printed. However, as the designer stresses, the human element is still essential in order to create a successful pattern. "You need an eye for colour, composition, and shape to make something work and to shape a coherent collection."[30]

Japan: Yoshiki Hishinuma and Hiroshi Awatsuji

Over the past thirty years Japan has emerged as an international leader in the application of new technology to textiles, while at the same time nurturing its rich craft traditions. As a result, Japanese textile and fashion design has flourished, acting as an inspiration and a catalyst for exciting new developments all over the world. Although Japan's reputation centres primarily on subtly textured woven fashion fabrics, the impact of colour and pattern has also been actively explored. In 1977, for example, the Issey Miyake Design Studio developed the technique of laser-beam printing to create geometric patterns in graduated tones, and during the 1990s

Top Fig. 7.43
Lily and *Leaf* *screen-printed wallpapers, designed and produced by Jocelyn Warner, 1999.* Part of the Larger Than Life collection, these patterns were created by scanning actual plants on the computer, then manipulating the resulting digital images to simplify their form.

Above Fig. 7.44
SA08e screen-printed silk taffeta furnishing fabric, designed by Leo Santos-Shaw and Margrèt Adolfsdóttir, produced by Santos & Adolfsdóttir, 1999. This pattern exploits the visual impact of early digital typography. Although apparently computer-generated, it was, in fact, designed by hand.

some of Issey Miyake's celebrated pleated garments have been adorned with printed images. Miyake's former assistant, Yoshiki Hishinuma, produced some highly original screen-printed textiles during the early 1980s, before turning his attention to experimental textured fabrics for his own fashion collections during the following decade. Hiroshi Awatsuji, the most innovative post-war Japanese printed textile designer, collaborated from 1964 with Fujie Textiles, founded in 1885, as well as designing for his own company, AWA, founded in 1988. Particularly striking were his elaborate multi-layered black and white patterns from the late 1980s, evoking fantastical flowers and imaginary textural terrain, and his painterly abstracts from the 1990s, printed or woven in variations of the same intense or subtle tones.

Japan: Jun'ichi Arai and the Nuno Corporation

The towering figure in Japanese textiles over the past two decades has been Jun'ichi Arai, who grew up in the craft-weaving centre of Kiryú, a small town north of Tokyo, and established himself as an independent designer in 1955. From 1979 to 1987 Arai ran a company called Anthologie, which supplied innovative woven fabrics to leading fashion designers such as Issey Miyake, Rei Kawakubo, and Yohji Yamamoto, produced in the workshops at Kiryú. Approaching weaving as a form of three-dimensional engineering, he created sensuous buckled and rippled fabrics, deliberately destabilizing the structure of the cloth by varying the tension of the yarns. Arai also pioneered the use of computers and scanners in translating complex textile designs for the loom. "Fine contemporary cloths are the results of the human spirit and new technology working hand in hand," he observed.[31]

In 1984 Arai co-founded the Nuno Corporation with Reiko Sudo. Nuno means "functional fabric," and the Nuno Corporation, which began as a specialist textiles shop in Tokyo, is now recognized as a world leader in the design of experimental contemporary fashion and interior textiles. Tapping into both high- and low-tech solutions, and using synthetic and natural fibres, Nuno has pushed forward the boundaries of textile design in terms of both technology and aesthetics. For Arai, textiles are a vehicle for tactile and sensory stimulation, and the designs he produced at Nuno exploited the textural and sculptural potential of textiles to the full. Although not a pattern designer himself, Arai sometimes incorporated patterns into his textiles. In 1987 he created a translucent knitted silk fabric called *Raschel Spider Web*, co-designed with his wife Riko Arai. In addition Jun'ichi Arai pioneered the development of combination jacquard weaving, in which yarns of different thicknesses were combined to create low-relief "woven structure patterns," such as *Bark* (1987). He also used metal-coated fabrics, created by vacuum-steaming aluminium on to polyester, as the basis for a series of designs called *Melted Off* (1988). An alkaline solution was used to "melt off" the metal in selected areas, creating free-flowing combed patterns that accentuated the billowing qualities of the cloth.

Although Jun'ichi Arai now works independently, Nuno's free-spirited approach to textiles has continued up to the present day under the inspired leadership of Reiko Sudo, the company's director and chief designer. Pattern design, although not Nuno's main focus, still crops up in its experiments, as in the Scrapyard fabrics (1994), decorated using rusty nails and iron plates, and the Rubber Band linens (1997), screen-printed with patterns of elastic bands built up from multiple layers of silicone resin (fig. 7.47).

Nuno also creates patterns using a modified version of warp-printing, and through applied decoration, such as embroidery and overstitching (*sashiko*). Abstract patterns are also a feature of its flocked, heat-shrunk, and salt-shrunk fabrics, although texture, colour, sheen, and translucency are the primary characteristics of these textiles. Nuno has exerted a huge impact on the textile industry internationally, with innovations in fashion fabrics spilling out into furnishings. Jun'ichi Arai, who now travels widely as an independent textile artist, continues to inspire designers throughout the world.

Coda: Who's afraid of pattern design?

Pattern design, which started on a high at the beginning of the 20th century, has since experienced many dramatic surges and abrupt declines. Driven forward by the birth of new artistic movements, the genius of individual designers, and the vision of enlightened manufacturers, it has been turned on its head at intervals throughout the century by technological innovations, economic upheavals, political unrest, and wars. Looking back, the high point of the century appears to have been the 1950s and 1960s, when contemporary pattern design flourished more vigorously and more widely than at any other time before.

Taste in pattern design continues to manifest itself in diverse ways. Generally, however, most people are much more fearful of pattern today than they were fifty years ago, which is why so many of the textiles and wallpapers on the market nowadays are extremely low-key. This is particularly so in the case of wallpapers, where the ultra-recessive currently reigns, typified by the recent work of the German textile designer Ulf Moritz for the wallpaper company Marburger (fig. 7.45). Moritz has collaborated with a number of leading European textile firms over the past forty years, including Ploeg during the 1960s, and, more recently, Sahco Hesslein. Widespread nervousness about pattern is also reflected in the prevailing vogue for minimalist Neo-Modern retro designs, with their neutered colours and pared-down forms.

Today our homes are relatively bereft of pattern, and after decades of indoctrination by firms such as Sanderson and Laura Ashley, calculated coordination reigns. When people come to redecorate their home, they tend to look for ready-made solutions, and are frightened of individuality. Patterned textiles and wallpapers were once a vital, stimulating element in our domestic environment, however. If we are brave, they can be again.

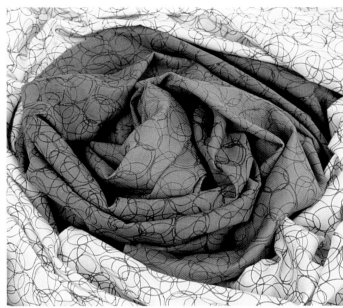

Above left Fig. 7.45
Wallpaper no.1741/71722, rotary screen-printed on non-woven fleece, designed by Ulf Moritz, produced by Marburger, 2001. Already renowned as a woven textiles designer, Ulf Moritz has recently collaborated with the German wallpaper company Marburger. Retro-Modern circle patterns in neutered colours form part of his vocabulary, along with this receding sphere design.

Left Fig. 7.46
Chevron, Padded Cell, and Needle digitally printed silk furnishing fabrics, designed by James Bullen, produced by James Bullen Design Ltd, 1998. These "virtual" patterns from the Trompe L'Oeil Illusionary Prints Collection were launched at James Bullen's degree show at the Royal College of Art. The designs were created by manipulating photographs on the computer, and the fabrics were printed using a digital ink-jet machine.

Above Fig 7.47
Rubber Band Scatter screen-printed linen furnishing fabric, designed and produced by the Nuno Corporation, 1997. This experimental pattern was created by photocopying a cluster of rubber bands. Silicone resin, dyed to match the colour of rubber bands, was used to print the fabric, repeated several times to build up the outlines in relief.

BIBLIOGRAPHY

Marianne Aav and Nina Stritzler-Levine, eds., *Finnish Modern Design*, Yale University Press, New Haven, 1998

Phyllis Ackerman, *Wallpaper – Its History and Use*, Tudor Publishing, New York, 1938

Alison Adburgham, *Liberty's – A Biography of a Shop*, Allen & Unwin, London, 1975

Diana Affleck, *Just New from the Mills*, Museum of American Textile History, North Andover, 1987

Anna Liisa Ahmavaara, *Finnish Textiles*, Otava, Helsinki, 1970

Pat Albeck, *Printed Textiles*, Oxford University Press, Oxford, 1969

Anni Albers, *On Designing*, Pellango Press, New Haven, 1959

Anni Albers, *On Weaving*, Studio Vista, London, 1965

American Federation of Arts, *Modern Wallpaper*, New York, 1948

Harry V. Anderson, "Contemporary American Designers," *The Decorators Digest*, March 1935

Isabelle Anscombe, *Omega and After – Bloomsbury and the Decorative Arts*, Thames & Hudson, London, 1981

Isabelle Anscombe, *A Woman's Touch – Women in Design from 1860 to the Present Day*, Virago, London, 1984

Paola Antonelli, Jörn Donner, Roberta Lord, and Juli Capella Samper, *Lindfors – Rational Animal*, Petomaani Oy, Helsinki, 2000

Sylvia Backemeyer, ed., *Making their Mark – Art, Craft and Design at the Central School 1896–1966*, Herbert Press, London, 2000

Howard Batho, "Textiles by Frank Dobson," *Journal of the Decorative Arts Society*, no. 17, 1993

Martin Battersby, *The Decorative Twenties*, Studio Vista, London, 1969

Martin Battersby, *The Decorative Thirties*, Studio Vista, London, 1971

Hazel Berriman, *Crysède – The Unique Textile Designs of Alec Walker*, Royal Institution of Cornwall, Truro, 1993

Bibliothèque Forney, *Papiers Peints 1925*, Société des Amis de la Bibliothèque Forney, Paris, 1976

Biennale di Firenze, *Emilio Pucci*, Florence, 1996

Helen Bieri and Bernard Jacqué, eds., *Papiers Peints Art Nouveau*, Skira, Milan, 1997

Roger Billcliffe, *Mackintosh Textile Designs*, John Murray, London, 1982

Dilys E. Blum, *The Fine Art of Textiles*, Philadelphia Museum of Art, Philadelphia, 1997

Sarah Bowness and Tim Nicholson, "The textile designs of Nancy Nicholson," *Apollo*, October 2001

Christine Boydell, *The Architect of Floors – Modernism, Art and Marion Dorn Designs*, Schoeser, Coggleshall, 1996

Christine Boydell, *Our Best Dresses – The Story of Horrockses Fashions Limited*, Harris Museum and Art Gallery, Preston, 2001 (exhibition guide)

Sarah E. Braddock and Marie O'Mahoney, *Techno Textiles – Revolutionary Fabrics for Fashion and Design*, Thames & Hudson, London, 1998

Andrea Branzi, *The Hot House – Italian New Wave Design*, Thames & Hudson, London, 1984

Yvonne Brunhammer, *The Art Deco Style*, Academy Editions, London, 1983

Hester Bury, *A Choice of Design 1850–1980*

– Fabrics by Warner & Sons, Warner & Sons, Braintree, 1981

Stephen Calloway, ed., *The House of Liberty – Masters of Style and Decoration*, Thames & Hudson, London, 1992

Camden Arts Centre, *Enid Marx – A Retrospective Exhibition*, London, 1979

Marianne Carlano, *Early Modern Textiles – From Arts and Crafts to Art Deco*, Museum of Fine Arts, Boston, 1993

Centro Design Montefibre, *Decorattivo 1 – UFO and Amorphous*, Studio Vista, London, 1976

Centro Design Montefibre, *Decorattivo 2 – Lines and Squares*, Idea, Milan, 1977

Hazel Clark, "Modern Textiles 1926–1939," *Journal of the Decorative Arts Society*, 1988

Chloë Colchester, *The New Textiles – Trends and Traditions*, Thames & Hudson, London, 1991

Ruggero Colombo, *Italian Textiles*, Frank Lewis, Leigh-on-Sea, 1961

Terence Conran, *Printed Textile Design*, Studio Publications, London, 1957

Crafts Council, *Colour into Cloth*, London, 1994

Jacques Damase, *Sonia Delaunay – Fashion and Fabrics*, Thames & Hudson, London, 1991

Ingeborg de Roode and Marjan Groot, *Amsterdamse School Textiel 1915–1930*, Uitgeverij Thoth, Bussum/Nederlands Textielmuseum, Tilburg, 1999

Jacques Deslandres and Dorothée Lalanne, *Poiret – Paul Poiret 1879–1944*, Thames & Hudson, London, 1987

Joanne Dolan and Lynn Felsher, *A Woman's Hand – Designing Textiles in America 1945–1969*, Fashion Institute of Technology, New York, 2000 (exhibition guide)

Magdalena Droste, *Bauhaus 1919–1933*, Bauhaus-Archiv, Berlin/Taschen, Cologne, 1998

Jane Ducas, "Past and Present," *Colefax and Fowler – Sixty Years 1934–1994*, Colefax and Fowler, London, 1994

Martin Eidelberg, ed., *Design 1935–1965 – What Modern Was*, Abrams, New York, 1991

Martin Eidelberg, ed., *Designed for Delight – Alternative Aspects of Twentieth-Century Decorative Arts*, Flammarion, Paris and New York, 1997

Sherman R. Emery, *The Stroheim & Romann Legacy*, Stroheim & Romann, New York, 1990

Carla Enbom, *Fujiwo Ishimoto – On the Road*, Amos Anderson Art Museum, Helsinki, 2001

E.A. Entwistle, *The Book of Wallpaper – A History and an Appreciation*, Arthur Barker, London, 1954

Ann Erickson, Delores Ginther, and Jo Ann Undem, *Alexander Girard Designs: Fabric and Furniture*, Goldstein Gallery, University of Minnesota, St Paul, 1985

Giovanni and Rosalia Fanelli, *Il Tessuto Moderno – Disegno, Moda, Architettura 1890–1940*, Vallechi, Florence, 1976

Giovanni and Rosalia Fanelli, *Il Tessuto Art Nouveau*, Cantini, Florence, 1986

Giovanni and Rosalia Fanelli, *Il Tessuto Art Déco e Anni Trenta*, Cantini, Florence, 1986

Michael Farr, *Design in Britain – A Mid-Century Survey*, Cambridge University Press, Cambridge, 1955

Maud Trube Ferrière, *Swiss Textiles*, Frank Lewis, Leigh-on-Sea, 1953

Grace Lovat Fraser, *Textiles by Britain*, Allen & Unwin, London, 1948

Iain Gale and Susan Irvine, *Laura Ashley Style*, Weidenfeld & Nicolson, London, 1987

Marjorie Orpin Gaylard, "Phyllis Barron and Dorothy Larcher," *Journal of the Decorative Arts Society*, no. 3, 1980

Madeleine Ginsburg, ed., *The Illustrated History of Textiles*, Studio Editions, London, 1991

Susanna Goodden, *A History of Heal's*, Heal & Son, London, 1984

Paul Greenhalgh, ed., *Art Nouveau 1890–1914*, V&A Publications, London, 2000

Brenda Greysmith, *Wallpaper*, Studio Vista, London, 1976

Ruth Grönwoldt, *Art Nouveau Textil – Dekor um 1900*, Württembergisches Landesmuseum, Stuttgart, 1980

Tricia Guild, *Tricia Guild's New Soft Furnishings*, Conran Octopus, London, 1990

Tricia Guild and Elizabeth Wilhide, *Tricia Guild on Colour – Decoration, Furnishing, Display*, Conran Octopus, London, 1992

Jean Hamilton, *An Introduction to Wallpaper*, HMSO, London, 1983

M.A. Hann and G.M. Thomson, *Tibor Reich (1916–1996)*, University Gallery, Leeds, 1997

Marilyn Oliver Hapgood, *Wallpaper and the Artist – From Dürer to Warhol*, Abbeville Press, New York, 1992

Jennifer Harris, *Lucienne Day – A Career in Design*, Whitworth Art Gallery, Manchester, 1993

Jennifer Harris, ed., *5000 Years of Textiles*, British Museum Press, London, 1993

Tanya Harrod, *The Crafts in Britain in the 20th Century*, Yale University Press, New Haven, 1999

H.G. Hayes Marshall, *British Textile Designers Today*, Frank Lewis, Leigh-on-Sea, 1939

David Hicks, *David Hicks on Decoration – With Fabrics*, Britwell Books, London, 1971

Katherine B. Hiesinger and George H. Marcus, eds., *Design Since 1945*, Philadelphia Museum of Art, Philadelphia, 1983

Frances Hinchcliffe, *Fifties Furnishing Fabrics*, Webb & Bower, London, 1989

Richard Horn, *Memphis – Objects, Furniture, and Patterns*, Running Press, Philadelphia, 1986

Lesley Hoskins, ed., *The Papered Wall*, Thames & Hudson, London, 1994

Lesley Hoskins, Mark Pinney, and Mark Turner, *A Popular Art – British Wallpapers 1930–1960*, Silver Studio Collection, Middlesex University, London, 1989

Antony Hunt, *Textile Design*, The Studio, London, 1937

Nigozi Ikoku, *British Textiles from 1940 to the Present*, V&A Publications, London, 1999

Lesley Jackson, *The New Look – Design in the Fifties*, Thames & Hudson, London, 1991

Lesley Jackson, *"Contemporary" Architecture and Interiors of the 1950s*, Phaidon, London, 1994

Lesley Jackson, *The Sixties – Decade of Design Revolution*, Phaidon, London, 1998

Lesley Jackson, *Robin and Lucienne Day – Pioneers of Contemporary Design*, Mitchell Beazley, London, 2001

J. Stewart Johnson, *American Modern 1925–1940 – Design for a New Age*, Abrams, New York, 2000

Lorraine Johnson and Gabrielle Townsend, *Osborne & Little – The Decorated Room*, Webb & Bower, London, 1988

John Brandon Jones, ed., *C.F.A. Voysey – Architect and Designer 1857–1941*, Lund Humphries, London, 1978

William Justema, *The Pleasures of Pattern*, Reinhold Book Corporation, New York, 1968

Kalmar Konstmuseum, *"Mästertryckeraren" – Erik Ljungberg, Floda*, Kalmar, 1980

Arne Karlsen, Bent Salicath and Mogens Utzon-Frank, eds., *Contemporary Danish Design*, The Danish Society of Arts and Crafts and Industrial Design, Copenhagen, 1960

Lois and William Katzenbach, *The Practical Book of American Wallpaper*, J.B. Lippincott, Philadelphia, 1954

Shirley Kennedy, *Pucci – A Renaissance in Fashion*, Abbeville Press, New York, 1991

Burkhard Kieselbach and Rolf Spilker, eds., *Rasch Buch 1897–1997*, Rasch, Bramsche, 1998

Brenda King, *Modern Art in Textile Design 1930–1980*, Whitworth Art Gallery, Manchester, 1989 (exhibition guide)

Brenda King, "Cresta Silks Ltd.," *Textile Society Magazine*, vol. 15, Spring 1991

Pat Kirkham, ed., *Women Designers in the USA 1900–2000*, Yale University Press, New Haven/Bard Graduate Center, New York, 2000

Joanne Kosuda-Warner, *Kitsch to Corbusier – Wallpaper from the 1950s*, Cooper-Hewitt Museum, New York, 1995 (exhibition guide)

Carol Dean Krute, *Cheney Textiles: A Century of Silk*, Wadsworth Atheneum, Hartford, Connecticut, n.d. (exhibition guide)

Susan Lambert, *Paul Nash as Designer*, Victoria & Albert Museum, London, 1975

Eric Larrabee and Massimo Vignelli, *Knoll Design*, Abrams, New York, 1981

Jack Lenor Larsen, *Jack Lenor Larsen – 30 Years of Creative Textiles*, Musée des Arts Décoratifs, Paris, 1981

Jack Lenor Larsen, *Furnishing Fabrics – An International Sourcebook*, Thames & Hudson, London, 1989

Jack Lenor Larsen, *Jack Lenor Larsen – A Weaver's Memoir*, Abrams, New York, 1998

Jack Lenor Larsen and Jeanne Weeks, *Fabrics for Interiors*, Van Nostrand Reinhold, New York, 1975

Edsel Larsson, ed., *Almedahls 1846–1996*, Almedahls AB, Gothenburg, 1996

Frank Lewis, *British Textiles*, Frank Lewis, Leigh-on-Sea, 1951

Frank Lewis, J.H. Mellor, and E.A. Entwistle, *A Century of British Fabrics 1850–1950*, Frank Lewis, Leigh-on-Sea, 1955

Helena Dahlbäck Lutteman, ed., *Stig Lindberg – Formgivare*, Nationalmuseum, Stockholm, 1982

Helena Dahlbäck Lutteman, ed., *Astrid Sampe – Swedish Industrial Textiles*, Nationalmuseum, Stockholm, 1984

Helena Dahlbäck Lutteman, *The Lunning Prize*, Nationalmuseum, Stockholm, 1986

Helena Dahlbäck Lutteman, ed., *Elsa Gullberg – Textil Pionjär*, Nationalmuseum, Stockholm, 1989

Catherine Lynn, *Wallpaper in America from the Seventeenth Century to World War I*, Barra Foundation/Cooper-Hewitt Museum, W.W. Norton, New York, 1980

Catherine McDermott, ed., *English*

Eccentrics – The Textile Designs of the Helen Littman, Phaidon, London, 1992

Pinucca Magnesi, *I sonetti grafici di Piero Fornasetti: tessuti e foulards*, Avigdor, Turin, 1989

Pinucca Magnesi and Giovanni Parolini, *Design e arte nel tessuto d'arredamento – Italia 1900–1940*, Avigdor, Turin, 1986

Annette Malochet, *Atelier Simultané di Sonia Delaunay 1923–1934*, Fabbri Editori, 1984

Edna Martin and Beate Sydhoff, *Swedish Textile Art*, Liberförlag, Stockholm, 1980

Leena Maunula and Rebecka Tarschys, *Annika Rimala 1960–2000 – Colour on our Life*, Museum of Art and Design, Helsinki, 2000

Patrick Mauriès, *Fornasetti – Designer of Dreams*, Thames & Hudson, London, 1991

David Revere McFadden, *Scandinavian Modern Design 1880–1980*, Abrams, New York, 1982

Susan Meller and Joost Elffers, *Textile Designs – 200 Years of Patterns for Printed Fabrics*, Thames & Hudson, London, 1991

Valerie Mendes, *British Textiles from 1900–1937*, V&A Publications, London, 1992

Valerie Mendes and Frances Hinchcliffe, *Ascher – Fabric, Art, Fashion*, Victoria and Albert Museum, London, 1987

Merrell Holberton, *Austerity to Affluence – British Art and Design 1945–1962*, Merrell Holberton/Fine Art Society/Rayner & Chamberlain, London, 1997

Katharina Metz, Ingrid Mössinger and Wieland Poser, *European Textile Design of the 1920s*, Edition Stemmle, Zurich, 1998

Ernst Wolfgang Mick, *Hauptwerke in des Deutsches Tapetenmuseums in Kassel*, Gakken, Tokyo, 1981

Betty Miles, *At the Sign of the Rainbow – Margaret Calkin James 1895–1985*, Felix Scribo, Alcester, 1996

Ritsuko Miyokawa, *Suké Suké*, Nuno Corporation, Tokyo, 1997

Ritsuko Miyokawa, *Shimi Jimi*, Nuno Corporation, Tokyo, 1998

Ritsuko Miyokawa, *Fuwa Fuwa*, Nuno Corporation, Tokyo, 1998

Ritsuko Miyokawa, *Kira Kira*, Nuno Corporation, Tokyo, 1999

Helena Moore, ed., *The Nicholsons: A Story of Four People and their Designs*, York City Art Gallery, York, 1988

Elizabeth Morano, *Sonia Delaunay – Art into Fashion*, George Baziller, New Yorks, 1986

Barbara Morris, *Liberty Design 1874–1914*, Pyramid Books, London, 1989

Jocelyn Morton, *Three Generations in a Family Textile Firm*, Routledge & Kegan Paul, London, 1971

Musée de l'Impression sur Étoffes, *Raoul Dufy, 1877–1953 – Créateur d'Etoffes*, Mulhouse, 1973

Musée Historique des Tissus, *Les Folles Années de la Soie*, Lyons, 1975

Museum of Modern Art, New York, *Textiles USA*, New York, 1956

Museum of Modern Art, Oxford, *Soviet Textiles, Fashion and Ceramics, 1917–1935*, Oxford, 1984

Colin Naylor, ed., *Contemporary Designers*, St. James Press, Chicago and London, 1990

Maria Neppert-Boehland, *German Textiles*, Frank Lewis, Leigh-on-Sea, 1955

Waltraud Neuwirth, *Wiener Werkstätte – Avantgarde, Art Déco, Industrial Design*, Waltraud Neuwirth, Vienna, 1984

Julia North, ed., *The Pattern Book*,

Mitchell Beazley, London, 2000

Heinrich Olligs, ed., *Tapeten: Ihre Geschichte bis zur Gegenwart*, Verlag Klinkhardt & Biermann, Braunschweig, 1969

Charles C. Oman and Jean Hamilton, *Wallpaper – A History and Illustrated Catalogue of the Collection of the Victoria and Albert Museum*, Sotheby/Victoria and Albert Museum, London, 1982

Kayoko Ota, *Zawa Zawa*, Nuno Corporation, Tokyo, 1999

Charlotte Paludan, "Marie Gudme Leth – A pioneer in Danish textile design," *Scandinavian Journal of Design History*, vol. 5, 1995

Verner Panton, *Verner Panton*, Basler Zeitung, Basle, 1986

Nicole Parrot, *Dessins d'Imprimés – Une Aventure dans le Tissu*, Syros, Paris, 1997

Linda Parry, *William Morris Textiles*, Weidenfeld & Nicolson, London, 1983

Linda Parry, *British Textiles from 1850 to 1900*, V&A Publications, London, 1993

Linda Parry, *Textiles of the Arts and Crafts Movement*, Thames & Hudson, London, 1988

Linda Parry, *William Morris and the Arts and Crafts Movement*, Studio Editions, London, 1989

Linda Parry, ed., *William Morris*, Philip Wilson/Victoria & Albert Museum, London, 1996

Alan Peat, *David Whitehead Ltd – Artist Designed Textiles 1952–1969*, Oldham Leisure Services, 1993

Niklaus Pevsner, *An Enquiry into Industrial Art in England*, Cambridge University Press, Cambridge, 1937

Barty Phillips, *Fabrics and Wallpapers – Design Sources and Inspirations*, Ebury Press, London, 1991

Leslie Piña, *Alexander Girard – Designs for Herman Miller*, Schiffer, Atglen, 1998

Sarah Postgate, *Patterns for Papers*, Webb & Bower, London, 1987

Alan Powers, *Modern Block Printed Textiles*, Walker Books, London, 1992

Lucy Pratt, "Ben Nicholson's block-printed textiles at the V&A," *Apollo*, October 1998

Dorte Raaschou, *Dansk Textiltryck 1930–86*, Udstilling Nicolaj, 1986

Barbara Radice, *Memphis*, Thames & Hudson, London, 1985

Steen Eiler Rasmussen, *Danish Textiles*, Frank Lewis, Leigh-on-Sea, 1956

Mathias Remmele and Alexander von Vegesack, eds., *Verner Panton – The Complete Works*, Vitra Design Museum, Weil-am-Rhein, 2000

Zandra Rhodes and Anne Knight, *The Art of Zandra Rhodes*, Jonathan Cape, London, 1984

Shirley Ann Roberts, *The Cotton Board and the Colour Design and Style Centre of Manchester 1940–1969*, University of Manchester, 1996 (MA thesis)

Mary Rose, ed., *The Lancashire Cotton Industry – A History since 1700*, Lancashire County Books, Preston, 1996

Elizabeth Rycroft, "Lewis Foreman Day 1845–1910," *Journal of the Decorative Arts Society*, no. 13, 1989, pp.19–26

Martha Saarto, *Finnish Textiles*, Frank Lewis, Leigh-on-Sea, 1954

Gill Saunders, *Wallpaper in Interior Decoration*, V&A Publications, London, 2002

Mary Schoeser, *Marianne Straub*, Design Council, London, 1984

Mary Schoeser, *Fabrics and Wallpapers – Twentieth-Century Design*, Bell & Hyman, London, 1986

Mary Schoeser, *Bold Impressions – Block-Printing 1910–1950*, Central Saint Martins College of Art & Design, London, 1995

Mary Schoeser, *International Textile Design*, Lawrence King, London, 1995

Mary Schoeser and Kathleen Dejardin, *French Textiles from 1760 to the Present*, Lawrence King, London, 1991

Mary Schoeser and Celia Rufey, *English and American Textiles from 1790 to the Present*, Thames & Hudson, London, 1989

P.R. Schwartz and R. de Micheaux, *A Century of French Fabrics*, Frank Lewis, Leigh-on-Sea, 1964

Scottish National Gallery of Modern Art, *Alastair Morton and Edinburgh Weavers*, Edinburgh, 1978

Anne Sebba, *Laura Ashley – A Life by Design*, Weidenfeld & Nicolson, London, 1990

Jill Seddon and Suzette Worden, eds., *Women Designing – Redefining Design in Britain between the Wars*, University of Brighton, Brighton, 1994

Richard E. Slavin, *Opulent Textiles – The Schumacher Collection*, Crown, New York, 1992

Greg Smith, ed., *Walter Crane 1845–1915 – Artist, Designer and Socialist*, Lund Humphries, London, 1989

Penny Sparke, ed., *Did Britain Make It? – British Design in Context 1946–86*, Design Council, London, 1986

Dr Fritz Stellwag-Carion, *Austrian Textiles*, Frank Lewis, Leigh-on-Sea, 1962

Stiftung Bauhaus Dessau, *Gunta Stölzl – Meisterin am Bauhaus Dessau*, Gerd Hatje, Stuttgart, 1997

Joyce Storey, *The Thames & Hudson Manual of Textile Printing*, Thames & Hudson, London, 1974

Tatiana Strizhenova, *Soviet Costume and Textiles 1917–1945*, Flammarion, Paris, 1991

Marian Boulton Stroud, ed., *An Industrious Art – Innovation in Pattern and Print at The Fabric Workshop*, The Fabric Workshop, Philadelphia/W.W. Norton & Co., New York, 1991

Pekka Suhonen, ed., *Phenomenon Marimekko*, Marimekko Oy, Helsinki, 1986

Akira Suzuki, *Boro Boro*, Nuno Corporation, Tokyo, 1997

Svensk Formgivning, *Hans Krondhal – Resor I Mönstervärlden*, Kalmar Konstmuseum/Regionmuseet I Skåne, Kristianstad, 1999

Inez Svensson, *Tryckta Tyger från 30-tal till 80-tal*, Liber Förlag, Stockholm, 1984

Tommy Tabermann and Tuija Wuori-Tabermann, *Spirit & Life*, Marimekko, Porvoo, 2001

Textilmuseum, *Stoffe um 1900*, Krefeld, 1977

Françoise Teynac, Pierre Nolot, and Jean-Denis Vivien, *Wallpaper – A History*, Thames & Hudson, London, 1981

Mark Hartland Thomas, *The Souvenir Book of Crystal Designs*, Council of Industrial Design, 1951

Christa C. Mayer Thurman, *Textiles in the Art Institute of Chicago*, The Art Institute of Chicago, Chicago, 1992

Christa C. Mayer Thurman, *Rooted in Chicago – Fifty Years of Textile Design Traditions* (*Museum Studies*, Vol. 23, no. 1), The Art Institute of Chicago, Chicago, 1997

Mark Turner, ed., *The Silver Studio Collection – A London Design Studio 1880–1963*, Lund Humphries, London, 1980

Mark Turner, ed., *Art Nouveau Designs from the Silver Studio Collection 1885–1910*, Middlesex Polytechnic, London, 1986

Mark Turner and Lesley Hoskins, *The Silver Studio of Design – A Design and Source Book for Home Decoration*, Webb & Bower/Michael Joseph, London, 1988

M.P.-Verneuil, *Exposition des Arts Décoratifs Paris 1925*, Éditions Albert Lévy, Paris, 1926

Victoria & Albert Museum, *English Chintz – Two Centuries of Changing Taste*, London, 1955 (exhibition guide)

Victoria & Albert Museum, *From East to West – Textiles from G.P. & J. Baker*, London, 1984

Angela Völker, *Textiles of the Wiener Werkstätte 1910–1932*, Thames & Hudson, London, 1994

Marcia J. Wade, *A Century of Opulent Textiles – The Schumacher Collection*, F. Schumacher & Co., New York, 1989

Kristina Wängberg-Eriksson, *Josef Frank – Textile Designs*, Bokförlaget Signum, Lund, 1999

Sigrid Wortmann Weltge, *Women's Work – Textile Art from the Bauhaus*, Thames & Hudson, London, 1993

Whitworth Art Gallery, *Modern Art in Textile Design*, Manchester, 1962

Whitworth Art Gallery, *Textiles/SIA*, Manchester, 1963

Whitworth Art Gallery, *Brown/Craven/ Dodd – 3 Textile Designers*, Manchester, 1965

Hans Wichmann, *Von Morris bis Memphis – Textilier der Neuen Sammlung Ende 19. Bis Ende 20. Jahrhundert*, Birkhäuser, Munich, 1990

Hans Wichmann, *Deutsche Werkstätten und WK-Werkband 1898–1990 – Aufbruch sum neuen Wohnen*, Prestel, Munich, 1992

Kerstin Wickman, *Ten Swedish Designers – Printed Patterns*, Raster Förlag, Stockholm, 2001

Leonie von Wilckens, *Geschichte der Deutschen Textilkunst – Vom spaten Mittelalter bis in die Gegenwart*, Verlag C.H. Beck, Munich, 1997

Nils G. Wollin, *Swedish Textiles 1930*, Bröderna Lagerström, Stockholm, 1930

Christine Woods, ed., *Sanderson 1860–1985*, Arthur Sanderson & Sons, London, 1985

Christine Woods, "The Magic Influence of Mr Kydd" – Blocked and Stencilled Wallpapers 1900–1925, Whitworth Art Gallery, Manchester, 1989 (exhibition guide)

Syd Graham Worth, *Textile Design Consultancy in the UK*, Manchester Metropolitan University, 1998 (PhD thesis)

WPM, *WPM 1899–1949 – The Pattern of a Great Organisation*, WPM, Manchester, 1949

I. Yasinskaya, *Soviet Textile Design of the Revolutionary Period*, Thames & Hudson, London, 1983

Nilgin Yusuf, *Georgina von Etzdorf – Sensuality, Art and Fabric*, Thames & Hudson, London, 1998

Erik Zahle, ed., *Scandinavian Domestic Design*, Methuen, London, 1963

NOTES
See Bibliography on pp.216–17 for full details of publications referred to below in abbreviated form in bold type.

CHAPTER ONEe
1. Quoted in Lois and William Katzenbach, "Imagination by the Roll," *Print*, July, 1952, p.12.
2. Quoted in **Wängberg-Eriksson, 1999**, p.39.
3. Quoted in Katzenbach, op. cit., pp.13–14.
4. "The Aims and Conditions of the Modern Decorator," *Journal of Decorative Art*, XV, 1895, p.82.
5. "An Interview with Mr Charles F. Annesley Voysey, *The Studio*, I, 1893, pp.231–7.
6. "Some recent designs by Mr C.F.A. Voysey," *The Studio*, VII, 1896, pp.209–18.
7. *The Studio*, I, 1893, op. cit., pp.231–7.
8. *Journal of Decorative Art*, XV, op. cit., p.82.
9. *Magazine of Art*, II, 1904, p.211.
10. Quoted in **Morton, 1971**, p.121.
11. "The Arts and Crafts Exhibition, 1896," *The Studio*, IX, pp.190–6.
12. Quoted in **Morris, 1989**, p.39.
13. **Morton, 1971**, p.194.
14. Quoted in **Morris, 1989**, p.26.
15. Ibid.
16. Quoted in **Bury, 1981**, p.35.
17. Quoted in **Brunhammer, 1983**, p.10.

CHAPTER TWO
1. **Neuwirth, 1984**, p.17.
2. **Branzi, 1984**, p.115.
3. Anni Albers, "Design – Anonymous and Timeless," *Magazine of Art*, New York, February 1947.
4. Raoul Dufy, "Les Tissus Imprimés," *Amour de l'Art*, no. 1, 1920.
5. Quoted in **Damase, 1991**, p.58.
6. Quoted in **Damase, 1991**, p.57.
7. Quoted in **Damase, 1991**, p.59.
8. Quoted in **Anscombe, 1981**, p.15.
9. Quoted in **Anscombe, 1981**, p.32.
10. **Hunt, 1937**, p.20.
11. **Hunt, 1937**, p.60.
12. **Hayes Marshall, 1939**, p.9.
13. **Hunt, 1937**, p.25.
14. "The Camera Works Out a New Theory of Design," *Vogue*, 1 February 1927, p.61.

CHAPTER THREE
1. **Hayes Marshall, 1939**, p.12.
2. **Hunt, 1937**, pp.21–2.
3. Quoted in **Scottish National Gallery of Modern Art, 1978**, pp.35–6.
4. **Hayes Marshall, 1939**, p.10.
5. **Hayes Marshall, 1939**, pp.10–11.
6. **Hunt, 1937**, p.25.
7. **Hunt, 1937**, p.24.
8. *St Ives Times*, 6 November 1925.
9. Ibid.
10. **Hunt, 1937**, p.50.
11. **Hunt, 1937**, p.7.
12. **Hayes Marshall, 1939**, p.326.
13. **Hunt, 1937**, p.56.
14. **Hunt, 1937**, p.58.
15. Quoted in **Woods, 1985**, p.37.
16. **Hayes Marshall, 1939**, p.161.
17. Quoted in **Morton, 1971**, p.297.
18. Quoted in **Scottish National Gallery of Modern Art, 1978**, p.5.
19. Quoted in **Hayes Marshall, 1939**, p.199.
20. Quoted in **Scottish National Gallery of Modern Art, 1978**, p.27.
21. **Hayes Marshall, 1939**, pp.122–5.
22. **Hayes Marshall, 1939**, p.118.
23. Ruth Reeves, "Design Creates Opportunities," *Craft Horizons*, May 1946, vol. 5, no. 13, p.6.
24. Ibid.
25. **Katzenbach, 1954**.
26. William Justema, "Mr Wallpaper," *Wallpaper and Wallcoverings*, August 1962, p.30.
27. **Zahle, 1963**, p.152.
28. Quoted in **Wängberg-Eriksson, 1999**, p.29.
29. Quoted in Charlotte Paludan, "Marie Gudme Leth –

a pioneer in Danish textile design," *Scandinavian Journal of Design History*, vol. 5, 1995, p.118.
30. **Zahle, 1963**, p.15.

CHAPTER FOUR
1. Paul Reilly, *Design*, August 1952.
2. James De Holden Stone, "Curtains in the Breeze," *The Studio*, February 1953, pp.49–50 (edited).
3. Ibid.
4. **Mark Hartland Thomas, 1951**, pp.1–2.
5. For further information on the Festival Pattern Group, see Lesley Jackson, "X-Ray Visions, *Crafts*, September–October 2001, pp.32–5.
6. Quoted in **Conran, 1957**, p.37.
7. Quoted in **Conran, 1957**, p.52. See also **Jackson, 2001**.
8. For further information on Mary White, a prolific freelance designer active from 1950 to 1957, see Ruth Marler, *"Something Fresher" – An Introduction to the 1950s Textiles of Mary White*, undergraduate thesis, Department of History of Art, Architecture and Design, Kingston University, UK, 1999/2000.
9. John T. Murray, "Furnishing fabrics for the mass market – The cheap need not be cheap-and-nasty," *Design*, December 1950, p.15.
10. **Conran, 1957**, p.50.
11. Misha Black, "Society of Industrial Artists 1930–1955," *The Ambassador*, no. 12, 1955, p.74.
12. Quoted in **Conran, 1957**, p.32.
13. "A source of pattern," *The Ambassador*, no. 2, 1956, pp.26–7.
14. Quoted in Donald Tomlinson, "Edinburgh Weavers," *The Studio*, September 1960, p.90.
15. **Morton, 1971**, p.419.
16. Michael Farr, "Fotexur," *Design*, April 1957, pp.44–53.
17. Quoted in **Conran, 1957**, p.48.
18. "Hand Produced Wallpapers," *Design*, January 1956, p.20.
19. John E. Blake, "Designing wallpa pers," *Design*, December 1955, p.19.
20. Blake, 1955, op. cit., p.21.
21. John E. Blake, "Wallpapers," *Design*, March 1957, p.33.
22. Ibid.
23. **Hiesinger and Marcus, 1983**, p.174 (edited).
24. Alvin Lustig, "Modern Printed Fabrics," *Design*, July 1952, pp.27–30 (edited).
25. Ibid.
26. Angelo Testa, "Design vs. Monkey Business," *Interiors*, February 1948, p.84.
27. Angelo Testa, "Angelo Testa," *Arts and Architecture*, July 1946, p.42.
28. *American Fabrics*, no. 3, 1948, p.85.
29. "The Lavernes – Partners in Design," *Craft Horizons*, Winter 1949, vol. 9, no. 4, pp.12–14.
30. Ibid.
31. Ibid.
32. Lustig, op. cit., p.30.
33. *American Fabrics*, no. 38, Fall 1956, p.33.
34. Ibid.
35. Lustig, op. cit., p.29.
36. Ibid.
37. **Kosuda-Warner, 1995**, p.3.
38. Lois and William Katzenbach, "Imagination by the Roll," *Print*, July 1952, p.21.
39. Quoted in Katzenbach, op. cit., p.23.
40. Katzenbach, op. cit., p.15.
41. Quoted in **Conran, 1957**, p.45 (edited).
42. **Zahle, 1963**, p.152.
43. Quoted in **Mauriès, 1991**, p.24.
44. Quoted in **Mauriès, 1991**, p.283.
45. Quoted in **Conran, 1957**, p.32.

CHAPTER FIVE
1. "The roots of contemporary," *The Ambassador*, no. 1, 1963, p.62.
2. **Sparke, 1986**, p.93.
3. Elizabeth Good, "Fabrics of convenience," *Design*, February 1969, p.40.
4. E-mail to author, September 2000.
5. **Ahmavaara, 1970**, p.3.

6. Quoted in **Naylor, 1990**, p.162.
7. Quoted in **Wickman, 2001**, p.16.
8. *The Ambassador*, no. 1, 1963, op. cit., p.56 (edited).
9. The Colour Design and Style Centre, established by the Cotton Board in 1940, was run initially by James Cleveland Belle, then by Donald Tomlinson from 1950 to 1964 and by Frederick Lyle from 1964 to 1969. *The Ambassador* was established by Hans and Elsbeth Juda in 1933 to promote the export of British textiles and fashion. Elsbeth Juda acted as the magazine's chief stylist and photographer until 1963, working under the name Jay. Hans Juda was the editor, and stayed on as an adviser after the magazine was sold to Thomson Publishing in 1963.
10. Corin Hughes-Stanton, "A shop with high standards," *Design*, July 1965, p.47.
11. "Hip Hip Heals!," *The Ambassador*, April 1966, p.79.
12. "CoID Design Awards," *Design*, June 1970, p.19.
13. "Furnishing Fabrics," *Design*, May 1968, p.42.
14. "Design Centre Awards 1963," *Design*, June 1963, p.44.
15. "Furnishing Fabrics," *Design*, May 1968, p.30.
16. *The Ambassador*, no. 1, 1963, op. cit., p.61.
17. *The Ambassador*, no. 1, 1963, op. cit., p.59.
18. Good, op. cit., p. 39.
19. Quoted in Jane Lott, "Young head on old shoulders," *Design*, June 1982, p.29.
20. "A new venture for Danasco," *House and Garden*, February 1961, p.19.
21. Advertisement, *Ideal Home*, May 1960.
22. Richard Carr, "Textiles for the seventies," *Design*, March 1970, p.42.
23. Quoted in **Woods, 1985**, p.52.
24. "English images for export," *The Ambassador*, no. 9, 1968, p.84.
25. Ibid.
26. Advertisement, *Architectural Review*, April 1964, pp.32–3.
27. "Vinyl wall-covering," *Design*, June 1969, p.54.
28. T.M.P. Bendixon, "Wallpapers," *Design*, February 1962, pp.44–8.
29. Quoted in **Naylor, 1990**, p.460.
30. Ibid.
31. **Hiesinger and Marcus, 1983**, pp.176–7.
32. Quoted in "Boris Kroll – Creative Force in the World of Weaving," *American Fabrics*, no. 48, Winter 1960, p.82.
33. Quoted in **Naylor, 1990**, p.312.
34. "An Interview with Jack Lenor Larsen," *Interior Design*, April 1978, p.252.
35. Quoted in Chee Pearlman, "Profile – Jack Lenor Larsen," *Interior Design*, March–April 1964, p.53.
36. "The Eclectic Eye," *Interiors*, June 1965, p.109.
37. Quoted in **Naylor, 1990**, p.323.
38. Quoted in "A Look at the Designers," *Wallpaper & Wallcoverings*, January 1966, p.21.
39. Ibid.
40. *Wallpaper & Wallcoverings*, op. cit., p.22.
41. *Dialogue 16*, Jack Denst Designs, Inc., c.1969.
42. Quoted in "Hats off to the designers," *United DeSoto Report*, June–July 1969.
43. "Anatomy of a Hot Line," *Wallpaper & Wallcoverings*, December 1969, pp.41–6 (edited).
44. "Bravo paces record year for wallcovering sales," *United DeSoto Report*, October 1969.
45. **Biennale di Firenze, 1996**, p.42.

CHAPTER SIX
1. **Hiesinger and Marcus, 1983**, pp.177–8.
2. Ibid.
3. Quoted in **Naylor, 1990**, p.164.
4. Quoted in **Wickman, 2001**, p.82.
5. Quoted in **Wickman, 2001**, p.74.
6. **Wickman, 2001**, p.88.
7. **Wickman, 2001**, p.74.
8. **Svensson, 1984**, p.150.
9. David Davies, "Colour it freely," *Design*, July 1975, p.40.
10. **Panton, 1986**, unpaginated.
11. **Sparke, 1986**, p.95.
12. "Studio One Wallcoverings," *Design*, April 1976, p.35.
13. "CoID Design Awards," *Design*, June 1970, p.18.

14. Bruce Clarke, "There's more than one way to save the textile industry," *Design*, June 1979, p.88.
15. Jacquey Visick, "Why British print design talent is blocked by British printers," *Design*, July 1978, pp.30–3 (edited).
16. Jack Lenor Larsen, "British Textile Designers – The Secret of Successful Foreign Competition," *Design*, December 1977, pp.28–9 (edited).
17. Howell Leadbeater, "Tom Worthington," *Design*, April 1974, p.75.
18. "Heal's Country Fabrics," *Design*, January 1976, p.27.
19. Jane Lott, "Young head on old shoulders," *Design*, June 1982, p.29.
20. Quoted in ibid.
21. **Gale and Irvine, 1987**, p.9.
22. **Gale and Irvine, 1987**, p.27.
23. Jacquey Visick, "From Nowhere Else," *Design*, July 1975, p.32.
24. **Larsen, 1981**, unpaginated.
25. Ibid.
26. "Frances Butler," *Fibrearts*, September–October 1978, pp.40–5.

CHAPTER SEVEN
1. **Stroud, 1991**, p.7.
2. **Branzi, 1984**, p.119.
3. **Centro Design Montefibre, 1977**, p.14.
4. **Eidelberg, 1997**, p.232.
5. Quoted in Jeremy Myerson, "All that jazz," *Design*,

February 1984, pp.44–5.
6. Quoted in **Wickman, 2001**, p.110.
7. **Svensson, 1984**, p.150.
8. Ibid.
9. **Naylor, 1990**, p.140 (edited).
10. Penny Sparke, "Bold strokes on a broad canvas," *Design*, June 1982, p.32.
11. **Suhonen, 1986**, p.143.
12. Quoted in **Naylor, 1990**, p.274.
13. Quoted in **Ducas, 1994**, p.1.
14. **Ducas, 1994**, p.5.
15. Ibid.
16. After working briefly for the carpet firm Templeton, Pat Etheridge joined the design studio at Sanderson in the mid-1960s. She turned freelance after eight years, but has continued to supply designs to Sanderson up to the present day, including many best-selling patterns. During the 1970s her agent was Brigitta Dehnert, herself a talented freelance designer active from the late 1950s to the early 1970s. During the late 1970s and early 1980s Etheridge designed flamboyant florals for clients in the United States and Japan. Subsequently she has worked closely with Colefax and Fowler, for whom she has created many successful floral chintzes, often mistaken for authentic period designs. Information from lecture given by Pat Etheridge entitled "Working Design: the practice today," at Designers at Work: the process and practice of pattern design, a study day held at the Museum of Domestic Design and Architecture,

Middlesex University, UK, 2 June 2001.
17. **Johnson and Townsend, 1988**, p.7.
18. Osborne & Little, company profile, 2001.
19. "Design Review," *Design*, January 1984, p.44.
20. "Cottons of character," *Design*, April 1983, p.24.
21. Quoted in Liz Jobey, "Learning on the job," *Design*, September 1981, p.44.
22. Geoffrey Yeandle, quoted in Jane Lott, "Young head on old shoulders," *Design*, June 1982, p.29.
23. **McDermott, 1992**, p.13.
24. Quoted in **Yusuf, 1998**, p.14.
25. Quoted in **Yusuf, 1998**, p.13.
26. *Fabric of Fashion*, Crafts Council Gallery, London, 8 November 2000–14 January 2001 (introductory text by Marie OMahony and Sarah E. Braddock).
27. Quoted in Caroline Roux, "Printed Matters," *The Guardian* (*Space* section), 15 February 2001, pp.12–13.
28. E-mail to author, 21 November 2000.
29. The large, London-based textile consultancy Deryck Healey International was a pioneer in this field during the mid-1970s with its Sci-tex installation, a computer-linked electronic sampling knitter. See Mark Brutton, "Textiles: A Suitable Case for Treatment," *Design*, December 1976, pp.44–7. It was in the field of jersey fabrics that computers were first adopted. See "A Brief Encounter with Instant Knitting," *Design*, April 1978, pp.42–7.
30. Interview with author, October 2000.
31. Quoted in **Naylor, 1990**, p.18.

GLOSSARY

Words in *italics* cross-refer to another entry.

Aerograph-sprayed Refers to pigments airbrushed on to textiles or wallpapers over stencils.

Aniline dye Chemical dye introduced to replace vegetable and mineral dye.

Batik Textile patterns created by applying a wax or starch *resist* before fabric is dyed.

Block-printing Labour-intensive method of hand-printing textiles and wallpapers using carved wooden blocks. Sometimes the wood is faced with linoleum, which is easier to cut. Pigment is transferred from the top surface.

Brocade Finely woven fabric with parts of the pattern picked out in colour. The effect resembles embroidery, although the coloured threads form part of the weave.

Combine Group of companies from the same area of manufacturing which form an alliance to control and promote trade in that sector.

Commission printer Company which undertakes printing work on a contract basis on behalf of clients including manufacturers, *converters*, and designers.

Converter Company without a manufacturing base, which arranges for goods to be made by others and then markets the end-products under its own name.

Damask Woven figured (patterned) *satin* cloth. The weft creates the design; the warp forms the background.

Digital-printing Computer-controlled ink-jet printing process. Currently used for textiles and occasionally for wallpapers.

Discharge-printing Textile printing process in which pigment is removed from a pre-dyed fabric using a bleaching agent.

Dobby-woven Refers to cloths with simple weaves produced on a dobby loom. Patterns are limited to small repeats.

Double cloth Reversible fabric composed of two interwoven layers of cloth.

Duplex-printed Reversible fabric printed on both sides of the cloth.

Éditeur French term for *converter*.

Engraved roller-printing High-volume, mass-production technique in which textiles and wallpapers are printed by machine using engraved or etched metal rollers. Pigment is transferred from depressions in the metal rather than from the roller's surface.

Flatbed screen-printing Semi-automated or fully automated process in which lengths of fabric or wallpaper are fed mechanically beneath a series of flat printing screens. Faster than *hand screen-printing* but slower than *rotary screen-printing*.

Flexo-printing Also known as flexography, a form of *surface-printing* in which rubber rollers cut in low relief are used to print patterns using solvent-based inks. High-volume, mass-production technique widely used in the wallpaper industry.

Hand screen-printing Manual *screen-printing* process in which pigment is forced through a fine gauze stretched over a frame. Used for textiles and wallpapers.

Ikat Fabrics in which the *warp* and/or *weft* threads are *resist*-dyed before weaving.

Jacquard-woven Refers to compound weaves produced on a jacquard loom. The process is used to create complex woven patterns.

Microfibres Synthetic fibres which are extremely fine.

Moquette Wool or mohair upholstery fabric in which the looped *warp* threads are partly cut to create a patterned pile.

Photogravure Process used to print wallpapers by machine using photochemically-engraved metal rollers.

Pigment dyes Insoluble colouring agents which sit on the surface of the cloth rather than soak into it.

Rayon Generic name for man-made fibres with a cellulose base, including acetate rayon and viscose rayon. Substantially cheaper than natural fibres, rayon is widely used as a substitute for cotton, linen, and silk.

Repeat One complete unit of pattern from a repeated design. Also describes the various different ways in which units of pattern are arranged in relation to each other, such as diagonally, rotationally, or mirrored.

Resist Pigment-resistant medium.

Roller-printed Generic description of textiles and wallpapers machine-printed using various types of rollers. Often used as shorthand term for *engraved roller-printing*.

Rotary screen-printing High-speed, fully automated *screen-printing* process, using cylinders made of perforated nickel mesh. The dye is forced out from the centre of the roller on to the cloth.

Satin Silk, cotton, or rayon fabrics with a lustrous finish. The sheen is created by running the warp threads over more than one weft.

Screen-printing Generic term for various stencil-like processes used to print textiles and wallpapers, either by hand or by machine. Pigment is forced through a gauze or fine metal mesh, previously treated with a *resist*. The resist acts as a barrier so that only the clear areas are printed.

Shadow tissue Fabric with a hazy, soft-edged pattern, created by printing the *warp* threads before weaving with a single-colour *weft*.

Surface-printing Generic term for various machine-printing process using surface rollers. Widely used to describe wallpapers printed using wooden rollers fitted with raised metal strips packed with felt. Pigment is transferred from the top surface.

Vat dye Fast or fadeless dye which penetrates deeply into the cloth.

Velvet and **velveteen** Silk or cotton fabrics with a soft, raised pile. In velvet the looped *warp* threads are cut to create the pile; in velveteen it is the *weft* threads

Warp Yarns running longitudinally through woven fabric.

Weft Yarns running horizontally across woven fabric.

Wooden roller-printing Machine *surface-printing* using carved wooden rollers. Used mainly for textiles, but occasionally for wallpapers.

AUTHOR'S ACKNOWLEDGMENTS

Of the many people who have assisted me with this book, four in particular have been outstandingly helpful. Christine Crawshaw has embraced the Herculean task of collating the illustrations for the book with her customary vigour and flair, making an invaluable contribution. Frances Pritchard has given me unparalleled access to the superb textile collections at the Whitworth Art Gallery (University of Manchester), as well as answering innumerable enquiries and masterminding a huge photography session. Lesley Hoskins has kindly read through my text and provided many helpful comments. I am also indebted to Ian Fishwick for his unflagging assistance with bibliographical research.

Foreign travel has been facilitated by support from the British Council, the Finnish Embassy, the Smithsonian Institution, the Swedish Institute, and the Swedish Ministry for Foreign Affairs. In Finland Sickan Park was extremely helpful, and in Sweden I was greatly assisted by Ann-Charlotte Biörnstad, Catarina Mannheimer, and Henrik Orrje. Of the many individuals and institutions around the world who responded to my (often repeated) requests for help, many were exceptionally helpful. I am particularly indebted to Christa C. Mayer Thurman at the Art Institute of Chicago; Dominique Deangeli Cayol at the Bibliothèque Forney, Paris; Rolf Danielsson and Pernilla Rassmussen at the Borås Textilmuseet; Joanne Kosuda-Warner and Gregory Herringshaw (Wallcoverings Department) at the Cooper-Hewitt, National Design Museum; John Davis at the Design Council Slide Library, Manchester Metropolitan University; Pat Etheridge; Anna Buruma at Liberty; Riika Finni at Marimekko; Natalie Zara at the Museum of Domestic Design & Architecture (MODA), Middlesex University; Barbro Hovstadius at the Nationalmuseum, Stockholm; Gerrit Rasch and Kirsten Polkamp at Rasch; Inger Cavallius and Jan Norrman at the Röhsska Museum, Gothenburg; Frederika Launert at Sanderson; Linda Parry and Margaret Scott (Textile Department) at the Victoria & Albert Museum; Sue Kerry at the Warner Archive; Jennifer Harris, Penny Haworth, and Christine Woods at the Whitworth Art Gallery.

Many other designers, companies, archives, and museums have provided valuable information and illustrations, and I would also like to thank the following: Birgitta Faxe at the Arkiv för Svensk Formgivning, Kalmar; Gunila Axén; Olivia O'Brien at Laura Ashley; Abigail Langston at G.P. & J. Baker; Bauhaus-Archiv, Berlin; Deborah Bowness; James Bullen; Linda Sandino at Camberwell College of Arts; Trudi Ballard at Colefax and Fowler; Susan Collier and Sarah Campbell at Collier Campbell; Barbara Duggan and Gillian Moss (Textiles Department) at the Cooper-Hewitt, National Design Museum; Roberta Frey Gilboe at the Cranbrook Art Museum; Guy Drean and Irma Faeh at Création Baumann; Neisha Crosland; Dallas Museum of Art; Helen David English Eccentrics; Deutsches Tapetenmuseum, Kassel; Dr Elisabeth Hackspiel-Mikosch at the Deutsches Textilmuseum, Krefeld; Eley Kishimoto; Xana Kudrjavcev-DeMilner at the Fabric Workshop and Museum, Philadelphia; Laurie Brewer and Lynne Felsher at the Fashion Institute of Technology, New York; Jenny Frean at First Eleven Studio; Sally Greaves-Lord; Ann Jones and Pamela McIntyre at Heriot-Watt University Archive; Tracy Kendall; Kerstin Jeanson and Jali Wahlsten at Kinnasand; Ulla Houkjaer and Charlotte Paludan at the Kunstindustrimuseum, Copenhagen; Kvadrat; Jack Lenor Larsen; Philip Sykas and Graham Worth at Manchester Metropolitan University; Sabine v. Breunig at Marburger; Ruth Marler; Lotus Stack at the Minneapolis Institute of Arts; Véronique Belloir at the Musée de la Mode et du Textile, Paris; Véronique de La Hougue at the Musée des Arts Décoratifs, Paris; Linda-Anne D'Anjou at the Musée des Beaux-Arts de Montréal; Bernard Jacqué at the Musée du Papier Peint, Rixheim; Musée Historique des Tissus, Lyons; Museum für Angewandte Kunst (MAK), Vienna; Marianne Aav and Johanna Kiuru at the Museum of Art and Design, Helsinki; Charlotte C. Niklas at the Museum of Fine Arts, Boston; Die Neue Sammlung, Munich; Ulysses Dietz at the Newark Museum; Elisabeth Pollock at Nobilis; Maria Maxén at the Nordiska Museet, Stockholm; Motoko Okubo at the Nuno Corporation; Charlotte Holt at Osborne & Little; Sophie Grattan-Bellew at the Paint & Paper Library; Rena Troxler at the Verner Panton Studio; Philadelphia Museum of Art; Alan Powers; Emilio Pucci; Victoria Richards; Shirley Roberts; Santos & Adolfsdóttir; Richard Slavin and Julia Davies at the Schumacher Archive; Svenskt Tenn; Ingela Håkansson, Birgitta Hahn, and Tom Hedqvist at the Tio-Gruppen; Timney Fowler; Alastair McAuley and Paul Simmons at Timorous Beasties; Isabel Tisdall; Venturi Scott Brown; Eva White (Archive of Art and Design), Nick Wise (Picture Library), and Gill Saunders (Prints and Drawings Department) at the Victoria & Albert Museum; Georgina von Etzdorf; Kristina Wängberg-Eriksson; Jocelyn Warner; Württembergisches Landesmuseum, Stuttgart; Sian Davies at Zoffany.

At Mitchell Beazley I am grateful to Jane Aspden and Mark Fletcher for their encouragement, and to everyone else at the company who has been involved in the production and promotion of this book. I would particularly like to thank Richard Dawes for the care and attention he has devoted to my text, Fiona Knowles for her clear, well-integrated design, and Hannah Barnes-Murphy for her skill in overseeing the project as a whole.

PICTURE CREDITS

Key: **AA** The Art Archive; **AB** Gift of Alan Buchsbaum,1980-66-2; **AG** Anonymous gift, D92.102.1; **AIC** © The Art Institute of Chicago; **AM** Gift of Alan Moss, D85.145.1; **ATL** Angelo Testa, Chicago, Illinois, 1921–1984. Panel entitled "Labyrinth," 1942–1952, weaving, 188.2 x 129.8cm. Gift of Angelo Testa; Alexander Demond Fund, 1982.164; **ATS** Angelo Testa, Chicago, Illinois, 1921–1984, Panel entitled "Skyscrapers," 1947–1952, weaving, 187.6 x 126.9cm, Gift of Angelo Testa; Alexander Demond Fund, 1982.167; **BA** Bauhaus-Archiv, Berlin/Photo © VG Bild Kunst Bonn, Germany; **BAL** The Bridgeman Art Library, London/Private Collection; **BF** Bibliothèque Forney, Ville de Paris; **BP** Bullen, Pijja Design Ltd.; **BR** Gift of Mr and Mrs Ben Rose through the Art Institute of Chicago, **(1)** 1989-62-5, **(2)** 1989-62-6, **(3)** 1989-62-7; **BRI** Gift of Ben Rose, Inc., 1969-104-2-d; **BRU** Photo Brunzel; **BSL** Photo Bokförlaget Signum, Lund; **BTM** Tekstilmuseet: The Swedish Museum of Textile History, Borås/Photo Jan Berg; **BU** Photo Bungartz; **CB** Création Baumann; **CF** Colefax and Fowler; **CH** Cooper-Hewitt, National Design Museum, Smithsonian Inst./Art Resource, NY; **CI** © Christie's Images Ltd 2002; **DACS (1)** © ARS, NY and DACS, London 2002, **(2)** © DACS 2002, **(3)** © ADAGP, Paris and DACS, London 2002, **(4)** © Angela Verren-Taunt 2002 All rights reserved, DACS, **(5)** © Eduardo Paolozzi 2002. All Rights Reserved, DACS; **DC** © Design Council Slide Collection at The Manchester Metropolitan University; **DCS** Design Council Slide Collection at The Manchester Metropolitan University; **DF** Photo Denis Farley, Montreal; **DG** Photo David Giles; **DM** Photo Daniel McGrath; **DMA** Dallas Museum of Art, 20th Century Design Fund, 1996.235; **DN** Die Neue Sammlung, The Museum of Design, Munich; **DS** Gift of Denst and Soderlund, 1952-126-1-1; **DTM** Deutsches Tapetenmuseum, Staatliche Museen Kassel; **EC** Gift of Elaine Lustig Cohen, D86.152.1; **EB** Estate of Edward Bawden; **EHK** Gift of Eleanor and Henry Kluck, 1985-84-6; **EK** Eley Kishimoto; **EMS** Gift of Esperanza and Mark Schwartz, by exchange, D93.263.1; **EO** Gift of the Estate of Ella Ostowsky, 1976-98-20; **EP** Laudomia Pucci and the Emilio Pucci Archives; **FW** Produced in collaboration with The Fabric Workshop and Museum, Philadelphia; **FIT** Courtesy of the Museum at The Fashion Institute of Technology, New York; **FS** Gift of F. Schumacher and Co., 1977-68-1; **GB** Gift of Geoffrey N. Bradfield, **(1)** D84.170.1, **(2)** D85.130.1; **GIM** Collection of State Historical Museum (GIM), Moscow; **GPJB** G. P. & J. Baker; **GR** Photo Giles Rivest, Montreal; **GVE** Courtesy of Georgina von Etzdorf; **HF** Gift of Helen Fioratti, by exchange, D88.114.1; **HG** © 1978 Estate of Duncan Grant, courtesy Henrietta Garnett; **HM** Gift of Herman Miller, Inc., D.84.115.1; **HT** Photo Hans Thorwid Nationalmuseum; **IH** Courtesy of Imperial Home Decor Group; IT Photo Ian Thomas; **JA** Koloman Moser, Austrian, 1868–1918, Austria, Vienna, sic Panel entitled "Mohnköpfe" (Poppyheads), 1900, silk, rayon, and cotton, satin weave, self-patterned by ground weft floats, 182.9 x 113cm, Restricted gift of Mrs Julian Armstrong, Jr., 1986.963; **JD** Gift of Jack Denst, 1969-45-3-3; **JL** Gift of Jack Lenor Larsen, **(1)** 1973-54-2, **(2)** 1968-47-1-c; **JM** Courtesy of Javier Mariscal; **JR** Gift of John Rombola, 1984-102-3; **JW** Jocelyn Warner; **JWF** Gift of Joy Wolf, 1981-64-1; **KAW** Gift of Katzenbach & Warren, Inc., 1959-134-1-e; **KC** Kunstindustrimuseum, Copenhagen, Photo © Ole Woldbye © Pernille Klemp; **KS** Kinnasand AB; **KV** Kvadrat A/S; **KW** Gift of Konwiser, Inc., 1956-151-6; **LA** © Laura Ashley Limited; **LAM** Gift of L. Anton Maix, Inc., 1956-125-2; **LM** Photo Lantz, Munich; LMS © L&M Services B.V. Amsterdam 20011114; **MA** Marburg Tapeten; **MADH** Museum of Art and Design, Helsinki; **MAK** MAK – Austrian Museum of Applied Art, Vienna; **MAR** Marimekko Corporation, Helsinki; **MCAG** © Manchester City Art Galleries; **MF** Photo Matt Flynn; **MMFA** The Montreal Museum of Fine Arts, Liliane and David M. Stewart Collection; **MMI (1)** D84.109.1, **(2)** D86.166.1; **MMT** Musée de la Mode et du Textile, coll. UCAD, photo Laurent-Sully Jaulmes; **MODA** MoDA – The Museum of Domestic Design & Architecture; **MPP** Musée du Papier Peint, Rixheim; **MTL** Musée des Tissus, Lyon/Photo Studio Basset; **NMS** The National Museum of Art, Stockholm; **NO** Nobilis; **NU** NUNO Corporation; **OPG** Octopus Publishing Group Ltd.; **PC** Private Collection; **PE** Photo Per Eriksson; **PM** 1983-8-1, Philadelphia Museum of Art: Gift of Marieta; **PP** Paint & Paper Library; **RA** Tapetenfabrik Gebr. Rasch GmbH & Co.; **RAH** Josef Hoffmann, Austrian, 1870–1956, Vienna, "Santa Sofia," 1912–17, ribbed silk, silk-screen painted, 135.7 x 114.6cm, Gift of Robert Allerton, 1924.217; **RAP** France, print, 20th century, silk, grey with blue birds and flowers, 640cm. Gift of Robert Allerton, 1924.205; **RG** Photo Richard P. Goodbody, New York; **RGW** Transfer from the Renwick Gallery, Washington D.C., 1995-152-1-52; **RM** © Alf Bokgren, Röhsska Museet, Göteborg, Sweden; **RSA** Rodchenko & Stepanova Archive; **SA** Santos & Adolfsdóttir; **SAN** By permission of Sanderson; **SH** Gift of Mrs Stanley Hanks, D85.148.1; **SKM** Photo SKM; **ST** Photo Steve Tanner; **SW** Gift of Sue Warner, 1991-57-1; **TB** Timorous Beasties; **TDF** Purchase, Textile Department Fund, 1978-176-3; **TF** Timney Fowler Design Studio; **TG** Courtesy of The Target Gallery, London; **TK** Gift of Teresa Kilham, 1958-88-12; **TR** Photo Tim Ridley; **TSA** Collection of State Museum reserve, Tsaritsino; **TSD** Ten Swedish Designers (Tio-Gruppen); **TW** TwentyTwentyOne; **UW** Gift of United Wallpaper Co., 1969-52-1-49; **UWP** Courtesy of United Wallpaper Co.; **VA** V&A Picture Library; **VAD** Gift of Various donors, 1980-77-3-112; **VP** Verner Panton Design; **VS** Gift of Vincent Scalia, 1982-35-3-23; **VSB** Venturi, Scott Brown and Associates; **WA** Courtesy of The Warner Archive; **WAR** © The Warner Archive; **WAG** The Whitworth Art Gallery, University of Manchester; **WL** Würtembergisches Landesmuseum Stuttgart; **WLK** Gift of William and Lois Katzenbach, 1969-167-2-49; **ÅL** Photo SKM/Åsa Lundén.

Endpapers NMS/ÅL; page 1 CI; p2 VA; p5 MAR; p6 top PP; p6 below TSD; p7 DC; figs. 1.1, 1.2, 1.3 VA; 1.4, 1.5, 1.6 WAG; 1.7 BAL; 1.8 VA; 1.9 WAG; 1.10 GPJB; 1.11 WAG; 1.12 VA; 1.13 WAG; 1.14, 1.15 MODA; 1.16, 1.17. 1.18, 1.19, 1.20, 1.21, 1.22 VA; 1.23 WAG; 1.24 VA; 1.25 GPJB; 1.26, 1.27, 1.28 WAG; 1.29 MPP; 1.30 KC; 1.31 VA; 1.32 MMT; 1.33 MPP; 1.34 WL; 1.35, 1.36 DTM; 1.37 DN; 1.38 DN/DACS(2); 1.39 AIC/JA; 1.40, 1.41 WL; 1.42 DN; 2.1 BF; 2.2, 2.3, 2.4, 2.5, 2.6, 2.7, 2.8 MAK; 2.9 MMFA/GR/EMS; 2.10, 2.11 MAK; 2.12 AIC/RAH; 2.13 CI; 2.14, 2.15 DN/BU; 2.16 MAK; 2.17 WAG; 2.18 BSL; 2.19 DN/BU; 2.20 WAG; 2.21 CH/TK; 2.22 DN/LM; 2.23 DN/LM; 2.24 RA; 2.25 VA/DACS(2); 2.26 BA/DACS(1); 2.27 VA/DACS(3); 2.28 BF/DACS(3); 2.29 VA; 2.30 AIC/RAP/DACS(3); 2.31 VA; 2.32 WAG; 2.33 MTL; 2.34, 2.35, 2.36 BF; 2.37 VA; 2.38, 2.39 BF; 2.40 BF/DACS(3); 2.41 BF; 2.42 MMT; 2.43 AA/LMS; 2.44 RSA; 2.45 GIM; 2.46 TSA; 2.47 GIM; 2.48, 2.49 VA/HG; 2.50, 2.51, 2.52 VA; 2.53 WAG; 2.54 VA; 2.55 MCAG; 2.56, 2.57 WAG; 2.58, 2.59, 2.60, 2.61, 2.62, 2.63 VA; 3.1 MCAG; 3.2, 3.3,VA; 3.4, 3.5, 3.6, 3.7 WAG; 3.8 VA; 3.9 VA/IT; 3.10, VA/EB 3.11, 3.12 VA; 3.13 WAG; 3.14 VA; 3.15 MCAG; 3.16, 3.17, 3.18 VA; 3.19 MCAG; 3.20, 3.21, 3.22 VA; 3.23 WAG; 3.24 WAG/DACS(4); 3.25 VA; 3.26 MCAG; 3.27 DCS/WA; 3.28, 3.29 VA/WA; 3.30, 3.31, 3.32 WAG; 3.33 VA; 3.34, 3.35 WAG; 3.36 CH/MF/EO; 3.37 CH/MF/WLK/IH; 3.38 RM; 3.39, 3.40 BTM; 3.41 NMS/HT; 3.42 NMS/ÅL; 3.43 BTM; 3.44 RM; 3.45, 3.46 PE; 3.47 KC; 4.1, 4.2 OPG/TG; 4.3, 4.4, 4.5 VA; 4.6, 4.7, 4.8, 4.9 WAG; 4.10 PC/DG; 4.11, 4.12, 4.13, 4.14 WAG; 4.15 WAG/DACS(5); 4.16 VA; 4.17, 4.18 WAG; 4.19 PC/DG; 4.20 WAG; 4.21 VA; 4.22 WAG; 4.23 DCS; 4.24, 4.25, 4.26 WAG; 4.27 CH/MF/BR(2); 4.28 AIC/ATL; 4.29 AIC/ATS; 4.30 CH/MF/BR(1); 4.31 CH/MF/BR(3); 4.32 CH/MF/EHK; 4.33 MMFA/RG/SH; 4.34 MMFA/RG/AM; 4.35 MMFA/GR/GB(1); 4.36 MMFA/DF/ HF; 4.37 MMFA/RG/EC; 4.38 DMA; 4.39 MMFA/RG/MMI(1); 4.40 MMFA/RG/GB(2); 4.41 MMFA/GR/AG/DACS(3); 4.42 CH/MF/KW; 4.43 CH/MF/LAM; 4.44 WAG; 4.45 VA; 4.46 CH/MF/VAD/IH; 4.47 CH/MF/KAW/IH; 4.48 CH/MF/JR; 4.49 CH/MF/DS; 4.50, 4.51 NMS/HT; 4.52 RM; 4.53, 4 54, 4.55 NMS/HT; 4.56 RM; 4.57 NMS/HT/DACS(2); 4.58, 4.59 RM; 4.60 NMS/HT; 4.61 RM; 4.62, 4.63 WAG; 4.64, 4.65 KC; 4.66 KC/DACS(2); 4.67 MAR; 4.68, 4.69 VA; 4.70 DN; 4.71, 4.72 VA; 4.73 RA; 4.74, 4.75 DN/LM; 4.76 DN; 5.1 WAG; 5.2, 5.3, 5.4 MAR; 5.5, 5.6 MADH; 5.7, 5.8 BTM; 5.9, 5.10 RM; 5.11 BTM; 5.12 RM; 5.13 WAG; 5.14 BTM; 5.15 NMS/SKM; 5.16 VP; 5.17 WAG; 5.18 DC; 5.19 WAG; 5.20 VA; 5.21, 5.22, 5.23, 5.24, 5.25, 5.26 WAG; 5.27, 5.28 VA/DM; 5.29 DC; 5.30 DCS/WA; 5.31, 5.32 WAG/WA; 5.33 DCS/WA; 5.34, 5.35, 5.36, 5.37 DCS; 5.38 OPG/TR/TW; 5.39 VA; 5.40 DC; 5.41 WAG; 5.42 SAN; 5.43, 5.44 DC; 5.45 WAG; 5.46 DC; 5.47, 5.48 WAG; 5.49 DC; 5.50, 5.51, 5.52, 5.53 WAG; 5.54 CH/MF/BRI; 5.55 MMFA/RG/HM; 5.56 CH/MF/JL(1); 5.57 CH/MF/JL(2); 5.58 FIT; 5.59 CH/MF/JD; 5.60 CH/MF/UW/IH; 5.61 CH/MF/RGW/UWP/IH; 5.62 EP; 6.1, 6.2, 6.3, 6.4, 6.5 TSD; 6.6 BTM; 6.7 RM; 6.8 TSD; 6.9 BTM; 6.10, 6.11 RM; 6.12 BTM; 6.13, 6.14 RM; 6.15 MAR; 6.16 MADH; 6.17 DN/LM; 6.18, 6.19 DN/BU; 6.20 VP; 6.21 DTM/BRU; 6.22, 6.23, 6.24 WAG; 6.25 DCS; 6.26, 6.27 DC; 6.28 WAG; 6.29 CH/MF/SW/WA; 6.30, 6.31, 6.32, 6.33, 6.34 DC; 6.35 LA; 6.36 VA; 6.37 CH/MF/FS; 6.38 CH/MF/TDF; 6.39 CH/MF/VS; 6.40 CH/MF/JWF; 6.41 CH/MF/AB; 7.1 KS; 7.2, 7.3 FW; 7.4 VSB; 7.5 MMFA/GR/MMI(2); 7.6 PM/JM; 7.7 NO; 7.8, 7.9, 7.10, 7.11 TSD; 7.12 BTM; 7.13 DN; 7.14 BTM; 7.15, 7.16 KS; 7.17 DN/BU; 7.18, 7.19 MAR; 7.20 KV; 7.21, 7.22 MAR; 7.23 CB; 7.24 CF; 7.25 VA/DM; 7.26 VA; 7.27 WAG; 7.28 DC; 7.29 TF; 7.30 VA/IT; 7.31 VA/WA; 7.32 WAR; 7.33 WAG/WA; 7.34 VA; 7.35 TB; 7.36 GVE; 7.37, 7.38 PP; 7.39 VA; 7.40 EK; 7.41 WAG; 7.42 DC; 7.43 JW; 7.44 SA; 7.45 MA; 7.46 BP; 7.47 NU.